SOMETHING ABOUT THE AUTHOR

SOMETHING ABOUT THE AUTHOR

Facts and Pictures about Contemporary Authors
and Illustrators of Books for Young People

Anne Commire

VOLUME 8

GALE RESEARCH
BOOK TOWER
DETROIT, MICHIGAN
48226

Also Published by Gale

CONTEMPORARY AUTHORS:
A Bio-Bibliographical Guide to
Current Authors and Their Works

(Now Covers About 45,000 Authors)

Special acknowledgment is due to the members of the *Contemporary Authors* staff (particularly Mary Reif Stevenson) who assisted in the preparation of this volume, and to Gale's art director, Chester Gawronski.

EDITORIAL ASSISTANTS
Linda Shedd, Rosemary DeAngelis Bridges

GRATEFUL ACKNOWLEDGMENT

is made to the following for their kind permission to reproduce copyrighted material.
■ **ABINGDON PRESS.** Illustration by Charles Cox from *Funny-Bone Dramatics* by Bernice Wells Carlson. Copyright © 1974 by Abingdon Press. / Illustration by Tim and Greg Hildebrandt from *The Remarkable Journey of Gustavus Bell* by Gloria Skurzynski. Copyright © 1973 by Abingdon Press. Both reprinted by permission of Abingdon Press. ■ **ATHENEUM PUBLISHERS.** Illustration by Erik Blegvad from *The Mushroom Center Disaster* by N. M. Bodecker. Copyright © 1974 by Erik Blegvad. / Illustration by N. M. Bodecker from *It's Raining Said John Twaining* by N. M. Bodecker. Illustration copyright © 1973 by N. M. Bodecker. /Illustration by Trina Schart Hyman from *Greedy Mariani* by Dorothy Sharp Carter. Illustration copyright © 1974 by Atheneum Publishers. /Illustration by Jochen Bartsch from *My Great-Grandfather and I* by James Krüss. Copyright © 1960 by Verlag Friedrich Oetinger, Hamburg. English translation © 1964 by Atheneum Publishers. All reprinted by permission of Atheneum Publishers. ■ **THE BOBBS-MERRILL CO.** Illustration by Gil Walker from *The Bounty's Boy* by I. G. Edmonds. Copyright © 1962 by I. G. Edmonds. /Illustration by Laurie Anderson from *Certainly, Carrie, Cut the Cake* by Margaret and John Travers Moore. Illustrations copyright © 1971 by Laurie Anderson. /Illustration by John R. Lane from *Two Muskets for Washington* by Don Oakley. Copyright © 1970 by Don Oakley. All reprinted by permission of The Bobbs-Merrill Co., Inc. ■ **BRADBURY PRESS.** Illustration by Giulio Maestro from *The Tortoise's Tug of War* by Giulio Maestro. Copyright © 1971 by Giulio Maestro. Reprinted by permission of Bradbury Press. ■ **COWARD, McCANN & GEOGHEGAN, INC.** Photograph by Hope Ryden from *The Wild Colt* by Hope Ryden. Copyright © 1972 by Hope Ryden. /Illustration by Charles Robinson from *The Terrible Wave* by Marden Dahlstedt. Copyright © 1972 by Marden Dahlstedt. Both reprinted by permission of Coward, McCann & Geoghegan, Inc. ■ **THOMAS Y. CROWELL CO.** Illustration by Arnold Spilka from *Robin Hood of Sherwood Forest* by Ann McGovern. Copyright © 1968 by Ann McGovern. /Illustration by Jacqueline Blass from *Elizabeth Gets Well* by Alfons Weber, M.D. Copyright © 1969 by Ex Libris Verlag, Zurich. Copyright © 1970 by International Publishing Consultants, Amsterdam. Both reprinted by permission of Thomas Y. Crowell Co. ■ **CROWELL-COLLIER PRESS.** Illustration from *Fanny Kemble* by Robert Rushmore. Copyright © 1970 by The Macmillan Co. /Illustration by John Wagner from *Spokesman for Freedom: The Life of Archibald Grimke* by Janet Stevenson. Copyright © 1969 by The Macmillan Co. Both reprinted by permission of The Macmillan Co. ■ **THE JOHN DAY CO., INC.** Illustration by Catherine Hanley from *Johnny Lost* by Mariana Prieto. Copyright © 1969 by The John Day Co., Inc. Reprinted by permission of The John Day Co., Inc. ■ **DELACORTE PRESS.** Illustration by Kiakshuk and Pudlo from *Eskimo Songs and Stories* translated by Edward Field. Copyright © 1973 by Dell Publishing Co. Illustration reprinted by permission of West Baffin Eskimo Cooperative, Cape Dorset, N.W.T. Canada. Reprinted by permission of Delacorte Press. ■ **T. S. DENISON & CO.** Illustration from *Tobuk, Reindeer Herder* by Velma R. Kvale. Copyright © 1968 by T. S. Denison & Co., Inc. Reprinted by permission of T. S. Denison & Co., Inc. ■ **DEVIN-ADAIR CO.** Illustration by John Henry Dick from *World of the Great White Heron* by Marjory Bartlett Sanger. Copyright © 1967 by the Devin-Adair Co. Reprinted by permission of the Devin-Adair Co. ■ **DIAL PRESS.** Illustration by Charles Lilly from *Philip Hall Likes Me. Maybe I Reckon* by Bette Greene. Pictures copyright © 1974 by The Dial Press. / Illustration by Steven Kellogg from *Matilda Who Told Lies and Was Burned to Death* by Hilaire Beloc. Pictures copyright © 1970 by Steven Kellogg. /Illustration by Steven Kellogg from *The Island of the Skog* by Steven Kellogg. Copyright © 1973 by Steven Kellogg. All reprinted by Dial Press. ■ **DODD, MEAD & CO., INC.** Illustration by Sam Savitt from *The Gallant Gray Trotter* by John T. Foster. Copyright © 1974 by John T. Foster. /Illustration by Manus Pinkwater from *Wizard Crystal* by Manus Pinkwater. Copyright © 1973 by Manus Pinkwater. /Illustration by Ted Lewin from *In Sheep's Clothing* by Darrell A. Rolerson. Copyright © 1972 by Darrell A. Roler-

son. /Illustration by Sam Savitt from *Wild Horse Running* by Sam Savitt. Copyright © 1973 by Sam Savitt. All reprinted by permission of Dodd, Mead & Co., Inc. ■ **DOUBLE-DAY & CO., INC.** Illustration by Tracy Sugarmen from *The Quiet Rebels* by Philip Sterling and Maria Brau. Copyright © 1968 by Doubleday & Co., Inc. /Illustration by Evelyn Copelman from *Runaway Teen* by Ann Finlayson. Copyright © 1963 by Doubleday & Co., Inc. /Illustration by Barbara Ninde Byfield from *The Book of Weird* by Barbara Ninde Byfield. Copyright © 1967 by Barbara Ninde Byfield. /Illustration by Barbara Corrigan from *Of Course You Can Sew!* by Barbara Corrigan. Copyright © 1971 by Barbara Corrigan. /Photograph by Celeste Scala Navarra from *Wheels for Kids* by John Gabriel Navarra. Copyright © 1973 by John Gabriel Navarra. All reprinted by permission of Doubleday & Co., Inc. ■ **E. P. DUTTON & CO., INC.** Illustration by Antony Maitland from *The Usurping Ghost* chosen by Susan Dickinson. Illustration copyright © 1970 by William Collins' Sons & Co., Ltd. /Illustration by Stefan Martin from *What's Under a Rock?* by Robert Gannon. Copyright © 1971 by Stefan Martin. /Illustration by Susan Perl from *A Flower Pot Is Not a Hat* by Martha Moffett. Illustration copyright © 1972 by Susan Perl. /Illustration by Hal Ashmead from *Gasoline Cowboy* by William Campbell Gault. Copyright © 1974 by William Campbell Gault. All reprinted by permission of E. P. Dutton & Co., Inc. ■ **FARRAR, STRAUS & GIROUX, INC.** Illustration by Natalie Babbitt from *Small Poems* by Valerie Worth. Illustration copyright © 1972 by Natalie Babbitt. /Illustration by Graham Oakley from *The Dragon Hoard* by Tanith Lee. Copyright © 1971 by Tanith Lee. /Illustration from *Brookie and Her Lamb* by M. B. Goffstein. Copyright © 1967 by M. B. Goffstein. /Illustration by Karl W. Stucklen from *People of the Dream* by James Forman. Copyright © 1972 by James Forman. /All reprinted by permission of Farrar, Straus & Giroux, Inc. ■ **FOLLETT PUBLISHING CO.** Illustration by Jean Cassels from *Battle on the Rosebush* by Marian S. Edsall. Illustration copyright © 1972 by Follett Publishing Co. /Illustration by Kelly Oechsli from *The Birthday Car* by Margaret Hillert. Copyright © 1966 by Follett Publishing Co. / Illustration by Jerry Pinckney from *The Great Minu* by Beth P. Wilson. Illustration copyright © 1974 by Follett Publishing Co. /Illustration by Henry James from *Safiri the Singer* by Eleanor B. Heady. Illustrations copyright © 1972 by Follett Publishing Co. All reprinted by permission of Follett Publishing Co. ■ **FUNK & WAGNALLS.** Illustration by Ernest Kurt Barth from *Adirondack Mountain Mystery* by Margaret Goff Clark. Copyright © 1966 by Margaret Goff Clark. Reprinted by permission of Funk & Wagnalls. ■ **GARRARD PUBLISHING CO.** Illustration by Cary from *Rosa Bonheur* by Olive Price. Copyright © 1972 by Olive Price. /Illustration by Victor Mays from *The Brave Balloonists* by Esther M. Douty. Copyright © 1974 by Esther M. Douty. /Illustration by Cyndy Szekeres from *Bedtime for Bears* by Adelaide Holl. Copyright © 1973 by Adelaide Holl. /Illustration by Victor Mays from *Sojourner Truth* by Helen Stone Peterson. Copyright © 1972 by Helen Stone Peterson. /Illustration by Gordon Laite from *Close to the Rising Sun* by Virginia Frances Voight. Copyright © 1972 by Virginia F. Voight. All reprinted by permission of Garrard Publishing Co. ■ **GROSSET & DUNLAP.** Illustration by Ruth Wood from *Barney Beagle Goes Camping* by Jean Bethell. Copyright © 1970 by Grosset & Dunlap. Reprinted by permission of Grosset & Dunlap. ■ **HARCOURT BRACE JOVANOVICH, INC.** Photograph by Victor Englebert from *Camera on Ghana* by Victor Englebert. Copyright © 1971 by Harcourt Brace Jovanovich, Inc. /Illustration by James Daugherty from *Abe Lincoln Grows Up* by Carl Sandburg. © 1926,1928, by Harcourt Brace Jovanovich, Inc. /Illustration by Harriet Pincus from *The Wedding Procession of the Rag Doll and the Broom Handle and Who Was in It* by Carl Sandburg. © illustrations by Harriet Pincus. /Photograph by Robert Vavra from *Felipe the Bullfighter* by Robert Vavra. /Illustration from *In the Village* by Hilde Heyduck-Huth. © Otto Maier Verlag, Ravensburg, 1968. © Burke Publishing Co., Ltd. 1969. All reprinted by permission of Harcourt Brace Jovanovich, Inc. ■ **HARPER & ROW, PUBLISHERS.** Illustration from *Stevie* by John Steptoe. Copyright © 1969 by John L. Steptoe. /Illustration by Ronald Himler from *Little Owl, Keeper of the Trees* by Ronald and Ann Himler. Illustration copyright © 1974 by Ronald Himler. /Illustration by Nicholasa Mohr from *Nilda* by Nicholasa Mohr. Copyright © 1973 by Nicholasa Mohr. /Illustration by Judith Gwyn Brown from *The Best Christmas Pageant Ever* by Barbara Robinson. Illustration copyright © 1972 by Judith Gwyn Brown. /Illustration by Ronald Himler from *Bunk Beds* by Elizabeth Winthrop. Illustration copyright © 1972 by Ronald Himler. /Illustration by Hans Guggenheim from *Balboa* by Jeannette Mirsky. Copyright © 1964 by Jeannette Mirsky. /Jacket by Edward Gorey from *Freaky Friday* by Mary Rodgers. Copyright © 1972 by Mary Rodgers. All reprinted by permission of Harper & Row, Publishers. ■ **HOLIDAY HOUSE.** Illustration by Glen Rounds from *Whitey's First Roundup* by Glen Rounds. Copyright © 1960 by Glen Rounds. /Illustration by Kelly Oechsli from *Upside Down Day* by Julian Scheer. Copyright © 1968 by Kelly Oechsli. /Illustration by Charles Schwartz from *When Animals Are Babies* by

PHOTOGRAPH CREDITS

Mr. Biddle lay in his hammock. He watched his four bird friends fly in. They were coming to have lunch with him, as usual. ■ (From *Mr. Biddle and the Birds* by Lonzo Anderson. Illustrated by Adrienne Adams.)

ABBOTT, Alice
See SPEICHER, Helen Ross (Smith)

ADAMS, Adrienne 1906-

PERSONAL: Born February 8, 1906, in Fort Smith, Ark.; daughter of Edwin Hunt (an accountant) and Sue (Broaddus) Adams; married John Lonzo Anderson (a writer, under name Lonzo Anderson), August 17, 1935. *Education:* Stephens College, B.A., 1925; attended University of Missouri, 1927, American School of Design, New York, 1929. *Residence:* Glen Gardner, N.J.

CAREER: Artist, illustrator, author of children's books. Taught in a rural school in Oklahoma, 1927-29; moved to New York City in 1929, working as a free-lance designer of displays, murals, textiles, greeting cards, and other materials; Childhood, Inc., New York, N.Y., designer of furniture and murals, art director, 1944-51; full-time illustrator, 1952—. *Awards, honors:* Runner-up for Caldecott Medal, 1960, for illustration of *Houses from the Sea*, and 1962, for illustration of *The Day We Saw the Sun Come Up*; Rutgers Award from Rutgers University College of Library Services, 1973, for "distinguished contribution to children's literature."

WRITINGS—Self-illustrated: *A Woggle of Witches*, Scribner, 1971; (compiler) *Poetry of Earth*, Scribner, 1972.

Illustrator: Lonzo Anderson, *Bag of Smoke*, Viking, 1942; Patricia Gordon, *The 13th is Magic*, Lothrop, 1950; Gordon, *The Summer is Magic*, Lothrop, 1952; Elizabeth Fraser Torjesen, *Captain Ramsay's Daughter*, Lothrop, 1953; Elizabeth Rogers, *Angela of Angel Court*, Crowell, 1954; Rumer Godden, *Impunity Jane*, Viking, 1954; Mary Kennedy, *Jenny*, Lothrop, 1954; Norma Simon, *The Baby House*, Lippincott, 1955; Beth Lipkin, *The Blue Mountain*, Knopf, 1956; Godden, *The Fairy Doll*, Viking, 1956; Priscilla Friedrich, *The Easter Bunny that Overslept*, Lothrop, 1957; Gordon, *The Light in the Tower*, Lothrop, 1957; Margaret Glover Otto, *Great Aunt Victoria's House*, Holt, 1957; Godden, *Mouse House*, Viking, 1957; Rachel Lyman Field, *The Rachel Field Story Book*, Doubleday, 1958; Godden, *Die Feen-puppe*, Boje Verlag, 1958; Godden, *The Story of Holly and Ivy*, Viking, 1958; Janice Udry, *Theodore's Parents*, Lothrop, 1958; Alice E. Goudey, *Houses from the Sea*, Scribner, 1959; Paula Hendrich, *Trudy's First Day at Camp*, Lothrop, 1959; Jeanne Massey, *The Little Witch*, Knopf, 1959.

Aileen Lucia Fisher, *Going Barefoot*, Crowell, 1960; Rumer Godden, *Candy Floss*, Viking, 1960; Jakob Ludwig

ADRIENNE ADAMS

Karl Grimm, *The Shoemaker and the Elves*, Scribner, 1960; Hans Christian Andersen, *Thumbelina*, Scribner, 1961; Fisher, *Where Does Everyone Go?*, Crowell, 1961; Alice E. Goudey, *The Day We Saw the Sun Come Up*, Scribner, 1961; Mary Francis Shura, *Mary's Marvelous Mouse*, Knopf, 1962; Clyde Robert Bulla, *What Makes a Shadow?*, Crowell, 1962; John L(onzo) Anderson, compiler, *A Fifteenth Century Cookry Boke*, Scribner, 1962; N. Saboly, *Bring a Torch, Jeannette, Isabella*, Scribner, 1963; Virginia Haviland, *Favorite Fairy Tales Told in Scotland*, Little, Brown, 1963; Shura, *The Nearsighted Knight*, Knopf, 1964; Grimm, *Snow White and Rose Red*, Scribner, 1964; Goudey, *Butterfly Time*, Scribner, 1964; Frances Carpenter, *The Mouse Palace*, McGraw, 1964; Hans Christian Andersen, *The Ugly Duckling*, Scribner, 1965; Fisher, *In the Middle of the Night*, Crowell, 1965; Jan Wahl, *Cabbage Moon*, Holt, 1965; Lonzo Anderson, *Ponies of Mykillengi*, Scribner, 1966; Andrew Lang, *The Twelve Dancing Princesses*, Holt, 1966; Barbara Schiller, *The White Rat's Tale*, Holt, 1967; Grimm, *Jorinda and Joringel*, Scribner, 1968; Lonzo Anderson, *Bag of Smoke*, Knopf, 1968; Lonzo Anderson, *Two Hundred Rabbits*, Viking, 1968; Leclaire Alger, *The Laird of Cockpen*, Holt, 1969.

Natalia Belting, *Summer's Coming In*, Holt, 1970; Carl Withers, *Painting the Moon*, Holt, 1970; Lonzo Anderson, *Mr. Biddle and the Bird*, Scribner, 1971; Lonzo Anderson, *Izzard*, Scribner, 1973; Irwin Shapiro, *"Twice upon a Time,"* Scribner, 1973; Lonzo Anderson, *Halloween Party*, Scribner, 1974.

SIDELIGHTS: "I love children's books, and I feel very lucky to be involved in them. As I became involved, I discovered the satisfactions of a field which can be as sweetly innocent of the rank business-and-profit taint as any I can hope for, simply because a book cannot succeed unless little children love it and wear out its cover and pages so thoroughly that librarians must reorder it for the library shelves; you can not tell a child what to like."

FOR MORE INFORMATION SEE: Illustrators of Children's Books, 1946-1956, Horn Book, 1958; *Horn Book*, April, 1965; *American Artist*, November, 1965; Diana Klemin, *The Art of Art for Children's Books*, C. N. Potter, 1966; *Illustrators of Children's Books, 1957-1966*, Horn Book, 1968; Lee Bennett Hopkins, *Books Are by People*, Citation, 1969; *Third Book of Junior Authors*, edited by de Montreville and Hill, H. W. Wilson, 1972; MacCann and Richard, *The Child's First Books*, H. W. Wilson, 1973

ADKINS, Jan 1944-

PERSONAL: Born November 7, 1944, in Gallipolis, Ohio; son of Alban B. (a contractor) and Dixie (Ellis) Adkins; married Deborah Kiernan, September 14, 1968; children: Sally. *Education:* Ohio State University, B.A., 1969. *Home:* Stockton Shortcut, Wareham, Mass. 02571. *Agent:* P. Knowlton, Curtis Brown, Ltd., 60 East 56th St., New York, N.Y. 10022.

JAN ADKINS, by Jan Adkins

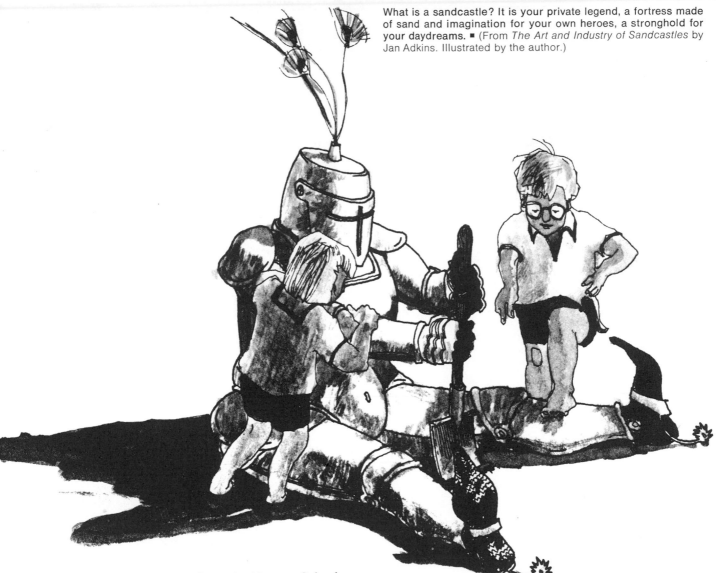

What is a sandcastle? It is your private legend, a fortress made of sand and imagination for your own heroes, a stronghold for your daydreams. ■ (From *The Art and Industry of Sandcastles* by Jan Adkins. Illustrated by the author.)

CAREER: Ireland & Associates Architects, Columbus, Ohio, designer, 1963-66, 1969; Buzzard Advertising Agency, Cambridge, Mass., 1973—. Writer, graphic designer, and illustrator, 1969—. *Awards, honors:* Jacobsen Short Story Award Ohio State University, 1969, for "One, Two"; nominated for National Book Award, 1972; Lewis Carroll Shelf Award, 1973; Brooklyn Museum Art Citation, 1972, 1973, 1974; Children's Book Showcase Award, 1974, for *Toolchest*.

WRITINGS: The Art and Industry of Sandcastles, Walker & Co., 1970; *The Craft of Making Wine*, Walker & Co., 1971; *How a House Happens*, Walker & Co., 1972; *Craft of Sail*, Walker & Co., 1973; *Toolchest* gtole booktnWalker OCo., 1974. Contributor to *Harper's*.

WORK IN PROGRESS: Inside: Seeing Beneath the Surface, for Walker; *Bread*, for Scribner; *Ship*, for Houghton.

SIDELIGHTS: "I write and I draw, but what I really do is learn. I learn about something that interests me, something I can find wonder in, and I try to explain it clearly—without losing the wonder. I'm a professional looker and learner, and a catcher-in-the-rye by vocation."

BARKER, Albert W. 1900-
(Reefe King, Hawk Macrae)

PERSONAL: Born, 1900; son of Edwin L. (an editor) and Jessie (Wineman) Barker; married Gertrude Rozan. *Address:* 15 St. Andrews Pl., Yonkers, N.Y. 10705. *Agent:* Oliver Swan.

WRITINGS—Juvenile: *Black on White and Read All Over: The Story of Printing* (Child Study Association book), Messner, 1971.

Adult novels—"Reefe King" series, published by Award Books: *Gift from Berlin*, 1969; *Apollo Legacy*, 1970.

"Hawk Macrae" series, published by Curtis Books: *If Anything Should Happen to Me*, 1973; *The Big Fix*, 1973; *The Dragon in Spring*, 1973; *The Blood of Angels*, 1974; *The Diamond Fix*, in press.

WORK IN PROGRESS: A new novel.

William Caslon, a young engraver, designed a style of type that became so popular that Benjamin Franklin arranged for the Declaration of Independence to be set in Caslon Type.
■ (From *Black on White and Read All Over* by Albert Barker.)

BARKER, Will 1908-
(Doug Demarest)

PERSONAL: Born March 25, 1908, in Troy, N.Y.; son of William, Jr. (manufacturer, president of William Barker Co.) and Florence (Herring) Barker. *Education:* Attended New York University. *Politics:* "Republican, more or less." *Religion:* Episcopalian. *Home and office:* 2000 Connecticut Ave., N.W., Washington, D.C. 20008.

CAREER: U.S. Department of Interior, Fish and Wildlife Service, Washington, D.C., writer and editor, 1949-54; free-lance writer, 1955—. Robert B. Luce, Inc., Washington, D.C., editorial consultant, 1962-63. G. S. Schirmer, Inc. (music publisher), New York, N.Y., copywriter. Lecturer at Montana State University Writers' Conference, 1958, Fredonia State Teachers College, 1960, Georgetown University Writer's Conference, 1961-69. Photographer-illustrator of own work. Actor in community theater, Washington, D.C. area. District of Columbia Action Committee for School Libraries, publicity, 1960-61. *Military service:* U.S. Army Air Corps., 1942-43.

MEMBER: American Museum of Natural History (associate), National Wildlife Federation (associate), Children's Book Guild of Washington, D.C. (secretary, 1960-61, program director, 1961-62). *Awards, honors:* National Wildlife Federation citation for work in conservation education, twice; citation from Stewart L. Udall, Secretary of Interior, for contribution to *Birds in Our Lives.*

WRITINGS: Familiar Animals of America (Outdoor Life Book Club selection), Harper, 1956; *Winter-Sleeping Wildlife*, Harper, 1958; *Familiar Insects of America*, Harper, 1960; *Wildlife in America's History*, Robert B. Luce, Inc., 1962; *Familiar Reptiles and Amphibians of America*, Harper, 1964; *Fresh Water Friends and Foes*, Acropolis, 1966. Contributor: *The Illustrated Library of Natural Sciences*, Simon & Schuster, 1958; *Time for Adventure*, Bobbs, 1960; *Beyond the Horizon*, Bobbs, 1960; *Birds in Our Lives*, Bureau of Sports Fisheries and Wildlife, 1966; *Joys and Journeys*, American Book Co., 1968; *High and Wide*, American Book Co., 1968; (contributor) Jean E. Haywood, *A Question of Choice*, Dickenson. Author of produced one-act play, "First Make Mad." Writer and editor of circulars, leaflets, papers, and brochures for U.S. Fish and Wildlife Service.

Contributor of nature column to *Science News Letter*; regular contributor to *American Forests*, and to *American Junior Red Cross News* and *American Junior Red Cross Journal*, 1956—; also contributor of articles, features, and verse to *American Field, Ford Times, Natural History, Science Digest, Sports Afield, Sports Illustrated, Kansas City Star, Milwaukee Journal*, other magazines and newspapers; contributor to *Book of Knowledge.*

SIDELIGHTS: "Mother and father were my first natural history teachers. My classroom was a ravine in Troy, New York, on the edge of which our white house was built—dining room and living room windows looked out over the ravine. From these windows the family—father, mother, sister and I—watched squirrels, rabbits, jays, various songbirds and sometimes one of the small predatory birds. We had a wildflower garden on the "bank", the upper sloping side of the ravine. Here we planted such wild plants as jack-in-the-pulpits (known in Great Britain as "lords-and-ladies"), wild geraniums, bloodroot, trilliums, various ferns including maidenhair. Bird boxes were put in trees along the edge of this ravine, where there were sugar maples. My father and I tapped these trees each spring, then took the sap home to boil down in an iron kettle to make syrup.

"First field trips were going to the Adirondack Mountains (N.Y.) each summer, to the Catskills in the spring, and to the shores of Lake Champlain on the Vermont side. On such trips I learned more about plant and animal lore—such as 'Leaves three, leave it be,' meaning stay away from poison ivy. I learned too that box tortoises (land turtles) love wild strawberries, always taking a dainty bite out of the biggest and the best berry. Years later, with my sister Florence and our Siamese cat, Miss Pu, on a leash, we were in Maryland's Gambril State Park. I noted that Fall that these animals all seemed to be moving in one direction when searching for spots to dig in (hibernate) for the winter.

"The entire family read omnivorously. Reading in such a way may have been an indication that I was to become a

WILL BARKER

writer, for most writers seem to be great readers from childhood. And my father got my sister and me all the books we wanted and also taught us how to use reference works such as dictionaries and encyclopedias.

"When I was a senior in Troy High School I won second place in an essay contest sponsored by the old *Troy Record*, a newspaper which is no more. The essay was about Troy, once a Dutch settlement known as Van der Hyden's Ferry. The prize was three dollars—the very first money I ever made from writing.

"I did not earn any more money from writing until I became a copy writer with G. Schirmer, Inc., music publishers. This job, I truly believe, was the start of my career as a writer. Right after I was discharged from the Army Air Corps (World War II) I began to write features and articles to submit to magazines. I did not sell anything at once, for I had to learn my craft by trial and error. Editors were often kind enough to scribble some helpful comment on a form rejection slip. One such remark that I recall was: 'Work to get away from exposition.' It was also soon after I was discharged from Service that I took a course in creative writing at New York University. The result of this course was that I could not write anything for a while.

"I studied the 'How-To' articles in various writers' magazines. This study, and writing hundreds of words, brought results. I sold an article about the Old West. This article was about a bad man of the Southwest and was called: 'Ben Thompson—Texas Terror.' I sold many more, including one about Sacagawea (Bird Woman) the girl guide for explorers Lewis and Clark. These sales were to the popular pulp magazines of the day—magazines in which many beginning writers got a start. Such sales encouraged me to continue writing. First sales are so very important. They mean recognition, seeing your name in print, and payment for your work.

"After what I call my 'New York interlude', I came to Washington (D.C.) and got a job with the Fish and Wildlife Service, United States Department of the Interior. I was a writer-editor in the Division of Information. I wrote popular publications and edited scientific papers. Members of the staff encouraged me to continue with my writing, including Rachel Carson (*The Sea Around Us* and *Silent Spring*), as well as Alastair McBain who wrote the foreword for my first book—*Familiar Animals of America*. My years with the Service were enormously rewarding, both as a writer and a naturalist. One reward was a long field trip to visit various National Wildlife Refuges about which I would write later. This trip took me to different parts of the United States where I saw animals new to me—antelope and yellow-bellied marmots in western Montana, yellow-headed blackbirds in northern North Dakota, otters (inland or river) in northern Michigan in the waters of Seney National Wildlife Refuge.

"While still with the Service, I sold an article to 'Natural History.' The article was about hibernation and winter sleep. This article was the basis for the book *Winter-Sleeping Wildlife*. I also sold 'Natural History' two features about unusual North American mammals. Harper editor Richard B. McAdoo read, and liked, these pieces in 'Natural History'. As a result of his liking my way of writing, he asked me to write about some of North America's mammals, with a short section on reptiles and amphibians.

This book is *Familiar Animals of America*, dedicated to my mother and father, my first natural history teachers. *Familiar Animals of America* is in the bibliographies of *Face of North America* (Peter Farb) and *Beyond Your Doorstep* (Hal Borland).

"Though I live in the city, Washington, D.C., I live only a short distance from the National Zoological Park, where I worked part of one summer in an office in the reptile house. I visit the Zoo frequently to see all kinds of animals, indigenous and exotic (imported). But the animals I love and study the most are the cats. I spent two years writing about my favorites among all the members in the animal kingdom. I have given this manuscript the working title *Cats and Their Cousins*. I hope it will be published within a reasonable time. I intend to continue to write—a profession which has been described as one of the loneliest."

Fifty Years of Children's Books, published by National Council of Teachers of English, lists *Winter-Sleeping Wildlife* as one of 250 most significant books for children in fifty-year period, 1910-60.

Syracuse University Library has "The Will Barker Papers," a collection of typescripts, family papers, correspondence (literary and historical), and ephemera in connection with Will Barker's writing and family history. He is also represented In the Kerlan Collection of juvenile literature at the University of Minnesota. Other Barker items at the Smithsonian Institution and with the Rensselaer County Historical Society, Troy, N.Y.

BEALER, Alex W(inkler III)   1921-

PERSONAL: Born March 6, 1921, in Valdosta, Ga.; son of Alex W., Jr. (in advertising) and Mary Louise (Peeples) Bealer; married Helen Eitel; children: Janet (Mrs. Ivan F. Bailey), Alex IV, Susan, Alice, Edmund. *Education:* Emory University, B.A., 1942; Northwestern University, graduate study, 1946. *Religion:* Presbyterian. *Residence:* Atlanta, Ga. *Office:* McRae & Bealer, Inc., 873 Spring St. N.W., Atlanta, Ga. 30308.

CAREER: Atlanta Journal, Atlanta, Ga., member of classified advertising department, 1945-46; Standard Oil Co., Chicago, Ill., advertising executive, 1946-48; Fuller & Smith & Ross (advertising agency), Chicago, Ill., copywriter, 1948-50; McRae & Bealer, Inc., Atlanta, Ga., executive vice-president, 1950—. Assistant state chairman of Georgia Republican Party, 1965-70. *Military service:* U.S. Marine Corps, 1942-45, 1950-52; became captain.

MEMBER: Artist-Blacksmiths Association of North America (president, 1973-74), First Advertising Agency Network (president, 1973-74), Atlanta Historical Society (trustee, 1973—), Commerce Club (Atlanta), Westville Historic Handicrafts (trustee, 1975—), Early American Industries Association. *Awards, honors:* Honorary Royal Consul of Sweden at Atlanta; Associated Press Award, 1965, for television script, "Only the Names Remain"; award for best juvenile book from Dixie Council of Authors and Journalists, 1972, and literary achievement award from Georgia Writers Association, 1973, for *Only the Names Remain*.

WRITINGS: The Picture-Skin Story (juvenile), Holiday House, 1957; *The Art of Blacksmithing*, Funk, 1969; *Only the Names Remain* (ALA Notable Book; *Horn Book* Honor List), Little, Brown, 1972; *Old Ways of Working Wood*, Barre, 1972. Author of television documentary, "Only the Names Remain," for WSB-Television, 1965. Contributor to magazines, including *Progressive Farmer* and *House Beautiful*. Editor of *The Anvils Ring*, quarterly newsletter of Artist-Blacksmiths Association of North America.

WORK IN PROGRESS: The Tools that Built America; *The Successful Craftsman*; *The Southerners*, for children.

SIDELIGHTS: "In preparing for my books since childhood I have lived from time to time with Indians, hunted and camped with them, entered into their lives to some extent. Also I have built my own blacksmith and woodworking shops where I work without the benefit of any power tools. I have talked and worked with old-time craftsmen who knew old tools and old techniques. Thus I have been able to a limited degree to recreate an atmosphere that has almost been lost and perhaps to salvage almost lost attitudes which can be of value to a modern, mechanized society and the individuals in that society."

HOBBIES AND OTHER INTERESTS: Travel, handicrafts, art, history.

FOR MORE INFORMATION SEE: "Blacksmith Workshop," a film made at Southern Illinois University, May, 1970.

ALEX W. BEALER

By this time, too, the Cherokees thought that finally they had learned the secret to a comfortable, civilized life—to live and let live. But the secret was no good unless everyone, white and Cherokee alike, felt the same way. Unfortunately this was not true. ■ (From *Only the Names Remain* by Alex W. Bealer. Illustrated by William Sauts Bock.)

BEHNKE, Frances L.

PERSONAL: Born in Fayette, Ala.; daughter of James Thomas and Lizzie (Newton) Berry; married John Alden Behnke (a science editor), December 30, 1957. *Education:* University of Arkansas, B.S., 1934; Emory University, M.S., 1940; Teachers College, Columbia University, Ed.D., 1959. *Politics:* Independent. *Religion:* Methodist. *Home:* 106 Morningside Dr., New York, N.Y. 10027. *Office:* Department of Science Education, Teachers College, Columbia University, 525 West 120th St., New York, N.Y. 10027.

CAREER: Barnard College, Columbia University, New York, N.Y., lecturer in chemistry, 1956-59; Hunter College, City University of New York, New York, N.Y., lecturer in science education, 1960-61; Teachers College, Columbia University, New York, N.Y., lecturer in science education, 1961-75. Director, Out-of-School Science Program. Consultant, Thomas Alva Edison Foundation. *Member:* American Association for the Advancement of Science (fellow), National Science Teachers Association, National Association of Biology Teachers (national vice-president, 1957), Association for the Education of Teachers of Science, Ornithology Society, Georgia Botanical Club, Iota Sigma Pi (president), Sigma Delta Epsilon, Pen and Brush Club.

WRITINGS: The Golden Adventure Book of Magnetism, Golden Press, 1962; *What We Find When We Look Under Rocks*, McGraw, 1969. Series editor, "Golden Adventure" series, Golden Press; series editor, "What We Find When ..." series, McGraw. Contributor to *School and Society, School Science and Mathematics, American Biology Teacher, American Physics Teacher, Chemical and Engineering News.* Editor, *Science World* Teaching Guides (high school edition). Editor of television scripts and school booklets.

WORK IN PROGRESS: The Changing World of Living Things for Holt; technical editor of three "Changing World" books on birds, the weather, and the decomposers.

SIDELIGHTS: "I hope that what I write for children will

catalyze questioning and creativity and will arouse sustained interest while providing information about natural phenomena. To be fully effective, this material would need assistance from parents, teachers and others associated with the young to provide constant encouragement for them to look for evidence, reasons and explanations. This would involve thinking things through rather than accepting glib opinions. Such a change in outlook could be an opening wedge to alternative ways of thinking and acting. This is the major goal of my writing.'' Behnke lived and studied in Marburg, Germany for two years.

HOBBIES AND OTHER INTERESTS: Futurology and futuristic studies. ''This involves the study of the future as a school subject. It can help young people see that science fiction may forecast the future.''

FRANCES L. BEHNKE

Look under a rock that has been there for a long time. ▪ (From *What We Find When We Look Under Rocks* by Frances L. Behnke. Illustrated by Jean Zallinger.)

BENEDICT, Rex   1920-

PERSONAL: Born June 27, 1920, in Jet, Okla.; son of Excel Edward (a farmer) and Violet (Lambert) Benedict; married Giusi Usai (now a secretary), January 5, 1966. *Education:* Northwestern State College, Alva, Okla., B.A., 1949; Oklahoma University, graduate study, 1949. *Home and office:* 23 West 88th St., New York, N.Y. 10024.

CAREER: Dance orchestra leader in Alva, Okla., 1939-41; translator and movie dubber in Rome, Italy, 1952-60; reader for various publishing houses in New York, N.Y., 1960—, and translator. *Military service:* U.S. Navy, 1941-45, 1951-53; served as naval aviator; became lieutenant; received Distinguished Flying Cross and three air medals.

WRITINGS: O ... Brother Juniper!, Pantheon, 1963; *Fantasano*, Corsair Press, 1967; *Good Luck Arizona Man*, Pantheon, 1972; *Goodbye to the Purple Sage*, Pantheon, 1973; *Last Stand at Goodbye Gulch*, Pantheon, 1974; *The Ballad of Cactus Jack*, Pantheon, 1975. Also wrote six volumes of poetry, Corsair Press, 1968-72.

Translator: *The Prayers of Man*, Obolensky, 1961; *Amorous Tales from the Decameron*, Fawcett, 1963; *Those Cursed Tuscans*, Ohio University Press, 1964; *One Moonless Night*, Braziller, 1964; *The Polka Dot Twins*, Braziller, 1964.

REX BENEDICT

SIDELIGHTS: "Thank heaven for children. Without them I never would have found my true medium as a novelist. Maybe I should also say thank heaven for the American West, since that's where my last four books have been set. I like to think I'm trying to do something special in my treatment of the West. It is heartening to find that the children who read the books seem to agree. Interestingly enough, many critics—especially London critics—agree also. The books have been called everything from 'Mozartian Westerns' to 'Don Quixote Westerns.' Actually that's pretty close to what I'm attempting.

"If you read the books closely you will see that I'm treating the West as a myth. My reality—made to order for young and open minds—is a literary or poetical reality. Being in the realm of poetry, anything can happen. And that's where the young reader comes in again: he will permit you to write anything, no matter how poetic, outrageous or exaggerated, so long as his or her fancy is caught and held. I don't think many novelists realize the complete sense of freedom one has when one writes for children. Complete freedom is a tremendous challenge. In fact it's kind of scary. Now, paradoxically, comes an interesting fact: much of my mail from readers comes from old people. Their excitement and delight at finding this Western heri-

tage set out so poetically is obvious. It's quite as if they were seeing it in a way they hadn't seen it before.

"I think I ought to say that, regarding the world of my books, my credentials are in order. As a kid I grew up in what had been the Cherokee Strip in Oklahoma. The old men, both Indian and White, were still around. Growing up in such an environment, one did not attach great importance to it for any particular reason. Not until years later, after I had roamed the world, did it occur to me that my own backyard contained endless treasures. That, coupled with my nature, my love for words and music, led inevitably to the reconstruction of my boyhood world. That it came out mythical and poetical is understandable. It is, I think, also logical that my West should turn out to be comic. Sad and comic would be a better way to say it, since that tone seems to prevail in every book.

"I guess what I'm trying to do is to create a world of my own out of the West, a world based on past reality, a literary reality with its own logic, dimensions, even, wherever possible, its own language. Some say the West as a medium for the arts is dead; I don't think it has yet got started . . . at least not properly. But that's just another beauty of it: it. now encompasses not only the original reality but also the Hollywood reality, the 'Street & Smith' reality, the Zane Grey reality, and so on. They are now part of the romance, the myth. My job is to tie them all together into my own special idea of reality and present them to—who else?—children . . . who will accept my offerings with complete faith.

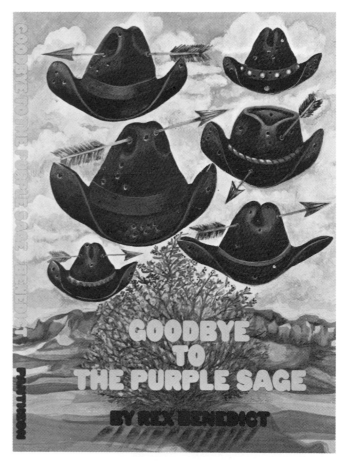

"That may sound a bit overblown for a writer of Westerns, but when one is dealing with the West and with children, one is, as I've said, permitted complete freedom of expression."

HOBBIES AND OTHER INTERESTS: "When not musing thusly, or playing the recorder, I listen to Mozart and Bach, trying to solve the mysteries, or read Mrs. Woolf."

FOR MORE INFORMATION SEE: Junior Literary Guild Catalogue, September, 1972, September, 1974; *New York Times Book Review,* June 3, 1973.

BERGER, Terry   1933-

PERSONAL: Born August 11, 1933, in New York, N.Y.; daughter of Morris A. (a dress manufacturer) and Belle (Otchet) Wapner; married Jerome Berger (director of King Features, Hearst Metrotone News), December 21, 1952; children: David, Susan. *Education:* Attended Vassar College, 1950-52; Brooklyn College (now Brooklyn College of the City University of New York), B.A., 1954; Hunter College (now Hunter College of the City University of New York), teaching degree, 1962. *Politics:* Liberal. *Religion:* Jewish. *Home:* 130 Hill Park Ave., Great Neck, N.Y. 11021.

TERRY BERGER

I Have Feelings
by TERRY BERGER

I have feelings. Some are good and some are bad, just like yours. ■ (From *I Have Feelings* by Terry Berger. Photographs by I. Howard Spivak.)

CAREER: Elementary school teacher in New York, N.Y., 1963-68.

WRITINGS—Juvenile: *Black Fairy Tales,* Atheneum, 1969; *I Have Feelings,* Behavioral Publications, 1971; *Lucky,* J. Philip O'Hara, 1974; *Being Alone, Being Together,* Advanced Learning Concepts, 1974; *A Friend Can Help,* Advanced Learning Concepts, 1974; *Big Sister, Little Brother,* Advanced Learning Concepts, 1974; *A New Baby,* Advanced Learning Concepts, 1974.

WORK IN PROGRESS: Book on divorce for children; *Not Everything Changes,* for Union of American Hebrew congregations; *I'm Not Good, I'm Not Bad,* for Windmill Books.

SIDELIGHTS: "I am happy doing books that help children understand their feelings. And I try to write them on the simplest level. I feel that my books are a sharing of my most intimate feelings.

"I am very grateful that I am able to write books for children. The simple truth and beauty that they require is always a challenge to me."

Black Fairy Tales is in the Kerlan Collection and was recorded by Caedmon. *I Have Feelings* has been made into a film by Jam Handy.

FOR MORE INFORMATION SEE: Time, October 18, 1971.

BERNARD, Jacqueline (de Sieyes) 1921-

PERSONAL: Born May 5, 1921, in Le Bourget du Lac, Savoie, France; daughter of Jacques Edouard (a diplomat) and Louise (Paine) de Sieyes; married Allen Bernard (a public relations writer), August 31, 1943 (divorced); children: Joel. *Education:* Attended Madeira School, Greenway, Va., 1935-39, Vassar College, 1939-41, and University of Chicago, 1941-42; has also attended evening classes at City College, New York, N.Y., intermittently, 1960—. *Religion:* None. *Home:* 552 Riverside Dr., New York, N.Y. 10027. *Agent:* Marie Rodell, 141 East 55th St., New York, N.Y. 10022.

CAREER: ABC News Service, Jamaica, N.Y., reporter, 1946-48; Pare Lorentz Associates, New York, N.Y., picture researcher, 1949-51; *Pageant* (magazine), New York, N.Y., editorial assistant, 1951-53; Filmstrip House, New York, N.Y., writer, 1953-57; advertising copywriter in New York, N.Y., with B. L. Mazel, Inc., 1957-59, and Young & Rubicam, 1959-61; Jewish Board of Guardians, New York, N.Y., public relations associate, 1963-68. Parents Without Partners (nation-wide organization for single parents and their children), co-founder and vice-president, 1957-58, currently an honorary member. *Member:* Authors Guild, National Emergency Civil Liberties Committee, American Civil Liberties Union, National Organization for Women.

WRITINGS: Journey Toward Freedom: The Story of Sojourner Truth (*Horn Book* Honor List; ALA Notable Book), Norton, 1967; *Voices from the Southwest*, Scholastic, 1972; *The Children You Gave Us*, Jewish Child Care Association, 1973.

WORK IN PROGRESS: Daughter of the Mines: A Life.

SIDELIGHTS: "Mostly I write about things I know little about and want an excuse to research (in the hope that others will be interested enough in what interests me to buy my book.) I find research, in general, endlessly fascinating and writing something to avoid as long as I possibly can.

"Of course, there always comes a time when I can no longer avoid that painful task. So I get to it, and usually it turns out okay although, for a long time, I don't believe it ever will. Lately I've been rebelling at spending so much of my life researching in library stacks—inevitable when writing about historical figures—and am now turning to journalism and real life biographies."

Richard Elman, in his review of *Journey Toward Freedom*, wrote that "the literal facts" of the career of the Negro woman evangelist who called herself Sojourner Truth "would be sufficiently challenging to any ambitious biographer. To the writer for children the problems further proliferate. . . . Jacqueline Bernard has succeeded on nearly every count." Robert Coles calls Bernard "a careful and lively writer, a historian as well as a storyteller." He says that to read her book is to gain "a thorough knowledge of the 19th-century America that struggled so hard over 'the race problem.'" Elman said in conclusion: "I learned from the author's quiet narrative ease and lucid prose, as well as from her careful unostentatious scholarship, her intelligent use of common speech, her choice of credible scenes and snatches of reconstructed dialogue."

In addition to her residence in France and the United States, Bernard has lived in Mexico.

HOBBIES AND OTHER INTERESTS: People, music (jazz, folk-rock, folk, blues, and classical), history, anthropology, science, art.

FOR MORE INFORMATION SEE: New York Times Book Review, November 26, 1967; *Book World*, January 21, 1968.

BETHELL, Jean (Frankenberry) 1922-

PERSONAL: Surname is pronounced *beth*-ell; born February 12, 1922, in Sharon, Pa.; daughter of Thomas Howard (an electrical engineer) and Helen (a teacher; maiden name, Rogers) Frankenberry; married Frederick L. Bethell (a construction executive), August 19, 1955. *Education:* Purdue University, B.S., 1943. *Home:* Oradell, N.J. 07649.

I think they are mad at me. ■ (From *Barney Beagle Goes Camping* by Jean Bethell. Illustrated by Ruth Wood.)

CAREER: National Broadcasting Co., New York, N.Y., writer for "Dave Garroway Show," 1950-52; Batten, Barton, Durstine and Osborn (advertising firm), New York, N.Y., copywriter, 1953; Benton & Bowles (advertising firm), New York, N.Y., copywriter, 1954-55; Wieboldt Stores, Inc., Chicago, Ill., advertising copy chief, 1956; Edward H. Weiss Advertising, Chicago, Ill., copywriter, 1957; Prentice-Hall, Englewood Cliffs, N.J., editor, 1974. *Member:* Pi Beta Phi.

WRITINGS: *Herman and Katnip,* Wonder Books, 1961; *Baby Huey,* Wonder Books, 1961; *The Monkey in the Rocket,* Grosset, 1962; *Barney Beagle,* Wonder Books, 1962; *Barney Beagle Plays Baseball,* Grosset, 1963; *The Clumsy Cowboy,* Wonder Books, 1963; *Ollie Bakes a Cake,* Wonder Books, 1964; *A Trick on Deputy Dawg,* Wonder Books, 1964; *How and Why Book of Famous Scientists,* Grosset, 1964; *Muskie and His Friends,* Wonder Books, 1964; *The Tale of Two Ducklings,* Wonder Books, 1964; *Luno the Soaring Stallion,* Wonder Books, 1964; *When I Grow Up,* Wonder Books, 1964; *Barbie Goes to a Party,* Grosset, 1964; *Barbie the Baby-Sitter,* Wonder Books, 1964; *Barbie Adventures to Read Aloud,* Wonder Books, 1964; *Barney Beagle and the Cat,* Grosset, 1965; *Hooray for Henry,* Grosset, 1965; *Petey, the Peanut Man,* Grosset, 1965; *When I Grow Up,* Grosset, 1965; *How to Care for Your Dog,* Four Winds, 1967; *Barney Beagle Goes Camping,* Grosset, 1970.

FOR MORE INFORMATION SEE: *New York Times Book Review,* May 9, 1965, November 5, 1967.

BLISHEN, Edward 1920-

PERSONAL: Born April 29, 1920, in Whetstone, Middlesex, England; son of William George (a civil servant) and Elizabeth Ann (Pye) Blishen; married Nancy Smith, November 4, 1948; children: Jonathan Edward, Nicholas Martin. *Education:* Educated in England. *Home:* 12 Bartrams Lane, Hadley Wood, Barnet, England. *Agent:* Irene Josephy, 35 Craven St., Strand, London W.C. 2, England.

CAREER: Employed in London, England, and vicinity, as journalist, 1937-41, preparatory schoolmaster, 1946-49, and teacher of English in secondary school, 1950-59; University of York, Heslington, England, part-time lecturer in department of education, 1963-65; full-time professional writer, Barnet, England, 1965—. Conductor for many years of British Broadcasting Corp. overseas program directed at young African writers. *Member:* P.E.N. (executive committee of English Center, 1962-66), Society of Author . . . (committee of management, 1971-74). *Awards, honors:* Carnegie Medal, 1970, for *The God Beneath the Sea.*

WRITINGS: *Roaring Boys,* Thames & Hudson, 1955; (editor) *Junior Pears Encyclopaedia,* Pelham Books, 1961, and annual revisions, 1962—; (editor) *Education Today,* BBC Publications, 1963; (editor) *Oxford Book of Poetry for Children,* Oxford University Press, 1963; *Town Story,* Anthony Blond, 1964; (editor) *Miscellany,* Oxford University Press, annually, 1964-69; (editor) *Come Reading* (anthology of prose for young readers), M. Joseph, 1967; *Hugh Lofting,* Bodley Head Monograph, 1968; (editor) *Blond's Encyclopedia of Education,* Anthony Blond, 1969; *This Soft Lot,* Thames & Hudson, 1969; (editor) *The School That I'd Like,* Penguin, 1969; (with Leon Garfield) *The God Beneath the Sea,* Kestrel, 1970; *A Cackhanded War,* Thames & Hudson, 1972; (with Leon Garfield) *The Golden Shadow,* Kestrel, 1973; *Uncommon Entrance,* Thames & Hudson, 1974; (editor) *The Thorny Paradise,* Kestrel, 1975.

WORK IN PROGRESS: With Christopher Cook, preparing *Pears Guide to the Modern World,* to be published in 1976; writing a novel set in a teachers' training college just after the Second World War.

SIDELIGHTS: "My chief frustrated ambition is to write a series of novels that would trace the extraordinary and often deeply painful changes brought about within a single family by the educational advance of the past seventy years."

BODECKER, N. M. 1922-

PERSONAL: Born January 13, 1922, in Copenhagen, Denmark. *Education:* Attended Technical Society's Schools (Copenhagen), School of Architecture, 1939-41, School of Applied Arts, 1941-44; also attended Copenhagen School of Commerce, 1942-44. *Residence:* Hancock, N.H.

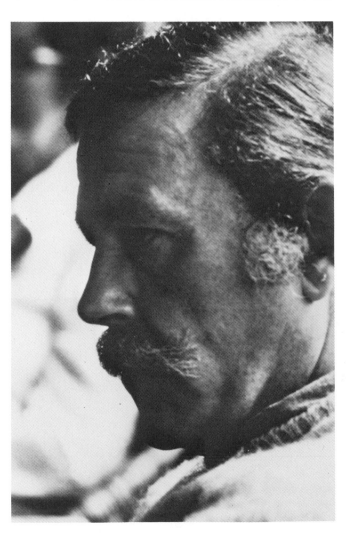

N. M. BODECKER

Something about the Author

Crack! went the ice.
Squeek! went the mice.
Home in her basket went little Miss Price.
■ (From *It's Raining Said John Twaining* by N. M. Bodecker. Illustrated by the author.)

CAREER: Free-lance writer and illustrator in Copenhagen, Denmark, 1944-52, and New York, N.Y., 1952—. *Military service:* Royal Danish Artillery, 1945-47. *Awards, honors:* Citation from Society of Illustrators, 1965, for *David Copperfield*; *Miss Jaster's Garden* was named among the Year's Ten Best Illustrated Books by the *New York Times Book Review*, 1973; *It's Raining Said John Twaining* received a Notable Book award from the American Library Association, 1973, was named among the Best Books of the Year by the School Library Association, 1973, among the Best Children's Books of the Year by the National Book League of the United Kingdom, 1973, received a Christopher award, 1974, and has been selected by A.I.E.A. as one of the twenty books to represent the United States at the Biennial of Illustration, Bratislava, 1976; *The Mushroom Center Disaster* was a Children's Book Showcase Title, 1975.

WRITINGS—Poems: *Digtervandring* (title means "Poets Ramble"), Forum, 1943; *Graa Fugle* (title means "Grey Birds"), Prior, 1946.

Juvenile: (Self-illustrated) *Miss Jaster's Garden*, Golden Press, 1972; (translator, illustrator, and editor) *It's Raining Said John Twaining* (Danish nursery rhymes; ALA Notable Book), Atheneum, 1973; *The Mushroom Centre Disaster*, Atheneum, 1974; (self-illustrated) *Let's Marry Said the Cherry, and Other Nonsense Poems*, Atheneum, 1974.

Poetry represented in the anthology *Ung Dansk Lyrik* (title means "Young Danish Poetry"), edited by Niels Kaas Johansen, Hirschsprung (Copenhagen), 1949.

Illustrator: Sigfred Pedersen, *Spillebog for Hus, Hjem og Kro* (title means "Book of Games for House, Home and Inn"), Erichsen (Copenhagen), 1948; Patric Dennis, *Oh!*

What a Wonderful Wedding, Crowell, 1953; Roger Eddy, *The Bulls and the Bees*, Crowell, 1956; Russell Lynes, *Cadwallader: A Diversion*, Harper, 1959; Mark Caine, *The S-Man*, Houghton, 1960; Agnes DeMille, *The Book of the Dance*, Golden Press, 1963; Charles Dickens, *David Copperfield*, Macmillan, 1966.

Illustrator—Juvenile: Edward Eager, *Half Magic*, Harcourt, 1954; Evan Commager, *Cousins*, Harper, 1956; Eager, *Knight's Castle*, Harcourt, 1956; Anne Barrett, *Songberd's Grove*, Bobbs-Merrill, 1956; Eager, *Magic by the Lake*, Harcourt, 1957; Commanger, *Beaux*, Harper, 1958; Eager, *The Time Garden*, Harcourt, 1958; Eager, *Magic Or Not*, Harcourt, 1959; Eager, *The Well Wishers*, Harcourt, 1960; Adeline Hull, *Sylvester, The Mouse with the Musical Ear*, Golden Press, 1961; Eager, *Seven Day Magic*, Harcourt, 1962; Miriam Schlein, *The Snake in the Carpool*, Abelard, 1963; Doris Adelberg, *Lizzie's Twins*, Dial, 1964; Josephine Gibson, *Is There a Mouse in the House?*, Macmillan, 1965; Mary Francis Shura, *Shoe Full of Shamrock*, Atheneum, 1965; Michael Jennings, *Mattie Fritts and the Flying Mushroom*, Windmill Books, 1973; Robert Kraus, *Good Night Little One*, Windmill Books, 1973; Kraus, *Good Night Richard Rabbit*, Windmill

If you follow the path, through the mole hills, you come at last to a small clearing full of white mushrooms. ■ (From *The Mushroom Center Disaster* by N. M. Bodecker. Illustrated by Erik Blegvad.)

Books, 1973; Kraus, *Good Night Little A.B.C.*, Windmill Books, 1973; Kraus, *The Night-Lite Calendar 1974*, Windmill Books, 1973; Kraus, *The Night-Lite Calendar 1975*, Windmill Books, 1974.

Contributor of illustrations: Celeste Andrews Seton and Clark Andrews, *Helen Gould Was My Mother-in-Law*, Crowell, 1953; Lynes, *Confessions of a Dilettante*, Harper, 1966; *Fun and Laughter: A Treasure House of Humor*, Reader's Digest, 1967; Henry F. Salerno, editor, *English Drama in Transition*, Pegasus, 1968; Helmut E. Gerber, editor, *The English Short Story in Transition*, Pegasus, 1968; John M. Munro, editor, *English Poetry in Transition*, Pegasus, 1968. Also contributor of illustrations to magazines, including *Holiday*, *McCall's*, *Saturday Evening Post*, *Esquire*, and *Ladies' Home Journal*.

WORK IN PROGRESS: The Day the Railroad Died (novel); *Travelling Light* (short stories); *Rook House* (autobiographical); *Good Morning, Dr. Yawning* (nonsense poems); *Pigeontoes' and Calicos'* (nursery rhymes); two novels for children, *Ben's Island* and *Colonel Crumpet's Little Journey*; and several picture books, *Who Is Mr. Giraffe?*, *Our House*, *The King with the Blooming Umbrella*, *Mrs. Richardson in the Chicken Coop*, and *The Story of Squilliam Squirt, and Other Stories*.

SIDELIGHTS: "I write and draw because that is what I was meant to do. I have never seriously considered any other occupation, though I have occasionally been sidetracked. I have many additional interests, but no other absolute needs. I write for children because I have retained strong emotional ties to the childhood condition and need to share my imaginings with a sympathetic audience." Bodecker's books have also been published in Canada, England, France, Sweden, Denmark, Italy, Germany, Holland, and Spain.

FOR MORE INFORMATION SEE: Illustrators of Children's Books, 1946-1956, Horn Book, 1958; *Illustrators of Children's Books, 1957-1966*, Horn Book 1968; *New York Times Book Review*, November 12, 1972, November 25, 1973; *New York*, December 17, 1973; *Horn Book*, October, 1974, December, 1974.

BRANDENBERG, Franz 1932-

PERSONAL: Born February 10, 1932, in Zug, Switzerland; son of Franz and Marie (Sigrist) Brandenberg; married Aliki Liacouras (an author and illustrator under name Aliki), March 15, 1957; children: Jason, Alexa Demetria. *Education:* Attended boarding school in Switzerland during his teens. *Home:* 473 West End Ave., New York, N.Y. 10024.

CAREER: Began apprenticeship with publisher and bookseller in Lucerne, Switzerland, 1949; continued in book trade, 1952-60, working in bookshops or publishing houses in London, Paris, and Florence; literary agent in New York, N.Y., 1960-72; writer for children, 1970—.

WRITINGS—All illustrated by his wife, Aliki: *I Once Knew a Man*, Macmillan, 1970; *Fresh Cider and Pie*, Macmillan, 1973; *No School Today*, Macmillan, 1975; *A Secret for Grandmother's Birthday*, Greenwillow Books, in press.

FRANZ BRANDENBERG

SIDELIGHTS: "When I was seven years old we moved to a small Swiss village, where 'nothing was going on.' I was determined to get the place moving by organizing shooting competitions, wrestling matches and performances of plays in my parents' car-less garage. The plays were my adaptations of fairy tales and historical events.

"My talent for organizing made me anything but popular with the other children. The losers in the competitions and matches would run away with the prizes (donated by my parents) before they could be awarded to the winners. Whoever didn't have a part in the plays would sabotage our performances, by pulling down the curtain and attacking the actors, or by staging a counter-performance in the spectator section of the garage.

"When I was thirteen, I went to boarding school, far from the village. . . . In Florence, in 1957, I met my wife, Aliki. We moved, first to Berne, then to Zurich. In 1960 we came to New York. In 1964 our son, Jason was born. In 1966 we had our daughter, Alexa.

"We like to spend our summers travelling, mostly in Europe."

FOR MORE INFORMATION SEE: Horn Book, October, 1973; *New York*, December 17, 1973.

BRIER, Howard M(axwell)   1903-1969

PERSONAL: Born March 20, 1903, in River Falls, Wis.; son of Warren Judson and Marion (Royce) Brier; married Grace Kjelstad, December 25, 1926; children: Warren, Nancy (Mrs. Peter Rybock). *Education:* University of Washington, Seattle, B.A., 1925, M.Ed., 1931; University of California, Berkeley, postgraduate study. *Politics:* Independent. *Religion:* Protestant.

CAREER: Seattle (Wash.) public schools, teacher of journalism and junior high principal, 1933-47; University of Washington, Seattle, 1947-69, associate professor and executive assistant at School of Communications. Sometime staff member of newspapers in Everett and Seattle, Wash., including *Seattle Post-Intelligencer.* Alberta Teachers' Association, writer's consultant for Banff Workshop, 1950-52; University of California, director of Journalism Seminar, 1961-64. Keep Washington Green Association, state director, 1940-48. *Member:* American Association of University Professors, Sigma Delta Chi, Phi Delta Kappa, Beta Theta Pi.

WRITINGS—All youth books except where noted: *Waterfront Beat*, Random, 1937; *Skycruiser*, Random, 1939; *Smoke Eater*, Random, 1941; *Skyfreighter*, Random, 1942; *Swing Shift*, Random, 1943; *Skyblazer*, Random, 1946; *Phantom Backfield*, Random, 1948; *Blackboard Magic*, Random, 1949; *Shortstop Shadow*, Random, 1950; *Cinder Cyclone*, Random, 1952; *Fighting Heart*, Doubleday, 1956; *Sawdust Empire* (adult book), Knopf, 1958. Contributor of stories to more than fifteen anthologies. Also contributor of more than 150 short stories and articles to magazines, including *Boys' Life, American Boy, St. Nicholas, Open Road, Boys' Today, Scholastic Editor.* Editor of *Student and Publisher*, 1955-64.

WORK IN PROGRESS: A novel for young people; short stories.

SIDELIGHTS: Nine of his twelve books have been Junior Literary Guild selections.

FOR MORE INFORMATION SEE: More Junior Authors, edited by Muriel Fuller, H. W. Wilson, 1963.

(Died October 3, 1969)

BROCK, Emma L(illian)   1886-1974

PERSONAL: Born June 11, 1886, in Fort Shaw, Mont.; daughter of Morton Richmere and Emma (Brownson) Brock. *Education:* University of Minnesota, B.A., 1908; studied at Minneapolis School of Art, 1910-14, Art Students League, New York, N.Y., 1917-18, 1921-28. *Politics:* Republican. *Religion:* Episcopalian. *Home:* 3719 Bryant Ave. South, Minneapolis, Minn. 55409.

CAREER: Minneapolis (Minn.) Public Library, assistant librarian, art department, 1914-17, 1918-21, 1928-32; New York (N.Y.) Public Library, assistant librarian, children's rooms, 1921-28; free-lance writer and illustrator of children's books. *Member:* Minnesota Artists, Authors League, Artists Guild, National Writers Club, Women's City Club (St. Paul, Minn.).

WRITINGS—Author and illustrator: *Runaway Sardine*, Knopf, 1929; *To Market, to Market*, Knopf, 1930; *Greedy Goat*, Knopf, 1931; *One Little Indian Boy*, Knopf, 1932; *The Hen That Kept House*, Knopf, 1934; *Little Fat Gretchen*, Knopf, 1932; *Drusilla*, Macmillan, 1937; *Pig with a Front Porch*, Knopf, 1937; *Nobodies Mouse*, Knopf, 1938; *Till Potatoes Grow on Trees*, Knopf, 1938, new edition, 1947; *Heedless Susan*, Knopf, 1939.

At Midsummer Time, 1940, *Then Came Adventure*, 1941, *Here Comes Kristie*, 1942, *Topsy Turvy Family*, 1943, *Uncle Bennie Goes Visiting*, 1944, *Mr. Wren's House*, 1944, *Umbrella Man*, 1945, *Bird's Christmas*, 1946, *Little Duchess*, 1948, *Kristie and the Colt*, 1949 (all published by Knopf).

Three Ring Circus, 1950, *Kristie's Buttercup*, 1952, *Kristie Goes to the Fair*, 1953, *Ballet for Mary*, 1954, *Plug Horse Derby*, 1955, *Come On-Along Fish*, 1957, *Skipping Island*, 1958, *Patty on Horse Back*, 1959, *Pancakes and the Merry-Go-Round*, 1960, *Plaid Cow*, 1961, *Mary's Secret*, 1962, *Mary's Magic Camera*, 1963, *Mary Makes A Cake*, 1964, *Sudden Mary on Roller Skates*, 1967 (all published by Knopf).

SIDELIGHTS: Here Comes Kristie was an N.B.C. television special.

HOBBIES AND OTHER INTERESTS: Reading, music.

(Died August 17, 1974)

EMMA L. BROCK

BROWER, Millicent

PERSONAL: Born in Jersey City, N.J. *Education:* Douglass College of Rutgers University, B.L. in Journalism. *Residence:* New York, N.Y.

CAREER: Radio, television, and stage actress (star of "Young Widder Brown," a radio serial). Radio reporter on "Dimension," WCBS-Radio, 1967. Feature writer, reporter, and drama critic, *Village Voice*, 1955, 1963; syndicated feature writer, Women's News Service; drama critic, *Broadside*, 1970. Appointed member of New York Mayor John V. Lindsay's Task Force on Noise Control.

WRITINGS: Ingenue (novel), Ballantine, 1959 (published in England as *Make Me a Star*, Panther, 1960); *I Am Going Nowhere* (poems for children), Putnam, 1972, (contributor) *The Scribner Anthology for Young People*, edited by Anne Diven, Scribner, 1976. Work is anthologized in *The Village Voice Reader*, edited by Daniel Wolf and Edwin Fancher, Doubleday, 1962. Contributor of fiction, nonfiction, and poetry to national and international magazines, including *Cricket* and *Elementary English*. Contributor to the report of the Task Force on Noise Control.

WORK IN PROGRESS: Several books for children; stories, lyric poetry, a book of limericks, and a new book of rhymes.

SIDELIGHTS: "*I Am Going Nowhere* resulted from a teaching experience in day care. I observed children reading and reciting all the old nursery rhymes and decided to try to write more modern ones. My rhymes were tried out in class; the children responded enthusiastically and the book was published soon afterwards.

"I find inspiration for my poems, both humorous and lyric, from observing life itself, from taking nature walks, from going to museums, art galleries and libraries; from old prints and books that I search out in thrift shops and curio shops; from conversations, from designs, from the simplest object.

"I began my career as an actress, and acted on the Broadway stage, on radio and on television. I have also been a syndicated writer for Women's News Service, a reporter for C.B.S. radio and the *Village Voice*. Currently, I write, act, and also substitute teach in day care."

FOR MORE INFORMATION SEE: Newsweek, July 9, 1956; *Village Voice*, March 4, 1959; *Variety*, September 24, 1969; *Elementary English*, November-December, 1973.

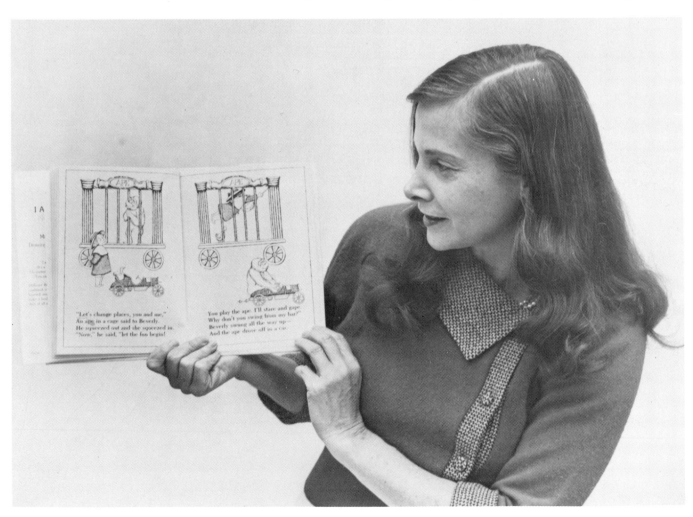

MILLICENT BROWER

"But you've got so many sweaters on you can't fit into school." ■ (From *I Am Going Nowhere* by Millicent Brower. Illustrated by Ronald Himler.)

This small town house has been successfully adapted for me by the practitioners of three or more compatible professions— alchemy, apothecary, and astrology. ■ (From *The Book of Weird* by Barbara Ninde Byfield. Illustrated by the author.)

Something about the Author

BARBARA NINDE BYFIELD

BYFIELD, Barbara Ninde 1930-

PERSONAL: Born March 28, 1930, in Abilene, Tex.; daughter of Harry W. and Rudisill (Freeman) Ninde; divorced; children: Barbery, Tamsen. *Education:* University of Wyoming, student, 1947-49. *Home:* 133 Christopher St., New York, N.Y. 10014.

WRITINGS—All self-illustrated: *The Eating in Bed Cookbook*, Macmillan, 1962; *The Glass Harmonica*, Macmillan, 1967; *The Haunted Spy*, Doubleday, 1969; *The Haunted Ghost*, Doubleday, 1971; *The Haunted Churchbell*, Doubleday, 1971; *The Book of Weird*, Doubleday, 1973; *Solemn High Murder* (adult mystery), Doubleday, 1975.

Illustrator: Donald Hutter, *Upright Hilda*, Bobbs, 1968; Seth M. Agnew, *The Giant Sandwich*, Doubleday, 1970; Harvey Swadow, *The Mystery of the Spanish Silver Mine*, Doubleday, 1971; Glendon Swarthout, *TV Thompson*, Doubleday, 1972; Herb Caen, *The Cable Car and the Dragon*, Doubleday, 1972; Armstrong, *Hadassah: Esther, The Orphan Queen*, Doubleday, 1972.

CAIN, Christopher
See FLEMING, Thomas J(ames)

CARLSON, Bernice Wells 1910-

PERSONAL: Born July 21, 1910, in Clare, Mich.; daughter of George Byron (a real estate broker) and Bernice (a concert singer; maiden name Cook) Wells; married Carl Walter Carlson (a professor emeritus of chemical engineering), September 10, 1935; children: Christine (Mrs. Paul J. Umberger), Philip, Marta. *Education:* Ripon College, A.B. *Politics:* Republican. *Religion:* Reformed Church in America. *Home and office:* Route 3, Box 332d, Skillmans Lane, Somerset, N.J. 08873.

CAREER: *State Journal*, Lansing, Mich., society editor, 1936-38, part-time feature writer, 1938-43; Franklin Township (N.J.) schools, substitute teacher, 1948-68. New Jersey Association for Retarded Children, member of executive board of Raritan Valley Unit, 1948-70. Active in Cub and Brownie Scout work. *Member:* Franklin Township Woman's Club, Franklin Township Conservation Club, Alpha Chi Alpha, Theta Alpha Phi, Pi Kappa Delta. *Awards, honors:* Distinguished Alumna citation, Ripon College; New Jersey Association of Teachers of English, Authors Award for children's books, 1963, 1965; New Jersey Writing Team of the Year (with Carl W. Carlson), 1966.

WRITINGS: *The Junior Party Book*, Cokesbury, 1939, revised edition, Abingdon-Cokesbury, 1948, *Make It Yourself*, 1950, *Do It Yourself*, 1952, *Fun For One or Two*, 1954, (contributor) *Christmas Programs*, 1954, *Act It Out*, 1956, *Make It and Use It*, 1958, *The Right Play for You*, 1960, (with David R. Ginglend) *Play Activities for the Retarded Child*, 1961, (with Kari Hunt) *Masks and Mask Makers*, 1961, *The Party Book for Boys and Girls*, 1963, *Listen! And Help Tell the Story*, 1965, (with Carl W. Carlson) *Water Fit to Use*, John Day, 1966, *You Know What? I Like Animals*, 1968, (with David Ginglend) *Recreation for Retarded Teenagers and Young Adults*, 1968, *Play a Part*, 1970, *Let's Pretend It Happened to You*, 1973, (with Ristiina Wigg) *We Want Sunshine in Our Houses*, 1973, *Funny-Bone Dramatics*, 1974 (all published by Abingdon except where otherwise noted). Contributor of articles to magazines and to *Childcraft Encyclopedia* and *Grolier Topical Encyclopedia*; contributor of feature stories to *Milwaukee Journal* and *Detroit News*.

WORK IN PROGRESS: A story-activity book, in collaboration with "an art teacher who was a Brownie Scout when I was her leader."

SIDELIGHTS: "Sometimes I think that my life as an author has been lucky because certain 'i's' and 'e's' came my way. When I was a child, my parents urged me and my

A ship like this sinks only once. ■ (From *Funny-Bone Dramatics* by Bernice Wells Carlson. Illustrated by Charles Cox.)

brother and sister to use *ingenuity* and *imagination* to do the things we wanted to do, using materials on hand. In high school, my teachers stressed *intellectual* curiosity: savoring the joy of learning with no practical use in mind. My husband and children gave me *encouragement* as I planned things for children to do and reported the most successful projects. All kinds of children, as individuals and in many kinds of groups, have responded, and still respond, with *enthusiasm* as we carry out ideas together.''

HOBBIES AND OTHER INTERESTS: Gardening, playing bridge, reading, working with children, flower arranging.

FOR MORE INFORMATION SEE: Sunday Home News, New Brunswick, N.J., April 20, 1952, March 13, 1960, March 5, 1961; *Saturday Review/World*, December 4, 1973.

BERNICE WELLS CARLSON

CARPELAN, Bo (Gustaf Bertelsson) 1926-

PERSONAL: Surname is pronounced *Car*-pel-an; born October 25, 1926, in Helsinki, Finland; son of Bertel Gustaf (an engineer) and Ebba (Lindahl) Carpelan; married Barbro Eriksson (a reservations clerk at Finnair), April 13, 1954; children: Anders, Johanna. *Education:* University of Helsinki, Ph.D., 1960. *Home:* Nyckelpigvaagen 2B, Tapiola, Finland.

CAREER: Poet and author; City Library, Helsinki, Finland, assistant chief librarian, 1963—. *Member:* Finnish-Swedish Authors Society, P.E.N. *Awards, honors:* Finnish State Prize and Nils Holgersson Prize, 1969, for *Baagen*.

WRITINGS—Books for children: Anders paa oen, Bonnier (Stockholm), 1959; *Anders i stan*, Bonnier, 1962.

Books for young people and adults: *Baagen: Beraettelsen om en sommar som var annorlunda*, Bonnier, 1968, translation by Sheila La Farge published as *Bow Island: The*

BO CARPELAN

liken Finland (essays), Soederstroem, 1961; *Den svala dagen*, 1961; (with others) *Aaret i norden* (nonfiction), Bonnier and Hasselbalch (Copenhagen), 1962; *73 dikter*, 1966; (compiler) *Finlandssvenska lyrikboken* (anthology), Forum (Stockholm), 1967; *Gaarden*, 1969; *Roesterna i den sena timmen* (novel), Bonnier, 1971; "Paluu nuoruuteen" (play), first produced in Helsinki, Finland, at Kansallisteatteri, in 1971; *Kaellan*, 1972.

Author of works for television, theater, and radio, including a radio play, "Voices at a Late Hour," produced by Canadian Broadcasting Corp.

WORK IN PROGRESS: A new collection of poems; a novel.

SIDELIGHTS: Carpelan himself made the designation that *Baagen* and *Paradiset* are books for teens *and* adults. He finds it "important to break down barrier between books for young people and books for adults." *Baagen* has been published in German, Polish, and Danish, in addition to the two editions in English. Both of the *Anders* titles have been translated into German and Polish, and *Anders paa oen* into Norwegian as well. Carpelan visited the United States in 1961.

CARTER, Dorothy Sharp   1921-

PERSONAL: Born March 22, 1921, in Chicago, Ill.; daughter of William Barnard (a professor of medicine) and Alice (Percy) Sharp; married Albert Edwin Carter (a foreign service officer), April 19, 1946; children: Robert Sharp, Janet E., Deborah C. (Mrs. Jeffrey Blank), Alice P. *Education:* Mills College, B.A., 1942, secondary teaching certificate, 1944; University of Texas, Austin, M.L.S., 1971. *Politics:* Independent. *Religion:* Episcopalian. *Home:* 208 Gannet Cove, Austin, Tex. 78746. *Agent:* Marilyn Marlow, Curtis Brown, Ltd., 60 East 56th St., New York, N.Y. 10022.

CAREER: High school English teacher in California, 1944-45; teacher of English in bi-national cultural center, San Jose, Costa Rica, 1945-46; free-lance writer.

WRITINGS: The Enchanted Orchard and Other Folktales of Central America, Harcourt, 1973; *Greedy Mariani and Other Folktales of the Antilles*, Atheneum, 1974. Contributor of short stories and articles to *Travel, Nature, Highlights for Children, Child Life*, and *Humpty Dumpty*.

WORK IN PROGRESS: Research in Latin American folktales.

SIDELIGHTS: "I grew up in Galveston, Texas. After graduating from Mills College, I taught for a year in California and was then sent by the Interamerican Schools Service to teach English in a bi-national cultural center in San Jose, Costa Rica. There I met my future husband, who was cultural attache in the American Embassy. We spent the next twenty-four years in the Foreign Service, mostly in Latin America (eleven years in Central and South America) and three years in Germany.

Story of a Summer That Was Different, Delacorte, 1972 (translation published in England as *The Wide Wings of Summer*, Heinemann, 1972); *Paradiset*, Bonnier, 1973.

Works for adults—Collections of poems, except as noted, most published simultaneously by Bonnier in Stockholm and Holger Schildt in Helsinki: *Som en dunkel vaerme*, 1946; *Du moerka oeverlevande*, 1947; *Variationer*, 1950; *Minus sju*, 1952; *Objekt foer ord*, 1954; *Landskapets foervandlingar*, 1957; *Studier i Gunnar Bjoerlings diktning 1922-1933* (doctoral dissertation), Svenska Litteratursaellskapet i Finland, 1960; (translator into Swedish with others) Eino S. Repo and Nils B. Stormbom, compilers, *Ny finsk lyrik* (anthology), 1960; (with others) *Jag lever i repub-*

"Now that my husband is retired, we divide our time between Lakeway, a resort development twenty-five miles west of Austin, and a small ranch on the Pedernales River, complete with pet deer, and other forms of wildlife. While working towards my Master's degree in Library Science at the University of Texas, I took on as an individual study project the collecting and translating of some Central American folktales. My professor sent the manuscript to Margaret McElderry, then at Harcourt, who accepted the collection for publication. That was *The Enchanted Orchard* and because of the fun I had doing it, I went on to make a similar collection of West Indian folktales, which became *Greedy Mariani*."

HOBBIES AND OTHER INTERESTS: Travel, foreign language study, wildlife of Texas, gardening, tennis.

"What are you doing, Compae Rabbit?"
"Brushing flies off your neck, Tiger."
(From *Greedy Mariani* by Dorothy Sharp Carter. Illustrated by Trina Schart Hyman.)

DOROTHY SHARP CARTER

CHARLOT, Jean   1898-

PERSONAL: Born February 7, 1898, in Paris, France; son of Henri and Anne (Goupil) Charlot; married Zohmah Day, May 26, 1939; children: Ann Maria, John Pierre, Martin Day, Peter Francis. *Politics:* Democrat. *Religion:* Roman Catholic. *Home:* 4956 Kahala Ave., Honolulu, Hawaii.

CAREER: Mexican government, Mexico City, mural painter, 1921-24; Carnegie Institute of Washington, D.C., staff artist in Yucatan, 1926-30; Art Students League, New York, N.Y., teacher, 1931-41; University of Georgia, Athens, artist-in-residence, 1941-44; Colorado Springs (Colo.) Fine Arts Center, director, 1947-49; University of Hawaii, Honolulu, professor, 1949-66, now retired. Painter of forty murals, mostly done in fresco, in churches, university and public buildings, and homes, in United States, Mexico, and Fiji; work exhibited at more than one hundred one-man shows; illustrator of some fifty books besides his own. Ryerson Lecturer at Yale University; summer lecturer at

Columbia University and University of California. *Military service:* French Army, Artillery, 1917-20, acting captain, 1940; became captain. *Member:* College Art Association, Hawaiian Historical Society. *Awards, honors:* Guggenheim fellowship, 1945-47, for writing in Mexico; D.F.A., Grinnell College, 1947; LL.D., St. Mary's College, Notre Dame, Ind., 1957; Benjamin Franklin Fellow, Royal Society of the Arts, 1972.

WRITINGS: (With Earl H. Morris and Ann Axtell Morris) *The Temple of the Warriors at Chichen Itza, Yucatan*, Volumes I and II, Carnegie Institute of Washington, 1931; (with J. Eric Thompson and Harry E. D. Pollock) *A Preliminary Study of the Ruins of Coba, Quintana Roo, Mexico*, Carnegie Institute of Washington, 1931; *Catalogue of Prints*, privately painted by Albert Carman, 1936; *Pictures and Picture Making* (lectures), privately printed by Disney Studios, 1938; *Art from the Mayans to Disney*, Sheed, 1939; (author of commentaries) *Charlot Murals in Georgia*, University of Georgia Press, 1945; *Guadalupe Posada: 100 Grabados en Madera*, Arsacio Vanegas Arroyo, 1945; (author of introduction) *Portrait of Latin America as Seen by Her Printmakers*, Hastings, 1946; (author of prologue) *Estampas de Yucatan Alfredo Zalce*, La Estampa Mexicana, 1946; *100 Original Woodcuts by Posada*, Taylor Museum, 1947.

Art-Making from Mexico to China, Sheed, 1950; *Dance of Death: 50 Drawings and Captions*, Sheed, 1951; (contributor) *Born Catholics*, Sheed, 1954; *Choris and Kamehameha*, Bishop Museum Press, 1958; *Mexican Art and the Academy of San Carlos, 1875-1915*, University of Texas Press, 1962; *Na'auao* (heroic comedy; produced by Honolulu Community Theatre, 1962), privately printed, 1962; *Mexican Mural Renaissance, 1920-1925*, Yale University Press, 1963; *Three Plays of Ancient Hawaii*, University of Hawaii Press, 1963; *Laukiamanui Kahiki*, privately printed, 1963; *Posada's Dance of Death*, Pratt Graphic Art Center, 1964; *Two Lonos* (play), privately printed, 1965.

(From *Secret of the Andes* by Ann Nolan Clark. Illustrated by Jean Charlot.)

JEAN CHARLOT

Other portfolios of work: *Picture Book* (lithographs), John Becker, 1933; *Mexihkanantli* (chromolithographs), La Estampa Mexicana, 1947; *Picture Book II* (lithographs), Dawson's Book Shop, 1974.

Adult books illustrated include: *The Book of Christopher Columbus*, Yale University Press, 1930; *Characters of the Reformation*, Sheed (London), 1936; Shakespeare, *Henry the Sixth, Part III*, Norton, 1940; *Carmen*, Limited Editions Club, 1941; *Secret of the Andes*, Viking, 1952; *Selections from Fornander's Hawaiian Antiquities and Folklore*, 1959; Thornton Wilder, *The Bridge of San Luis Rey*, Limited Editions Club, 1962.

Children's books illustrated include: *Tawynmore*, Doubleday, 1931; *A Child's Good Night Book*, Scott, 1942; *Two Little Trains*, Scott, 1949; Margaret Wise Brown, *Fox Eyes*, Pantheon, 1951; Ann Nolan Clark, *Secret of the*

Andes, Viking, 1952; Joseph Krumgold, *And Now Miguel*, Crowell, 1953; Clyde Robert Bulla, *Poppy Seeds*, Crowell, 1955; *Hester and the Gnomes*, Whittlesley House, 1955; *Julio*, Abelard, 1955; Anita Brenner, *Dumb Juan and the Bandits*, Young Scott, 1957; Miriam Schlein, *Kittens, Cubs and Babies*, Scott, 1959; Anita Brenner, *The Timid Ghost*, Scott, 1966; Claire H. Bishop, *Martin De Porres: Hero*, Houghton, new edition, 1973.

Also writer of script for three films in color and sound; articles in magazines.

WORK IN PROGRESS: Ancient Hawaiian culture; further Hawaiian plays, one in the Hawaiian language.

SIDELIGHTS: His one-act play, "Spirit Island," was produced at Kennedy Theater, University of Hawaii, and his one-act "Laukiamanuikahiki" was sponsored at Punahou School by the Hawaiian Historical Society. He has been commissioned to do a portrait of Hawaiian King Kamehameha I for the atomic submarine of that name.

FOR MORE INFORMATION SEE: More Junior Authors, edited by Muriel Fuller, H. W. Wilson, 1963; *Illustrators of Children's Books: 1957-1966*, Horn Book, 1968.

CHERRYHOLMES, Anne
See PRICE, Olive

CHORAO, (Ann Mc)Kay (Sproat) 1936-

PERSONAL: Surname is pronounced Shoe-*row*; born January 7, 1936, in Elkhart, Ind.; daughter of James McKay (a lawyer) and Elizabeth (Fleming) Sproat; married Ernesto A. K. Chorao (an artist), June 10, 1960; children: Jamie, Peter, Ian. *Education:* Wheaton College, Norton, Mass., B.A., 1958; graduate study at Chelsea School of Art (London), 1958-59. *Home:* 290 Riverside Dr., New York, N.Y. 10025.

CAREER: Artist, illustrator of children's books, and writer. *Awards, honors: Albert's Toothache* was a Children's Book Showcase Title, 1975, and named one of the 50 Best Books by the American Institute of Graphic Arts, 1974; *Ralph and the Queen's Bathtub* was selected for the American Institute of Graphic Arts Children's Book Show, 1973/74.

WRITINGS—Self-illustrated books for children: *The Repair of Uncle Toe*, Farrar, Straus, 1972; *A Magic Eye for Ida*, Seabury, 1973; *Ralph and the Queen's Bathtub*, Farrar, Straus, 1974; *Ida Makes a Movie*, Seabury, 1974; *Maudie's Umbrella*, Dutton, in press.

Illustrator: Judith Viorst, *My Mama Says*, Atheneum, 1973; Madeline Edmonson, *Witch's Egg*, Seabury, 1974; Barbara Williams, *Albert's Toothache*, Dutton, 1974; Winifred Rosen, *Henrietta: The Wild Woman of Borneo*, Four Winds, 1975; Barbara Williams, *Kevin's Garden*, Dutton, 1975.

WORK IN PROGRESS: Illustrations for *Someday I Will Take Care of You*, by Barbara Williams.

"I was raised mainly in a mid-western suburb with pretty tree-lined streets, wide lawns (where sprinklers twirled all summer), and colonial houses in which two children and a cocker spaniel were standard. (I had one brother and one dog, Tuffy.) We lived in Beachwood Village outside Cleveland, Ohio.

"I went to an excellent school named Laurel, where the girls wore dismal gym bloomers for gym and utilitarian green uniforms at all other times, and where lipstick was not allowed, but where creativity was. The art department was far better than the one at Wheaton College, where I later went. And the English department put great stress on creative writing. The training was good.

"After four (somewhat wasted) years in college, I went for a year of travel and study in England. At Chelsea School of Art I met my future husband and studied drawing and painting. Ernesto Chorao and I were married in 1960, and lived in San Francisco until 1962, when we moved to New York. All three sons were born in New York—Jamie (1962), Peter (1964), and Ian (1968).

"Our life here is quite different from the one I knew as a child. We feel our children are getting a far broader view of life. They are exposed to all kinds of people, all kinds of life styles, to say nothing of the museums, plays, etc. (To balance all that we spend summers in a cottage on Lake Huron, in Canada.)

Ida felt she might cry. Right on her meringue glacé. ■ (From *Ida Makes a Movie* by Kay Chorao. Illustrated by the author.)

KAY CHORAO

"I like to think I write for my children, and sometimes I do. *Ralph and The Queen's Bathtub* was written with Peter in mind from the beginning. But usually I simply write what occurs to me and draw on my own feelings.

"When I illustrate, I try to express the text as appropriately as possible. When I read *Albert's Toothache*, for example, I knew the illustrations had to be soft and big. That's how the text 'felt' to me. With *The Witch's Egg* they had to be crisper, black and feathery. With *Maudie's Umbrella*, there had to be a feeling of a soft scurrying mole's world. Her eyesight was terrible, so I thought it would be fun to have hidden faces in the gnarled trees, growing things, and everyday objects, which Maudie rushed blindly past. I suppose the point is to create a personal world within the world confined by those book covers!"

CLARK, Margaret Goff 1913-

PERSONAL: Born March 7, 1913, in Oklahoma City, Okla.; daughter of Raymond Finla and Fanny (Church) Goff; married Charles Robert Clark, 1937; children: Robert Allen, Marcia Almeda. *Education:* Columbia University, summer student, 1934; State University of New York, College of Education at Buffalo, B.S. in Education, 1936. *Home:* 5621 Lockport Rd., Niagara Falls, N.Y. *Agent:* Caroline S. Lehman, Box 1697, Stuart, Fla. 33494.

CAREER: Elementary school teacher in Niagara, N.Y., 1933-34, Buffalo, N.Y., 1934-39; teacher of creative writing in adult education programs, 1960-61; teacher at Georgian College Summer School of the Arts, Huntsville, Ontario, Canada, 1974-75. Formerly deputy town clerk, Niagara, N.Y. *Member:* National League of American Pen Women (Western New York branch), Association of Professional Women Writers (president, 1960-61), Mystery Writers of America, Alpha Delta Kappa, Delta Kappa Gamma.

WRITINGS: The Mystery of Seneca Hill, Watts, 1961; *The Mystery of the Buried Indian Mask*, Watts, 1962; *Mystery of the Marble Zoo*, Funk, 1964; *Mystery at Star Lake*, Funk, 1965; *Adirondack Mountain Mystery*, Funk, 1966; *The Mystery of the Missing Stamps*, Funk, 1967; *Danger at Niagara*, Funk, 1968; *Freedom Crossing*, Funk, 1969; *Benjamin Banneker*, Garrard, 1971; *Mystery Horse*, Dodd, 1972; *Their Eyes on the Stars*, Garrard, 1973; *John Muir*, Garrard, 1974; *Death at Their Heels*, Dodd, 1975; *The Mysterious Hole* (talking book), International Learning Co., 1975. More than two hundred short stories in *American Girl, Ingenue, Teen Talk, The Instructor*, and other American and Canadian magazines.

It was not a grandstand seat. There were too many leaves and branches in the way, but by ducking this way and that, he could observe part of Birch Knoll Manor. ■ (From *Adirondack Mountain Mystery* by Margaret Goff Clark. Illustrated by Ernest Kurt Barth.)

Contributor to anthologies: *The New People and Progress*, Scott, 1955; *Let's Read*, Henry Holt, 1955; *Arrivals and Departures*, Allyn & Bacon, 1957; *Stories to Live By*, Platt, 1960; *Time of Starting Out*, Watts, 1962; *Acting, Acting*, Watts, 1962; *Pressing Onward*, Pacific Press, 1964; and to the *Encyclopedia Britannica'* Reading Series. Twenty-five one-act plays and numerous poems also have been published.

SIDELIGHTS: Margaret Clark began writing when her two children were young and the age level of the stories grew with the children. "Every day that it is possible I write from nine o'clock to noon, continuing for an hour or so after lunch, also if possible. I write at a desk in an upstairs bedroom of the hundred-year-old house where we live outside the city of Niagara Falls."

"I write for young people and of course for myself. Most of my books grow out of my own experiences. Places especially turn me on. For instance, my husband and I spend every summer at our cottage in Ontario, Canada, at the edge of Algonquin Park, a huge semi-wilderness of forest, lakes, and streams. After several years of canoeing, fishing, and camping in the park, the background was a part of me. I had to write a story about the park and the creatures who inhabit it. *Death at Their Heels* was the result, the story of two stepbrothers fleeing through Algonquin, pursued by a deadly enemy. I hope the tension of the story keeps the reader turning pages to see what happens next while he

MARGARET GOFF CLARK

learns something about the ways of bears, loons, and wolves and observes how two boys, miles apart at the beginning, come together through shared experience and thoughts."

In 1962, Clark was adopted by the Seneca Indians.

HOBBIES AND OTHER INTERESTS: Archaeology, history, travel, swimming.

FOR MORE INFORMATION SEE: Niagara Falls Gazette, July 31, 1960, March 11, 1962, April 19, 1964, August 16, 1964, October 23, 1973; *Buffalo Evening News*, March 9, 1964; *Buffalo Courier-Express*, December 19, 1971.

CLARK, Mavis Thorpe
(Mavis Latham)

PERSONAL: Born in Melbourne, Victoria, Australia; daughter of John Thorpe (a contractor) and Rose Matilda (Stanborough) Clark; married Harold Latham; children: Beverley Jeanne (Mrs. Ralph Henderson Lewis), Ronda Faye (Mrs. Peter Hall). *Education:* Attended Methodist Ladies' College, Melbourne. *Home:* 2 Crest Ave., Melbourne, Victoria 3103, Australia.

CAREER: Writer since her school days. *Member:* International P.E.N. (Australia Centre; vice-president of Melbourne branch, 1968, 1971, 1973, 1974; president of Melbourne branch, 1969), Australian Society of Authors (member of management committee), Fellowship of Australian Writers. *Awards, honors:* Commendation by Children's Book Council of Australia for *The Brown Land Was Green*, 1956, and *Blue Above the Trees*, 1968, and Book of the Year Award for *The Min-Min*, 1967; Deutscher Jugendbuchpreis (German Children's Book Award) for German editions of *Spark of Opal*, 1971, and *Iron Mountain*, 1973.

WRITINGS—Novels for young teens, except as noted: *Dark Pool Island*, Oxford University Press, 1949; *The Twins from Timber Creek*, Oxford University Press, 1949.

Home Again from Timber Creek, Oxford University Press, 1950; *Jingaroo*, Oxford University Press, 1951; *Missing Gold*, Hutchinson, 1951; *The Brown Land Was Green*, Heinemann, 1956, special school edition, Heinemann, 1957, reissued with new illustrations, Lansdowne Press, 1967, Hodder & Stoughton, 1975; *Gully of Gold*, Heinemann, 1958, reissued with new illustrations, Lansdowne Press, 1969; *Pony from Tarella*, Heinemann, 1959, reissued with new illustrations, Lansdowne Press, 1969; (under name Mavis Latham) *John Batman* (short biography), Oxford University Press, 1962.

They Came South, Heinemann, 1963, reissued with new illustrations, Lansdowne Press, 1971; *Fishing* (textbook), Oxford University Press, 1963; *The Min-Min*, Lansdowne Press, 1966, Macmillan (New York), 1969, Hodder & Stoughton, 1975; *Blue Above the Trees*, Lansdowne Press, 1967, Meredith, 1969, Hodder & Stoughton, 1975; *Spark of Opal*, Lansdowne Press, 1968, Macmillan (New York), 1973; *The Pack-tracker* (textbook), Oxford University Press, 1968; *The Opal Miner* (textbook), Oxford University Press, 1969; *Nowhere to Hide*, Lansdowne Press, 1969.

Iron Mountain, Lansdowne Press, 1970, Macmillan (New York), 1971, Hodder & Stoughton, 1975; *Iron Ore Mining* (textbook), Oxford University Press, 1971; *New Golden Mountain*, Lansdowne Press, 1973; *Wildfire*, Hodder & Stoughton, 1973, Macmillan (New York), 1974; *The Sky is Free*, Hodder & Stoughton, 1974.

Adult biographies: *Pastor Doug*, Lansdowne Press, 1965, revised edition, 1972; *Strolling Players*, Lansdowne Press, 1972.

Formerly contributor of short stories and articles to adult magazines and author and adapter of scripts for children's radio programs.

WORK IN PROGRESS: A children's novel set in the Kimberleys.

SIDELIGHTS: "I started to write while still at school and, at fourteen, wrote a full-length children's book which was published in serial form by the *Australasian*, a weekly newspaper of the time. For some years after marriage I wrote mainly adult short stories and articles, while also adapting and scripting serials for children's radio programmes. I believe that the writing craft is one that has to be practised constantly if thought processes and word fluency are to be retained. For this reason I am thankful that during this busy time, I kept working at some form of writing, even though it was not books. When my daughters started at school, I felt I could tackle a full-length manuscript again.

MAVIS THORPE CLARK

"I can't explain, even to myself, why I have concentrated on novels for children or, more accurately, for the young teen-ager. But I suppose we each fulfil our given role.

Adult biography, however, does attract me and if I ever give up writing for young people, which is most unlikely, it will be to concentrate on this field. The two biographies I have published to date have been extremely rewarding projects, especially *Pastor Doug*. This book led me into deep research of Australia's Indigenous people and their problems, thereby widening my horizon and developing within me an appreciation of the universality of man.

"Many of my novels are set against some particular Australian background. . . . I have travelled thousands of miles in search of material, criss-crossing this vast country from east to west and north to south. I've travelled to Europe and Asia but the spell of my own wide red land lures me continually and sets me on the lonely dusty Outback track. There is the tremendous reward of friends in out-of-the-way places and glimpses of lives that are lived so simply yet so richly with the earth of the world's oldest continent. These intangible joys are the real reward of the writer."

Pastor Doug was updated when Pastor Doug Nicholls was created a Knight of the British Empire in 1972 and became Sir Douglas Ralph Nicholls, the first Aboriginal to receive such an honor. Mavis Thorpe Clark's other adult biography, *Strolling Plays*, has a youth-oriented theme, since it is the story of Joan and Betty Rayner, who presented children's theater in many parts of the world (including nine years in America) before establishing their Australian Children's Theatre.

Pastor Doug and two youth books, *Blue Above the Trees* and *The Min-Min* have been transcribed into Braille. In addition to Australian and American editions of *Min-Min*, the book has been published in German and Japanese and in paperback in England by William Collins.

FOR MORE INFORMATION SEE: New York Times Book Review, January 25, 1970.

CLARK, Walter Van Tilburg 1909-1971

PERSONAL: Born August 3, 1909, in East Oreland, Me.; son of Walter Ernest (a teacher, economist, president of University of Nevada) and Euphemia Murray (Abrams) Clark; married Barbara Frances Morse, October 14, 1933 (deceased); children: Barbara Anne Clark Salmon, Robert Morse. *Education:* University of Nevada, B.A., 1932, M.A., 1932; University of Vermont, M.A., 1934. *Politics:* Democrat. *Home address:* P.O. Box 5546, Reno, Nev. 89503. *Agent:* International Famous Agency, 1301 Avenue of the Americas, New York, N.Y. 10019. *Office:* University of Nevada Press, Reno, Nev.

CAREER: Cazenovia Central School, Cazenovia, N.Y., teacher of English, drama, sports, 1936-45; head of an English department, and tennis coach, Rye, N.Y., 1945; University of Montana, Missoula, assistant professor of English, 1953-56; San Francisco State College (now California State University), San Francisco, Calif., professor of English, director of creative writing, 1956-62; University of Nevada, Reno, writer-in-residence, 1962-71. Visiting lecturer in creative writing, University of Iowa writers' workshop, and Stanford University writers' workshop. Visiting lecturer or professor at other universities, including University of Utah, University of Wyoming, University of California, University of Illinois, University of Missouri, and University of Arkansas. Fellow in writing at Center for Advanced Studies, Wesleyan University, 1960-61, Rockefeller Foundation lecturer in writing, Reed College, University of Washington, and University of Oregon. *Member:* American Association of University Professors, Authors Guild, American Civil Liberties Union, Sierra Club, Western Historical Association, Western Literary Association, Phi Kappa Phi. *Awards, honors:* O. Henry Memorial Award, 1945, for "The Wind and the Snow of Winter"; Litt.D., Colgate University, 1957.

WRITINGS—All published by Random House (except as indicated): *The Ox-Bow Incident* (novel), 1940, published with an introduction by Clifton Fadiman, Heritage, 1942, published with an afterword by W. P. Webb, New American Library, 1960; *The City of Trembling Leaves* (novel), 1945 (published in England as *Tim Hazard*, Kimber, 1951); *The Track of the Cat* (novel), 1949; *The Watchful Gods, and Other Stories* (contains "Hook," "The Wind and the Snow of Winter," "The Rapids," "The Anonymous," "The Buck in the Hills," "Why Don't You Look Where You're Going?," "The Indian Well," "The Fish Who Could Close His Eyes," "The Portable Phonograph," "The Watchful Gods"), Random, 1950; (author of foreword) *Robert Cole Caples: A Retrospective Exhibition, 1927-63* (cataloge), [Reno], 1964. Contributor to *Saturday Review, Holiday, Western Review, Pacific Spectator, Chrysalis, New York Times, New Yorker, Nation,* and *New York Herald Tribune.*

WORK IN PROGRESS: A biography of Alfred Doten, tentatively titled *The Delegation from Pluckville,* for University of Nevada-University of California Presses; an edition of Doten's journals (1849-1903), for University of Nevada-University of California Presses.

SIDELIGHTS: "Hate cities: too many people ... with nothing else alive except in a zoo or on a leash, which is not really being alive.... Loved the Maine country and seashore and the farm. Lots of space and sky and weather, all sorts of things growing wild and in gardens (had one of my own to ruin from the time I was five).... The deep interest in all kinds of life which I developed then has never left me.

It was a hard letter to write. He would stare at the fire with glazed eyes, wake up with a shiver and look around him, put the pencil to the paper, and then relapse into that staring again.
■ (From the movie *"The Ox-Bow Incident,"* © 1943 by 20th Century-Fox.)

It was a big pine with its top shot away by lightning. It had a long branch that stuck out straight on the clearing side, about fifteen feet from the ground. We'd all spotted that branch.
■ (From the movie *"The Ox-Bow Incident,"* © 1943 by 20th Century-Fox.)

On the farm, too, by way of my mother's piano, my father's fine story-telling and reading aloud to us, King Arthur, Robin Hood, Indian and frontier tales, Greek, Roman and Nordic gods and heroes, the Bible, much else, and the kind interest of a neighbor who was a painter, I developed the love of reading and writing, music and art which have also continued.

"My first painting I can remember, a very wet and mingled water-color of the first football game I ever saw. . . . My first poem I cannot remember, but have been told it was a quatrain about a pair of rubbers. Unfortunately for posterity, both masterpieces have been lost. Also wrote many very adventurous and very short short-stories, even serials of a distinctly cliff-hanging variety, all of which were 'published' in a very local weekly paper, *The Clark News*, to which I also contributed poems and illustrations."

Clark was interested in teaching, writing, sports, art and music (though mostly just as looker and listener), hiking and camping, outdoor life in general, and socializing. "My favorite diversion, by long odds, is socializing, just sitting around with a beer or more in all kinds of places, talking to all kinds of people about all kinds of things." Other interests: Chess, history (particularly western history as told by those who were personally involved in it, by way of journals, memoirs, letters, etc.), Indian lore, geology, mining and ranching methods (as necessary knowledge for stories).

He believed that "the most important concerns of the human race now, all of it everywhere, must be birth control and natural conservation, the preservation and even, where possible, the restoration, of other forms of life and of all natural resources."

The Ox-Bow Incident was filmed by 20th Century Fox, 1943; *The Track of the Cat* was filmed by Warner Brothers, 1954. Clark's works have been translated into twenty languages, including Arabic, Urdu, Korean, and Japanese.

FOR MORE INFORMATION SEE: Books, October 12, 1940, October 7, 1950; *New Yorker*, October 12, 1940; *New York Times*, October 13, 1940, May 27, 1945, June 5, 1949, September 24, 1950, November 12, 1971; *Saturday Review of Literature*, October 26, 1940, June 2, 1945, June 4, 1949, September 30, 1950; *Atlantic*, October, 1940; *New Republic*, December 2, 1940; *New York Herald Tribune Weekly Book Review*, June 5, 1949; *San Francisco Chronicle*, June 5, 1949; *Christian Science Monitor*, June 11, 1949; *Catholic World*, July, 1949; *Arizona Quarterly*, 1951; *College English*, February, 1952; *Western Review*, winter, 1956; *Bulletin of Bibliography*, September-December, 1956; *Critique*, winter, 1959; *Washington Post*, November 12, 1971; *Variety*, November 17, 1971; *Newsweek*, November 22, 1971; *Time*, November 22, 1971; *Publishers' Weekly*, November 29, 1971.

(Died November 11, 1971)

COBB, Vicki 1938-

PERSONAL: Born August 19, 1938, in New York, N.Y.; daughter of Benjamin Harold (a labor arbitrator) and Paula (Davis) Wolf; married Edward S. Cobb (a psychology professor), January 31, 1960; children: Theodore Davis, Joshua Monroe. *Education:* University of Wisconsin, student, 1954-57; Barnard College, B.A., 1958; Teachers College, Columbia University, M.A., 1960. *Home:* 410 Riverside Dr., New York, N.Y. 10025.

CAREER: Scientific researcher in Rye, N.Y., at Sloan-Kettering Institute and Pfizer & Co., 1958-61; science teacher in high school in Rye, N.Y., 1961-64; Teleprompter Corp., New York, N.Y., hostess and principal writer of television series, "The Science Game," 1972—. Creative Televisions for Children, Inc., owner and creator of television programs, 1972—. *Member:* Authors' Guild, Authors League. *Awards, honors:* Cable television award, 1973, for "The Science Game," best educational show.

WRITINGS—All juvenile: *Logic*, Watts, 1969; *Cells*, Watts, 1970; *Gases*, Watts, 1970; *Making Sense of Money*, Parents' Magazine Press, 1971; *Sense of Direction: Up, Down, and All Around*, Parents' Magazine Press, 1972; *Science Experiments You Can Eat*, Lippincott, 1972; *How the Doctor Knows You're Fine*, Lippincott, 1973; *The Long and Short of Measurement*, Parents' Magazine Press, 1973; *Heat*, Watts, 1973; *Arts and Crafts You Can Eat*,

Cooks and scientists work with chemicals, though to a cook sodium chloride is salt and tartaric acid is cream of tartar. ■ (From *Science Experiments You Can Eat* by Vicki Cobb. Illustrated by Peter Lippman.)

Lippincott, 1974; *Supersuits*, Lippincott, 1975. "What It's Made Of," a series of four filmstrips for Educational Design, Inc. Editor, "McGraw-Hill text Films," Elementary Science Study Prints section, 1970.

WORK IN PROGRESS: Book on magic tricks for Lippincott.

SIDELIGHTS: "It's my guess that most juvenile nonfiction is read by children who are, for one reason or another, already interested in the subject matter. I try to reach the uninitiated—those who will read other nonfiction as a result of reading my books. I try to make 'heavy' subjects more approachable by using a slightly irreverent tone and always relating content to what a child already knows about life and nature."

FOR MORE INFORMATION SEE: Horn Book, October, 1972.

COHEN, Daniel 1936-

PERSONAL: Born March 12, 1936, in Chicago, Ill.; son of M. Milton and Sue (Greenberg) Cohen; married Susan Handler (a writer), February 2, 1958; children: Theodora. *Education:* University of Illinois, journalism degree, 1958. *Home and office:* 49 Canal St., Port Jervis, N.Y. 12771. *Agent:* Henry Morrison, Inc., 58 West 10th St., New York, N.Y. 10011.

CAREER: Science Digest (magazine), New York, N.Y., managing editor, 1960-69; writer for adults and young people, 1969—. *Member:* Author's Guild, National Association of Science Writers, Audubon Society, Appalachian Mountain Club.

VICKI COBB

WRITINGS—All published by Dodd: *Myths of the Space Age*, 1967; *Mysterious Places*, 1969; *A Modern Look at Monsters*, 1970; *Masters of the Occult*, 1971; *Voodoo, Devils, and the New Invisible World*, 1972, *The Far Side of Consciousness*, 1974.

For young people: *Secrets from Ancient Graves*, Dodd, 1968; *Vaccination and You*, Messner, 1968; *The Age of Giant Mammals*, Dodd, 1969; *Animals of the City*, McGraw, 1969; *Night Animals*, Messner, 1970; *Conquerors on Horseback*, Doubleday, 1970; *Talking with Animals*, Dodd, 1971; *Superstition*, Creative Education Press, 1971; *A Natural History of Unnatural Things*, Dutton, 1971; *Ancient Monuments and How They Were Built*, McGraw, 1971; *Watchers in the Wild*, Little, Brown, 1972; *In Search of Ghosts*, Dodd, 1972; *The Magic Art of Foreseeing the Future*, Dodd, 1973; *How Did Life Get There?*, Messner, 1973; *Magicians, Wizards, and Sorcerers*, Lippincott, 1973; *How the World Will End*, McGraw, 1973; *Shaka: King of the Zulus*, Doubleday, 1973; *ESP: The Search Beyond the Senses*, Harcourt, 1973; *The Black Death*, Watts, 1974; *The Magic of the Little People*, Messner, 1974; *Curses, Hexes, and Spells*, Lippincott, 1974; *Intelligence: What Is It?*, M. Evans, 1974; *Not of the World*, Follett, 1974; *Human Nature Animal Nature*, McGraw, 1974; *The Spirit of the Lord: Revivalism in America*, Four Winds, 1975; *The New Believers: Young Religion in America*, Evans, 1975; *Monsters, Giants and Little Men from Mars*, Doubleday,

... there has been a tremendous amount of confusion and misinformation about gorilla behavior. ■ (From *Watchers in the Wild* by Daniel Cohen. Illustrated by John Hamberger.)

1975; *Animal Territories*, Hastings House, 1975; *The Magic of Reincarnation*, Dodd, 1975; *The Body Snatchers*, Lippincott, 1975; *The Human Side of Computers*, McGraw, in press; *The Ancient Visitors*, Doubleday, in press; *The Science of Spying*, McGraw, in press; *Altered States of Consciousness*, Watts, in press; *The Greatest Monsters in the World*, Dodd, in press.

WORK IN PROGRESS: Biofeedback, for Harcourt; *Animal Ghosts*, for Doubleday.

SIDELIGHTS: "A person who spends as much time writing as I do does not have a great deal of extra time for exciting hobbies or interesting vacations. In fact, I haven't taken a vacation in years, and doubt if I would remember how to enjoy one. I do some traveling in connection with my work, however, and over the last couple of years have been doing a bit of lecturing at colleges as well—so I do get around a bit.

"Those books that I think have been most successful, are the books that I write for myself. That is, I find a subject I think is interesting, and want to know more about. Then I look around for a publisher who is willing to finance my curiosity. I have been pretty lucky in finding them. It is difficult for me to manufacture interest in a subject, just because there is supposed to be a market for books on that subject.

"What with my wife now being a full-time writer too, our house resembles a combination office and zoo—we have a lot of animals. Just the other day one of my cats ate a contract for a Japanese edition of one of my books. The contract came on onion skin paper, and the cat loves onion skin paper.

"I used to think that all writers were rich. I know better now. Most of us get along, and I'm not going to cry poverty, but if your aim in life is to make a lot of money you are probably better off at the racetrack. However, I find writing a satisfying life. I find that many of my contemporaries get pretty nervous as they approach the age of forty.

DANIEL COHEN

Some start waking up at two in the morning wondering what they are doing with their lives, or where it is all going. But that doesn't happen to me (though I may wake up at two in the morning wondering how I am going to get it all done). There is always a new project to think about, a new area to be explored.''

FOR MORE INFORMATION SEE: New York Times Book Review, April 16, 1972 (Middletown, N.Y.) *Sunday Record*, December 3, 1972; (Port Jervis, N.Y.) *Union Gazette*, July 22, 1974.

COHEN, Robert Carl   1930-

PERSONAL: Born September 24, 1930; son of Isadore Wolf and Ida (Gabriel) Cohen; married Helene Konidare (a motion picture producer), June 21, 1961; children: Dianna, Julia. *Education:* University of California, Los Angeles, B.A., 1952, M.A., 1954, further study, 1959-61; also did graduate work at Sorbonne, University of Paris, 1956-57, and University of Southern California, 1961-62. *Politics:* Registered Democrat. *Religion:* "Optimist." *Address:* c/o Random House, 201 East 50th St., New York, N.Y. 10022.

Sometimes people decide that being tanned is better than being pale. Sometimes they decide the opposite. ■ (From *The Color of Man* by Robert Carl Cohen. Photographs by Ken Heyman.)

CAREER: Columbia Broadcasting System-Television, New York, N.Y., writer for "Adventure Show," 1954; Jean Image Films, Paris, France, writer-designer for cartoon production, 1956; National Broadcasting Co.-Television, New York, N.Y., special correspondent in China, 1957; public lecturer on "the world around us," 1959-65; National Educational Television (WNEW-TV), Chicago, Ill., special producer, 1964-65; Metro-Goldwyn-Mayer Studios, supervisor of minority training program, 1972-73. *Military service:* U.S. Army, 1954-56. *Member:* Writers Guild of America, West. *Awards, honors: The Color of Man* was an American Library Association Notable Book of 1968.

WRITINGS: The Color of Man (*Horn Book* Honor List), Random House, 1968, revised edition, 1973; *Black Crusader: A Biography of Robert Franklin Williams*, Lyle Stuart, 1972.

Television specials: "Inside East Germany," 1959; "Inside Red China," 1961; "Committee on Un-American Activities," 1962; "Three Cubans," 1965.

Motion picture scripts: "Cudjoe, the Maroon," produced 1974.

WORK IN PROGRESS: Screenplay of Harry Rhodes' *A Chosen Few*, published by Bantam, 1965.

SIDELIGHTS: "My motivation is to attempt to understand the nature of life through dealing with the primary problems which torment humanity: racism, ideology, etc., and to then share whatever insights I may have reached through the media of books, films, TV, and other means of communication. I do this because I have found that the most satisfactory means for solving problems is to study the factors causing them, and to then try to either adjust those factors or otherwise manipulate the situation so as to eliminate or alleviate the effects of the contradictions. My profession is, therefore, education, but always tempered by concern with esthetics because I believe that important subjects require effective presentation.''

FOR MORE INFORMATION SEE: Young Readers' Review, September, 1968; *Horn Book*, August, 1969.

COLLIER, James Lincoln   1928-
(Charles Williams)

PERSONAL: Born June 27, 1928, in New York, N.Y.; son of Edmund and Kathrine (Brown) Collier; married Carol Burrows, September 2, 1952 (divorced); children: Geoffrey Lincoln, Andrew Kemp. *Education:* Hamilton College, A.B., 1950. *Home:* 519 West 121st St., New York, N.Y. 10027. *Agent:* John Cushman Associates, 25 West 43rd St., New York, N.Y.

CAREER: Free-lance writer. *Awards, honors: My Brother Sam is Dead* was nominated for the National Book Award, 1974, and is a Newbery Honor Book.

WRITINGS: Cheers, Avon, 1961; *Somebody Up There Hates Me*, Macfadden, 1962; (under pseudonym Charles Williams) *Fires of Youth*, Hutchinson, 1963; *The Hypocritical American*, Bobbs, 1964. Contributor of six hundred articles to magazines.

Juveniles: *Battleground*, Grosset, 1965; *A Visit to the Firehouse*, Grosset, 1966; *The Teddy Bear Habit*, Grosset, 1967; *Which Musical Instrument Shall I Play?*, Grosset, 1969; *Danny Goes to the Hospital*, Grosset, 1970; *Rock Star* (Child Study Association Book Award), Four Winds, 1970; *Why Does Everybody Think I'm Nutty?*, Grosset, 1971; *Practical Music Theory*, Grosset, 1971; *The Hard Life of the Teenager*, Four Winds, 1972; *It's Murder at St. Basket's*, Grosset, 1972; *Inside Jazz*, Four Winds, 1973; *Jug Bands and Handmade Music*, Grosset, 1973; *The Making of Man*, Four Winds, 1974; *My Brother Sam is Dead*, Four Winds, 1974.

SIDELIGHTS: "I am a specialist in social science reporting, and have worked extensively in sex education and related fields. I am also a musician, which accounts for my writing on music. I have lived in Paris and London, travelled widely in Europe and report regularly from there."

JAMES LINCOLN COLLIER

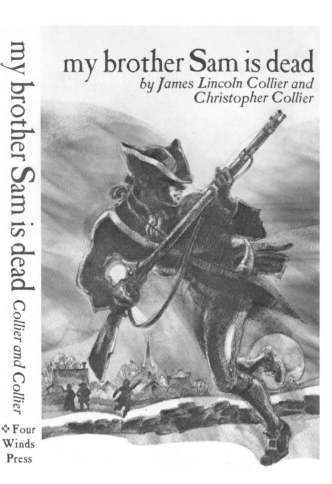

(From *My Brother Sam is Dead* by James Lincoln Collier. Jacket designed by Karl W. Stuecklen.)

CONNOLLY, Jerome P(atrick)   1931-

PERSONAL: Born January 14, 1931, in Minneapolis, Minn.; son of Walter Joseph (an accountant) and Gladys (Webb) Connolly; married Phyllis Emily Underwood, May 30, 1956 (divorced, 1972); married Elma Grace Hollenbach (a free-lance artist), April 15, 1973; children: (first marriage) Anne Marie, Ellen Louise. *Education:* University of Minnesota, B.S., 1955. *Home:* Tetonia, Idaho 83452. *Office:* Arts Etc., Inc., Tetonia, Idaho 83452.

CAREER: Illinois State Museum, Springfield, staff artist, 1957-60; Natural Science for Youth Foundation, Westport, Conn., staff artist, 1960-65; free-lance artist, working principally on diorama backgrounds for natural history museums, 1965—. Has painted more than eighty diorama backgrounds for seventeen museums and nature centers, among them Museum of History and Technology at Smithsonian Institution, William Penn Memorial Museum, Harrisburg, Pa., Illinois State Museum, Science Museum, St. Paul, and Carnegie Museum, Pittsburgh; illustrator of nature books. Had one-man show at Abercrombie & Fitch, New York, 1972; work also has been shown at Society of Animal Artists Annual, New York, and Hudson Valley Art Association Annual, White Plains. *Military service:* U.S. Army, 1951-53; served in Korea. *Member:* Society of Animal Artists, Society of Illustrators.

JEROME P. CONNOLLY

ILLUSTRATOR: Eugene V. Mohr, *The Study of Fishes Made Simple*, Doubleday, 1962; Ross E. Hutchins, *Lives of an Oak Tree*, Rand McNally, 1962; Sarah Regal Reidman, *Naming Living Things: The Grouping of Plants and Animals*, Rand McNally, 1963; Peter Farb, *The Face of North America*, Harper, 1963; Ross E. Hutchins, *The Travels of Monarch X*, Rand McNally, 1966; Ross E. Hutchins, *The Last Trumpeters*, Rand McNally, 1967; Dorothy Wood, *The Cat Family*, Harvey House, 1968; Dorothy Wood, *The Deer Family*, Harvey House, 1969; Ross E. Hutchins, *Adelbert, the Penguin*, Rand McNally, 1969; Alice Hopf, *Butterfly and Moth*, Putnam, 1969; Phyllis Connolly, *Cheers for Chippie*, Harvey House, 1969; Ross E. Hutchins, *Little Chief of the Mountains*, Rand McNally, 1970; Ross E. Hutchins, *The Saga of Pelorus Jack*, Rand McNally, 1971; Lillian Brady, *Aise-ce-Bon: A Raccoon*, Harvey House, 1971.

WORK IN PROGRESS: Illustrating a book on the white-tail deer, by Lillian Brady.

SIDELIGHTS: "The American illustrators have always interested me, because when I was growing up abstract art had a stranglehold on the art world and I wanted no part of it. When I moved to the New York area I made the rounds of the publishing houses with my samples of art work and discovered how hard it was to break in, and yet the quality of art work used was usually not that good. And I've always felt that publishers should have 'talent scouts' for finding new artists because I am convinced that for every good 'found' artist there are probably five or six others *just as good*, who are lost or unknown, out in the sticks. . . .

"On the books illustrated, I had to do the color separations, so each color was done on a separate sheet of frosted acetate. The art work was done in black and greys and the color that sheet was to be printed was put on the bottom of the sheet along with the book title and page number. Some books were done using pencil, others were a combination of pencil and ink. Sometimes I used an air brush and ink to blend, but I found out later I could use a pencil and a lot of rubbing with cotton to get a smooth blend. . . . My favorite book was *Adelbert, the Penguin*. It was fun to do and I think overall, my best."

COOK, Joseph J(ay) 1924-

PERSONAL: Born February 19, 1924, in Brooklyn, N.Y.; son of Joseph and Ida (Madaii) Cook; married Mary J. Plummer, 1947; children: Joseph, Garret. *Education:* Drake University, B.A., 1949; State University of New York, New Paltz, M.S., 1953; Columbia University, post-graduate study. *Home:* 25 O'Hara Pl., Halesite, N.Y. 11743.

CAREER: Union Free Schools at Valley Stream, N.Y., teacher, 1949-50, Merrick, N.Y., teacher, 1950-55, curriculum coordinator, 1955-61, Levittown, N.Y., principal, 1961-69; Hofstra University, Hempstead, N.Y., lecturer, 1965—. *Military service:* U.S. Army, three years. *Member:* Authors' Guild, Association of University Professors.

WRITINGS: (With William L. Wisner) *Your First Book of Salt Water Fishing*, Essy, 1961; (with William L. Wisner) *Killer Whale!*, Dodd, 1963; (with W. L. Wisner) *The Phantom World of the Octopus and Squid*, Dodd, 1965; (with W. L. Wisner) *The Warrior Whale*, Dodd, 1966; (with William J. Romeika) *Better Surfing For Boys*, Dodd, 1967; (with W. L. Wisner) *The Nightmare World of the Shark*, Dodd, 1968; *The Electronic Brain: How it Works*, Putnam, 1969; *The Curious World of the Crab*, Dodd, 1970; *Famous Firsts in Baseball*, Putnam, 1971; *The Nocturnal World of the Lobster*, Dodd, 1972; *The Changeable World of the Oyster*, Dodd, 1973; (with W. L. Wisner) *Blue*

The calico crab is also known as the Dolly Varden crab. Dolly Varden, a character from Charles Dicken's novel *Barnaby Rudge*, became famous for her large straw hat trimmed with cherry-colored ribbons. ■ (From *The Curious World of the Crab* by Joseph J. Cook.)

Whale: Vanishing Leviathan, Dodd, 1973; (with Ralph W. Schreiber) *Wonders of the Pelican World*, Dodd, 1974; (with Joseph J. Cook II) *Famous Firsts in Basketball*, Putnam, 1975; (with W. L. Wisner) *Coastal Fishing*, Dodd, 1976; *The Incredible World of the Herring*, Dodd, in press. Reading analyst for Random House, Inc.

SIDELIGHTS: "I have lived near the ocean since childhood, and have always been interested in sea and shore life, and all forms of sports. My books are expressions of those things that interest and fascinate me, and I try to impart my wonder and enthusiasm to readers of all ages.

"Some of my books are based on actual experience while others are the result of research—or a combination of both. My aim is to casually instruct and entertain in books that deal with subjects that interest me, and which I hope will interest others."

CORRIGAN, Barbara 1922-

PERSONAL: Born April 30, 1922, in Attleboro, Mass.; daughter of Owen H. (a jewelry manufacturer) and Florence (Hasler) Corrigan. *Education:* Massachusetts College of Art, Certificate in Design, 1944. *Politics:* Independent ("lean toward liberal Democrat"). *Home:* 18 Hayward St., Attleboro, Mass. 02703.

CAREER: Bresnick & Solomont (advertising agency), Boston, Mass., staff artist, 1944-45; free-lance designer and illustrator with own studio in Boston, Mass., 1945-61; self-employed at home in Attleboro, Mass., 1961—, first as artist, later as sewing teacher and custom dressmaker. *Awards, honors:* Work included in Book Jacket Designers' Guild annual exhibit, 1950, 1951, 1952.

WRITINGS—Author and illustrator: *Of Course You Can Sew: Basics of Sewing for the Young Beginner*, Doubleday, 1971; *I Love to Sew*, Doubleday, 1974.

Illustrator: Virginia Pasley, *The Christmas Cookie Book*, Atlantic-Little, Brown, 1949; Ogden Nash, *Parents Keep Out*, Little, Brown, 1951; Wilma Lord Perkins, reviser, *The Boston Cooking School Cook Book*, Little, Brown, 1951; Virginia Pasley, *The Holiday Candy Book*, Atlantic-Little, Brown, 1952; Joan Lowell, *Promised Land*, Duell, Sloan & Pearce, 1952; Ruth Wakefield, *The Toll House Cook Book*, Little, Brown, 1953; Heloise Frost, *Early American Recipes*, Phillips Publishers, 1953; L. Belle Pollard, *Experiences in Homemaking*, Ginn, 1954; Laura Sootin, *Let's Go to a Bank*, Putnam, 1957; Naomi Buchheimer, *Let's Go to the Telephone Company*, Putnam, 1958; Helen Boyd Higgins, *Old Trails and New*, Friendship, 1960; H. Allen Smith, *Waikiki Beachnik*, Little, Brown, 1960; L. Belle Pollard, *Experiences with Clothing*, Ginn, 1961; Ruth Stempel, *Hello, Joe*, Whitman Publishing, 1961; Tirsa Saavedra Scott, *Como se Dice?*, Ginn, 1963; Margil Vanderhoff, *Clothes: Part of Your World*, Ginn, 1968. Also illustrator of spelling books and a sewing program published by Ginn.

WORK IN PROGRESS: How to Make Something Out of Practically Nothing, for Doubleday; research for an ecological history of a river near her home.

SIDELIGHTS: "I never had any idea of becoming a writer, but who can predict how things will turn out? Ever since I can remember I liked to draw and sew. I went to the Massachusetts College of Art with every intention of majoring in fashion design, but the stimulating experiences of art school, the exposure to new ideas and people, art exhibitions, etc., changed my attitudes and ambitions, so I switched to the general design course.

"After graduation, I did some advertising art work for a while, but it gradually became apparent that book publishing was a more congenial field for me. I designed many book jackets, and illustrated a number of books—cook books, children's and text books.

"After working on several sewing text books for junior high and high school students, I began to feel that students must be quite bored and frustrated with the way that sewing was being taught to them. I felt that if I had the opportunity I could teach sewing in a way that would stimulate their enthusiasm rather than turning them off. The result was my first book, *Of Course You Can Sew*. It presents only as much as I think children of about ten to fourteen want to know. If they really take pleasure in their early learning experience, they will be eager to learn more later as their coordination and powers of concentration mature.

BARBARA CORRIGAN

"By this time I was working at home, and feeling more and more that I did not want to spend the rest of my life working over a drawing board. I had done too much of it, and inspiration dried up.

"Finally I returned to my first love, sewing and designing. I put into practice some of the ideas from my book, with sewing classes for both children and adults. This has been quite a successful project, and I have enjoyed working with people. It's much more stimulating than turning out little drawings all day, with no company but a radio. The teaching experience also gave me the ideas for my second and third books on sewing.

"I also do a lot of custom dressmaking, and love working with fabrics. When I have time to do any creative work, instead of painting I prefer to do applique wall hangings, several of which have been in *Woman's Day*.

"I live with my elderly mother and two pampered cats in the gingerbready Victorian house where I was born. That may not sound very exciting, but there never seems to be enough time for all the things I would enjoy doing.

Before you start to sew, be sure that you have all the equipment you need and a comfortable and convenient place in which to work. ■ (From *Of Course You Can Sew!* by Barbara Corrigan. Illustrated by the author.)

"I love working in the garden—even the grubby, dirty part of it. The house is on the bank of a small river, and the surroundings turn into a jungle if I don't keep at it.

"I've always been a wildlife enthusiast, feed the birds and keep records of them, and have done some observation and research on the river, its environs and wildlife. At present there are two white ducks that I feed and talk to, and they reward me by attracting flocks of wild mallards in the winter. Recently we have had raccoons and an opossum—and this is almost the middle of the city!

"I've never been a joiner of organizations, but I am very strong for Women's Lib, and like to get together with friends to discuss politics and world affairs.

"My present ambition is to win the Massachusetts lottery, so I can retire to a house in the unspoiled country (if such a place still exists), and turn it into my own private wildlife sanctuary.

HOBBIES AND OTHER INTERESTS: "I love to read (and must confess to a weakness for detective stories), do double crostics, take color photographs, listen to classical music and jazz."

CURRY, Peggy Simson 1911-

PERSONAL: Born December 30, 1911, in Dunure, Ayrshire, Scotland; daughter of William Andrew (a rancher) and Margaret (Anderson) Simson; married William Seeright Curry (chairman of English department at Casper College), July 21, 1937; children: Michael Munro. *Education:* University of Wyoming, B.A., 1936. *Politics:* Republican. *Religion:* Presbyterian. *Home and office:* 3125 Garden Creek Rd., Casper, Wyo. 82601. *Agent:* August Lenniger, 437 Fifth Ave., New York, N.Y. 10016.

CAREER: Casper College, Casper, Wyo., instructor in creative writing, 1952—; author. Lecturer at various colleges and writers' conferences, 1952—. Poet-in-residence, State of Wyoming poetry-in-schools program, 1971—. *Member:* Western Writers of America, Kappa Kappa Gamma, P.E.O. Sisterhood. *Awards, honors:* Spur award, Western Writers of America, 1957, 1970; Kappa Kappa Gamma Distinguished Alumni award, 1964; University of Wyoming Distinguished Alumni award, 1968.

WRITINGS: Fire in the Water (novel), McGraw, 1951; *Red Wind of Wyoming* (poetry), Allan Swallow, 1955; *So Far from Spring* (novel), Viking, 1956; *The Oil Patch* (novel), McGraw, 1959; *Creating Fiction from Experience*, Writer, Inc., 1964; *A Shield of Clover* (juvenile novel), McKay, 1970. Contributor to *New York Times, Saturday Evening Post, Christian Science Monitor, Poet* (India), *Reader's Digest, Audubon, Good Housekeeping, Collier's, Toronto Star,* and *Boys' Life.* Poet's column in *Chicago Sunday Tribune* and in other publications.

WORK IN PROGRESS: Shindig, a novel; a book of poems.

SIDELIGHTS: "I write to share those experiences that stir my emotional responses. Everything that I write—a poem, a short story or a book—begins with emotional im-

PEGGY SIMSON CURRY

pact whether that impact is simply curiosity or anger or delight. What I am pushed to put on paper may be anything from the way winter grass looks beside a frozen pond to the multi-colored experiences of rounding up cattle in Colorado, living in an oil field settlement in Wyoming, or thirty nights spent at sea with the herring fishermen off the west coast of Scotland. A song, a sunset, a few words heard in a bus—anything that strikes my imagination may be the beginning of days at the typewriter.

"I have strong sense of place and special information. I try to bring these to the reader along with characterization and plot. I never see people as isolated but always part of the earth, sky and wildlife in that place where they are. Often I draw special information from those things that are part of my own life—fossil hunting, trout fishing, hiking in wilderness, study of history and poetry and people.

"I keep notebooks that list descriptions of people and places, bits of conversation, exciting phrases that sometimes drift through my mind while I'm doing simple household chores, memorable quotations from my reading, emotional responses and dreams.

"Even as I am stimulated to write by what I feel, I hope the reader will be stimulated to feel by what I write. All that I write is based on what James Stephens says so briefly and beautifully in *The Crock of Gold*. 'The head does not hear anything until the heart has listened.'"

CURTIS, Peter
See LOFTS, Norah (Robinson)

DAHLSTEDT, Marden 1921-

PERSONAL: Born August 14, 1921, in Pittsburgh, Pa.; daughter of Glenn Stewart (a hardware store owner) and Lillian (Seigler) Armstrong; married Richard Robert Dahlstedt (a newspaperman), May 26, 1945; children: Ellen Christina (Mrs. Richard Douglas Irwin, II). *Education:* Chatham College, A.B., 1942; Slippery Rock State College, Library Science, 1964. *Politics:* Democrat. *Religion:* Protestant. *Home:* 2613 Bay Ave., Beach Haven Gardens, N.J. 08008. *Agent:* McIntosh & Otis, Inc., 18 East 41st St., New York, N.Y. 10017.

CAREER: West Deer Junior High School, Cheswick, Pa., librarian, 1964-68; Beach Haven Elementary School, Beach Haven, N.J., librarian, 1971—. Co-owner with husband of The Attic, an antique shop, Beach Haven Gardens, N.J. *Member:* American Association of University Women, New England Poetry Society, Pittsburgh Poetry Society. *Awards, honors:* Borestone Mountain Poetry Award, 1960.

Indeed, it seemed as if Aunt Ella were right—the whole Little Conemaugh River seemed to be running down their street! ■ (From *The Terrible Wave* by Marden Dahlstedt. Illustrated by Charles Robinson.)

MARDEN DAHLSTEDT

WRITINGS: The Terrible Wave, Coward, 1972; *Shadow of the Lighthouse*, Coward, in press; *Thereaway*, Putnam, in press. Author of a column on antiques, "The Corner Cupboard," in *Beach Haven Times*.

WORK IN PROGRESS: A contemporary juvenile novel.

DANIEL, Hawthorne 1890-

PERSONAL: Born January 20, 1890, in Norfolk, Neb.; son of David Rush (a physician) and Nancy Ann (Kyner) Daniel; married Nelle Ryan (an economic and historical researcher), October 26, 1922; children: Nancy Nelle. *Education:* Attended U.S. Naval Academy, 1908, Iowa State College, 1909-10; courses at Columbia University, 1914-16, New York University, 1915-16. *Politics:* Democrat. *Religion:* Congregationalist. *Home:* 37 Standish Ave., Colonial Heights, Tuckahoe, N.Y. 10710. *Agent:* Brandt & Brandt, 101 Park Ave., New York, N.Y. 10017.

CAREER: Omaha Bee, Omaha, Neb., reporter, 1915; *World's Work*, member of editorial staff, 1916-23; *Boys' Life*, managing editor, 1923-25; American Museum of Natural History, New York, N.Y., editor of *Natural History*, curator of printing and publishing, 1926-35, secretary of scientific staff, 1927-35; *Commentator*, managing editor,

1936-39. War correspondent with Navy in Asiatic-Pacific theater and in Europe, 1945. Lecturer in United States and Canada. *Military service:* U.S. Navy, served in European waters, 1917; became ensign; U.S. Tank Corps, 1918-19, served in England and France; became lieutenant. *Member:* U.S. Naval Academy Alumni Association; Princeton University Club, Explorers Club (both New York). *Awards, honors:* Medal of Oregon Trail Memorial Association for *End of Track*, 1937; Navy commendation for service as war correspondent, 1946; citation, Assembly of Captive European Nations, for *The Ordeal of the Captive Nations*, 1960.

WRITINGS: In the Favour of the King, Doubleday, 1922; *Ships of the Seven Seas*, Doubleday, 1925, revised edition, Dodd, 1930; *The Clipper Ship*, Dodd, 1928; (with Herbert S. Dickey) *The Misadventures of a Tropical Medico*, Dodd, 1929; *End of Track* (biography of James H. Kyner), Caxton, 1936; *Householder's Complete Handbook*, Little, 1936, revised edition, 1939; *North America: Wheel of the Future*, Scribner, 1942; *Islands of the Pacific*, Putnam, 1943; *Islands of the East Indies*, Putnam, 1944; *For Want of a Nail*, McGraw, 1948; *Judge Medina: A Biography*, Wilfred Funk, 1952; (with Jan Cwiklinski) *The Captain Leaves His Ship*, Doubleday, 1954; (with Francis Minot) *The Inexhaustible Sea*, Dodd, 1954; (with Emily Smith Warner) *The Happy Warrior*, Doubleday, 1956; *The Ordeal of the Captive Nations*, Doubleday, 1958; *The Hartford of Hartford*, Random House, 1960; *Public Libraries for Everyone*, Doubleday, 1961; *Ferdinand Magellan: A Biography*, Doubleday, 1964; (with Milton E. Miles) *A Different Kind of War*, Doubleday, 1967.

HAWTHORNE DANIEL

39

Historical novels for teen-age readers: *The Gauntlet of Dunmore*, Macmillan, 1926; *The Honor of Dunmore*, Macmillan, 1927; *The Seal of the White Buddha*, Coward, 1928; *The Red Rose of Dunmore*, Macmillan, 1928; *Bare Hands*, Coward, 1929; *Peggy of Old Annapolis*, Coward, 1930; *The Shadow of the Sword*, Macmillan, 1930; *Dorothy Stanhope—Virginian*, Coward, 1931; *Shuttle and Sword*, Macmillan, 1932; *The Lost Professor*, Coward, 1933; *Broken Dykes*, Macmillan, 1934; *Head Wind*, Macmillan, 1936; *Uncle Sam's Navy*, Grosset, 1940; *Whampoa*, Crowell, 1941; *Fogbound*, Winston, 1943.

Ghost writer of ten books in collaboration with prominent individuals in fields of business, law, exploration, big game hunting, Americanism. Contributor of articles and short stories to magazines.

WORK IN PROGRESS: Historical research and research on certain phases of World War II; book for Doubleday.

SIDELIGHTS: Daniel visited the Arctic in his earlier years, has since traveled in Europe many times, around the world twice. Of his books, ten have been published in England, and some of these have been translated into a total of five European languages, as well as Chinese, Burmese, Japanese, Arabic, and other Asiatic languages. Four teen-age novels have been translated for publication in France, and others are in process of being translated.

HOBBIES AND OTHER INTERESTS: Sailing, archery, woodworking.

DEMAREST, Doug
See BARKER, Will

DESMOND, Alice Curtis   1897-

PERSONAL: Born September 19, 1897, in Southport, Conn.; daughter of Lewis Beers and Alice (Beardsley) Curtis; married Thomas C. Desmond, August 16, 1923. *Education:* Miss Porter's School, graduate, 1916. *Politics:* Republican. *Religion:* Episcopalian. *Home:* P.O. Box 670, Newburgh, N.Y. 12550.

CAREER: Writer, primarily for young people. *Member:* National League of American Pen Women, Society of Women Geographers, National Association of Women Artists, New York State Historical Association, Society of American Historians (fellow), Society for Colonial History, Woman's National Republican Club, Colonial Dames of America, Society of Mayflower Descendants, Daughters of the American Revolution, Founders and Patriots of America, Junior League, Collectors Club, Pen and Brush Club, Colony Club (New York). *Awards, honors:* Litt.D., Russell Sage College, 1946; fellow, Rochester Museum of Arts and Sciences, 1946; juvenile award, National League of American Pen Women, 1949; Pintard fellow, New York Historical Society, 1972.

WRITINGS: Far Horizons, McBride, 1931; *South American Adventures*, Macmillan, 1934; *Soldier of the Sun*, Dodd, 1939; *The Lucky Llama*, Macmillan, 1939; *Feathers*, Macmillan, 1940; *For Cross and King*, Dodd, 1941; *Jorge's Journey*, Macmillan, 1942; *Martha Washington*, Dodd, 1942; *The Sea Cats*, Macmillan, 1944; *Glamorous Dolly*

ALICE CURTIS DESMOND

Madison, Dodd, 1946; *The Talking Tree*, Macmillan, 1949.

Alexander Hamilton's Wife, Dodd, 1952; *Barnum Presents: General Tom Thumb*, Macmillan, 1954; *Bewitching Betsy Bonaparte*, Dodd, 1958; *Your Flag and Mine*, Macmillan, 1960; *George Washington's Mother*, Dodd, 1961; *Teddy Koala: Mascot of the Marines*, Dodd, 1962; *Sword and Pen for George Washington*, Dodd, 1964; *Marie Antoinette's Daughter*, Dodd, 1967; *Cleopatra's Children*, Dodd, 1971.

Contributor to anthologies, including: *Roads to Travel*, 1936; *Boys of the Andes*, 1941; *Wonder and Laughter*, 1947; *Adventures in Reading Exploration*, 1947; *People and Progress*, 1947; *Told Under Spacious Skies*, 1952; *A Book of Gladness*, 1953. Articles, short stories, and verse in magazines and newspapers.

WORK IN PROGRESS: Another book on the Romans.

SIDELIGHTS: "I've kept two careers going. From childhood I liked to paint, and was enrolled at the Parson's Art School in New York, where I met my husband. He encouraged my writing. I put away my paints to please him, bought myself a typewriter, and went to Columbia's School of Journalism to try to become a writer. I took every course in writing Columbia taught, except juvenile writing. That, I never expected to do. But it became my life work.

40

"I first wrote articles, adult fiction, and verse for the leading American newspapers and magazines. A series of my travel articles for the *New York Sun*, later syndicated by the North Atlantic Newspaper Alliance, grew into my second book, *South American Adventures*. Then World War II came along. No one was going anywhere. At least, not for pleasure. Since you couldn't sell travel material, I drifted into the juvenile field, writing about children in foreign countries. I have been happily turning out books for young people ever since."

DICKINSON, Susan 1931-

PERSONAL: Born December 26, 1931, in Surrey, England; daughter of William Croft (a university professor) and Margery (Tomlinson) Dickinson; married Arnold Gibson (an insurance consultant), February 11, 1961; children: Sophie Elizabeth, Emily Jane. *Education:* Attended St. Margaret's School, Edinburgh; University of Edinburgh, M.A., 1953. *Politics:* Liberal. *Religion:* Presbyterian. *Home:* 2 Westmoreland Rd., London S.W.13, England. *Office:* William Collins, Sons & Co. Ltd., 14 St. James's Pl., London S.W.1, England.

He was chubby and squat and even paler than Hoag, with a low forehead beneath lank, wet-looking hair, and black eyes set wide apart in a fat, stupid-looking face. ■ (From *The Usurping Ghost* chosen by Susan Dickinson. Illustrated by Antony Maitland.)

CAREER: Thomas Nelson & Sons Ltd., editorial assistant in educational books, Edinburgh, Scotland, 1954-56, assistant editor of children's books, London, England, 1956-59; William Collins, Sons & Co. Ltd., London, England, children's books editor, 1960—.

WRITINGS: (Compiler) *The Restless Ghost and Other Encounters and Experiences*, Collins, 1970, published in America as *The Usurping Ghost and Other Encounters and Experiences*, Dutton, 1971; (compiler) *The Case of the Vanishing Spinster and Other Mystery Stories*, Collins, 1972, published in America as *The Drugged Cornet and Other Mystery Stories*, Dutton, 1973; (editor) *Mother's Help: For Busy Mothers and Playground Leaders*, Collins, 1972.

WORK IN PROGRESS: Editing a collection of original stories for children under five; abridging *Vanity Fair* for Collins "Classics for Today" series.

SIDELIGHTS: "Main interest is old children's books, but generally lack the money to buy them! As an editor of new children's books, find the changes in the last hundred years fascinating. Love exploring old castles and churches, possibly partly due to the fact that my father was a professor of mediaeval history, so we were brought up on ancient monuments of which Scotland has plenty."

FOR MORE INFORMATION SEE: Horn Book, February, 1972.

DICKSON, Naida 1916-
(Grace Lee Richardson)

PERSONAL: Born April 18, 1916, in Thatcher, Ariz.; daughter of Charles Edmund (a pioneer lawyer, teacher, and doctor) and Daisie (Stout) Richardson; married C. Eugene Dickson, December 25, 1942; children: Charles Edmund and Clarence Eugene (twins). *Education:* Utah State University, B.S., 1940, M.S., 1944. *Politics:* Conservative Republican. *Religion:* Church of Jesus Christ of Latter-Day Saints (Mormon). *Home:* 23500 Old Rd. #23, Newhall, Calif. 91321.

CAREER: Elementary and junior high school teacher in Payson, Utah, 1939-40, Weber County, Utah, 1943-44, 1947-48, Ontario, Calif., 1953-57, San Bernardino and Riverside Counties, Calif., 1963-68, and Los Angeles County, Calif., 1970—. Social case worker in Cache and Weber Counties, Utah, 1941-43; Upland Public Library, assistant juvenile librarian, 1958-59; California Institute for Women (prison), correctional counselor, 1961-63.

WRITINGS—For children, all self-illustrated except where noted: *The Littlest Helper*, Denison, 1971; *The Best Color* (not self-illustrated), Denison, 1971; *In the Meadow*, Denison, 1971; *I'd Like*, Denison, 1971; *The Story of Harmony Lane*, Golden Press, 1972; *The Toad that Couldn't Hop*, Denison, 1972; *Just the Mat for Father Cat*, Denison, 1972; *About Doctors of Long Ago*, Children's Press, 1972; *The Happy Moon*, Denison, 1972; *Big Sister and Tagalong Teddy*, Denison, 1973; *The Biography of a Honeybee*, Lerner Press, 1974. Editor, *Washington Terrace Spokesman*, Ogden, Utah, 1943-44. Contributor of poems and stories to magazines and anthologies.

NAIDA DICKSON

WORK IN PROGRESS: Four children's books for Denison; research on "Bigfoot" or "Sasquatch," for a book.

SIDELIGHTS: "I tend to work in waves—with tremendous surges of enthusiasm which last for a time (two to five years) and then subside for a time while some other interest takes over. For a period I entered prize contests and won a lot of prizes—then nothing. I write copiously for two or three years—sell a lot of stuff, then seem to wane. Then I go into a fever of art work for a few months or a couple of years. Now I'm doing puzzles at a furious pace, constructing for several word puzzle magazines.

"I am deeply, devoutly religious, convinced of the total verity of my faith, which inspires me to excellence. I've always adored children, and delight in my five grandchildren. I write for kids because I like them and understand how they think. (My 'child' ego state is very lively. Refer to Eric Berne to explain *that*.)

"I like to draw, for fun or to accomplish some purpose. I'll never be a great artist because artistic perfection has never seemed deeply important to me. But I did want to illustrate some of my own books and am delighted to have accomplished this."

"DR. A"
See SILVERSTEIN, Alvin

DODGE, Bertha S(anford) 1902-

PERSONAL: Born March 23, 1902, in Cambridge, Mass.; married Carroll W. Dodge (a professor), October 12, 1925; children: Anne Caroline (Mrs. W. Dale Hooper), Mary Lavina (Mrs. Darrell Van Citters). *Education:* Radcliffe College, A.B., 1920; Massachusetts Institute of Technology, M.S., 1922. *Home:* 312 Maple St., Burlington, Vt. 05401.

CAREER: Formerly held variety of teaching positions in science and mathematics at high school and college freshman level. Ran year-long radio program on St. Louis (Mo.) City Hospital, 1944. Editorial work on technical publications of the American Society of Tool and Manufacturing Engineers. International Institute, board member, 1956-59. *Member:* National Writers' Club, Society of Technical Writers, Authors' League of America, National League of American Penwomen, Wednesday Club (St. Louis; honorary), League of Vermont Writers (president, 1970-71).

WRITINGS: Introduction to Chemistry, Mosby, 1948; *The Story of Nursing*, Little, Brown, 1954, 2nd edition, 1965; *Plants That Changed the World*, Little, Brown, 1959; *Engineering is Like This*, Little, Brown, 1963; *Hands That Help: Careers for Medical Workers*, Little, Brown, 1967; *Potatoes and People*, Little, Brown, 1970; *What Everyone Knows*, Eldridge, 1971; *Big is So Big*, Coward, 1972; *The Story of Inscription Rock*, Phoenix, 1975. Has contributed short stories, articles on educational matters, Latin America, historical personages, etc. to magazines.

SIDELIGHTS: "Though I am generally considered to be a writer of nonfiction, I have to my credit some published short stories and some longer manuscripts that might be classified as fiction though based on solid historical fact. Personally, I find no basic differences between writers of fiction and of nonfiction. Both must use the same tools—words—both must strive to use them effectively, without distortion of meaning, and sparingly, saying what is to be said as briefly as possible.

"My own education bore heavily upon the science end, though of course one had to have courses in the so-called 'cultural' area. Both as an undergraduate and as a graduate student, science was my area of specialization and, in retrospect, I think such training a not-so-bad background for a would-be writer. A serious student of science must learn to observe without bias, record observations with honesty and precision, interpret them with a trained and disciplined mind.

"While I was in college, I saw myself as the Great Scientist of the century. When, presently, I reflected upon such a career, I began to prefer myself in the role of Great Communicator of Ideas. Very few editors with whom I then tried to communicate shared my vision. However, after many frustrating years, one editor did suggest the need of a story of nursing for teenagers and why didn't I write one. By then I was ready to try my hand at anything any editor

Wise colonists learned to eat native foods. Admitted, potatoes were not mentioned in the Bible—but neither was America. ■ (From *Potatoes and People* by Bertha S. Dodge. Illustrated by John Kaufmann.)

might be willing to read. I had, at that point, to find out about nursing, past, present, future. The process of seeking, finding, and sifting this material has shaped my whole attitude towards writing and given me perspective on this matter of being an author.

"I had always, from early childhood, been required to read a daily stint—not specially selected books save that they should be by writers with a respect for language. It didn't take me long to learn that if I made the right choice, there could be a great deal of joy in reading. Today, I believe that reading is a writer's best friend and not only in the sense of others reading and buying his books. Communication has to be a two-way street and to communicate with the present and future, it is well to be aware of what has already been communicated and how. Science, for instance, has a long history and only by being aware of this history can we truly understand how science got where it is and whither we may expect it to go in the future. One need not be too solemn about this for the mistakes and misconceptions of the past look notably funny in the light of today's knowledge. Yet, just possibly, they can teach us that some of this cherished 'knowledge' of today may look equally funny in the future. Whatever one writes—fact or fancy—fiction or nonfiction—a background of acquaintance with the past gives a perspective all writers need.

"For whom do I intend my books? For anyone who can read them. Though I am proud to be listed as a writer of books for young people, the only one of my published works that is beamed towards a special age is *Big is So Big*, which deals with concepts of basic measurements in a manner (hopefully) to engage the interest of children in the first to third grades. Paradoxically, I came to perceive the need for such a book some years ago when I was a humble assistant in a college freshman mathematics course and found my class rather hazy on the subject of units of measurement. So, when an editor of a science series approached me for a book for the quite young, this was the book I wanted to write. Having tested it on two eight-year-old grandchildren, I believe it may serve its end.

"How do I get my ideas? Variously. The nursing books were an editor's suggestion. The two plant books are the outgrowth of my husband's (and my) travels and interests. Actually the latter book was the outgrowth of the first for when the first was to be translated into German, the German editor asked for two extra chapters, one of them being on potatoes. I refused then but did not forget the suggestion as the second book reveals.

"*Hands that Help* was the outgrowth of my doctor-pathologist daughter's insistence that I write a book on paramedical careers and that I, with my scientific background and writing experience, was better equipped to do it than many others. The work incidental to this book provided material for a one-act playlet called "What Everyone Knows" dealing with William Harvey's rejection of witchcraft at a time (early 1600's) when everyone knew all about witches save the man who discovered the circulation of the blood.

"To sum up, though science-related subjects are the most likely to receive sympathetic notice from an editor, I am still stubbornly engaged in pursuing historical events for their own sakes. A writer who seriously believes in the importance for the future of an understanding of the inter-

BERTHA S. DODGE

play of past and present can hardly help becoming involved in events of a nonscientific kind."

Bertha Dodge has travelled extensively in Latin America with husband, a botanist. Speaks Spanish, German; reads Portugese, French. Particularly interested in weavings and textiles; her collection of Guatemalan Indian weavings has been shown in museums.

DOOB, Leonard W(illiam) 1909-

PERSONAL: Born March 3, 1909, in New York, N.Y.; son of William and Florence (Lewis) Doob; married Eveline Bates, March 21, 1936; children: Christopher, Anthony, Nicholas. Education: Dartmouth College, B.A., 1929; Duke University, M.A., 1930; University of Frankfurt, postgraduate student, 1930-32; Harvard University, Ph.D., 1934. Home: Clark Rd., Woodbridge, Conn. Office: Department of Psychology, Yale University, 333 Cedar St., New Haven, Conn.

CAREER: Duke University, Durham, N.C., assistant instructor in psychology, 1929-30; Dartmouth College, Hanover, N.H., instructor of sociology, 1932-33; Yale University, New Haven, Conn., 1934—, started as instructor, became professor of psychology, 1950, chairman of council

on African Studies, 1958, and director of social science, 1963. U.S. Government, positions with various agencies concerned with psychological warfare, 1940-45, including coordinator of inter-American Affairs, chief of analysis section, 1940-42; War Department Section G-2, consulting psychologist, 1942-43; Office of War Information, chief of Bureau of Overseas Intelligence, 1943-44, policy coordinator of overseas bureau, 1944-45. Institute for Propaganda Analysis, member of advisory board, 1938-40. National Academy of Sciences, senior staff member of committee on human environments in Africa, 1958-60. Member: Society for Cross Cultural Research, Phi Beta Kappa, Sigma Xi. Awards, honors: Guggenheim fellow, 1960-61.

WRITINGS: Propaganda: Its Psychology and Technique, Holt, 1935; (with M. A. May) Competition and Cooperation, Social Science Research Council, 1937; (with J. Dollard and others) Frustration and Aggression, Yale University Press, 1939; The Plans of Men, Yale University Press, 1940; Public Opinion and Propaganda, Holt, 1948, 2nd edition, Shoe String, 1966.

Social Psychology, Holt, 1952; Becoming More Civilized, Yale University Press, 1960; Communication in Africa, Yale University Press, 1961; Patriotism and Nationalism, Yale University Press, 1964; (editor) Ants Will Not Eat Your Fingers: A Selection of Traditional African Poems, Walker, 1966; (editor) A Crocodile Has Me By the Leg (Horn Book Honor List), Walker, 1967; (editor) Resolving Conflict in Africa, Yale University Press, 1970; Patterning of Time, Yale University Press, 1971; Social Psychology: An Analysis of Human Behavior, Greenwood Press, 1971. Contributor to technical journals. Assessing editor, Journal of Social Psychology, 1965—.

DOUTY, Esther M(orris)

PERSONAL: Born March 24, in New York State; daughter of John Charles and Rosalie (Bien) Morris; married Harry M. Douty (now associate commissioner, U.S. Bureau of Labor Statistics), August 16; children: Christopher Morris, Harriet Taylor. Education: Duke University, A.B.; University of North Carolina, graduate student. Politics: Independent. Religion: Unitarian Universalist. Home: 4612 Butterworth Pl. N.W., Washington, D.C. 20016.

CAREER: Orange County, N.C., social worker. Director of workshop in junior biography, Writers' Conference, Georgetown University, 1960—; lecturer on junior biography, Writers' Institute, George Washington University, 1961. Member: Children's Book Guild (president, 1961-62), Phi Beta Kappa. Awards, honors: Boys' Clubs of America certificate award for Ball in the Sky, 1957.

WRITINGS: Story of Stephen Foster, Grosset, 1954; Ball in the Sky: John Wise, America's Pioneer Balloonist, Henry Holt, 1956; Patriot Doctor: The Story of Benjamin Rush, Messner, 1959; America's First Woman Chemist—Ellen Richards, Messner, 1961; Under the New Roof: Five Patriots of the Young Republic, Rand Mcnally, 1965, Forten the Sailmaker (ALA Notable Book), Rand McNally, 1968; Mr. Jefferson's Washington, Garrard, 1970; Charlotte Forten: Free Black Teacher, Garrard,

1971; *The Brave Balloonists. America's First Airmen*, Garrard, 1974; *Hasty Pudding and Barbary Pirates: A Life of Joel Barlow*, Westminster, 1975. Contributor to various publications including *American Heritage*, *New Republic*, and *Reporter*.

WORK IN PROGRESS: An adult historical mystery novel, a true story dealing with an early president of the United States.

SIDELIGHTS: "For the benefit of anyone who is flirting with the idea of going into historical or biographical writing, I usually make two basic mistakes which they might well avoid. One, I choose subjects whose contributions are great but who themselves are relatively obscure, and two, I do far too much original research for a young people's biography. A well-known subject is his own publicity; an obscure one must battle his way for the reader's consideration. From my own experience and from that of other writers I know, the sad fact is that the reviewers rarely realize that a juvenile biography often represents as much scholarly digging as an adult biography. (The research for my book on James Forten, for example, took three years.) Consequently, credit is seldom given for all that hard work, and this is somewhat discouraging to the author—somewhat discouraging, but not entirely, because the inner satisfaction that comes from a research job thoroughly and accurately done is not to be discounted, nor is the pleasure of doing it.

He felt even more certain now that they were riding ahead of a great storm. Heavy cumulus clouds were rolling in the distance, and the air had a strange milklike appearance. ■ (From *The Brave Balloonists* by Esther M. Douty. Illustrated by Victor Mays.)

"I might comment also on one other aspect of writing for young people—the current fashion for what is termed 'realism' in juvenile books. Now why is the presentation of the dark side of human nature considered 'real' and the portrayal of the finer qualities of the human spirit looked upon as sentimental claptrap?

"After all, what is 'real?' Is not health as real as sickness? Is not courage as real as cowardice? Is not love as real as hate? And finally, basically, is not good as real as evil?

"Observe a group of young children watching a television play or a movie. Do they not cheer on the 'good guy?' And they don't have to be told who the good guy is either. Why is this? Can it be that *instinctively* they know that their security lies only in the triumph of the 'good' and that destruction awaits them in the triumph of evil?

"Personally, I feel that the belief that children will grow up stronger and better able to 'cope' if they are early made aware of degrading circumstances in the lives of some families is a mistake. This knowledge can come later when young readers have more understanding and can place

ESTHER M. DOUTY

these unfortunate circumstances in proper perspective. When a child is young, he needs adult models who are heroes, people who can make the child's own striving, and the world about him, seem worthwhile. He needs reading to give him courage and a belief in the invincibility of the human spirit, *his* spirit. Let not the world be lost to him before he even enters the fray.''

HOBBIES AND OTHER INTERESTS: Collecting and coloring antique steel engravings relating to the American scene, and experimenting with the old art of transferring them to glass.

DURRELL, Gerald (Malcolm)   1925-

PERSONAL: Surname accented on first syllable; born January 7, 1925, in Jamshedpur, India; son of Lawrence Samuel (a civil engineer) and Louisa Florence (Dixie) Durrell; younger brother of Lawrence Durrell, the novelist; married Jacqueline Sonia Rasen (now her husband's personal assistant), 1951. *Education:* Educated by private tutors in France, Italy, Switzerland, and Greece; with specialized study in natural history under Theodore Stephanides of Athens. *Politics:* None. *Home and office:* Jersey Wildlife Preservation Trust, Les Augres Manor, Trinity, Jersey, Channel Islands. *Agent:* Curtis Brown Ltd., 13 King St., Covent Garden, London W.C. 2, England.

GERALD DURRELL

Then the reluctant donkeys had to be led out one by one and tethered to each other and then finally the horse was tethered to them as the leader. ■ (From *The Donkey Rustlers* by Gerald Durrell. Illustrated by Robin Jacques.)

CAREER: Whipsnade Zoological Park, Whipsnade, Bedfordshire, England, student keeper, 1945-46; Jersey Zoological Park, Trinity, Jersey, Channel Islands, founder, 1958, now honorary director, converted Park into the Jersey Wildlife Preservation Trust. Leader and underwriter of zoological collecting expeditions to remote parts of Africa, South America, Australia, and Southeast Asia, 1946—(made filming expedition to New Zealand, Australia, and New Zealand for B.B.C. television series, ''Two in the Bush,'' 1962). Member of advisory board, Wildlife Youth Service of World Wild Life Fund. *Military service:* None; rejected as medically unfit. *Member:* Zoological Society of London (fellow), Royal Society of Literature (fellow), Royal Geographical Society (fellow), Bombay Natural History Society, Nigerian Field Society, Fauna Preservation Society, British Ornithologists Union, Australian Mammal Society, Malayan Nature Society, American Zooparks Association, International Institute of Arts and Letters (fellow). *Awards, honors:* National Association of Independent Schools award, 1956, for *Three Tickets to Adventure.*

WRITINGS: The Overloaded Ark, Viking, 1953; *Three Singles to Adventure*, Hart-Davis, 1954, published as *Three Tickets to Adventure*, Viking, 1955; *The Bafut Beagles,*

Viking, 1954; *The New Noah* (juvenile), Collins, 1955, Viking, 1964; *The Drunken Forest*, Viking, 1956; *My Family, and Other Animals*, Viking, 1956; *A Zoo in My Luggage*, Viking, 1957; *Encounters with Animals*, Hart-Davis, 1958; *Island Zoo*, Collins, 1960, Macrae Smith, 1963; (compiler) *My Favourite Animal Stories*, Lutterworth, 1961, McGraw, 1963; *The Whispering Land*, Hart-Davis, 1961, Viking, 1962; *Look at Zoos*, Hamish Hamilton, 1963; *Menagerie Manor*, Hart-Davis, 1964, Viking, 1965; *Two in the Bush*, Viking, 1966; *Rosy is My Relative* (first novel), Viking, 1968; *Donkey Rustlers*, Viking, 1968; *Birds, Beasts, and Relatives*, Viking, 1969; *Fillets of Plaice*, Viking, 1971; *Catch Me a Colobus*, Viking, 1972; *Bevy of Beasts*, Simon & Schuster, 1973. Contributor to *New York Times, Reader's Digest, Harper's, Mademoiselle, Atlantic, Holiday, Show*, and other publications in England, United States, Canada, Australia, and New Zealand.

SIDELIGHTS: Gerald Durrell was born in Jamshedpur, India, in 1925. In 1928 his family returned to England, in 1933 they went to live on the Continent and eventually they settled on the island of Corfu, where they lived until 1939. During this time Durrell made a special study of zoology, and kept a large number of the local wild animals as pets. In 1945 he joined the staff of Whipsnade Park as a student keeper. In 1947 he financed, organized and led his first animal collecting expedition to the Cameroons. This gave rise to his first book, *The Overloaded Ark.*

The highlight of his varied career came in 1959 when he achieved his lifelong ambition of owning his own zoo, which he established in the Channel Island of Jersey. In 1963 this became the Jersey Wildlife Preservation Trust, the sole object of which is the keeping and breeding of those animals threatened with extinction in the wild state. Because of this they are treated accordingly. *Time* reported: "The 32 green and rolling acres are warmed by the

gulf stream, and animals have spacious cages with privacy when they want it. Durrell warns against expecting animals to take an automatic liking to each other. 'We humans seem to think we have a monopoly on love. How would you feel if you were locked for thirty years in a cage with a partner you couldn't stand?'"

Speaks French and Greek and some Spanish.

HOBBIES AND OTHER INTERESTS: Reading, photography, drawing, and swimming.

FOR MORE INFORMATION SEE: New York Times Book Review, May 13, 1973; *Time*, September 24, 1973.

ECKERT, Horst 1931-
(Janosch)

PERSONAL: Born March 11, 1931, in Zaborze, Poland; son of Johann (a shopkeeper) and Hildegard E. (Glodny) Eckert. *Education:* Attended gymnasium in Zaborze, 1940-43, and textile design school in Krefeld, Germany, 1947-49. *Religion:* None. *Home:* Kaiserstrasse 37, Munich, Germany.

CAREER: Author and illustrator of children's books.

His boots are dusty
But his face shines
■ (From *How Does a Czar Eat Potatoes?* by Anne Rose. Illustrated by Janosch.)

WRITINGS—All under Janosch and all self-illustrated except as indicated: *Onkel Poppoff kann auf Baeume fliegen*, Domino, 1964; *Das Auto hier heisst Ferdinand*, Deutscher Buecherbund, 1965; *Das Apfelmaennchen*, Parabel, 1965, translation published as *Just One Apple*, Walck, 1966; *Heute um neune hinter der Scheune*, Parabel, 1965, translation published as *Tonight at Nine*, Walck, 1967; *Ratemal, wer suchen muss*, Parabel, 1966; *Hannes Strohkopp und der unsichtbare Indianer*, Parabel, 1966; *Leo Zauberfloh: Oder, Wer andern eine Grube graebt*, Domino, 1966; *Poppoff und Piezke*, Parabel, 1966; *Der Josa mit der Zauberfiedel*, Parabel, 1967, translation published as *Joshua and the Magic Fiddle*, World Publishing, 1968; *Schlafe, lieber Hampelmann*, Parabel, 1967; *Raubenkoenig Muckelbass*, Domino, 1967; *Herr Wurzel und sein Zauberkuenstler*, Paulus, 1968; *Boellerbam und der Vogel*, Middelhauve, 1968, translation by Refna Wilkin published as *Bollerbam*, Walck, 1969; *Has Anyone Seen Paul? Who Will Be He?*, translated from the German by Margaret Green, Dobson, 1969; *Der Maeuse-Sheriff: Luegengeschicten aus dem Wilden Westen, er logen von einer Maus*, Bitter Verlag, 1969; *Das Regenauto*, Ellermann (Munich), 1969, translation published as *The Magic Auto*, Crown, 1971; *Ach lieber Schneeman*, Parabel, 1969, translation published as *Dear Snowman*, World Publishing, 1970; *Drei Raeuber und ein Raben Koenig*, Parabel, 1969, translation by Elizabeth Shub published as *The Thieves and the Raven*, Macmillan, 1970.

Leo Zauberfloh; oder die Leowenjagd in Oberfimmel, Bitter Verlag, 1970; *Komm nach Iglau, Krokodil*, Parabel, 1970, translation published as *The Crocodile Who Wouldn't Be King*, Putnam, 1971; *Cholonek oder der liebe Gott aus Lehm*, Bitter Verlag, 1970; *Flieg Vogel flieg*, Parabel, 1971; *Loewe Spring*, Parabel, 1971; *Ene bene Bimmelbahn*, Parabel, 1971; *Lari fari Mogelzahn*, Parabel, 1971; *Autos Autos viel Autos*, illustrated by Friedrich Kohlsaat, Beltz Verlag, 1971; *Janosch erzahlt Grimms Marchen*, Beltz Verlag, 1972; *Bilder und Gedichte fuer Kinder*, Westermann Verlag, 1972; *Schulfiebel 1*, Westermann Verlag, 1972; *Ich bin ein grosser Zottelbaer*, Parabel, 1972; *Wohin Rast die Feuerwehr*, [Munich], 1972; *Familie Schmidt*, Rowohlt Verlag, 1974; *Hottentotten grüne Motten*, Rowohlt Verlag, 1974; *Das starke Auto Ferdinand*, Parabel, 1975.

Illustrator: Mischa Damjan (pseudonym), *Filipo und sein Wunderpinsel*, Nord-Sued Verlag, 1967, translation published as *The Magic Paintbrush*, Walck, 1967; Jozef Wilkon, *Die Loewenkinder*, Middelhauve, 1968; Hans-Joachim Gelberg, *Die Stadt der Kinder*, Bitter Verlag, 1969; Jack Prelutzky, *Lazy Blackbird, and Other Verses*, Macmillan, 1969; Hans Baumann, *Der Wunderbare Ball Kada lupp*, Betz (Munich), 1969, translation published as *Gatalop, The Wonderful Ball*, Walck, 1971; Beverly Cleary, *Die Maus auf dem Motorrad*, Union Verlag, 1972; Cleary, *Mauserich Ralf Haut ab*, Union Verlag, 1972; Walter D. Edmonds, *Das Mauschaus*, Loewes Verlag, 1972. Also illustrator of *Bonko*, by Hans Baumann, 1972, and *Die lustigen Abenteur des Kasperl larifari*, by Franz-Graf von Pocci, 1972; Anne Rose, *How Does the Czar Eat Potatoes?*, Lothrop, 1973; James Krüss; *Der Kleine Flax*, Oetinger Verlag, 1975.

FOR MORE INFORMATION SEE: New York Times, November 3, 1968; *National Observer*, November 4, 1968; *Library Journal*, September 1, 1970.

EDMONDS, I(vy) G(ordon) 1917-

PERSONAL: Born February 15, 1917, in Frost, Tex.; son of Ivy Gordon (an oil field worker) and Delia (Shumate) Edmonds; married Reiko Mimura, July 12, 1956; children: Annette. *Education:* Attended high school in Hillsboro, Tex. *Residence:* Cypress, Calif. *Agent:* Scott Meredith Literary Agency, Inc., 580 Fifth Ave., New York, N.Y. 10036. *Office:* Northrop Corp., Hawthorne, Calif. 90250.

CAREER: U.S. Air Force, aerial photography and public relations assignments, 1940-63, spent half of service in overseas posts and retired as chief master sergeant; Federal Civil Service, public relations work in Los Angeles, Calif., 1963-68; Northrop Corp., Hawthorne, Calif., industrial editor, 1968-72, Anaheim, Calif., division public relations, 1972—. Writer. *Member:* Writers Guild of America, West. *Awards, honors*—Military: Distinguished Flying Cross, Air Medal, and Bronze Star Medal.

WRITINGS—mainly juvenile: *Solomon in Kimono* (folklore), Pacific Stars and Stripes, 1956; *Ooka: More Tales of Solomon in Komono*, Pacific Stars and Stripes, 1957; *Ooka the Wise* (folklore), Bobbs, 1961; *The Bounty's Boy*, Bobbs, 1962; *Hollywood RIP*, Regency, 1963; *Isometric and Isotonic Exercises*, Monarch, 1964; *Joel of the Hanging Gardens*, Lippincott, 1966; *Trickster Tales* (folklore), Lippincott, 1966; *Our Heroes' Heroes*, Criterion, 1966; (with John J. Gribbons) *Young Sportsman's Guide to Gymnastics and Tumbling*, Thomas Nelson, 1966, published as *Gymnastics and Tumbling*, Cornerstone Library, 1971; *Lassie and the Wild Mountain Trail*, Whitman Publishing, 1966; *Rat Patrol: Iron Monster Raid*, Whitman Publishing, 1967; *Revolts and Revolutions*, Hawthorn, 1969.

Khmers of Cambodia: The Story of a Mysterious People, Bobbs, 1970; *Hot Rodding for Beginners*, Macrae Smith, 1970; *Taiwan: The Other China*, Bobbs, 1971; *The Pos-*

HORST ECKERT

sible Impossibles of Ikkyu the Wise (folklore), Macrae Smith, 1971; *Motorcycling for Beginners*, Macrae Smith, 1972; *The Magic Man* (biography), Thomas Nelson, 1972; *Thailand, the Golden Land*, Bobbs, 1972; *Drag Racing for Beginners*, Bobbs, 1972; *Jet and Rocket Engines*, Putnam, 1973; *The New Malaysia*, Bobbs, 1973; *Mao's Long March*, Macrae Smith, 1973; *Minibikes and Minicycles*, Archway, 1973; *China's Red Rebel*, Macrae Smith, 1974; *Automotive Tuneups for Beginners*, Macrae Smith, 1974; *Pakistan*, Holt, 1975; *Micronesia: America's Outpost in the Pacific*, Bobbs, 1975; *United Nations: Successes and Failures*, Bobbs, 1975; *Ethiopia: Land of the Lion of Judah*, Holt, 1975; *The Magic Makers*, Thomas Nelson, in press. Has also written forty-five additional adult books under five pseudonyms.

SIDELIGHTS: "I attempted to write my first story when I was ten years old (in 1927) after seeing a Lon Chaney horror film called 'London after Midnight.' I got three pages and couldn't go any farther. But the desire to be a writer, born there, never wavered and I never wanted to be anything else.

"My particular interests are history, folklore and travel, and these are reflected in my books for young people. I first became interested in folklore after hearing a native 'talking chief' on the British island of Nanumea in the Ellice group tell the folk account of the island's birth. Since that time I have collected authentic folk tales in all the many countries I have visited. This resulted in three collections of folk tales, *Ooka the Wise*, *Trickster Tales*, and *The Possible Impossibles of Ikkyu the Wise*.

"On the histories that I write, I deal only with countries I have visited and always make a trip back while writing a book to check on changes and to keep my information current. During these trips I keep digging for folk tales I have not heard. These folklore books evolve slowly. I have been collecting now for four years on one tentatively titled, *Waves of a Mighty Sea*, and have not yet started to write it.

"While the majority of my books for children have received good reviews, the comment that has pleased me most was in a letter I received from a young man who had read *Hot Rodding for Beginners*. 'The way you wrote it,' he said, 'made it easy to understand.' That pleased me so much because that is exactly what I try to do in my writing for young people—make it easy to understand.

"I work hard to make these books 'easy to understand' without writing down to my audience. This has been especially true in the automotive series. The idea behind these books is that automobile shop manuals, textbooks and the like assume too much knowledge on the part of the reader. They are good for people who know something about mechanics, but no absolute beginner can take them and do work. I try to include those things which are usually omitted as being self-evident, but which aren't. I aim at the interested but completely uninformed who want to begin on their own.

Tinkler jumped up to run but the old sailor stuck out his wooden leg. The boy fell over it, sprawling on the cobble-stones with a jolt that knocked the wind from him. ▪ (From *The Bounty's Boy* by I. G. Edmonds. Illustrated by Gil Walker.)

I. G. EDMONDS

"I also aim for 'easy understanding' in my histories. In these I strive to tell *why* as well as *what*. Every one I have written are countries with whom the United States has been directly involved and affected. In addition to the story of the country, I strive to show why the United States became involved in these countries and the effect it has had. This is done without taking sides.

"I try to emphasize those aspects of the past that illuminate the present. For example, in *The Khmers of Cambodia*, if one understands the actions of the kings of Cambodia from the fall of Angkor in 1329 to the conquest of the country by the French in the late 19th century, then one will understand the seemingly peculiar actions of Prince Sihanouk in trying to play Russia and the United States against each other in the days preceeding the present Cambodian war. The old kings preserved Cambodian independence by adroitly playing one foreign enemy against the other. It did not work with Sihanouk in the end, but you can see and understand his actions even if you do not agree with them."

EDSALL, Marian S(tickney) 1920-

PERSONAL: Born April 24, 1920, in Chicago, Ill.; daughter of Harry F. and Hazel (Dickover) Stickney; married James VanAllen Edsall (director of planning and construction at University of Wisconsin), November 20, 1943; children: Sandra Lee (Mrs. Patrick O'Brien). *Education:* Wellesley College, B.A., 1941. *Home:* Deer Run Heights, Cross Plains, Wis. 53528. *Office:* Coordinated Library Information Program, Inc., Box 1437, 3030 Darbo Dr., Madison, Wis. 53701.

CAREER: Meyer Both Advertising Agency, Chicago, Ill., copywriter, 1941-43; Community Plan Office, Champaign, Ill., publications director, 1953-54; University of Illinois, Champaign, publicity director for television station WILL, 1961-63; Visual Educational Consultants, Middleton, Wis., editor, 1967-68; Wisconsin Division for Library Services, Madison, director of cooperative library information program, 1970—. Trustee at various times of library boards in Champaign, Middleton, and Dane County. *Member:* American Library Association, National Audubon Society, Wisconsin Library Association, Friends of Wisconsin Libraries. *Awards, honors:* Named Wisconsin Library Trustee of the Year by Wisconsin Library Association, 1971.

WRITINGS—Juvenile: *Our Auto Trip*, Rand McNally, 1952; *Battle on the Rosebush: Insect Life in Your Backyard*, Follett, 1972. Staff writer for several trailer and travel magazines; free-lance writer for other periodicals. Editor, *Camping Horizons* (bimonthly magazine), 1960-62, and of newsletters.

WORK IN PROGRESS: A book on library promotion.

HOBBIES AND OTHER INTERESTS: Outdoor life and nature, particularly at a vacation retreat in the isolated Canadian woods.

A male monarch butterfly has one distinctive marking, a small black [dot] on the upper surface of each hind wing. ■ (From *Battle on the Rosebush* by Marian S. Edsall. Illustrated by Jean Cassels.)

MARIAN S. EDSALL

BLOSSOM ELFMAN

ELFMAN, Blossom, 1925-

PERSONAL: Born November 4, 1925, in New York, N.Y.; daughter of Herman (a jeweler) and Lillian (Blackman) Bernstein; married Milton Elfman (a teacher), March 7, 1948; children: Richard Elliot, Daniel Robert. *Education:* University of California, Los Angeles, B.A., 1948; University of Southern California, M.A., 1965. *Home:* 476 Greencraig Rd., Brentwood, Los Angeles, Calif. 90049. *Agent:* Barthold Fles Literary Agency, 507 Fifth Ave., New York, N.Y. 10017.

CAREER: Teacher at public schools in Los Angeles, Calif., 1962-72.

WRITINGS: The Girls of Huntington House (novel; ALA Notable Book), Houghton, 1972.

WORK IN PROGRESS: A second book on the subject of pregnant teens, *When The Bough Breaks.*

SIDELIGHTS: "*The Girls of Huntington House* relates in part my experiences as a teacher in several maternity homes."

EMBERLEY, Barbara A(nne)

PERSONAL: Maiden surname, Collins; married Edward Randolph Emberley; children: Rebecca Anne, Michael Edward. *Education:* Attended Massachusetts College of Art. *Home:* 6 Water St., Ipswich, Mass.

CAREER: Writer of children's books.

WRITINGS—Illustrated by husband, Ed Emberley: *Night's Nice*, Doubleday, 1963; *Paul Bunyan*, Prentice-Hall, 1963; *Yankee Doodle*, Prentice-Hall, 1965; *One Wide River to Cross*, Prentice-Hall, 1966; *Drummer Hoff*, Prentice-Hall, 1967; *Simon's Song* (Junior Literary Guild selection), Prentice-Hall, 1969.

HOBBIES AND OTHER INTERESTS: Herb gardening, collecting antiques for 1690 saltbox Colonial home in Ipswich, Mass., sailing along the Northeast coast.

FOR MORE INFORMATION SEE: Lee Bennett Hopkins, *Books Are By People*, Citation Press, 1969; *New York Times Book Review*, November 9, 1969; Selma G. Lanes, *Down the Rabbit Hole*, Atheneum, 1971; *Third Book of Junior Authors*, edited by de Montreville and Hill, H. W. Wilson, 1972.

EMBERLEY, Ed(ward Randolph) 1931-

PERSONAL: Born October 19, 1931, in Malden, Mass.; son of Wallace Akin and Evelyn (Farrell) Emberley; married Barbara A. Collins (now writer of children's books); children: Rebecca Anne, Michael Edward. *Education:* Massachusetts College of Art, B.F.A.; also studied at Rhode Island School of Art. *Religion:* Protestant. *Home:* 6 Water St., Ipswich, Mass.

CAREER: Writer and illustrator of children's books, and magazines; illustrator of textbooks. *Military service:* U.S. Army, two years. *Awards, honors: New York Times* award for best-illustrated book, 1961, for *The Wing on a Flea,* and 1965, for *Punch and Judy;* Caldecott Medal, 1968, for *Drummer Hoff.*

WRITINGS Author and illustrator: *The Wing on a Flea,* Little, Brown, 1961; *The Parade Book,* Little, Brown, 1962; *Cock A Doodle Doo,* Little, Brown, 1964; *Punch and Judy,* Little, Brown, 1965; *Rosebud,* Little, Brown, 1966; *London Bridge Is Falling Down,* Little, Brown, 1967; *Green Says Go,* Little, Brown, 1968; *Ed Emberley's Drawing Book of Animals,* Little, Brown, 1969; *Ed Emberley's Drawing Book: Make a World,* Little, Brown, 1972; *Klippity Klop,* Little, Brown, 1973; *Ed Emberley's Drawing Book of Faces,* Little, Brown, 1975.

Illustrator of six books written by wife, Barbara Emberley: *Night's Nice,* Doubleday, 1963; *Paul Bunyan,* Prentice-Hall, 1963; *Yankee Doodle,* Prentice-Hall, 1965; *One Wide River to Cross,* Prentice-Hall, 1966; *Drummer Hoff,* Prentice-Hall, 1967; *Simon's Song,* Prentice-Hall, 1969.

Illustrator: Ruth Bonn Penn, *Mommies Are for Loving,* Putnam, 1962; Franklyn M. Branley, *The Big Dipper,* Crowell, 1962; Mary Kay Phelan, *The White House,* Holt, 1962; Roma Gans, *Birds Eat and Eat and Eat,* Crowell, 1963; Leslie Waller, *American Inventions,* Holt, 1963; Franklyn M. Branley, *Flash, Crash, Rumble and Roll,* Crowell, 1964; Richard Schackburg, *Yankee Doodle,* Prentice-Hall, 1965; L. Schatz, *Rhinoceros? Preposterous.,* Steck-Vaughn, 1965; Dorothy Les-Tina, *Flag Day,* Crowell, 1965; Paul Showers, *Columbus Day,* Crowell, 1965; M. C. Farquhar, *Colonial Life in America,* Holt, 1965; Augusta Goldin, *The Bottom of the Sea,* Crowell, 1966; Augusta Goldin, *Straight Hair, Curly Hair,* Crowell, 1966; Leslie Waller, *The American West,* Holt, 1966; Judy Hawes, *Ladybug, Ladybug, Fly Away Home,* Crowell, 1967; Heywood Broun, *The Fifty-First Dragon,* Prentice-Hall, 1968; Leslie Waller, *Clothing,* Holt, 1969; Ian Serraillier, *Suppose You Met a Witch,* Little, Brown, 1973.

SIDELIGHTS: "I realize that being a children's book illustrator doesn't give me credentials to speak with authority about the art education of young children. (I'm not, after all, an expert in education . . . nor children . . . nor, for that matter, art.) But it does give me a platform and, while I have I'm going to use it. I'm not one to beat around the bush, either. So let's get to it. I want to talk about that old classroom monster—copying. Most particularly, copying in art, and what it does or doesn't do for pupils.

"Do you tolerate rubber-stamp art in your classroom (every child's house turns out just like the beautiful one Jack built with his trusty crayon)? Do you pass out precut triangles, or squares, or whatever for art projects? Do you let your kids use their worksheets as coloring books? Do you give 1 . . . 2 . . . 3-type recipes for concocting take-homes (with the noble intent, no doubt, of giving the parents a chance at recognizing what they're being gifted with)? Are you giving your kids a one-way ride on the easy street to artistic damnation?

"In *Creative Mental Growth,* for example, authors Viktor Lowenfeld and W. Lambert Brittain make no bones about their position: 'Experimental research,' say they, 'has given us *ample proof* that imitative methods have a detrimental effect on a child's creativeness.'

"In the same book, Dr. Irene Russell gets more specific: 'After coloring the (math) work book birds,' she tells us, 'the child has lost his creative sensitivity and self-reliance.' And then she treats us to an aviary of those infamous colored creatures, presumably to prove her point.

"No doubt, most of today's artists, teachers of art and teachers of teachers (and lots of plain people, too) agree with Lowenfeld and Brittain that copying is, at the very least, inhibiting and, more likely downright destructive. But is it?

"I submit that copying can, indeed, be a source of both information and inspiration for the little copy kittens in your classroom. The fact is, some of the artists whose work we most admire today copied to learn. Consider, for example . . .

". . . The Egyptian of antiquity. For century upon century, he produced virtually the same sculptures and paintings. And still, millenniums later, his starched-and-ironed figures doing their ankle-breaking, side-stepping thing across the museum wall, awe and inspire us.

ED EMBERLEY

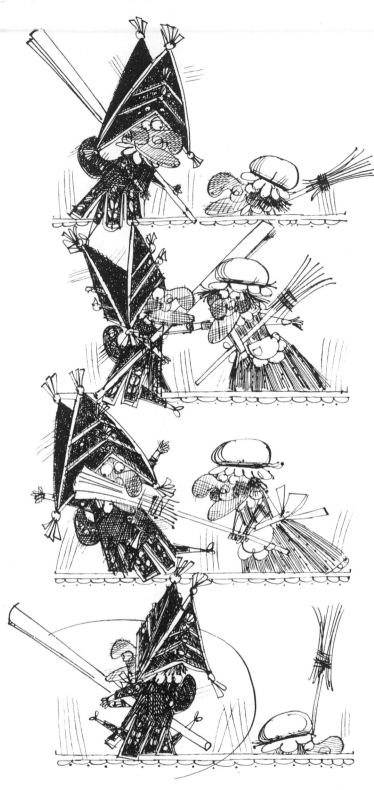

JUDY: Well, what do you want, old lobster nose? ■ (From *Punch and Judy* by Ed Emberley. Illustrated by the author.)

"... or the Eskimo sculptor. Never, through the years, has he wielded his tools without reference to the past. Each time, he mixes anew the discoveries and techniques of the artists who have gone before with a little bit of himself. And we value his work as much for its copying of the past, as for the little something new he injects into it.

"... or, if you prefer name-dropping, let's drop "Michaelangelo." According to *I Michaelangelo Sculptor*, the glorifier of the Sistine Chapel 'was forever' ... playing hookey to sketch the Giottos in Santa Croce or the Massaccios in the Brancacci Chapel."

"... or Van Gogh, who unabashedly copied Millet and Delacroix. Late in his career, he wrote his brother, Theo: 'Heaps of people do not copy. Heaps of others copy. I started by chance, and I find it teaches me things. Above all, it gives me consolation.'

"I have to admit that my ego, training and the kind of 'ample evidence' referred to by Lowenfeld and Brittain once made it difficult for me to endorse any and all kinds of copying. But Van Gogh and the Eskimos set me to thinking ... if copying can bring consolation to a Van Gogh, why can't it do the same for our children? Do they never need this kind of consolation?

"... if imitative methods destroy the creative sensibility and selfreliance of a child wielding a crayon or brush, why doesn't it destroy that of the pint-size musician-in-the-making endlessly pounding out scales on a piano? Did it, after all, destroy Beethoven ... or Casals?

"... does the aspiring ballerina's painful miming of the marvelous leaps and arabesques of a Fonteyn condemn her to mediocrity? Nonsense.

"Isn't it about time we learned that artistic achievement—in whatever medium—is a sum total of the past and the present? That the artist is, in a very special way, both the protector of the past—a guardian of history, so to speak—and a unique chronicler of his own age? That plagiarism—copying for profit—is one thing; the subtle resurrection of the culture of one generation to the enrichment of a later one, quite another.

"Such thoughts inevitably bring me back to my own beginnings as an artist in grade school. In that long ago, I remember, I could recreate a lot of the folk heroes of the day—Popeye, Donald Duck and others like them—by parroting their complicated and, unfortunately, 'onetime use' curves.

"I suppose I got a lot of satisfaction—maybe even some Van Gogh-style consolation—from this kind of copying. But what can you do with Popeye's slipped biceps once you've learned to draw them?

"I can also remember that, at about the same time, I learned to draw by following a diagram that showed me how to turn some simple shapes and a few lines into a tank. That was thirty years ago. While I have long since forgotten how to draw Popeye and his friends, I can still use the 'vocabulary' of the simple shapes to draw a tank. That's a kind of copying, a kind of repetition, that sticks to the artistic ribs. And it offers the possibility of ever more fulfilling discoveries.

"It was remembrances of those tanks past that led me to develop a whole 'graphic vocabulary'—mostly circles, triangles and rectangles—to provide a 'basic lexicon' for creating some 400 objects. The result: *Make a World*, a drawing book published by Little, Brown that invites kids to copy . . . copy . . . copy.

"The method used in *Make a World* is not new, of course. And it certainly is not the only worthwhile copy method. But it does make every child an instant expert . . . and an instant experimenter. And, since the book was conceived as entertainment, it's fun too.

"If a child gets satisfaction or consolation from imitating the creations of another—let him go to it. Before you know it, he'll modify, embellish, improvise to create something of his very own. And, best of all, he'll enjoy! Enjoy!"

HOBBIES AND OTHER INTERESTS: Bicycling, cross-country skiing, gardening, boating, printing limited editions of children's books (his imprint is Bird in Bush Press), making toys, collecting antiques for 1690 saltbox colonial home. Emberley says he has "4000 extra interests," ranging from playing the guitar to sailing.

FOR MORE INFORMATION SEE: Illustrators of Children's Books: 1957-1966, Horn Book, 1968; Lee Bennett Hopkins, *Books Are By People*, Citation Press, 1969; *New York Times Book Review*, November 9, 1969, November 3, 1974; *Time*, December 21, 1970; Hoffman and Samuels, *Authors and Illustrators of Children's Books*, Bowker, 1972; *Third Book of Junior Authors*, edited by de Montreville and Hill, H. W. Wilson, 1972; MacCann and Richard, *The Child's First Books*, H. W. Wilson, 1973; *Wilson Library Bulletin*, October, 1974.

ENGLEBERT, Victor   1933-

PERSONAL: Surname is pronounced Engla-berre; born February 5, 1933, in Brussels, Belgium; son of Joseph (a musician) and Rosa (Leberzorg) Englebert; married Lucienne Girard, April, 1955 (divorced, 1972); married Martha Jaramillo, September 21, 1972; children: (first marriage) Barbara, Eric. *Education:* Self-educated. *Religion:* None. *Home:* Apartado aereo, 8221 Cali, Colombia.

CAREER: Professional photographer living in Germany, 1952-54, Zaïre, 1955-57, Canada, 1960-61, United States, 1961-73, Colombia, 1974—. *Military service:* Belgian Army, 1952-54. *Member:* American Society of Magazine Photographers, American Society of Picture Professionals.

WRITINGS—Books for children illustrated with own photographs: *Camera on Africa: The World of an Ethiopian Boy*, Harcourt, 1970; *Camera on Ghana: The World of a Young Fisherman*, Harcourt, 1971; *Camera on the Sahara: The World of Three Young Nomads*, Harcourt, 1971; *The Goats of Agadez*, Harcourt, 1973. Writer and illustrator of *National Geographic* features; photographs and articles have appeared in National Geographic books.

WORK IN PROGRESS: Books on the Tuareg nomads of the Sahara and on Colombia.

SIDELIGHTS: "Became photographer to help satisfy an urge to travel and explore. Started to write to help sell my

At school the classes are taught in English, Ghana's official language, although at home Kwabla and his friends speak Ewe, the language of their tribe. ■ (From *Camera on Ghana* by Victor Englebert. Photographs by the author.)

pictures. But now take pictures and write for sheer pleasure. Have studied a dozen or more primitive tribes in Africa, Asia, South America, mostly to write *National Geographic* articles, and so am interested in anthropology. I speak fluently French, English, Spanish, and less well, Dutch, German, and Portuguese.''

FAITHFULL, Gail 1936-
(Gail Faithfull Keller)

PERSONAL: Born November 20, 1936, in New York, N.Y.; daughter of George Edward (a lawyer) and Lucia (Turner) Faithfull; divorced; children: Bayard Faithfull Keller, Elizabeth Coburn Keller. *Education:* Rosemary Hall, student, 1951-54; Vassar College, A.B., 1958; Union Theological Seminary and Columbia University, M.A. (joint degree), 1960. *Politics:* Democrat. *Home:* 1 Delsmere Ave., Delmar, N.Y. 12054. *Office:* Albany Academy for Girls, 140 Academy Rd., Albany, N.Y. 12208.

CAREER: Assistant to minister of Presbyterian church in Yonkers, N.Y., 1958-59; Rosemary Hall, Greenwich, Conn., instructor in ancient and biblical history, 1960-61; *Columbia Encyclopedia*, New York, N.Y., researcher for religious entries, 1963; Albany Academy for Girls, Albany, N.Y., assistant to headmaster, director of guidance, and teacher of English and history, 1969—. Ordained elder of Westminster Presbyterian Church, Albany, 1974; chairperson of executive council, Focus: A Coalition of Emmanuele Baptist, Trinity United Methodist, First and Westminster Presbyterian Churches, Albany.

WRITINGS: (Under name Gail Faithfull Keller) *Jane Addams* (juvenile), Crowell, 1971.

GAIL FAITHFULL

WORK IN PROGRESS: Research on educational trends and on ancient history, especially the ancient Near East.

SIDELIGHTS: "I am still seriously considering going into the ministry, but my present occupation and preoccupation is girl's education, K-12.''

FEELINGS, Thomas 1933-
(Tom Feelings)

PERSONAL: Born May 19, 1933, in Brooklyn, N.Y.; son of Samuel (a taxicab driver) and Anna (Nash) Feelings; married Muriel Grey (a school teacher), February 18, 1968 (divorced, 1974); children: Zamani, Kamili. *Education:* Attended School of Visual Art, 1951-53, 1957-60. *Home:* c/o Anna Morris, 21 St. James Pl., Brooklyn, N.Y. 11205.

CAREER: Ghana Publishing Company, Ghana, West Africa, illustrator for *African Review*, 1964-66; Government of Guyana, Guyana, South America, teacher of illustrators for Ministry of Education, 1971—; artist and illustrator. Has worked as free-lance illustrator for Ghana television programs and for newspapers and other businesses in Ghana. *Military service:* U.S. Air Force, illustrator in Graphics Division in London, England, 1953-57. *Awards, honors:* Caldecott Honor Book runner-up for best illustrated children's book, 1972, for *Moja Means One*; *Black Pilgrimage* was runner-up for Coretta Scott King award, received Woodward School annual book award, and Brooklyn Museum citation, all 1973; School of Visual Art outstanding alumni achievement award, 1974.

WRITINGS—For children: *Black Pilgrimage* (ALA Notable Book; *Horn Book* Honor List), Lothrop, 1972.

Illustrator: Letta Schatz, *Bola and the Oba's Drummers*, McGraw, 1967; Eleanor Heady, compiler, *When the Stones Were Soft: East African Folktales*, Funk, 1968; Jullius Lester, editor, *To Be a Slave*, Dial, 1968; Osmond Molarsky, *Song of the Empty Bottles*, Walck, 1968; Robin McKown, *The Congo: River of Mystery*, McGraw, 1968; Nancy Garfield, *The Tuesday Elephant*, Crowell, 1968; Kathleen Arnot, *Tales of Temba: Traditional African Stories*, Walck, 1969; Ruskin Bond, *Panther's Moon*, Random House, 1969; Rose Blue, *A Quiet Place*, F. Watts, 1969; Lester, compiler, *Black Folktales*, Baron, 1969.

Muriel Feelings, *Zamani Goes to Market*, Seabury, 1970; Jane Kerina, *African Crafts*, Lion Press, 1970; Muriel Feelings, *Moja Means One*, Dial, 1971; Muriel Feelings, *Jambo Means Hello*, Dial, 1974.

WORK IN PROGRESS: An extensive illustrated book dealing with the history of slavery of the black man in North America; an illustrated autobiography.

SIDELIGHTS: "My main interest has been the Black People of the world. In this connection I have traveled and drawn from life in East and West Africa and South America.

"Because I tend to overpaint and had to find a medium and a method that would limit this tendency, I experimented for many years until I found that tissue paper solved this problem for me. It also gave my work a luminous quality that I could not get in any other way.

To show everyone how strong he could be, Zamani took hold of each basket and slowly dragged them across the compound until he reached the big trees. ■ (From *Zamani Goes to Market* by Muriel Feelings. Illustrated by Tom Feelings.)

"I prepare my art in several stages. When I complete my first drawing I transfer it in pencil onto a rough-textured board. Then I go over it with a pen filled with water-soluble black ink. I call this my *base* art.

"I then paint the areas of the picture that I want to remain light or highlighted in the final painting with white water-based tempera paint. Then I lay a sheet of wet tissue paper over the complete board. This causes the black ink and white tempera to run into each other, creating wonderful shades and forms and 'accidents' that I use or fight to control in the final painting. This 'wet into wet' stage is what makes the process particularly exciting to me, for I *never* know what will happen here.

"While the tissue is still wet I paint ink washes into the darker areas and more white tempera, sometimes mixed with ink, into the lighter areas or over darker sections. Then the process of rewetting and painting into different sections continues until I feel I've captured the right mood and the painting is finished.

"Finally, if I feel the painting needs it, I use linseed oil to darken some areas and to bring out the base line drawing."

TOM FEELINGS

FOR MORE INFORMATION SEE: *Negro Digest* now *Black World*, September, 1967, August, 1971; *Sepia*, September, 1969; Lee Bennett Hopkins, *Books Are by People*, Citation Press, 1969; *Third Book of Junior Authors*, edited by de Montreville and Hill, H. W. Wilson, 1972; *New York Times Book Review*, May 7, 1972; *Saturday Review*, May 20, 1972; *Horn Book*, August, 1972.

FEELINGS, Tom
See FEELINGS, Thomas

FEIFFER, Jules 1929-

PERSONAL: Born January 26, 1929, in Bronx, New York; son of David (who held a variety of jobs from dental technician to salesman) and Rhoda (a fashion designer; maiden name, Davis) Feiffer; married Judith Sheftel (formerly picture editor with *American Heritage*), September 17, 1961; children: Kate. *Education:* Attended Art Students League, New York, N.Y., 1946, Pratt Institute, 1947-48, 1949-51. *Agent:* Robert Lantz, 111 West 57th St., New York, N.Y.

CAREER: Assistant to Will Eisner cartoonist, 1946-51; drew syndicated cartoon, "Clifford," 1949-51; held various odd jobs, 1953-56, including a job making slide films, a job as writer for Terrytoons, and one designing booklets for an art firm; cartoonist for *Village Voice* (cartoons now syndicated by Hall Syndicate), 1956—. *Military service:* U.S. Army, Signal Corps, 1951-53; worked in a cartoon animation unit. *Member:* National Committee for a Sane Nuclear Policy (sponsor), Authors League of America, Dramatists Guild, Committee of the Professions, P.E.N.

WRITINGS: Sick, Sick, Sick (cartoons), McGraw, 1958; *Passionella, and Other Stories* (cartoons), McGraw, 1959; *The Explainers* (cartoons), McGraw, 1960, a satirical review written by Feiffer was produced with the same title at Playwrights Cabaret Theater, Chicago, 1961; *Boy, Girl, Boy, Girl* (cartoons), Random, 1961; "Crawling Arnold" (one-act play), first produced at Gian-Carlo Menotti's Festival of Two Worlds, Spoleto, Italy, 1961; *Feiffer's Album* (cartoons), Random, 1963; *Harry: The Rat With Women* (novel), McGraw, 1963; *Hold Me!* (cartoons), Random, 1963; (editor and annotater) *The Great Comic Book Heroes*, Dial, 1965; *The Unexpurgated Memoirs of Bernard Mergendeiler* (cartoons), Random, 1965; "Little Murders" (play), first produced at Yale School of Drama, 1966, then at Broadhurst Theatre, New York, 1967, first American play produced by Royal Shakespeare Co., London, 1967, very successfully revived off-Broadway at Circle-in-the-Square, 1969; *Feiffer's Marriage Manual*, Random, 1967; *Feiffer on Civil Rights*, Anti-Defamation League, 1967; *God Bless* (play), 1968; *The White House Murder Case* (play), Grove, 1969; *Pictures at a Prosecution* (drawings), Grove, 1970; "Carnal Knowledge," Farrar, 1971.

Illustrator: Robert Mines, *My Mind Went All to Pieces*, Dial, 1959; Norton Juster, *The Phantom Tollbooth*, Random, 1961.

Feiffer draws his cartoons easily, but he sometimes rewrites his captions 15 times. Once he has completed the strip, his contract specifies that no one can tamper with his words. He maintains he has no trouble finding new material

"Why, my cabinet members can do all sorts of things. The duke here can make mountains out of molehills. The minister splits hairs. The count makes hay while the sun shines. The earl leaves no stone unturned. And the undersecretary," he finished ominously, "hangs by a thread. Can't you do anything at all?"
■ (From *The Phantom Tollbooth* by Norton Juster. Illustrated by Jules Feiffer.)

each week: "There really is no deliberate search for material," he told *Mademoiselle*, "because once I start doing *that* I separate myself from what I'm doing. Really the strips are a normal outgrowth of how I feel from time to time. This doesn't mean I don't sit down and worry about what I'm going to do this week. But what comes up, I discover looking back later, always had something directly to do with what I was feeling about some particular situation at that particular moment. . . ."

Feiffer believes that he has been influenced to a greater degree by writers rather than by cartoonists. Among cartoonists, he most admires Saul Steinberg. "The drawing style has been most influenced by a combination of people," he says, "from William Steig to Robert Osborn to Andre Francois. The writing began, I guess, being patterned after Benchley."

An animated cartoon, "Munro," based on a Feiffer story, was filmed by Rembrandt Films, 1961, and won an Oscar as the best short-subject cartoon; "The Feiffer Film," a re-creation of some of his cartoons, was released in 1965; "The Apple Tree," a musical by Jerry Bock and Sheldon Harnick, produced in 1966, consists of three playlets, one based on Feiffer's "Passionella." *Harry: The Rat With Women* was made into a play and first produced at Institute of Arts, Detroit, 1966.

FOR MORE INFORMATION SEE: Time, February 9, 1959, May 26, 1961, June 28, 1963; *New Republic*, June 6, 1960; *Mademoiselle*, January, 1961; *Horizon*, November, 1961; *Commentary*, November, 1961; *Newsweek*, November 13, 1961, May 8, 1967; *New York Times Book Review*, June 30, 1963; *Life*, July 17, 1965; *Village Voice*, April 13, 1967, May 4, 1967; *New York Times*, April 23, 1967, April 27, 1967.

FIELD, Edward 1924-

PERSONAL: Born June 7, 1924, in Brooklyn, N.Y. *Education:* Attended New York University. *Home:* 97 Perry St., New York, N.Y. 10014.

CAREER: Writer. Has done narrations for film documentaries. *Military service:* U.S. Army Air Forces, 1942-46. *Awards, honors:* Lamont Poetry Selection, 1962, for *Stand Up, Friend, With Me*; Guggenheim fellowship, 1963; Shelley Memorial Award, 1975.

WRITINGS: Stand Up, Friend, With Me (poems), Grove, 1962; *Variety Photoplays*, Grove, 1967; *Eskimo Songs and Stories*, Delacorte, 1973.

JULES FEIFFER

She was really turning into stone from the legs up. ■ (From *Eskimo Songs and Stories* translated by Edward Field. Illustrated by Kiakshuk and Pudlo.)

FINKEL, George (Irvine)   1909-1975
(E. M. Pennage)

PERSONAL: Born May 13, 1909, in Durham, England; son of George Edward (a farmer) and Grace Amy (Stephenson) Finkel; married Lena Almond, January, 1930; children: Ian Derek, Anne Deirdre (Mrs. Leslie Beckhouse), Christopher Thomas George, David Michael. *Education:* Educated at Bede Collegiate School, 1919-26, and in Royal Navy. *Politics:* "Floating voter." *Religion:* Anglican. *Home:* 18 Coolabah Rd., Valley Heights, New South Wales, Australia. *Office:* University of New South Wales, Kensington, New South Wales, Australia.

CAREER: Started in chemical engineering; became aviator, flying pioneer routes in Africa, 1935-39; career officer in Royal Navy, 1938-58, leaving service with rank of lieutenant commander; University of New South Wales, Kensington, New South Wales, Australia, planning engineer, 1958-69. Author. *Member:* Australian Society of Authors, Childrens Book Council of New South Wales.

WRITINGS: The Mystery of Secret Beach, Angus & Robertson, 1962; *Ship in Hiding*, Angus & Robertson, 1963; *Cloudmaker*, Roy, 1965; *The Singing Sands*, Angus & Robertson, 1966; *Twilight Province*, Angus & Robertson, 1967, published in America as *Watchfires to the*

GEORGE FINKEL

"In 1954 was Commandant of a Naval Training School in Australia, and all my junior trainees over 5'7" (1.73m) were drafted to form the Royal Guard for Her Majesty Queen Elizabeth II on the occasion of the first visit by a reigning monarch to this country. This left me with very little to do for five months (training the guard, the visit, and leave at the end of it, in none of which I had any part). So I began writing again, and have been doing so ever since. It took me seven years to write an acceptable book, but most of what I have written since 1961 has been published.

"I usually write a first draft in pencil, rubbing out and rewriting a good deal of this. Then I write a typed draft, and drastically edit out about 15% of this. The third draft is the one that goes to the publisher.

"Once I begin a book I work on it some part of every day. If I have to travel I cut out writing until I'm home again. It takes me five to eight months to write a full-length novel. The Topic Books (about 6,000 words each) took about ten days, but my wife did the third typing. We were working to a deadline.

I now live in the Blue Mountains, with a State Forest Reserve at the bottom of the garden. There are wallabies and wombats, currawongs and lorikeets and kookaburras in it (also dogs and cats!). For some odd reason most cats in Australia are black and white, like Walt Disney's Figaro.

"Some of the books written and rejected during my apprenticeship period have been re-hashed since I achieved publication, and have found print in their second incarnation. *Loyall Virginian* is one of them."

HOBBIES AND OTHER INTERESTS: Desert travel, Anglo-Saxon and Byzantine history, ancient voyages.

(Died, 1975)

North, Viking, 1968; *Long Pilgrimage*, Viking, 1968; *The Loyall Virginian*, Angus & Robertson, 1969, published in America as *The Loyal Virginian*, Viking, 1969; *Journey to Jorsala*, Angus & Robertson, 1969; *James Cook: Royal Navy*, Angus & Robertson, 1970; *The Peace-Seekers*, Angus & Robertson, 1970; *Pilgrim of Fortune*, Angus & Robertson, 1972; *The Dutchman Bold*, Angus & Robertson, 1972; (under pseudonym E. M. Pennage) *The Stranded Duck*, Angus & Robertson, in press; (under pseudonym E. M. Pennage) *The Crew of the "Ingrid"*, Angus & Robertson, in press. Monthly motoring columnist in *Avalon News*, New South Wales. Twelve topic books for the South Australian Education Department, published by Thomas Nelson Ltd.

SIDELIGHTS: "I began writing verse for the school magazine at the age of eleven, and wrote verse steadily until my mid-twenties. Had two poems published and paid for. Then the muse was swamped by the necessity of having to earn a living. Wrote four official publications for Royal Navy, 1942/43. (Sorry! Official Secrets Act and all that!)

ANN FINLAYSON

Libby wanted to stay where she was, close to the earth. But she was afraid to wait. The street was directly ahead, beyond another screen of bushes. ■ (From *Runaway Teen* by Ann Finlayson. Illustrated by Evelyn Copelman.)

FINLAYSON, Ann 1925-

PERSONAL: Born March 25, 1925, in New York, N.Y.; daughter of Frank Lathrop and Anna (Neacy) Finlayson. *Education:* Northwestern University, B.S.J., 1945. *Politics:* Usually Democratic. *Religion:* Roman Catholic. *Home and office:* 33 North Western Hwy., Blauvelt, N.Y. 10913.

CAREER: Popular Publications, New York, N.Y., editor, 1950-51, editor and staff writer for *True Story*, 1951-60; free-lance writer, mostly for confession magazines, 1960-63; Rutledge Books, Inc., New York, N.Y., editor, 1963-64; free-lance copy editor and proofreader for book publishers and free-lance writer, mostly for young people, 1965—.

WRITINGS: Runaway Teen, Doubleday, 1963; *A Summer to Remember*, Doubleday, 1964; *Animal Habits*, Golden Press, 1965; *Decathlon Men*, Garrard, 1966; *Stars of the Modern Olympics*, Garrard, 1967; *Champions at Bat: Three Power Hitters*, Garrard, 1970; *Redcoat in Boston*, Warne, 1971; (editor of condensation) Elswyth Thane, *Dawn's Early Light*, Hawthorn, 1971; *Rebecca's War*, Warne, 1972; (with Harold B. Gill) *Colonial Virginia*, Nelson, 1973; *Greenhorn on the Frontier*, Warne, 1974; *House Cat*, Warne, 1974; *Colonial Maryland*, Nelson, 1974.

HOBBIES AND OTHER INTERESTS: Walking, reading, watching television, knitting, talking, browsing in hardware and stationary stores.

FLEISCHMAN, (Albert) Sid(ney) 1920-

PERSONAL: Born March 16, 1920, in Brooklyn, N.Y.; son of Reuben and Sadie (Solomon) Fleischman; married Betty Taylor, 1942; children: Jane, Paul, Anne. *Education:* San Diego State College, B.A., 1949. *Home and office:* 305 Tenth St., Santa Monica, Calif. 90402. *Agent:* Collins-Knowlton-Wing, Inc., 60 East 56th St., New York, N.Y. 10022.

CAREER: First aspirations were for a career as a magician, and Fleischman put together a two-hour magic show with the aid of another high school student and took it on tour the summer of 1936. After the war he turned to short-story writing for a time, decided to finish his college education, and then worked as a reporter on a San Diego (Calif.) newspaper until it suspended publication. Full-time writer since. *Military service:* U.S. Naval Reserve, 1941-45; became yeoman aboard destroyer escort with duty in the Philippines, Borneo, China. *Member:* Writers Guild of America West, Western Writers of America.

AWARDS, HONORS: New York Herald Tribune Spring Book Festival Award, 1962, for *Mr. Mysterious and Company*; Western Writers of America Spur Award, 1963, Southern California Council on Literature for Children and Young People Award, 1964, Boys' Clubs of America Award, 1964, all for *By the Great Horn Spoon!*; Commonwealth Club of California Juvenile Book Award, 1966, for *Chancy and the Grand Rascal*; Lewis Carroll Shelf Award, 1969, for *McBroom Tells the Truth*; *Book World* Spring Book Festival Award, 1971, for *Jingo Django*; George C. Stone Center for Children's Books, Recognition of Merit Award, 1972, for *By the Great Horn Spoon!*; Southern California Council on Literature for Children and Young People Award, 1972; Society of Children's Book Writers Golden Kite Awards, 1974, for *McBroom the Rainmaker*.

WRITINGS: The Straw Donkey Case, Phoenix Press, 1948; *Murder's No Accident*, Phoenix Press, 1949; *Shanghai Flame*, Gold Medal, 1951; *Look Behind You Lady*, Gold Medal, 1952; *Danger in Paradise*, Gold Medal, 1953; *Counterspy Express*, Ace Books, 1954; *Malay Woman*, Gold Medal, 1954; *Blood Alley*, Gold Medal, 1955.

Yellowleg, Gold Medal, 1960; *Mr. Mysterious & Company*, (Junior Literary Guild selection; *Horn Book* Honor List), Atlantic Monthly Press, 1962; *The Venetian Blonde*, Gold Medal, 1963; *By the Great Horn Spoon!* (Junior Literary Guild selection), Atlantic Monthly Press, 1963; *The Ghost in the Noonday Sun* (Junior Literary Guild selection), Atlantic Monthly Press, 1965; *McBroom Tells the Truth*, Norton, 1966; *Chancy and the Grand Rascal* (*Horn Book* Honor List), Atlantic Monthly Press, 1966; *McBroom and the Big Wind*, Norton, 1967.

Longbeard the Wizard (Junior Literary Guild selection), Atlantic-Little, Brown, 1970; *McBroom's Ear*, Norton, 1970; *Jingo Django* (Junior Literary Guild selection, ALA Notable Book), Atlantic-Little, Brown, 1971; *McBroom's*

Zoo, Grosset, 1971; *The Wooden Cat Man*, Atlantic Monthly Press, 1972; *McBroom the Rainmaker*, Grosset, 1973; *Mr. Mysterious' Secrets of Magic*, Atlantic-Little, Brown, 1974; *The Ghost on Saturday Night*, Atlantic-Little, Brown, 1974.

Films: Film version of *Blood Alley*, 1955; "Goodbye, My Lady," based on novel by James Street, 1956; "Lafayette Escadrille," 1958; The Deadly Companions," based on *Yellowleg*, 1961; "Scalawag," 1973.

By the Great Horn Spoon! was filmed by Walt Disney and released under the title, "Bullwhip Griffin," 1967; *The Ghost in the Noonday Sun* was filmed in England with Peter Sellers, 1974.

SIDELIGHTS: "When I knew very little about writing, I wrote very fast. I once did a mystery novel in three weeks. I couldn't do that today. I compose very slowly. My first draft is a kind of finished draft. I put paper and carbons in the typewriter and chip out each sentence with care.... I will stay with that page until I think it is as good as I can make it. On some days I will get only one page of work finished; on other days, five or six.

"While this method of working might drive other writers

SID FLEISCHMAN

Since you said your last words two-three times already this afternoon, let's get on with it. ■ (From *Bullwhip Griffin* by Sid Fleischman. Illustrated by Eric von Schmidt.)

out of their minds, it has taught me to write it right—the first time. To think it out before I commit a thought to paper. And I feel that one's best creative time is when the ideas are forming on paper—not during the rewrite process.

"Writing *Mr. Mysterious* was a treat. As I finished each chapter I read it to my children. When I couldn't figure out what was to happen next I asked them for ideas...."

HOBBIES AND OTHER INTERESTS: Magic, astronomy, playing classical guitar.

FOR MORE INFORMATION SEE: Junior Literary Guild Catalogue, February, 1962, March, 1971; Eleanor Cameron, *The Green and Burning Tree*, Atlantic-Little, Brown, 1969; *Horn Book*, April, 1970, August, 1971, December, 1971, February, 1973, August, 1974; *New York Times Book Review*, October 17, 1971; *Third Book of Junior Authors*, edited by de Montreville and Hill, H. W. Wilson, 1972.

63

Something about the Author

FLEMING, Thomas J(ames) 1927-
(Christopher Cain, T. F. James, J. F. Thomas)

PERSONAL: Born July 5, 1927, in Jersey City, N.J.; son of Thomas James and Katherine (Dolan) Fleming; married Alice Mulcahey (a writer), January 19, 1951; children: Alice, Thomas, David, Richard. *Education:* Fordham University, A.B., 1950, graduate study in social work, 1951. *Politics:* Democrat. *Home:* 315 East 72nd St., New York, N.Y. 10021. *Agent:* Malcolm Reiss, Paul R. Reynolds & Son, 12 East 41st St., New York, N.Y. 10017.

CAREER: Yonker's Herald Statesman, reporter, 1951; *Reader's Digest*, assistant to Fulton Oursler, 1951-52; Oursler Estate, literary executor, 1952-54; *Cosmopolitan Magazine*, associate editor, 1954-58, executive editor, 1958-60. *Military service:* U.S. Navy, 1945-46; became seaman first class. *Member:* Society of American Historians, New York American Revolution Round Table (chairman), University Club, Dutch Treat Club, New York Historical Society. *Awards, honors:* Brotherhood award of National Conference of Christians and Jews, for article, "Religious Abuse," published in *Cosmopolitan*, 1963; Achievement Award in Communication Arts, Fordham University, 1961; Encaenia Award, 1965; Award of the Colonial Dames of America for best book on American history, 1969, 1971; Award of Merit from American Association of State and Local History for "brilliantly illuminating littleknown aspects of state and local history," 1974.

WRITINGS: Now We Are Enemies, St. Martins, 1960; *All Good Men*, Doubleday, 1961; *The God of Love*, Doubleday, 1963; *Beat the Last Drum: The Siege of Yorktown*, St. Martins, 1963; *One Small Candle: The Pilgrims First Year in America*, Norton, 1964; *King of the Hill*, New American Library, 1966; (editor) *Affectionately Yours, George Washington: A Self-Portrait in Letters of Friendship*, Norton, 1967; *A Cry of Whiteness*, Morrow, 1967; *West Point: The Men and Times of the U.S. Military Academy*, Morrow, 1969; *The Man from Monticello: An Intimate Life of Thomas Jefferson*, Morrow, 1969; *Romans, Countrymen, Lovers*, Morrow, 1969; *The Sandbox Tree*, Morrow, 1970; *The Man Who Dared the Lightening: A New Look at Benjamin Franklin*, Morrow, 1971; (editor) *Benjamin Franklin: A Biography in His Own Words*, Newsweek, 1972; *The Forgotten Victory*, Reader's Digest Press, 1973; *The Good Shepherd*, Doubleday, 1974.

For young readers: *First in Their Hearts: A Biography of George Washington*, Norton, 1968; *Battle of Yorktown*, American Heritage, 1968; *Behind the Headlines: Great Moments in American Newspaper History*, Doubleday, 1970; *The Golden Door: The Story of American Immigration*, Grosset, 1970; *Thomas Jefferson*, Grosset, 1971; *Give Me Liberty: Black Valor in the Revolutionary War*, Scholastic, 1971; *Benjamin Franklin*, Four Winds, 1973. Contributor to *New York Times Magazine, Reader's Digest, American Heritage* and other magazines.

SIDELIGHTS: "My special interest is in the impact of history on individual lives, the use to which men put political power. I am also interested in the role of religion in this intersection of history, politics and power. It is the interplay of these forces, and above all their impact on personal lives in America, past and present, that fascinates me."

FORMAN, James Douglas 1932-

PERSONAL: Born November 12, 1932, in Mineola, Long Island, N.Y.; son of Leo Erwin (a lawyer) and Kathryn (Forman) Forman; married Marcia Fore, September 3, 1956; children: Karli. *Education:* Princeton University, A.B., 1954; Columbia University, LL.B., 1957. *Home:* 2 Glen Rd., Sands Point, Port Washington, N.Y. 11501. *Agent:* Theron Raines, 244 Madison Ave., New York, N.Y. 10016. *Office:* 290 Old Country Rd., Mineola, Long Island, N.Y. 11501.

CAREER: Practice of law, 1957—. *Member:* Lightning Fleet 142 (sailboats; past president).

WRITINGS: (With wife, Marcia Forman) *Islands of the Eastern Mediterranean* (booklet), Doubleday, 1959; *The Skies of Crete*, Farrar, Straus, 1963; *Ring the Judas Bell*, Farrar, Straus, 1965; *The Shield of Achilles*, Farrar, Straus, 1966; *Horses of Anger*, Farrar, Straus, 1967; *The Traitors*, Farrar, Straus, 1968; *The Cow Neck Rebels*, Farrar, Straus, 1969; *My Enemy, My Brother*, Meredith, 1969; *Ceremony of Innocence*, Hawthorn, 1970; *So Ends This Day*, Farrar, Straus, 1970; *Song of Jubilee*, Farrar, Straus, 1971; *Law and Disorder*, Thomas Nelson, 1971; *Capitalism: Economic Individualism to Today's Welfare State*, F. Watts, 1972; *Communism: From Marx's Manifesto to*

JAMES D. FORMAN

It was in the early spring following his eighth winter that the boy went looking for visions and a name. The white men had baptized him and called him Ephraim, but that was their name, not his own. ■ (From *People of the Dream* by James Forman. Jacket designed by Karl W. Stuecklen.)

20th Century, F. Watts, 1972; *Socialism: Its Theoretical Roots and Present-Day Development*, F. Watts, 1972; *People of the Dream*, Farrar, Straus, 1972.

WORK IN PROGRESS: Chief Joseph, a biography of the Nez Perce leader in the last major Indian war.

AVOCATIONAL INTERESTS: Travel, photography (some photographs appear in his works), and antique arms of the eighteenth century.

BIOGRAPHICAL/CRITICAL SOURCES: Best Sellers, May 1, 1967, November 1, 1968, November 1, 1969, January 15, 1971, July 15, 1971; *Young Readers' Review*, June, 1967, November, 1968; *Saturday Review*, June 28, 1969; *New York Times Book Review*, November 30, 1969; *Library Journal*, June 15, 1970.

FOSTER, John T(homas) 1925-

PERSONAL: Born July 19, 1925, in Chicago, Ill.; son of George Peter (an attorney) and Helen (McLaughlin) Foster; married Elizabeth Rhodes, June 3, 1949; children: Carol W. Faulkner (stepdaughter), Norah S., John, Jr. *Education:* University of Wisconsin, student, 1943; Florida Southern College, B.A., 1950; University of Florida, further study, 1950-51. *Home:* R.D. 1, Box 387, Fairview Ave., Montauk, N.Y. 11954. *Agent:* Lurton Blassingame, 60 East 42nd St., New York, N.Y. 10017. *Office:* New York Ocean Science Laboratory, Montauk, N.Y. 11954.

CAREER: Newspaper reporter in Lakeland, Fla., 1951-53,

and Wilmington, N.C., 1953-55; *Dixie Roto*, New Orleans, La., staff writer and assistant editor, 1955-66; *Suffolk Sun*, Deer Park, N.Y., editor of *Dawn*, weekend magazine, 1966-68; Long Island University, Brookville, N.Y., assistant to director of public relations, 1968-70; New York Ocean Science Laboratory, Montauk, technical writer, 1970—. *Military service:* U.S. Naval Reserve, active duty, 1943-46; served in the Pacific. *Awards, honors:* State (North Carolina) Associated Press award, 1954; Regional Associated Press award, 1965; National Alumni Association award, 1971.

WRITINGS: Rebel Sea Raider, Morrow, 1966; *Marco and the Tiger* (juvenile), Dodd, 1966; *Guadalcanal General*, Morrow, 1967; *Marco and the Sleuth Hound* (juvenile), Dodd, 1967; *Sir Francis Drake*, Garrard, 1967; *Southern Frontiersman: The Story of General Sam Dale*, Morrow, 1968; *Napoleon's Marshall*, Morrow, 1969; *Mississippi Wonderland*, Dodd, 1969; *General John J. Pershing*, Garrard, 1970; *Marco and That Curious Cat* (juvenile) Dodd, 1971; *The Hundred Days*, Watts, 1972; *The Gallant Gray Trotter*, Dodd, 1974; *The Flight of the Lone Eagle*, Watts, 1974. Contributor to national magazines in Canada, Europe, and the United States.

SIDELIGHTS: "When I was a boy growing up in Oak Park, Illinois, outside Chicago, my older brother George spent a great deal of time with me. Far, far more than any older brother I have ever heard of, even though he had many good friends his own age. George took me to my first

JOHN T. FOSTER

By the time the third heat was called, the track was in complete darkness and the judges had to light candles to see their watches. ■ (From *The Gallant Gray Trotter* by John T. Foster. Illustrated by Sam Savitt.)

movie (Charlie Chaplin's 'City Lights') and many after that, and on numerous roundtrip bus and elevated train rides to the Loop—five cents for bus, three for train—and long hikes in the Forest Preserves near our home.

"The first words I remember George saying to me are, 'Come on, I'll tell you a story.' Then we would go into the library in our house, a dark, gloomy room lined from floor to ceiling with books—my father's and grandfather's lawbooks mostly, but also encyclopedias, reference books, sets of Dickens, Twain, Stevenson, and Conan Doyle, along with individual novels—especially mysteries.

"And then George would tell me a story, making it up as he went along. I don't remember any of the stories now, but George's tastes ran to pirates, galloping horsemen at midnight, the click-clock of a flintlock pistol being cocked, a tap on the window at the height of a storm—that sort of thing.

"As I grew older, George began to read me stories in that shadowy, spooky room with the doors closed and a single parchment-shaded lamp on. His preference ran to Ambrose Bierce, Saki, and Conan Doyle.

"The times I remember best were during a chill, moaning Chicago winter night with a square, shiny black chunk of coal crackling and popping in the fireplace, and George's deep, resonant voice reading. 'It was a cold morning in the early spring, and we sat after breakfast on either side of a cheery fire in the old room at Baker Street. A thick fog. . . .'

"Two of my mother's sisters were librarians in the Chicago Public Library. They, too, told me stories and also read to me. When I started to write, they helped me with my research. My Aunt Bernadine still helps me. I also get a great deal of aid from my wife, Dusty. She reads everything I write (including this) before I mail it, and I weigh her comments carefully, almost always following her advice. My Marco Fennerty character is largely based upon her.

"As much as possible I try to experience what my characters are going through. The ruined fort with its roomful of tiny skulls, which plays such a big part in *Marco and the Sleuth Hound*, was based upon an actual fort that I explored in the swamps outside New Orleans. The house in *Marco and That Curious Cat* is patterned after Shadows on the Teche, a beautiful plantation house on Bayou Teche in New Iberia, Louisiana, which I visited many times.

"Most of my research, however, has been in public libraries. I could not have written *The Gallant Gray Trotter* if it hadn't been for the librarians that I acknowledge in that book."

HOBBIES AND OTHER INTERESTS: Travel, walking, swimming, rowing, reading, watching suspense films.

FOR MORE INFORMATION SEE: Christian Science Monitor, October 5, 1967; *New York Times Book Review*, November 5, 1967; *Book World*, November 9, 1969, Part II.

FROMAN, Robert (Winslow) 1917-

PERSONAL: Born May 25, 1917, in Big Timber, Mont., grew up in Caldwell, Idaho; son of Harry Hunter and Muriel (Nolen) Froman: married Elizabeth Hull (deceased). *Home:* Santa Cruz, Calif.

CAREER: Free-lance writer, 1945—.

WRITINGS: One Million Islands for Sale, Duell, 1953; *The Nerve of Some Animals*, Lippincott, 1961; *Man and the Grasses*, Lippincott, 1963; *Wanted: Amateur Scientists* (Junior Literary Guild selection for older members). McKay, 1963; *Quacko and the Elps* (Junior Literary Guild selection), McKay, 1964; *Faster and Faster* (Junior Literary Guild selection), Viking, 1965; *Our Fellow Immigrants*, McKay, 1965; *Spiders, Snakes, and Other Outcasts*, Lippincott, 1965; *The Many Human Senses*, Little, Brown, 1966; *Baseball-Istics*, Putnam, 1967; *Science of Salt*, McKay, 1967; *Billions of Years of You*, World, 1967; *The Great Reaching Out*, World, 1968; *Science, Art, & Visual Illusions*, Simon & Schuster, 1970; *Street Poems* (Junior Literary Guild selection), McCall, 1971; *Bigger &*

ROBERT FROMAN

Up three

worn

steps,

Through a heavy door,

Into

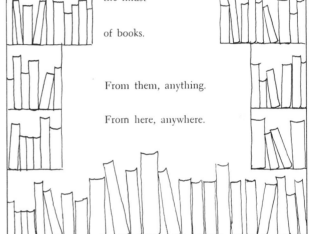

the midst

of books.

From them, anything.

From here, anywhere.

(From *Street Poems* by Robert Froman.)

Smaller, Crowell, 1972; *Hot & Cold & In Between*, Grosset, 1971;·*Racism*, Delacorte, 1972; *Rubber Bands, Baseballs & Doughnuts*, Crowell, 1972; *Venn Diagrams*, Crowell, 1972; *The Wild Orphan*, Scholastic, 1972; *Thomas, the Tiger Teacher*, Scholastic, 1973; *Less Than Nothing is Really Something*, Crowell, 1973; *Mushrooms and Molds*, Crowell, 1973; *Arithmetic for Human Beings*, Simon & Schuster, 1974; *Seeing Things: A Book of Poems*, Crowell, 1974; *A Game of Functions*, Crowell, 1974; *Mr. Harry Know-It-All*, Macmillan, 1975; *The Stuff of You*, Macmillan, 1974; *Angles*, Crowell, 1976; *A Song about You*, Doubleday, 1976. Approximately two hundred articles on varied topics in popular magazines.

WORK IN PROGRESS: A new book of poems; several books on math including *Strange Numbers* for adults; a series of books on physics for beginning readers; a screenplay for adults; a novel for adults.

SIDELIGHTS: "In the Idaho town where I grew up the schools were boring, and I learned almost entirely from the books in our Carnegie Public Library. But it did not have many readable books on science, so I didn't learn much science. I made up my mind when I was twelve that I wanted to be a free-lance writer and I began writing for magazines in 1941, became a free lance in 1945, and will remain one for life.

"Gradually discovered the sciences as subjects to learn and write about, not just the physical sciences but also psychology, social science, and math. Then in 1962 I made the best discovery of all—that it is far more satisfying to write for young readers than for the magazines.

"Some of my science books for young readers have grown out of articles I wrote for magazines, and in the books I was able to go much deeper into the subjects. Now I'm beginning to vary my work, writing poetry and fiction as well as books on science and also writing books and screenplays for adults. But trying to make certain aspects of science and math as exciting for young readers, as they are for me, will always be one of my favorite occupations."

FOR MORE INFORMATION SEE: Junior Literary Guild Catalogue, March, 1971; *Saturday Review*, May 20, 1972; *Horn Book*, October, 1972, June 6, 1973, February, 1974.

GANNON, Robert (Haines)   1931-

PERSONAL: Born March 5, 1931, in White Plains, N.Y.; son of John Albert (a business executive) and Dorothy B. Gannon; second marriage to June Ormay, June 20, 1963 (divorced); married Marcia Hayes (an author), August 23, 1971; children: Pricilla. *Education:* Miami University, Oxford, Ohio, student, 1949-53. *Politics:* Liberal. *Religion:*

ROBERT H. GANNON

The quantity of life beneath a rock is enormous. The population of a square foot of ground—most of them microscopic—can number more than the human inhabitants of the entire planet. ■ (From *What's Under a Rock?* by Robert Gannon. Illustrated by Stefan Martin.)

Nondenominational. *Home:* R.D. 1, Box 114, Port Matilda, Pa. 16870. *Agent:* Theron Raines, 244 Madison Ave., New York, N.Y. 10016. *Office:* 228 Burrowes, Pennsylvania State University, University Park, Pa. 16802.

CAREER: Leo Burnett Co., Inc., New York, N.Y., publicist, 1955-57; Daniel J. Edelman & Associates, New York, N.Y., public relations account executive, 1957-59; freelance writer, 1959—. Lecturer in nonfiction at Pennsylvania State University, University Park, 1974—. Trustee of D & H Canal Historical Society, High Falls, N.Y., 1963-69; mayor of High Falls, 1967-69. *Military service:* U.S. Army, 1953-55. *Member:* Society of Magazine Writers, Authors Guild, National Association of Science Writers, American Association for the Advancement of Science.

WRITINGS: How to Raise and Train a Scottish Terrier, T. F. H. Publications, 1960; *How to Raise and Train an English Springer Spaniel*, T. F. H. Publications, 1961; *How to Raise and Train an Irish Setter*, T. F. H. Publications, 1961; *How to Raise and Train an English Cocker Spaniel*, T. F. H. Publications, 1962; *Start Right with Goldfish*, T. F. H. Publications, 1964; *Start Right with Tropical Fish*, T. F. H. Publications, 1964; *The Complete Book of Archery*, Coward, 1964; (with John Walsh) *Time Is Short and the Water Rises: Operation Gwamba–The Story of the Rescue of 10,000 Animals from Certain Death in a South American Rain Forest*, Dutton, 1967; *What's Under a Rock?* (juvenile), Dutton, 1971; (editor) *Great Survival*

Adventures (juvenile), Random House, 1973. Contributor to *Reader's Digest, Saturday Evening Post, True, Popular Mechanics, Family Circle* (former columnist), *Science Digest*, and other magazines. Science adventure editor of *Popular Science*, which has published more than ninety of his pieces, 1968—; editor, *Natural Life Styles*, 1972-73.

WORK IN PROGRESS: Research for a possible book on home fires; magazine assignments.

GAULT, William Campbell 1910-

PERSONAL: Born March 9, 1910, in Milwaukee, Wis.; son of John H. and Ella (Hovde) Gault; married Virginia Kaprelian, August 29, 1942; children: William Barry, Shelley Gault Amacher. *Education:* Attended University of Wisconsin, 1929. *Politics:* "Revolutionary Republican." *Religion:* "Faith in man." *Home and office:* 482 Vaquero Lane, Santa Barbara, Calif. 93111. *Agent:* Don Congdon, Harold Matson Co., Inc., 22 East 40th St., New York, N.Y. 10016.

CAREER: Free-lance writer, and author of mysteries and juvenile fiction. Has worked, at various times, as waiter, busboy, shoe sole cutter, hotel manager, and mailman. Secretary, Channel Cities Funeral Society. *Military service:* U.S. Army, 1943-45. *Awards, honors:* Edgar award from Mystery Writers of America, 1952, for *Don't Cry for Me*; award from Boys' Club of America, 1957, for *Speedway Challenge*; honorable mention from Southern California Council on Literature for Children and Young People, 1968.

WRITINGS—Mystery novels: Don't Cry for Me, Dutton, 1952; *The Bloody Bokhara*, Dutton, 1952; *The Canvas Coffin*, Dutton, 1953; *Blood on the Boards*, Dutton, 1953; *Run, Killer, Run*, Dutton, 1954; *Ring Around Rosa*, Dutton, 1955; *Day of the Ram*, Random House, 1956; *Square in the Middle*, Random House, 1956; *The Convertible Hearse*, Random House, 1957; *Night Lady*, Fawcett, 1958; *Sweet Wild Wench*, Fawcett, 1959; *The Wayward Widow*, Fawcett, 1959; *Death out of Focus*, Random House, 1959; *Come Die with Me*, Random House, 1959; *Million Dollar Tramp*, Fawcett, 1960; *Vein of Violence*, Simon & Schuster, 1961; *The Hundred Dollar Girl*, Dutton, 1961; *County Kill*, Simon & Schuster, 1962; *Dead Hero*, Dutton, 1963. Author of three additional novels published by Fawcett and Ace Books.

Juveniles; all published by Dutton: *Thunder Road*, 1952; *Mr. Fullback*, 1953; *Gallant Colt*, 1954; *Mr. Quarterback*, 1955; *Speedway Challenge*, 1956; *Bruce Benedict, Halfback*, 1957; *Rough Road to Glory*, 1958; *Dim Thunder*, 1958; *Drag Strip*, 1959.

Dirt Track Summer, 1961; *Through the Line*, 1961; *Two Wheeled Thunder*, 1962; *Road Race Rookie*, 1962; *Wheels of Fortune: Four Racing Stories*, 1963; *Little Big Foot*, 1963; *The Checkered Flag*, 1964; *The Long Green*, 1965; *The Karters*, 1965; *Sunday's Dust*, 1966; *Backfield Challenge*, 1967; *The Lonely Mound*, 1967; *The Oval Playground*, 1968; *Stubborn Sam*, 1969.

Quarterback Gamble, 1970; *The Last Lap*, 1972; *Trouble at Second*, 1973; *Gasoline Cowboy* (Junior Literary Guild Selection), 1974; *Wild Willie, Wide Receiver*, 1974; *The Underground Skipper*, 1975; *The Big Stick*, 1975. Contributor of about three hundred short stories to magazines, including *Grit* and *Saturday Evening Post*.

WORK IN PROGRESS: A juvenile about hockey; an adult mystery.

SIDELIGHTS: "As a person, I am not too exciting. I love sports, but was a very bad high school football player and presently a fifteen-handicap golfer, despite my persistence. This I will say about sports, in the professional ranks, it is one area of endeavor where everybody gets the pay and acclaim he honestly earns, not what chicanery and a public relations man can earn him. Black or white, male or female, if you cut the mustard, you get a piece of the cake, to discombobulate the metaphor. All I got out of high school football was a bad knee, which the U.S. Army fixed for me in 1943, so I could serve them better. All I got out of golf is the laughs of my competitors.

"I came out to California in 1949 to get away from those Milwaukee winters, and left the Los Angeles area in 1958 to get away from the smog. But Santa Barbara is growing, too. Where is there left to hide? At the age of sixty-four, I took my first European trip: London, Paris, Lausanne, Venice, Florence, Rome. I saw more art in three weeks than I had seen in my previous sixty-four years. I was not really floored until I saw Michelangelo's David, when I had to cry. What an experience!

"I have this strange feeling the good (and understandable) major novelists are no longer around. I don't mean the

WILLIAM CAMPBELL GAULT

We were coming up behind the stragglers now, the tail end of the posse. They resented being lapped, and displayed it. The upper half of this team tried to show no resentment, only superiority. ■ (From *Gasoline Cowboy* by William Campbell Gault. Jacket designed by Hal Ashmead.)

genius type: I mean the Hemingway, Fitzgerald, John Dos Passos, Steinbeck, O'Hara, Maugham, etc. But maybe I am getting old and I was never too literate.''

Gault's mystery novels have been translated into fourteen languages.

GOFFSTEIN, M(arilyn) B(rooke)   1940-

PERSONAL: Born December 20, 1940, in St. Paul, Minn.; daughter of Albert A. (an electrical engineer) and Esther (Rose) Goffstein; married Peter Schaaf (a photographer and concert pianist), August 15, 1965. *Education:* Bennington College, B.A., 1962. *Religion:* Judaism. *Home:* 697 West End Ave., New York, N.Y. 10025.

CAREER: Author and illustrator; has had several one-man exhibitions of pen and ink and watercolor drawings in New York, N.Y., and St. Paul, Minn. *Awards, honors: Sleepy People* and *Across the Sea* were selected for the American Institute of Graphic Arts' Children's Book Show of 1965-66, 1967-68; *The Gats!* was an honor book in *Book Week's* Children's Spring Book Festival, 1966; *Across the Sea* was one of the *New York Times'* 15 Best Children's Books, 1968; *Goldie the Dollmaker* was one of the *New York Times'* Outstanding Children's Books, 1969, and nominated for the Dorothy Canfield Fisher Award, 1970; *A Little Schubert* was one of the *New York Times'* 10 Children's Books, 1972; *Me and My Captain* was one of the *New York Times'* Outstanding Children's Books, 1974.

M. B. GOFFSTEIN

70

(From *Brookie and Her Lamb* by M. B. Goffstein. Illustrated by the author.)

but all he could sing was, Baa baa baa   and all he could read was, Baa baa baa

WRITINGS—All self-illustrated: *The Gats!*, Pantheon, 1966; *Sleepy People*, Farrar, Straus, 1966; *Brookie and Her Lamb*, Farrar, Straus, 1967; *Across the Sea*, Farrar, Straus, 1968; *Goldie the Dollmaker*, Farrar, Straus, 1969; *Two Piano Tuners*, Farrar, Straus, 1970; *The Underside of the Leaf* (novel without illustrations), Farrar, Straus, 1972; *A Little Schubert* (with record of five Schubert waltzes by Peter Schaaf), Harper, 1972. *Me and My Captain*, Farrar, Straus, 1974; *Daisy Summerfield's Style* (novel), Delacorte, 1975; *Fish for Supper*, Dial, 1976.

SIDELIGHTS: "The dignity and pleasure of being professional, like *Goldie the Dollmaker*, is to work and work in solitude—until it looks like you didn't have to work at all."

FOR MORE INFORMATION SEE: Selma G. Lanes, *Down the Rabbit Hole*, Atheneum, 1971; *Graphis 155*, Volume 27, 1971/72; *Fourth Book of Junior Authors*, H. W. Wilson, in press.

GREEN, Morton   1937-

PERSONAL: Born May 18, 1937, in Los Angeles, Calif.; son of Sidney (owner of a small business) and Ruth (Tenner) Green. *Education:* University of California, Los Angeles, B.A. and Secondary School Teaching Credential, 1960; University of Southern California, School Librarianship Credential and M.S.L.S., 1964. *Politics:* Independent. *Religion:* Religious Science. *Home:* 1829 Westholme Ave., Los Angeles, Calif. 90025.

CAREER: Los Angeles city schools, Los Angeles, Calif., junior high school teacher, 1960-61; West Los Angeles Regional Library, Los Angeles, Calif., librarian trainee, 1962-64; Arcadia Public Library, Arcadia, Calif., reference and young adult librarian, 1964-70; Los Angeles City Public Library, Los Angeles, Calif., adult librarian at Robertson Branch, 1970-73, substitute librarian, 1973—. Substitute librarian, Los Angeles Community College District, 1974—. *Member:* Society of Children's Book Writers, Southern California Council on Literature for Children and Young People, Young Adult Reviewers of Southern California (member of executive board, 1965-70).

WRITINGS: Garden of Mystery (easy-reading adaptation of Nathaniel Hawthorne's "Rappaccini's Daughter"), Leswing Press, 1973; *Blue Skies Magic* (picture book), Ginn, 1974. Stories included in textbooks published by Noble, Globe Book, Science Research Associates, and other publishers. Contributor of stories, articles, poems, and plays to education journals, Scholastic Magazines, *Photoplay, Los Angeles*, and others.

WORK IN PROGRESS: An easy-reading biography of Henry Kissinger, combined with a simplified survey of contemporary United States foreign relations. Also, more picture books and beginning to read books.

SIDELIGHTS: "Since 1973 I have worked in about twenty-five branches and the Central Children's Room of Los Angeles Public Library, as a substitute librarian. This has given me an invaluable insight into the reading interests of children in different environments. Non-writers always want to know where writers get their 'ideas.' I can only say that the writer learns to set his mind in a certain way, and then relaxes, knowing that ideas will come to him. The writer learns to become atuned to the Universal Mind, in which all ideas already exist in their complete forms. Knowing the craft and mechanics of writing is important, but achieving this mental 'set' is critical for success."

MORTON GREEN

GREEN, Sheila Ellen 1934-
(Sheila Greenwald)

PERSONAL: Born May 26, 1934, in New York, N.Y.; daughter of Julius (manufacturer) and Florence (Friedman) Greenwald; married George Green (a New York surgeon), February 18, 1960; children: Samuel, Benjamin. *Education:* Sarah Lawrence College, B.A., 1956. *Politics:* Democrat. *Religion:* Jewish. *Home:* 175 Riverside Dr., New York, N.Y. 10024.

CAREER: Illustrator, writer. Has illustrated for *Harper's, Gourmet, The Reporter*, and other magazines.

WRITINGS—Juveniles, all self-illustrated: *A Metropolitan Love Story*, Doubleday, 1962; *Willie Bryant and the Flying Otis*, Norton, 1971; *Mat Pit and the Tunnel Tenants*, Lippincott, 1972; *The Hot Day*, Bobbs, 1972; *Miss Amanda Snap*, Bobbs, 1973; *The Secret Museum*, Lippincott, 1974.

Illustrator: Marie L. Allen, *Pocketful of Poems*, Harper, 1957; Carol Ryrie Brink, *The Pink Motel*, Macmillan, 1959; Florence Laughlin, *The Little Leftover Witch*, Macmillan, 1960; Miriam Dreifus, *Brave Betsy*, Putnam, 1961; Grace V. Curl, *Come A-Witching*, Bobbs, 1964; Laura H. Fisher, *Amy and the Sorrel Summer*, Holt, 1964; Barbara Rinkoff, *Remarkable Ramsey*, Morrow, 1965; Hila Colman, *Boy Who Couldn't Make Up His Mind*, Macmillan, 1965; Anne Mallett, *Who'll Mind Henry?*, Doubleday, 1965; Florence Laughlin, *Seventh Cousin*, Macmillan, 1966; Mary J. Roth,

Lizzie did the woodwork, replacing the old porch boards while Jennifer slapped paint over the shingles. Lizzie had a fierce angry way of hammering that sometimes surprised Jennifer and made her laugh. ■ (From *The Secret Museum* by Sheila Greenwald. Illustrated by the author.)

Pretender Princess, Morrow, 1967; James Playsted Wood, *When I Was Jersey*, Pantheon, 1967; Emma V. Worstell, *Jump the Rope Jingles*, Macmillan, 1967; Jean Bothwell, *Mystery Cup*, Dial, 1968; M. Jean Craig, *New Boy on the Sidewalk*, Norton, 1968. Also contributor to *Cricket* and *New York Times*.

SIDELIGHTS: "I started drawing too far back to remember and I did it all the time, as a habit, as a way to amuse myself. After illustrating other peoples' books for a number of years, I decided to try writing my own and found this doubly rewarding. I write down ideas that appeal to me—some work out, some don't. *The Hot Day* was based on an incident from my father's childhood, *Willie Bryant* on situations my own children have experienced, and *Amanda Snap* on a turn in the old fairy tale. I write and draw because I enjoy writing and drawing. My books are intended for whoever enjoy my pleasure in these things."

FOR MORE INFORMATION SEE: Charm Magazine, August, 1959; *New York Times*, May 29, 1961.

SHEILA GREEN

Something about the Author

GREENE, Bette 1934-

PERSONAL: Born June 28, 1934, in Memphis, Tenn.; married Donald S. Greene (a physician), June 14, 1959; children: Carla, Jordan. *Education:* Attended University of Alabama, 1952, and Columbia University, 1955. *Home and office:* 338 Clinton Rd., Brookline, Mass. 02146. *Agent:* Sheldon Fogelman, 10 East 40th St., New York, N.Y. 10016.

CAREER: Writer. *Awards, honors:* New York Times outstanding book award for *Summer of My German Soldier*, 1973; nominated for National Book Award, 1974, for *Summer of My German Soldier*; Golden Kite Society children's book writer's award, 1974, for *Summer of My German Soldier*; *New York Times* outstanding book award, 1974, for *Philip Hall Likes Me, I Reckon Maybe*, which was also a Newbery Honor Book, 1975.

WRITINGS: Summer of My German Soldier (autobiographical; (ALA Notable Book), Dial, 1973; *Philip Hall Likes Me, I Reckon Maybe* (Junior Literary Guild selection), Dial, 1974. Author of a screenplay for *Summer of My German Soldier*.

WORK IN PROGRESS: A novel, publication expected in 1977.

FOR MORE INFORMATION SEE: Philadelphia Inquirer, December 28, 1973; *Boston Evening Globe*, December 28, 1973.

BETTE GREENE

"Beth, honey, you is so smart about most things. How come the good Lord made you so dumb about Philip Hall?"
" 'Cause Philip Hall likes me. I reckon maybe. He's always inviting me over to his very own farm, now ain't that the truth."
■ (From *Philip Hall likes me. I reckon maybe* by Bette Greene. Illustrated by Charles Lilly.)

GREENWALD, Sheila
See GREEN, Sheila Ellen

GUILLAUME, Jeanette G. (Flierl) 1899-

PERSONAL: Born May 6, 1899, in Buffalo, N.Y.; daughter of Frederick Adam and Louise M. J. (Boller) Flierl; married Roland Phillip Guillaume, 1918; children: David F., Barbara F. (Mrs. A. J. Hathaway III), Jonathan F. *Education:* University of Buffalo, Ed.B.; additional study at University of New Hampshire, University of Hawaii, and State University of New York at Buffalo. *Religion:* Unitarian Universalist. *Home:* 5210 Main St., Williamsville, N.Y.; (summer) Brookhill, Rushford, N.Y.

CAREER: Teacher, nursery school director, 1942-52; Village Nursery School, Williamsville, N.Y., owner and director, 1952—. Participant in Head Start program for State University of New York at Buffalo; evaluator for Early Push Program for Far West Laboratory for Research and Development; specialist for Head Start for Office of Economic Opportunity. Neighborhood House, Buffalo, board member; Family Service Society, advisory committee; Community Welfare Council, advisory committee; Williamsville-Amherst Historical Society, trustee. *Member:* New York State Association for Education of children (state secretary; program chairman, Buffalo chapter), Early Childhood Education Council of Western New York (president), National League of American Pen Women (president).

WRITINGS: (With Mary Lee Bachmann) *Amat and the Water Buffalo*, Coward, 1962. Articles in *Parents' Magazine, Instructor*, and professional journals; radio and television scripts for children's programs and educational programs.

WORK IN PROGRESS: I Don't Know Who You Are.

SIDELIGHTS: "My first major writing took place when I was teaching at the pre-school level and realized how uncertain and concerned parents were about their young children. I began making notes of situations, parent's attitudes, and ended up writing a program for radio entitled 'Janet Williams Chats About Children' which was sold by the Hayhurst Advertising Agency of Toronto, Canada to Canadian Canners, and was used to promote and advertise their baby foods. The program was also used by American stations, but the Canadian programs were broadcast throughout Canada and received wide recognition.

"Later the same material was used, using the same name, as a television program over station WGR-TV, Buffalo, N.Y., with the same listener reaction of many letters from interested and concerned parents.

"I also wrote a play for children, 'The Piano and the Toy Box,' which allowed for participation by the children and was presented a number of times in this area, one as part of the Christmas program for children at the Albright-Knox Gallery in Buffalo, where two performances were given. The play was also published in *The Instructor*. I wrote additional sequences and these, together with the original play, were broadcast as a series over WNED-TV, Buffalo.

"*Amat and the Water Buffalo* was written because of interest in an AFS (American Field Service) student who was attending a local school and was beautifully illustrated by Kurt Wiese.

Guillaume has traveled extensively in this country, and visited Europe three times.

HOBBIES AND OTHER INTERESTS: Houses and gardens, reading, music, people.

HAHN, Hannelore 1926-

PERSONAL: Born November 9, 1926, in Dresden, Germany; daughter of Arthur and Helen (Brach) Hahn; children: Tina Stoumen. *Education:* Attended Black Mountain College, 1945-47, Whittier College, 1947; University of Southern California, B.A., 1952. *Home:* 1628 York Ave., New York, N.Y. 10028. *Agent:* Evelyn L. Singer Agency, P.O. Box 163, Briarcliff Manor, N.Y. 10510.

CAREER: Atlantis Productions, Inc. (educational films), Hollywood, Calif., research assistant, 1956-57; U.S. Information Service, New York, N.Y., exhibit coordinator for two U.S. Department of State exhibits, 1958-59; American Institute of Physics, New York, N.Y., historical and biographical research, 1962-65; Chermayeff & Geismar Associates, New York, N.Y., exhibit research for U.S. Pavilion at Expo 67, Montreal, 1965-66. Founder-director, Phoenix House Poetry Workshops, Phoenix House Foundation, New York, N.Y., 1970-73; New York City Parks, Recrea-

HANNELORE HAHN

tion and Cultural Affairs Administration, special projects, 1966—. International Women's Arts Festival/International Women's Year 1975, chairperson (literature committee); producer-writer, *Women/Voices 1975*, literary showcase for women writers.

AWARDS, HONORS: Mademoiselle, New York, N.Y. guest editor, 1952; *Prix de Paris* finalist, *Vogue*, 1952; 1970 Spring Poet, New York Poetry Forum; Guest Poet, "Free Time," Channel 13, 1971; Guest Poet, *The New York Quarterly*, 1971; 1972 Valentine Poet, The New York Poetry Forum; honorable mention winner, Rego Award 1972, The New York Poetry Forum.

WRITINGS: Take a Giant Step, Little, Brown, 1960. Contributor to *The Saturday Book*, Number 20, London, 1960, and to *Mademoiselle*. Contributor to *The Black Mountain Project*, North Carolina Museum of Art, Raleigh, N.C., 1972. Poems published in *The New York Quarterly*, Summer 1970, Winter 1972, Summer 1972; *Image*, April 1971; *Poetry Roundtable*, 1972; *Charlie Magazine*, 1971; *International Who's Who in Poetry Anthology*, 1972.

Translator: *Substation to the Great Beyond* (scientific correspondence of Albert Einstein), Princeton University Press, 1975; Volker Braun, *For Neruda, For Chile*, Beacon Press, 1975.

WORK IN PROGRESS: Second Skin, an autobiography.

SIDELIGHTS: "I became involved with the ex-addicts at Phoenix House because we had in common: a shattered past, an intense experience which caused suffering, an intense need to begin life again, and the question: how do I start? If I cannot go back, how do I go forward?

"*Substation to the Great Beyond* is, in part, a portrait of a family of upperclass German-Austrian merchant Jews in the process of immigrating to the United States in the Fall of 1938. It is also the story of the daughter; her struggles in trying to become an American and later, as an American, trying to become a woman and a person."

HALL, Anna Gertrude   1882-1967

PERSONAL: Born February 9, 1882, in West Bloomfield, N.Y.; daughter of Myron Edwin (a farmer) and Anna (Sterling) Hall. *Education:* Leland Stanford Junior University, A.B., 1906; New York State Library School, B.L.S., 1916. *Politics:* Democrat. *Religion:* Presbyterian. *Home:* Apartment 209, 850 Webster St., Palo Alto, Calif.

CAREER: Stanford University, Palo Alto, Calif., library cataloger, 1906-14; Endicott (N.Y.) Free Library, librarian, 1915-18; New York State Department of Education, Albany, library organizer, 1918-21; librarian of county library, Pendleton, Ore., 1923-27, of public library, Longview, Wash., 1929-32, of Palo Alto Medical Clinic, Palo Alto, Calif., 1948-62. *Member:* American Library Association.

WRITINGS: The Library Trustee, American Library Association, 1937; *Nansen*, Viking, 1940; *Cyrus Holt and the Civil War*, Viking, 1964. Author of pamphlets and articles in library field.

(Died February 8, 1967)

HANSON, Joan   1938-

PERSONAL: Born June 25, 1938, in Appleton, Wis.; daughter of Jack Ray (a dentist) and Jeanne (Glennon) Benton; married Dale Hanson (a banker) July 15, 1961; children: Tucker, Timmy. *Education:* Carleton College, B.A., 1960. *Home:* 15416 Afton Hills, Lakeland, Minn. 55043.

CAREER: New England Deaconess Hospital, Boston, Mass., laboratory technician, 1960-62; University of Minnesota, Medical School, Minneapolis, cancer research laboratory technician, 1963-66; writer and illustrator of children's books.

WRITINGS—Self-illustrated: *The Monster's Nose Was Cold*, Lerner-Carolrhoda, 1970; *I Don't Like Timmy*, Lerner-Carolrhoda, 1971; *Alfred Snood*, Putnam, 1972; *Homonyms*, Lerner, 1972; *Homographs*, Lerner, 1972; *Antonyms*, Lerner, 1972; *Synonyms*, Lerner, 1972; *More Synonyms*, Lerner, 1973; *More Antonyms*, Lerner, 1973; *Homographic Homophones*, Lerner, 1973; *More Homonyms*, Lerner, 1973; *I Won't Be Afraid*, Lerner, 1974; *I'm Going to Run Away from Home*, Platt & Munk, in press.

Illustrator: Gloria Patrick, *This Is . . .*, Lerner-Carolrhoda, 1969; Eve Holmquist, *The Giant Giraffe*, Carolrhoda, 1973.

WORK IN PROGRESS: What If There's a Big Black Spider with Long Furry Legs Under My Bed?

SIDELIGHTS: "My writing and illustrating seem to be closely allied to the ages of my boys—I started when they

JOAN HANSON

Pull

(From *Antonyms* by Joan Hanson. Illustrated by the author.)

became old enough to talk and give me ideas. The first books were preschool, then older level. The books are based on their experiences and my experiences with them."

HOBBIES AND OTHER INTERESTS: Reading, painting, sailing, tennis, and skiing.

HAWK, Virginia Driving
See SNEVE, Virginia Driving Hawk

HAYES, William D(imitt) 1913-

PERSONAL: Born March 5, 1913, in Goliad, Tex.; son of Arthur John (a musician) and Grace (Singleton) Hayes; married Kathryn Hitte (author of books for children), April 2, 1960. *Education:* Arizona State University, student, 1932-34; University of Missouri, Bachelor of Journalism, 1938. *Mailing address:* 8202 East Osborn Rd., Scottsdale, Ariz. 85251.

CAREER: NEA Service (news syndicate), Cleveland, Ohio, syndicated cartoonist, 1942-43; U.S. Information Service, newscast writer in San Francisco, Calif., 1945-46, artist for *Amerika* magazine in New York, N.Y., 1946-52; Scholastic Magazines, New York, N.Y., artist, 1954-68, free-lance writer, artist and cartoonist, 1968—. *Military service:* U.S. Army Air Forces 1943-44. *Member:* Authors Guild of Authors League of America, Mystery Writers of America.

WRITINGS: (Self-illustrated) *Indian Tales of the Desert People*, McKay, 1957; (self-illustrated) *Project: Genius*, Atheneum, 1962; (self-illustrated) *The Monkey Tree*, Putnam, 1963; (self-illustrated) *The Millionth Landing*, American Book Co., 1963; *That Amazing Machine*, American Book Co., 1964; *Johnnie and the Tool Chest*, Atheneum, 1963; *Curious Carlos*, American Book Co., 1964; *Mystery at Squaw Peak*, Atheneum, 1965; (self-illustrated) *Project Scoop*, Atheneum, 1966; *Hold That Computer!*, Atheneum, 1968; (with Kathryn Hitte) *Mexicali Soup*, Parents' Magazine Press, 1970; (self-illustrated) *How the True Facts Started in Simpsonville and Other Tales*, Atheneum, 1972.

WILLIAM D. HAYES
(self-portrait in oils)

Illustrator: Lilian Moore, *Important Pockets of Paul*, McKay, 1954; Myra Stillman and Beulah Tannenbaum, *Understanding Time*, McGraw, 1958; George Barr, *Young Scientist Takes a Ride*, McGraw, 1960; Paul E. Blackwood, *Push and Pull*, McGraw, 1966; Mary E. Cober, *Remarkable History of Tony Beaver*, McKay, 1968; and others. Contributor of stories to *Humpty Dumpty's Magazine* and to publications of Scholastic Magazines and to reading texts; cartoons published in Colliers and other national magazines, and in newspapers.

HOBBIES AND OTHER INTERESTS: Photography, walking and bicycling, Eastern art, travel, portrait painting.

HEADSTROM, Richard 1902-

PERSONAL: Born February 21, 1902, in Cambridge, Mass.; son of John Birger and Anna (Wiebe) Headstrom; married Ruth H. Hemmerdinger, November 17, 1920; children: John Richard. *Education:* Attended Massachusetts Institute of Technology and Harvard University. *Home:* 1144 Cornish St., Aiken, S.C. 29801.

CAREER: Educator and head of science departments in private and public schools, 1941-64. Illustrator of his own books and articles. New England Museum of Natural History, associate curator of botany, 1938-43; Worcester Museums of Science, Worcester, Mass., curator of entomology, 1942-64; Town of Dover, Mass., town entomologist, member of tree committee, 1953-56; Town of Medway, Mass., member of conservation committee, 1962-64. *Member:* Entomological Society of America, National Association of Biology Teachers, New England Association of Biology Teachers, Massachusetts Audubon Society, American Association of Physics Teachers (New England section), American Museum of Natural History, New England Association of Chemistry Teachers, Boston Geological Society, Massachusetts Teachers Association, Boston Mineral Club.

WRITINGS: The Origin of Man, Princeton University Press, 1921; *The Story of Russia*, Stokes, 1933; *Adventures With a Microscope*, Stokes, 1941; *Birds' Nests*, Washburn, 1949; *The Living Year*, Washburn, 1950; *Birds' Nests of the West*, Washburn, 1951; *Garden Friends and Foes*, Washburn, 1954; *Adventures With a Hand Lens*, Lippincott, 1962; *Adventures With Insects*, Lippincott, 1963; *Adventures with Water Animals*, Lippincott, 1964; *Nature in Miniature*, Knopf, 1968.

A Complete Field Guide to Nests, Washburn, 1970; *Lizards as Pets*, Lippincott, 1971; *Whose Track Is It?*, Washburn, 1971; *Frogs, Toads, and Salamanders as Pets*, Washburn, 1972; *Spiders of the United States*, Barnes & Noble, 1973; *Your Insect Pet*, David McKay, 1973; *Beetles of the United States*, Barnes & Noble, 1974; *Families of Flowering Plants*, Barnes & Noble, 1976; *Lobsters, Crabs, Shrimps, and their Relatives*, Barnes & Noble, in press. Contributor of some twenty-five hundred essays and articles in the fields of philosophy, literature, and science to professional journals, magazines, and newspapers, and to such encyclopedias as *The Encyclopedia of the Biological Sciences*, *Encyclopedia Britannica*, and the *Woman's Home Companion Garden Book*. Columnist, *Boston Transcript*, 1939-41, *Boston Globe*, 1941-45, *Worcester Telegram*, 1964—, *The State*, Columbia, S.C., 1965-67.

SIDELIGHTS: "I have been interested in the sciences and in writing since an early age. I wrote my first book(?) about the age of ten; it consisted merely of pasting pictures of birds in a notebook and then writing a legend about each bird. It didn't amount to anything of course but perhaps it was prophetic of later work. I still have the book incidentally.

"I sold my first article to *Nature Magazine* when I was about twenty years of age. And did a considerable amount of publishing in philosophy, literature and science in the middle twenties, contributing to various magazines, including the *Personalist*, official publication of the department of philosophy of the University of Southern California. Then obtained a contract to do a history of Russia from Stokes which came out as *The Story of Russia* in 1933.

"Following publication of my book on Russia, I gradually began to turn my attention to the sciences. I went into teaching in private schools and at the same time became curator of the David Mason Little Museum of Natural History, a small private museum. After several years of teaching in private schools, I decided that public schools offered a more secure future. I also became associated with the *Boston Transcript* as a columnist and after its demise became associated with the *Boston Globe* in the same capacity. Both columns were on natural history and were directed essentially to children. Meanwhile I had transferred my museum interests to the New England Museum of Natural History.

RICHARD HEADSTROM

"I began teaching at a rather late time in life but from the time I began I have carried on a most intensive program of teaching, writing, and museum work for some twenty-odd years or until my retirement from teaching in 1964. During this period, in addition to my regular teaching activities, I have conducted science workshops for teachers, who participated in them for credit towards advanced degrees and salary increments and most of which were sponsored by the schools where I taught as well as by the museums with which I have been associated. I have also been nature counselor in camps for boys and girls and served as a consultant to the boy and girl scouts in nature study. Which serves to show that I have been closely associated with children of school age for a great many years as well as with teachers and with others not engaged in school work.

"I have conducted classes in school during Saturday mornings throughout the winter as well as all day during the Christmas recess, something unheard of in school circles and at my pupils' express request; and have conducted a course in nature study in Sunday school instead of the usual bible subjects, an innovation both unique and successful.

"My writing schedule consists of a stint at the typewriter every day. I do not limit myself to any length of time or to any certain amount of work each day although I do have some idea of what I want to accomplish at each sitting. A day's work may result in only a few pages but it is sur-

prising how the pages mount up after a while. I have twice written two books at the same time, not literally but figuratively, having worked on one book in the morning and the other in the afternoon. I have written most of my books within six months or less though *Nature in Miniature* required about a year and *The Story of Russia* about two. Most of my books I have illustrated myself.

"As for ideas for my books and essays and articles, they seem to pop into my mind quite naturally although quite a few have been written by request. The material for my books and essays has been obtained in a variety of ways: by extensive reading, by teaching, by research, and by field work or field trips. I have done a fair amount of travelling too. Teaching and writing has been hard work and it has not always been clear sailing. There have been disappointments to be sure and certain rewards as when you hear of someone having profited by your teaching or having enjoyed one of your books."

HOBBIES AND OTHER INTERESTS: "The humanities, such as history, philosophy, and literature; also gardening. Though retired from teaching science, still continue to take an active interest in the various sciences."

FOR MORE INFORMATION SEE: Boston Sunday Globe, May 24, 1942; *Middleborough* (Mass.) *Gazette*, October 20, 1955, March 4 and 15, 1956; *Milford* (Mass.) *News*, March 22, 1962, September 11, 1962; *Worcester* (Mass.) *Evening Gazette*, September 23, 1963; *Worcester* (Mass.) *Telegram*, February 2, 1964, September 18, 1965; *The State*, Columbia, S.C., June 26, 1966, March 22, 1970, August 27, 1972; *Chronicle* (Augusta, Ga.), June 3, 1970, April 2, 1971, January 6, 1972; *Augusta Herald* (Ga.), June 4, 1970.

HEADY, Eleanor B(utler) 1917-

PERSONAL: Surname rhymes with "ready"; born March 13, 1917, in Bliss, Idaho; daughter of Arthur Harrison and Effie (Carrico) Butler; married Harold F. Heady (a professor of ecology), June 12, 1940; children: Carol Marie (Mrs. Don De Maria), Kent Arthur. *Education:* University of Idaho, B.A., 1939. *Politics:* Liberal Republican. *Religion:* Congregationalist. *Home and office:* 1864 Capistrano Ave., Berkeley, Calif. 94707. *Agent:* Marilyn Marlow, Curtis Brown Ltd., 60 East 56th St., New York, N.Y. 10022.

CAREER: Has worked as a high school English teacher, radio announcer, and script writer. Member of board of directors, Concerned Berkeley Citizens. *Member:* League of American Penwomen, California Writers' Club (president, 1972-74), Berkeley City Club.

WRITINGS—Juvenile: *Jambo, Sungura*, Norton, 1965; *When the Stones Were Soft: East African Fireside Tales*, Funk, 1968; *Coat of the Earth*, Norton, 1968; *Brave Johnny O'Hare*, Parents' Magazine Press, 1969; *Tales of the Nimipoo*, World Publishing, 1970; (with Harold F. Heady) *High Meadow*, Grosset, 1970; *Safiri the Singer*, Follett, 1972; *The Soil That Feeds Us*, Parents' Magazine Press, 1972; *Sage Smoke*, Follett, 1973; *Dolls You Can Make*, Lothrop, 1974; *Traveling Plants*, Parents' Magazine Press, in press. Contributor to *Ranger Rick's Nature Magazine*, *Cricket*, and *Highlights for Children*.

WORK IN PROGRESS: With Harold F. Heady, *Range and Wildlife Management in the Tropics*, for Longman's Green.

SIDELIGHTS: "I was born in Idaho and grew up on a ranch in the Snake River Valley. I began writing as a small child, but did little serious work until later years. All my early attempts were in verse, some of which were published when I was in my early teens and twenties.

"Educated at the University of Idaho at Moscow where I earned a B.A. in English, I taught in Rockland High School in southern Idaho, then married Harold F. Heady, whom I met while attending the University.

"I lived in New York State on a wildlife experimental forest, then in Minnesota and Montana. In Montana I worked as operator-announcer-writer at the local radio station in Bozeman. While working there I wrote my first children's stories for broadcast over a weekly story-telling series. From these efforts came the first published story for children.

"We lived in Texas for five years. While there my children took up most of the time and little writing developed. Then we moved to Berkeley where we have lived in the same house on Capistrano Avenue for over twenty-three years.

ELEANOR B. HEADY

Many years ago Tebetebe was monkey king of the forest. ■ (From *Safiri the Singer* by Eleanor B. Heady. Illustrated by Harold James.)

"I followed my professor husband to Africa where he went to study the grasslands. While there I collected stories for my African folklore books, *Jambo Sungura, When the Stones were Soft*, and *Safiri the Singer*.

"Returning to the state of my birth, I collected the folklore of the Nez Perce Indians of northern Idaho. The resulting book was *Tales of the Nimipoo*. This has been adopted as a reading text in Idaho schools.

"Following a year in Australia and New Zealand, I wrote *Brave Johnny O'Hare*, a picture story in verse for small children based on an Australian Aboriginal folk tale.

"We make frequent trips to various parts of the world. There's a story behind every bush, a nature book in every stone, and a verse in every cloud."

FOR MORE INFORMATION SEE: New York Times Book Review, May 5, 1965; *Saturday Review*, September 21, 1968.

HENSTRA, Friso 1928-

PERSONAL: Born February 9, 1928, in Amsterdam, Netherlands; son of Sytze (an artist) and Anna Henstra; married Maria Sligting, March 7, 1952; children: Sylvia. *Education:* Studied at National College of Art, Amsterdam. *Home:* Nieuwe Herengracht 13, Amsterdam, Netherlands.

CAREER: Artist. Started as painter, switched to sculptor in 1950, and then to free-lance illustrating. Instructor at College of Art, Arnhem, 1969—. *Military service:* Dutch Army, 1948-50; served in Indonesia. *Member:* Beroepsvereniging Grafisch Vormgevers-Nederland (Society of Graphic Designers-Netherland). *Awards, honors:* Pomme d'Or at Bratislavia Biennale, 1969, for illustrations of *The Practical Princess*; Citation of Merit, 1970, and Gold Medal, 1971, from Society of Illustrators; *Stupid Marco*

and *The Round Sultan* were Honor Books in the Annual Chicago Book Clinic Exhibition, 1971; *The Silver Whistle* was selected as one of the fifty best books of the year by American Institute of Graphic Arts, 1972.

■ (From *Petronella* by Jay Williams. Illustrated by Friso Henstra.)

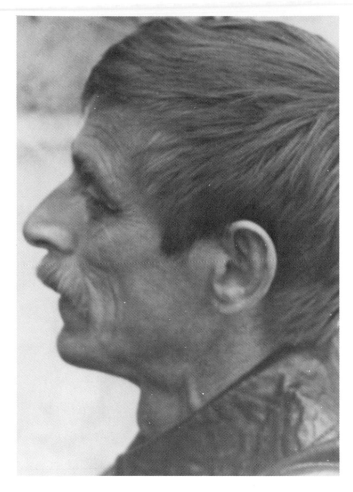

FRISO HENSTRA

CAREER: Art teacher in Frankfurt am Main, Germany, 1953-57; free-lance artist exhibiting in one-woman and group shows in Essen, Kassel, Frankfurt am Main, and elsewhere in Germany, 1958—; author and illustrator of children's books, 1961—. *Awards, honors:* Premio Grafico-Preis (first prize for illustration) at International Children's Book Show in Bologna, Italy, 1967, for *Drei Voegel (Three Birds)*; *The Three Birds, In the Forest, In the Village,* and *When the Sun Shines* were included among the Child Study Association of America Children's Books of the Year, 1971.

WRITINGS—Author and illustrator; all published in Germany by Otto Maier, except as noted: *Wenn die Sonne scheint,* 1961, translation published as *When the Sun Shines,* Harcourt, 1971; *Im Kinderland* (title means "In Nurseryland"), 1962; *Kommt in den Wald,* 1963, published as *In the Forest,* Harcourt, 1971; *Drei Voegel,* 1966, published as *The Three Birds,* Harcourt, 1971; *Thomas im Dorf,* 1967, published as *In the Village,* Harcourt, 1971; *Jahreszeiten-Bilderbuch* (title means "Seasons of the Year Picture Book"), 1968; *Fahrzeuge* (title means "Vehicles"), 1968; *Kinderspiele* (title means "Children's Games"), 1969; *Malen und Zeichnen* (title means "Paint and Draw"), two books, 1969; *Weihnachten* (title means "Christmas"), 1971; *14 Bilder zum Weitermalen* (title means "Fourteen Pictures to Paint"), 1971; *Schau, was ich gefunden hab* (title means "Look What I Have Found"), 1973; *3 Malmappen Religion* (title means "Three Painting Folders for Religion"), Benziger, 1973.

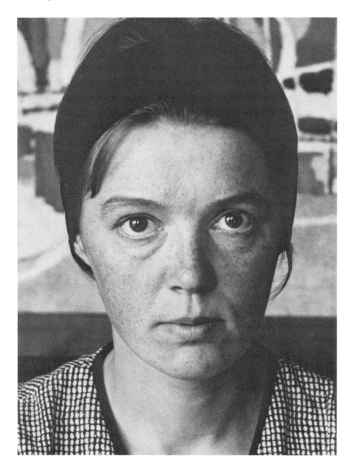

HILDE HEYDUCK-HUTH

ILLUSTRATOR—All published by Parents' Magazine Press, except as noted: Jay Williams, *The Practical Princess,* 1969; Jay Williams, *School for Sillies,* 1969; Jay Williams, *Stupid Marco,* 1970; Barbara Walker, *The Round Sultan,* 1970; Jay Williams, *The Silver Whistle,* 1971; Jay Williams, *Seven at One Blow,* 1972; Jay Williams, *The Youngest Captain,* 1972; Jay Williams, *Petronella,* 1973; Jay Williams, *Forgetful Fred,* 1974; Jane Yolen, *The Little Spotted Fish,* Seabury, in press. Also has done illustrations for *Cricket* (children's magazine) and other magazines, newspapers, weeklies, television, and book covers.

SIDELIGHTS: Henstra supported himself for a time in the early 1950's by doing cartoons; the first one appeared in *Mandril,* a Dutch satirical magazine. He and Jay Williams met during one of the latter's trips to Holland and they became good friends as well as an author-illustrator team.

HEYDUCK-HUTH, Hilde   1929-

PERSONAL: Born March 18, 1929, in Niederweisel, Germany; daughter of Reinhard (a clergyman) and Irmgard (Eick) Huth; married Christof Heyduck (a stage designer), 1956; children: Nikolaus. *Education:* Studied at Hochschule fuer bildende Kuenste (Academy of Art), Kassel, Germany, 1949-53. *Home:* Waldstrasse 36, 6113 Babenhausen, West Germany.

This morning
Tom climbed the pear tree
and picked the ripe pears
to put in his basket.

(From *In the Village* by Hilde Heyduck-Huth. Illustrated by the author.)

WORK IN PROGRESS: A book on animals for children six-to-ten.

SIDELIGHTS: "I studied painting and pedagogy. In addition I am interested in psychology. I think that it is very important for one's later life, what kind of pictures one has seen in their early years. When my son was small, I made the first children's book. I observed him and learned what was particularly interesting or gave pleasure to him. All my later books and workbooks were a result of direct contact with children."

FOR MORE INFORMATION SEE: Horn Book, June, 1971.

HILLERT, Margaret   1920-

PERSONAL: Born January 22, 1920, in Saginaw, Mich.; daughter of Edward Carl (a tool and die maker) and A. Ilva (Sproull) Hillert. *Education:* Bay City Junior College, A.A., 1941; University of Michigan, R.N., 1944; Wayne University (now Wayne State University), A.B., 1948. *Residence:* Berkley, Mich. *Office:* Whittier School, 815 East Farnum, Royal Oak, Mich. 48067.

CAREER: Primary school teacher in public schools of Royal Oak, Mich., 1948—. Poet and writer of children's books. *Member:* International League of Children's Poets, Society of Children's Book Writers, Emily Dickinson Society, Poetry Society of Michigan, Detroit Women Writers. *Awards, honors:* Numerous awards for poems from Poetry Society of Michigan.

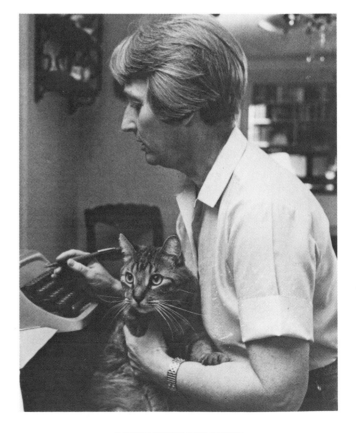

MARGARET HILLERT

82

Here we go.
■ (From *The Birthday Car* by Margaret Hillert. Illustrated by Kelly Oechsli.)

WRITINGS—Children's Poetry: *Farther Than Far*, Follett, 1969; *I Like to Live in the City*, Golden Books, 1970; *Who Comes to Your House?*, Golden Books, 1973; *Come Play with Me*, Follett, 1975; *The Sleepytime Book*, Western, 1975.

Children's books; all published by Follett: *The Birthday Car*, 1966; *The Little Runaway*, 1966; *The Yellow Boat*, 1966; *The Snow Baby*, 1969; *Circus Fun*, 1969; *A House for Little Red*, 1970; *Little Puff*, 1973.

Children's stories retold; all published by Follett: *The Funny Baby*, 1963; *The Three Little Pigs*, 1963; *The Three Bears*, 1963; *The Three Goats*, 1963; *The Magic Beans*, 1966; *Cinderella at the Ball*, 1970.

Contributor of poems to *Horn Book, Christian Science Monitor, McCall's, Saturday Evening Post, Jack and Jill, Western Humanities Review, Poet Lore, Cricket*, and others.

SIDELIGHTS: "I have been writing poems ever since I was in the third grade, and so now I write mostly poetry—both for children and grownups—but I just love to read, so I have written books with very easy words for children 'just-beginning-to-read' so that they can have the fun of really reading for themselves. In my poetry and stories I write about things I like myself: *cats*, Teddy bears, biking, *cats*, colored leaves, *cats*, etc. I sit or lie on the couch and write everything with a pencil I've had for about thirty-five years before I type it. One of my cats usually sits on my chest and 'helps'—or sits on my lap at the typewriter. I get up very early in the morning, *every* morning, even Saturdays and Sundays and vacations. I like walking and playing tennis and working in my yard and reading and reading and reading. . . ."

FOR MORE INFORMATION SEE: Rachel M. Hilbert, *Michigan Poets*, Ann Arbor, 1964; J. R. Le Master, *Poets of the Midwest*, Young Publications, 1966; Lee Bennett Hopkins, *Pass the Poetry, Please*, Citation Press, 1972.

HILTON, Ralph 1907-

PERSONAL: Born September 10, 1907, in Mendenhall, Miss.; son of R. T. (an attorney) and Myrtis (Cruise) Hilton; married Mary Jane Kendall, February 20, 1935 (deceased); married Dorothy M. Asnip, April 27, 1972; children: Mary Jane (Mrs. Peter B. Field). *Education:* George Washington University, B.A., 1929. *Home:* 43 North Sea Pines Dr., Hilton Head Island, S.C. 29925. *Agent:* A. Watkins, Inc., 77 Park Ave., New York, N.Y. 10016.

RALPH HILTON

CAREER: Newspaper correspondent in Mexico City, Mexico, 1931-32; Associated Press, staff writer and editor in New Orleans, New York, Dallas, Richmond, and Washington, D.C., 1933-43; U.S. Department of State, Foreign Service officer, 1943-64, with posts in Lima, Peru, 1943-45, San Jose, Costa Rica, 1946, Buenos Aires, Argentina, 1947-49, public affairs adviser, assistant Secretary of State for Inter-American Affairs, 1955-56, counselor, American Embassy, Asunción, Paraguay, 1957-58, director of UNESCO relations staff, 1959; special assistant to administrator, Bureau of Security and Consular Affairs, 1960; executive secretary, Joint Board of Examiners, U.S. Information Agency, 1962-63; Career Foreign Service, retired, Consul-General, 1964. Editor, co-founder, "The Island Packet," 1970. *Member:* Foreign Service Association, National Press Club (Washington, D.C.), Overseas Press Club of America (New York).

WRITINGS: Worldwide Mission: The Story of the United States Foreign Service (juvenile), World Publishing, 1970; (editor) *The Gentlemanly Serpent*, University of South Carolina Press, 1974. Editor, "The Island Packet," 1970—.

HIMLER, Ann 1946-

PERSONAL: Born May 1, 1946, in Camden, N.J.; daughter of Chester John (an engineer) and Anna (Bar-

ANN and RONALD HIMLER

A family of field mice scurried across the path in front of him. Little Owl called out to them, but they were shy and quickly ran into the tall grass. ■ (From *Little Owl, Keeper of the Trees* by Ronald and Ann Himler. Illustrated by Ronald Himler.)

rington) Danowitz; married Ronald Norbert Himler (an illustrator of children's books), June 18, 1972; children: Daniel Damien (stepson), Anna Grace. *Education:* Immaculata College, student, 1964-66; Dickinson College, B.A., 1968; University of Pennsylvania, M.A., 1971. *Religion:* Russian Orthodox. *Home and office:* 680 West End Ave., Apt. 4-D, New York, N.Y. 10025.

CAREER: Library Company of Philadelphia, Philadelphia, Pa., cataloguer, 1970; University of Pennsylvania, Philadelphia, instructor in Russian, 1971.

WRITINGS: (With husband, Ronald Himler) *Little Owl: Keeper of the Trees* (juvenile), Harper, 1974; *Waiting for Cherries*, Harper, 1976.

WORK IN PROGRESS: A novel for children, about an itinerant tinker in eighteenth-century Ireland.

HOLL, Adelaide (Hinkle)

PERSONAL: Born December 9, in Pittsburgh, Pa.; daughter of Lester Earl and Bertie (Smith) Hinkle; married Walter E. Holl; married Leonard Davis Wesson; children: Linda Holl Veffer, Thomas Richard. *Education:* Attended Cleveland School of Art, Western Reserve University; Capital University, B.A., B.S. in Education, Ohio State University, M.A. *Home:* 5 Tudor Place, New York, N.Y.

CAREER: Madison Township School, Ashville, Ohio, teacher; Worthington School, Worthington, Ohio, teacher; Artists and Writers Press, New York, N.Y., writer, educational consultant; Random House, New York, N.Y., editor; now free-lance author. *Member:* National Education Association, Author's Guild of America, Ohioana Library Association, Pi Lambda Theta. *Awards, honors:* Valley Forge classroom teacher's medal, 1960; Capital University, Outstanding Alumna Award, 1967.

WRITINGS: *Sylvester, The Mouse with the Musical Ear*, Golden Press, 1961; *Golden Reading Workbook*, Golden Press, 1961; *George the Gentle Giant*, Golden Press, 1962; *Lizette*, Lothrop, 1962; *Zeke the Raccoon*, Heath, 1962; *A Real Kitten*, Heath, 1962; *Colors Are Nice*, Golden Press, 1962; *The Thinking Book*, Golden Press, 1963; *Sir Kevin of Devon*, Lothrop, 1963; *Jamie Looks*, Golden Press, 1963; *Listening for Sounds*, Golden Press, 1963; *Time and Measuring*, Golden Press, 1963; *Adventures with Words*, Golden Press, 1963; *Dogs, Cats, Birds, and Bats*, Golden Press, 1963; *Magic Tales*, C. E. Merrill, 1964; *Mrs. McGarity's Peppermint Sweater*, Lothrop, 1965; *The Rain Puddle*, Lothrop, 1965; *Runaway Giant*, Lothrop, 1967; *The Remarkable Egg*, Lothrop, Lee & Shepard, 1968; *Bright, Bright Morning*, Lothrop, Lee & Shepard, 1969; *One Kitten for Kim*, Addison-Wesley (Weekly Reader

It was almost winter. . . . But small bear didn't want to go to bed. ■ (From *Bedtime for Bears* by Adelaide Holl. Illustrated by Cyndy Szekeres.)

Children's Book Club Selection), 1969; *North is for Polar Bears*, L. W. Singer Co.; *Journey to the Sea*, L. W. Singer Co., 1968; *The Runaway Hat*, L. W. Singer Co., 1969; *Hooray for Mike*, L. W. Singer Co.; *Have You Seen My Puppy?*, Random House, 1968; *Moon Mouse*, Random House (A Weekly Reader Children's Book Club Selection), 1969; (with Kjell Ringi) *The Man Who Had No Dream*, Random House, 1969.

An ABC of Cars, Trucks and Machines, American Heritage Publishing Co., 1970; *Hide-and-Seek ABC*, Platt and Munk, 1971; *My Father and I*, Franklin Watts, 1973; *Teacher's Manual, Student Record Book* (for 2 Pilot Libraries), Science Research Associates; *Teacher's Manual for Magic Tales and Giants and Fairies*, Charles E. Merrill; *Teacher's Manual for The Golden Beginning Readers*, Golden Press; *Teacher's Guide for Educational Experiences Filmstrips*, Education Department, Western Publishing Company; *Parent's Guide to First Adventures In Learning*, Western Publishing Co.; *The Parade*, Franklin Watts; *Bedtime for Bears*, Garrard Publishing Co., 1973; *Too Fat to Fly*, Garrard Publishing Co., 1973; *The Long Birthday*, Garrard Publishing Co., 1974; *Gus Gets the Message*, Garrard Publishing Co., 1974; *Pretending*, Holt Rinehart and Winston; *The Mystery of Pine Valley Zoo*,

ADELAIDE HOLL

Holt Rinehart and Winston; *Let's Count*, Addison Wesley; *My Weekly Reader Picture-Word Book*, Xerox Co. for Weekly Reader Book Club; *Most-of-the-Time Maxie*, Weekly Reader Book Club; *The Poky Little Puppy's First Christmas*, Western Publishing, 1973; *The Little Viking*, Western Publishing, 1975; *Wonderful Tree*, Western Publishing, 1974. Contributor of column, "Teacher's Viewpoint," to *Columbus* (Ohio) *Dispatch*.

HOLLAND, Isabelle 1920-

PERSONAL: Born June 16, 1920, in Basel, Switzerland; daughter of Philip (a U.S. Foreign Service officer) and Corabelle (Anderson) Holland. *Education:* Attended private and boarding schools in England, and University of Liverpool for two years; Tulane University, B.A., 1942. *Politics:* Independent. *Religion:* Christian. *Home:* 1199 Park Ave., New York, N.Y. 10028. *Agent:* Jane Wilson, John Cushman Associates, 25 West 43rd St., New York, N.Y. 10036.

CAREER: Worked for several magazines, including *McCall's*, after finishing college; Crown Publishers, Inc., New York, N.Y., publicity director, 1956-60; J. B. Lippincott Co., New York, N.Y., publicity director, 1960-66; *Harper's*, New York, N.Y., assistant to publisher, 1967-68; G. P. Putnam's Sons, New York, N.Y., publicity director, 1968-69; free-lance writer, 1969—. *Member:* Authors Guild, P.E.N.

ISABELLE HOLLAND

WRITINGS—Novels for young people, except as noted: *Cecily* (adult fiction), Lippincott, 1967; *Amanda's Choice*, Lippincott, 1970; *The Man Without a Face*, Lippincott, 1972; *Heads You Win, Tails I Lose*, Lippincott, 1973; *Kilgaren* (adult), Weybright, 1974; *Trelawny* (adult), Weybright, 1974; *Journey for Three*, Houghton, 1975; *Of Love and Death and Other Journeys*, Lippincott, 1975. Short stories have been published in *Collier's* and *Country Gentleman*.

SIDELIGHTS: Lived in Guatemala City, where her father's assignment took the family when she was four, and then in northern England. "Then the war came and my father dispatched my mother and me to the States, which was the first time I had lived in my own country, and that took some adjusting."

HOBBIES AND OTHER INTERESTS: All things Spanish—music, fiestas, the sound of the language; cats.

FOR MORE INFORMATION SEE: New York Times Book Review, May 3, 1970.

HUBBELL, Patricia 1928-

PERSONAL: Born July 10, 1928, in Bridgeport, Conn.; daughter of Franklin H. and Helen (Osborn) Hubbell; married Harold Hornstein (now a newspaper editor), March 10, 1954; children: Jeffrey, Deborah. *Education:* University of Connecticut, B.S., 1950. *Politics:* Independent. *Religion:* Unitarian Universalist. *Home:* R.F.D. 1, Norton Rd., Easton, Conn. 06880.

CAREER: Reporter for *Newtown Bee*, Newtown, Conn., 1950-51, and *Westport Town Crier*, Westport, Conn., 1951-54; *Bridgeport Sunday Post*, Bridgeport, Conn., horse and dog columnist, 1958-68; free-lance writer specializing in gardening and nature, 1968—.

WRITINGS: The Apple Vendor's Fair, Atheneum, 1963; *8 a.m. Shadows*, Atheneum, 1965; *Catch Me a Wind*, Atheneum, 1968.

SIDELIGHTS: "I came to write my books by simply setting down poems as they occurred to me. Basically, I write for pure pleasure—because I like the sound of the words, the rhythm of the phrases, the delight of playing with words, thoughts and dreams. I first started writing when I was about eleven-years old. I often sat on the limb of a maple tree in front of my house and watched the patterns of the clouds, the leaves, the wind-ruffled grasses. As I watched, I set down my thoughts, and they came out poems.

"I was brought up in the beautiful small town of Easton, Connecticut, where I still live. Since I have always delighted in my surroundings, my poems reflect this.

"After I graduated from the University of Connecticut, where I studied everything from English literature to livestock judging, I went to work for a weekly newspaper. Some of my poems were first published there. Most of the poems in *The Apple Vendor's Fair, 8 a.m. Shadows*, and *Catch Me a Wind*, were written while I lived in a very old house in Easton, with my husband and two small children. The house was built long before the Revolutionary War and

PATRICIA HUBBELL

its wide-board floors, huge stone chimney and moss-encrusted roof provided many ideas for poems. I used to sit at the kitchen table and write, while Jeff and Debbie played.

"I've always loved animals, especially horses, and ride nearly every day. We've always had an abundance of animals around the place, including ponies, horses, sheep, cats, chickens, a goat, a guinea pig and many dogs. I love to garden and have a rock garden and a wild flower garden as well as a vegetable garden. I paint and do craft work—a little bit of everything from making mobiles to macrame, weaving and applique. It seems to me crafts and painting and even gardening are a lot like writing poems—you are always arranging and rearranging, whether it is with words, plants, paints or fabrics. Somehow a pattern emerges, and reflects your delight in some aspect of the world."

HUGHES, Richard (Arthur Warren) 1900-

PERSONAL: Born April 19, 1900, in Weybridge, Surrey, England; son of Arthur and Louisa Grace (Warren) Hughes; married Frances Catharine Ruth Bazley, January 8, 1932; children: Robert Elystan-Glodrydd, Penelope Hughes Minney, Lleky Susanna Hughes Papastavrou, Catharine Phyllida Hughes Wells, Owain Gardner Collingwood. *Education:* Attended Charterhouse School, 1913-18; Oriel College, Oxford, B.A., 1922. *Home:* North Wales, also Tangier, Morocco; *Mailing address:* c/o Chatto and Windus, 40-42 William IV St., London W.C.2. *Agent:* Harold Ober Associates, Inc., 40 East 49th St., New York, N.Y. 10017.

CAREER: Full-time writer. As a young man, lived (more for amusement than of necessity) as a tramp, a beggar, and a pavement artist in Europe and, during two brief visits, in the United States; once conducted an expedition through Central Europe and has traveled on his own through Canada, the West Indies, and the Near East, as well as Europe and America; University of London, London, England, Gresham Professor of Rhetoric, three years during the 1920's. Co-founder of the Portmadoc Players, a Welsh theatrical company, 1923; first vice-chairman of Welsh National Theatre, 1924 (resigned, 1936); from the middle 1940's until 1955, he was primarily engaged with writing filmscripts for Ealing Studios, Ealing, London, England. *Wartime service:* British Army, 1918; became second lieutenant, British Admiralty, 1940-45; became Deputy Principal Priority Officer; decorated, 1946.

MEMBER: Royal Society of Literature (fellow), American Academy of Arts and Letters (honorary), National Institute of Arts and Letters (honorary), United University Club, Pratt's Club (both London); Royal Welsh Yacht Club (Caernavon). *Awards, honors:* Femina-Vie Heureuse prize, for *A High Wind in Jamaica*; member, Order of the British Empire, 1946, for wartime service; D.Litt., University of Wales, 1956; Arts Council Award, 1961, for *The Fox in the Attic*; Welsh Arts Council Award, 1974, for services to literature.

WRITINGS: The Sisters' Tragedy (one-act play, produced in London under the sponsorship of John Masefield, 1922), Basil Blackwell, 1922; *Gipsy-Night, and Other Poems*, W. Ransom (Chicago), 1922; *A Rabbit and a Leg* (plays; contains *The Sisters' Tragedy* [see above], *A Comedy of Good and Evil* [produced at Abbey Theatre, Dublin, and at Birmingham Repertory Theatre, London, 1924, revived and produced on Broadway as "Minnie and Mr. Williams," 1948], *The Man Born to Be Hanged*, and *Danger*), Knopf, 1924 (published in England as *The Sisters' Tragedy, and Other Plays*, Chatto & Windus, 1924), reissued as *Plays*, Harper, 1966; (editor) John Skelton, *Poems*, Heinemann, 1924; *A Moment of Time* (stories), Chatto & Windus, 1926; *Confessio Juvenis* (collected poems), Chatto & Windus, 1926; *The Innocent Voyage* (novel), Harper, 1929 (published in England as *A High Wind in Jamaica*, Chatto & Windus, 1929, then reissued with that title in America, Harper, 1930).

Richard Hughes: An Omnibus (stories, poems, and plays), Harper, 1931; *The Spider's Palace, and Other Stories* (juvenile), Chatto & Windus, 1931, Harper, 1932; *In Hazard* (novel), Harper, 1938; *Don't Blame Me!* (children's stories), Harper, 1940; (with John Dick Scott) *The Administration of War Production*, H.M.S.O., 1955; *The Fox in the Attic* (novel; first of a projected four or five volume work entitled *The Human Predicament*), Harper, 1961; *Liturgical Language Today*, Church in Wales Publications, 1962; *Gertrude's Child* (juvenile), Harlan Quist, 1966; *Gertrude and the Mermaid* (juvenile), Harlan Quist, 1967; *The Wooden Shepherdess* (novel: second volume of *The Human Predicament*), Harper, 1973. Contributor to literary journals in England and the United States. Author of the world's first radio play, January, 1924, as well as subsequent radio scripts.

The Innocent Voyage was dramatized by Paul Osborn and produced on Broadway in 1943. The script was included in Burns Mantle's *The Best Plays of 1943-44* and was published separately by Dramatic Publishing Co. in 1946. The novel was also filmed by 20th Century-Fox and released as "A High Wind in Jamaica" in 1965.

WORK IN PROGRESS: Third volume of *The Human Predicament.*

SIDELIGHTS: Hughes started writing when he was six; he insisted that his mother write down his stories before he himself was able to. Now, although he has published only four novels, his reputation as a novelist of distinction derives from the consistently high quality of his prose.

It has been suggested, by Cyril Connelly and others, that, it is Hughes' *lack* of style which distinguishes his writing. Perhaps what is meant is that Hughes so completely achieves the vitalization of his characters that the reader is unconscious of the author's control of action and dialogue. Hughes himself admits that, in a sense, he relinquishes his own style to the "style" of each character. "All characters are different facets of the author," he told *Christian Science Monitor.* "I use a stream of consciousness to describe [an incident] as it appeared to the last person who spoke though not in his words." Selma G. Lanes cites the effectiveness of Hughes' narrative method for children in her review of *Gertrude's Child* which, she says, "goes further than any young children's book in memory to reach 'beyond the words yet available to a child' into that realm where, as [Maurice] Sendak himself noted, 'fantasy and feeling lie deeper than words.'"

Hughes now has little enthusiasm for his early work, even though critics still discuss the novel that was some forty years ago. *"High Wind* and *In Hazard* are both so remote from me," he says. "Now I am only interested in what I am going to write. I want to bring *The Human Predicament* down to the end of the war. There should be three or four volumes more, but I will be about 140 years old when I finish them."

Hughes was asked if he considered writing a pleasure. "Pleasure," he answered, "suggests something voluntary. If one is under a compulsion, 'pleasure' is not the right word."

FOR MORE INFORMATION SEE: Times Literary Sup-

All at once, she found she had had enough of the storm: it had become intolerable, instead of a welcome distraction. ■ (From the movie *"A High Wind in Jamaica,"* copyright © 1965 by 20th Century-Fox.)

Duryea Brothers, Walck, 1968; *Joe Namath, Superstar*, Walck, 1968, revised, 1974; *Let's Go Yaz: The Story of Carl Yastrzemski*, Walck, 1968; *Stock Car Racing: Grand National Competition*, Walck, 1968; *Blue and White Abroad: The United States in International Automobile Racing*, Walck, 1969; *Thirty-one and Six: The Story of Denny McLain*, Walck, 1969; *Earl the Pearl: The Story of Earl Monroe*, Walck, 1969, revised, 1974; *Steam Cars of the Stanley Twins*, Walck, 1969; *Bradley of the Knicks*, Walck, 1970; *Championship Trail: The Story of Indianapolis Racing*, Walck, 1970; *Racing Cars*, Walck, 1970; *Here Comes Bobby Orr*, Walck, 1971; *Johnny Bench*, Walck, 1971; *Behind the Wheel: Great Road Racing Drivers*, Walck, 1971; *Cars Against the Clock: The World Land*

plement, September 26, 1929, July 9, 1938, October 6, 1961; *New Statesman*, October 5, 1929; *Christian Science Monitor*, August 10, 1938, March 2, 1967; *New Yorker*, October 8, 1938; *Springfield Republican*, October 9, 1938; *Saturday Review*, February 3, 1962; *New York Times Book Review*, February 4, 1962; *Commonweal*, March 30, 1962; *Catholic World*, May, 1962; *Critique*, Volume IX, number 1, 1967; *Book Week*, April 23, 1967; Brian Doyle, *The Who's Who of Children's Literature*, Schocken Books, 1968; Carolyn Riley, *Contemporary Literary Criticism/1*, Gale Research, 1973.

JACKSON, Robert B(lake) 1926-

PERSONAL: Born November 11, 1926, in Hartford, Conn.; son of Blake Smith and Frieda (Welz) Jackson. *Education:* Amherst College, A.B., 1950; Columbia University, M.S., 1953. *Home:* 31 Parkland Dr., Woodbury, Conn. 06798.

CAREER: East Orange (N.J.) Public Library, coordinator of readers' service, 1953-66. *Military service:* U.S. Army, 1945-46; became sergeant. *Member:* Authors' Guild, American Auto Races Writers, Broadcasters' Association.

WRITINGS: (With Harold L. Roth) *New Jersey Public Libraries and Adult Education*, New Jersey Association for Adult Education, 1961; (with John F. Moran) *Services to Community Agencies and Organizations*, American Library Association, 1961; *Sports Cars*, Walck, 1963; *Road Racing, USA*, Walck, 1964; *Road Race Round the World: The 1908 New York to Paris Race*, Walck, 1965; *Grand Prix at the Glen*, Walck, 1965; *The Remarkable Ride of the Abernathy Boys*, Walck, 1967; *Gasoline Buggy of the*

On April 5, 1910, Bud and Temple Abernathy set out from Cross Roads, Oklahoma, bound for New York City. Their ages were ten and six. ■ (From *The Remarkable Ride of the Abernathy Boys* by Robert B. Jackson.)

Speed Record, Walck, 1971; *Jabbar: Giant of the NBA*, Walck, 1972; *Can-Am Competition: World's Fastest Sports Car Racing*, Walck, 1972; *Supermex: The Lee Trevino Story*, Walck, 1973; *Classic Cars*, Walck, 1974; *Waves, Wheels and Wings: Museums of Transportation*, Walck, 1974; *Quarter-Mile Combat: The Explosive World of Drag Racing*, Walck, 1975. Book reviewer, *Library Journal*.

SIDELIGHTS: "My writing career began during a discussion with Beman Lord about Mr. Lord's manuscript on cars. We agreed there was a real need for an informative book for younger children on sports cars and sports-car racing, and before I knew it, I had been talked into going ahead by myself to write the book. I've always had an avid interest in cars and sports-car events. I once crossed France in a boxcar and once owned an MG-TC with right-hand drive and spidery wire wheels. The memory of that car is still cherished and I hope to do a story about it one day.

"Both personally and professionally, I have strong feelings about writing style. I avoid insulting children with patronizing 'talk-down' statements as such writing made me

ROBERT B. JACKSON

pretty angry as a youngster. I admire the smooth, seemingly effortless communication that authors sweat blood to achieve. Gene Olsen, Asimov, and Dr. Seuss are some of my favorite writers for children.

"Each time I sit down at the typewriter, I find it to be an exasperating, humbling, yet uniquely satisfying process. It involves many drafts, much staring out of the window and worrying. I am never completely satisfied with a draft, even the final one, but I get as close to absolute clarity and smoothness as I practically can. However, I'm always spotting possible improvements, even in published things. Two things from my childhood reading strongly influenced my writing today: the importance of action; the need to explain some factors which adults take for granted, but which children question."

"As a librarian, I look back now on the books I read as a child with some dismay. I'm ashamed to admit to a terrible hang-up on the Tom Swift series; also waded through (how?) all of the Horatio Alger atrocities; and contrary to children's librarians' opinions, I was fascinated by the 'Oz' series. My reading tastes have changed and now I read both British and American contemporary literature, along with all that automotive stuff—technical, racing and historical."

JAMES, T. F.
See FLEMING, Thomas J(ames)

JANOSCH
See ECKERT, Horst

JENSEN, Virginia Allen 1927-

PERSONAL: Born September 21, 1927, in Des Moines, Iowa; daughter of Byron Gilchrist and Elsa (Erickson) Allen; married Flemming Jakob Jensen (a management consultant), March 21, 1953; children: Merete, Annette, Kirsten. *Education:* Bennington College, B.A., 1950; University of Minnesota, graduate study. *Home:* Kildeskovsvej 21, DK-2820 Gentofte, Denmark. *Office:* International Children's Book Service, Kildeskovsvej 21, DK-2820 Gentofte, Denmark.

CAREER: International Children's Book Service, Gentofte, Denmark, director, 1960—. Member of board of directors of Danish section of International Board on Books for Young People. *Member:* Danish Authors' Union. *Awards, honors:* Honorable mention from Finnish Authors' Union, 1971, for *Lars Peter's Bicycle*; Nordic Cultural Fund grant, 1973 and 1974, for the promotion of Nordic children's literature; *The Nisse from Timsgaard*, runner-up for the Margaret Batchelder Award, 1974; research grant from the Danish Ministry of Cultural Affairs, 1975.

WRITINGS—Juvenile: *Lars Peter's Birthday*, Abingdon, 1959; *Hop Hans*, Gyldendal, 1966; *Lars Peters cykel*, Gyldendal, 1968, published in England as *Lars Peter's Bicycle*, Angus & Robertson, 1970; *Sara and the Door*, Hodder & Stoughton, 1975.

VIRGINIA ALLEN JENSEN

Translator from the Danish: Ib Spang Olsen, *The Marsh Crone's Brew*, Abingdon, 1960; Thea Bank Jensen, *Play with Paper*, Macmillan, 1962; Olsen, *The Boy in the Moon*, Abingdon, 1963; Susanne Palsbo, *Droll, Danish, and Delicious*, Hoest & Sons, 1966; Thoeger Birkeland, *When the Cock Crows*, Coward, 1968, published in England as *The Wastelanders*, Angus & Robertson, 1972; Birkeland, *The Lemonade Murder*, Coward, 1971; Olsen, *Where is Martin?*, Angus & Robertson, 1969, published in America as *Cat Alley*, Coward, 1971; Olsen, *Smoke*, Coward, 1972; Wilhelm Bergsoee, *The Nisse from Timsgaard*, Coward, 1972; Olsen, *The Little Locomotive*, Coward, 1975; Birkeland, *The Lemonade Murder*, Angus & Robertson, 1975; Birkeland, *The New Boy*, Angus & Robertson, in press.

HOBBIES AND OTHER INTERESTS: Theater, dance, puppets, music, bicycling, hiking, swimming, cooking.

JOHNSON, Eric W(arner) 1918-

PERSONAL: Born March 22, 1918, in Philadelphia, Pa.; son of Walter James (interior decorator) and Edith (Warner) Johnson; married Gay Gilpin, November 26, 1949; children: Rebecca Warner, Jeffrey Gilpin, Emily Cooper. *Education:* Harvard University, A.B., 1940, M.A., 1941. *Religion:* Society of Friends. *Home:* 6110 Ardleigh St., Philadelphia, Pa. 19138. *Office:* Germantown Friends School, Philadelphia, Pa. 19144.

CAREER: American Friends Service Committee, Philadelphia, Pa., relief and refugee worker in Portugal, Morocco, Algeria, Egypt, and India, 1942-44, head of Far Eastern Work, 1944-46, Quaker international affairs representative, 1952-54, director, voluntary international service assignments, 1961-62; Friends' Central School, Philadelphia, Pa., headmaster, 1948-52; Germantown Friends School, Philadelphia, Pa., head of junior high school, 1954-61, vice-principal, 1962-71, teacher of English and sex education, 1971-74, teacher of sex education, 1974—; consultant to schools, 1974—. *Member:* National Council of Teachers of English (former director, member, committee on English in junior high school), Society for the Scientific Study of Sex.

WRITINGS: Improve Your Own Spelling, McGraw, 1956, 3rd edition, 1962; *How to Live Through Junior High School*, Lippincott, 1959, revised edition, 1975; (with Frank Jennings) *Four Famous Adventures*, Harcourt, 1962; *Love and Sex in Plain Language*, Lippincott, 1965, 2nd revised edition, Bantam, 1974; (with Mildred Dawson and others) *Language for Daily Use* (grades 1-8), Harcourt, 1965; (with E. M. Pumphrey) *Adventures For You*, 2nd edition, Harcourt, 1968; (with Corinne Johnson) *Love and Sex and Growing Up*, Lippincott, 1970; *Sex: Telling it Straight*, Lippincott, 1970; *The Stolen Ruler*, Lippincott, 1970; *Escape into the Zoo*, Lippincott, 1971; *V.D.*, Lippincott, 1973, Bantam, 1974; *How to Do English: A Handbook*, Bantam, 1975; *Life into Language*, Bantam, 1975. Occasional contributor to magazines.

SIDELIGHTS: "I got started writing books when I was a seventh-grade English teacher. I found there was no practical book to help kids learn to spell on their own, so I devised a method, tried it out in classes over a couple of years and then put it into the book *Improve Your Own Spelling*. Next, as principal of the junior high school at Germantown Friends School, I found that parents kept coming to me and other teachers asking the same sorts of questions over and over, questions about the school life, the home life, the social and sexual lives of their kids, and it seemed to me that a book trying to answer some of these questions, and giving some background about adolescence would be useful. So during summer vacation in New Hampshire in 1958 I wrote *How to Live through Junior High School*.

"While I was writing *HTLTJHS*, I looked around for a good, plain, non-moralizing book on love and sex and growing up, and I couldn't find one that I thought met the need. Therefore, after a lot of consulting with experts, I wrote *Love and Sex in Plain Language* for the sort of students I teach. This was followed by *Love and Sex and Growing Up*, for fourth-through-sixth graders and written with my sister-in-law.

"The two books I most enjoyed writing were story books for children aged five-through-nine, *The Stolen Ruler* and *Escape into the Zoo*. The first was based on an experience that happened to a student of mine, Claude, when he was in first grade. His teacher accused him of stealing his *own* ruler and hit him on the hand with it. I turned this into a sort of home-and-school-detective story where Claude and his friend Otis sleuth out who did steal the ruler. This was followed by a sequel when Fred, Claude's very independent cat, escaped *into* a zoo, ended up cowering in the cage of a tiger, and had to be rescued.

"I do my writing on days off from school (for several years I have taken Tuesdays off) in an 8 x 10 study I built for myself in the woods, 220 feet behind our house. I can make all the mess I want there and don't have to straighten it up, and my wife, if she needs me, calls me in by turning off the lights by means of a switch in the cellar of our house."

Claude saw that under the notebook, now no longer hidden, was a ruler—his ruler. ■ (From *The Stolen Ruler* by Eric W. Johnson. Illustrated by June Goldsborough.)

ERIC W. JOHNSON

93

That afternoon the snow came down thicker. It drifted up against the houses. It piled up on the roofs. It covered the trees and bushes in lovely white. ■ (From *Mole and Troll Trim the Tree* by Tony Johnston. Illustrated by Wallace Tripp.)

JOHNSTON, Tony 1942-

PERSONAL: Born January 30, 1942, in Los Angeles, Calif.; daughter of David L. (a golf professional) and Ruth (Hunter) Taylor; married Roger Johnston (a banker), June 25, 1966; children: Jennifer, Samantha. *Education:* Attended University of California, Berkeley, 1959-60; Stanford University, B.A., 1963, M.Ed., 1964. *Home:* 75A Willow, Brooklyn Heights, N.Y.

CAREER: Teacher in the public elementary schools, Pasadena, Calif., 1964-66; McGraw-Hill Publishing Co., New York, N.Y., editing supervisor, 1966-68; Harper & Row Publishers, Inc., New York, N.Y., copy editor (and miscellaneous related jobs) of children's books, 1969.

WRITINGS: The Adventures of Mole and Troll, Putnam, 1972; *Fig Tale*, Putnam, 1974; *Mole and Troll Trim the Tree*, Putnam, 1974.

HOBBIES AND OTHER INTERESTS: Cooking, tennis, archaeology.

KELLER, Charles 1942-

PERSONAL: Born March 30, 1942. *Home:* 162 19th St., Union City, N.J. 07087.

WRITINGS: Ballpoint Bananas, Prentice-Hall, 1972; *Too Funny for Words*, Prentice-Hall, 1973; *Laugh Lines*,

CHARLES KELLER

94

What is red, white and blue and yellow all over?

The Star Spangled Banana.

(From *The Star-Spangled Banana* by Charles Keller and Richard Baker. Illustrated by Tomie de Paola.)

Prentice-Hall, 1973; *Going Bananas*, Prentice-Hall, 1974; *Star Spangled Bananas*, Prentice-Hall, 1974; *Punch Lines*, Prentice-Hall, 1975.

WORK IN PROGRESS: Anthology of American humor.

KELLER, Gail Faithfull
See FAITHFULL, Gail

KELLOGG, Steven 1941-

PERSONAL: Born October 26, 1941, in Norwalk, Conn.; son of Robert E. and Hilma Marie (Johnson) Kellogg; married Helen Hill, 1967; stepchildren: Pamela, Melanie, Kimberly, Laurie, Kevin, Colin. *Education:* Rhode Island School of Design, B.F.A., 1963 (spent senior year in Italy on honors fellowship); American University, graduate study, 1965. *Home:* Bennett's Bridge Rd., Sandy Hook, Conn. 06482. *Agent:* Sheldon Fogelman, 10 East 40th St., New York, N.Y. 10016.

CAREER: Artist, and author and illustrator of children's books. Instructor in etching at American University, 1966;

also has taught printmaking and painting. Paints and etchings have been exhibited. *Awards, honors: Matilda Who Told Lies and Was Burned to Death*, which he illustrated, was chosen as one of ten best picture books of 1970 by *New York Times* and received Brooklyn Museum ABC Award; *Can I Keep Him?* was awarded Dutch Zilveren Griffel ("best picture book in Dutch), 1974, and named one of best books of the year by *School Library Journal*; *There Was an Old Woman* was chosen as one of the "ten best picture books" by the *New York Times*, 1974; *The Mystery of the Missing Red Mitten* was a Children's Book Showcase Title, 1974.

STEVEN KELLOGG

WRITINGS—Self-illustrated: *The Wicked Kings of Bloon* (Junior Literary Guild selection), Prentice-Hall, 1970; *Can I Keep Him?* (Junior Literary Guild selection), Dial, 1971; *The Mystery Beast of Ostergeest*, Dial, 1971; *The Orchard Cat*, Dial, 1972; *Won't Somebody Play With Me?*, Dial, 1972; *The Island of the Skog*, Dial, 1973; (reteller) *There Was an Old Woman*, Parents' Magazine Press, 1974; *The Mystery of the Missing Red Mitten*, Dial, 1974.

Illustrator: George Mendoza, *GWOT!*, Harper, 1967; Jim Copp, *Martha Matilda O'Toole*, Bradbury, 1968; Mary Rodgers, *The Rotten Book*, Harper, 1969; Eleanor B. Heady, *Brave Johnny O'Hare*, Parents' Magazine Press, 1969; Miriam Young, *Can't You Pretend?*, Putnam, 1970; Ruth Loomis, *Mrs. Purdy's Children*, Dial, 1970; Fred Rogers, *Mister Rogers Songbook*, Random House, 1970; Hillaire Belloc, *Matilda Who Told Lies and Was Burned to Death*, Dial, 1970; Peggy Parish, *Granny and the Desperadoes*, Macmillan, 1970; Jan Wahl, *Crabapple Night*, Holt, 1971; Ann Mallett, *Here Comes Tagalong*, Parents' Magazine Press, 1971; Aileen Friedman, *The Castles of the Two Brothers*, Holt, 1972; Jan Wahl, *The Very Peculiar Tunnel*, Putnam, 1972; Joan L. Nodset, *Here Comes Cat*, Harper, 1973; Jeanette Caines, *Abby*, Harper, 1973; Doris H. Lund, *You Ought to See Herbert's House*, Watts, 1973; Cora Annett, *How the Witch Got Alf*, Watts, 1975; Hillaire Belloc, *The Yak, the Python, and the Frog* (Junior Literary Guild selection), Parents' Magazine Press, 1975; Alice

(From *The Island of the Skog* by Steven Kellogg. Illustrated by the author.)

During the first few days of the voyage the mice feasted on chocolate waffles and coconut cherry cheese pie. Between meals they dreamed of their island and tanned their pelts in the sun.

Something about the Author

Bach, *The Smartest Bear and His Brother Oliver*, Harper, 1975; Margaret Mahy, *The Boy Who Was Followed Home*, Watts, in press. Contributor to *Family Circle*.

WORK IN PROGRESS: Writing and illustrating *Best Friends*, for Dial.

SIDELIGHTS: "I have always wanted to write and illustrate picture books, and, the more deeply involved in it I become, the more I find it to be an endlessly broad and fascinating art form. I enjoy illustrating my own books, and I love the challenge of devising the right visual accompaniment for the manuscripts of other authors.

"My books are intended for all who enjoy picture books, and yet I realize that children are distinct individuals, and a book that will be meaningful and special to one child will perhaps not interest another. I think it is important that there be a wide range of picture books available so that this individuality is encouraged.

"In regard to techniques, I employ a variety of materials and variations in style in an effort to bring the unique characteristics of each picture book to the point of highest intensity."

FOR MORE INFORMATION SEE: Junior Literary Guild Catalogue, March, 1971.

KEY, Alexander (Hill) 1904-

PERSONAL: Born September 21, 1904, in La Plata, Md.; son of Alexander Hill (cotton dealer) and Charlotte (Ryder) Key; married Alice Towle, December 21, 1945; children: Zan. *Education:* Attended Chicago Art Institute, 1921-23. *Religion:* "Freethinker." *Home:* Wayah Valley Road, Franklin, N.C. *Agent:* McIntosh and Otis, Inc., 18 East 41st St., New York, N.Y. 10017.

CAREER: Painter, illustrator, free-lance writer. Began as book illustrator in Chicago, illustrating first book at 19, while still a student. Later taught art in Chicago at Studio School of Art. Began writing juvenile books and stories in 1929; then adult fiction and magazine article writing followed. *Military service:* U.S. Navy, 1942-45, became lieutenant commander. *Awards, honors:* American Association of University Women Award for *The Forgotten Door*, 1965; Lewis Carroll Shelf Award, 1972, for *The Forgotten Door*.

ALEXANDER KEY

WRITINGS—Juveniles: *Red Eagle*, Volland, 1930; *Liberty or Death*, Harper, 1931; *Caroliny Trail* (Junior Literary Guild selection), Holt, 1941; *Cherokee Boy*, Westminster, 1957; *Sprockets*, Westminster, 1963; *Rivets and Sprockets*, Westminster, 1964; *The Forgotten Door*, Westminster, 1965; *Bolts, a Robot Dog*, Westminster, 1966; *Mystery of the Sassafras Chair*, Westminster, 1967; *Escape to Witch Mountain*, Westminster, 1968; *The Golden Enemy* (Junior Literary Guild selection), Westminster, 1969; *The Incredible Tide*, Westminster, 1970; *Flight to the Lonesome Place*, Westminster, 1971; *The Strange White Doves*, Westminster, 1972; *The Preposterous Adventures of Swimmer*, Westminster, 1973; *The Magic Meadow*, Westminster, 1975.

Adult novels: *The Wrath and the Wind*, Bobbs, 1949; *Island Light*, Bobbs, 1950. Contributor to *Saturday Evening Post, Argosy, Elks, Cosmopolitan, American Mercury*, and others.

Illustrator: Rannie B. Baker, *In the Light of Myth*, Row, Peterson, 1925; O. M. Fuller, *The Book of Dragons*, McBride, 1931; Jeannette C. Nolan, *The Young Douglas*, McBride, 1934; Cecile Hulse Matschet, *Suwannee River*, Farrar, Straus, 1938; Cecile Hulse Matschet, *Ladd of the Big Swamp*, Winston, 1954; Thomas Helm, *Monsters of the Deep*, Dodd, 1962; J. M. Lyback, *Indian Legends*, Lyons, 1963.

SIDELIGHTS: "I've always called my Maryland birth a bio-geographical accident, for I'm almost a native Floridian. I say almost, for at this point I can hardly call any state my own. The first Keys settled in Virginia, circa 1670—the old place in Sussex County is still standing—but about a century-and-a-half ago thirteen members of the family died of yellow fever in thirteen days, so the three remaining members fled over the mountains to Muscle Shoals and were doing very nicely until that rascally Sherman came along, followed by the carpetbaggers. So the tattered Keys fled once more, this time to a log cabin in Florida.

"Anyway, after the Maryland incident, my first six years were spent on the Suwannee River, where my father had one of the first sawmills and cotton gins in the region—both burned by 'night-riders' just before his death. Night-riders were bands of plundering rascals who killed and burned if they didn't like someone's politics or economics. (The Suwannee was really wild in those days, and I could write a book about it.) My mother was killed in an accident soon after, and I spent an erratic youth with various relatives, attending no less than fourteen schools until, at seventeen, I took something or other by the horns and headed for Chicago to study at the Chicago Art Institute.

"A bank failure put me out on the street at nineteen, trying to make art pay. It did, in the nick of time, but only after I'd grown a mustache and put on a pair of horn-rimmed glasses to make me look older, and attired myself in a borrowed suit to give the impression of prosperity. I owed three months rent and was downright hungry the day I sold my first drawing to a publisher.

"In those days I often wished Chicago would slide over into the lake and vanish, but it was sixteen years before I could acquire a battered Ford and means enough to leave

Suppose I really did have to float for a hundred years! I'd be just plain cuckoo. ∎ (From *Rivets and Sprockets* by Alexander Key. Illustrated by the author.)

it. The Depression had come and I was practically forced into writing as the only means of getting drawing commissions. I wrote and/or illustrated for most of the juvenile magazines, illustrated scores of school books and began writing reams of blood-and-thunder for the pulp magazines. It was a check from *Cosmopolitan* that finally took me away from Illinois and down to the Gulf Coast.

"There, I was presently the owner of a curious old home and a curious old sloop, and spent some interesting years writing sea stories for the *Post* and other periodicals. Then the world blew up and I suddenly found myself in the Navy.

"When World War II was over I returned to my old love, the Gulf Coast. But the magic was gone, and fast-growing Florida was finally too much for me. After three novels and some gallons of drawing ink, the Keys took a scouting trip, with the result that the following spring saw them in a remote corner of the Smoky Mountains, building a new studio home. We have been here ever since.

"In between books I have been painting for a long time, and my pictures hang in many private collections. In both painting and writing I try to awaken in people a response to the greater world that exists beyond paving. The world we've created is a pretty sad one, and our only hope of making it better is through the young. Their minds are still open. Anyway, I long ago reached the point where I feel that the young are the only ones worth writing for."

Escape to Witch Mountain was filmed by Buena Vista (Disney), 1975.

FOR MORE INFORMATION SEE: Helen Ferris, *Writing Books for Boys and Girls*, Doubleday, 1952; *Horn Book*, April, 1974.

KING, Reefe
See BARKER, Albert W.

KLEIN, H. Arthur

PERSONAL: Married Mina C. Klein (an author and editor); children: Laura, David. *Education:* Stanford University, A.B.; Occidental College, M.A.; postgraduate study at Columbia University, University of California, Los Angeles, and European universities. *Religion:* Jewish. *Mailing address:* P.O. Box 3, Malibu, Calif. 90265.

CAREER: Writer (has done newspaper work, publicity, copywriting, feature writing). *Member:* Authors League of America, National Association of Science Writers, U.S. Surfing Association, American Civil Liberties Union, Phi Beta Kappa, Malibu Township Council.

WRITINGS: (Translator with wife, Mina C. Klein, and others, and editor and annotator) *Hypocritical Helena, Plus a Plenty of Other Pleasures* (verses based on picture-stories of German artist-satirist, Wilhelm Busch), Dover, 1962; (translator with wife and others, and editor and annotator) *Max and Moritz, With Many More Mischief-Makers* (verses from Wilhelm Busch), Dover, 1962; *Graphic Worlds of Peter Bruegel the Elder*, Dover, 1963; *Masers and Lasers*, Lippincott, 1963; *Bioluminescence*, Lippincott, 1965; *Surfing*, Lippincott, 1965; *Fuel Cells*, Lippincott, 1966; (editor with wife, M. C. Klein) *Surf's Up!*, Bobbs, 1966; (with Mina C. Klein) *Peter Bruegel the Elder: Artist of Abundance*, Macmillan, 1968; (with Mina C. Klein) *Great Structures of the World*, World Publishing, 1968.

Holography, Lippincott, 1970; (with Mina C. Klein) *Temple Beyond Time: The Story of the Site of Solomon's Temple at Jerusalem*, Van Nostrand, 1970; *The New Gravitation: Key to Incredible Energies*, Lippincott, 1971; (with Mina C. Klein) *Israel: Land of the Jews*, Bobbs, 1972; (with Mina C. Klein) *Käthe Kollwitz: Life in Art*, Holt, 1972; *Oceans and Continents in Motion: An Introduction to Continental Drift and Global Tectonics*, Lippincott, 1972; (with Don James) *Surf-riding*, Lippincott, 1972; (with Mina C. Klein) *The Kremlin: Citadel of History*, Macmillan, 1973; *The World of Measurements: Masterpieces, Mysteries, and Muddles of Metrology*, Simon & Schuster, 1974; (editor and translator with Mina C. Klein) B. Traven, *The Kidnapped Saint and Other Stories*, L. Hill & Co., in press; (with Mina C. Klein) *Hitler's Hang-Ups*, Dutton, in press. Also, writer and producer of soundfilm, "Bruegel's Seven Deadly Sins," made from engravings of the same name.

H. ARTHUR KLEIN

SIDELIGHTS: "An intellectual rolling stone, I finally gave up attempting to confine myself to literary or artistic interests on the one hand and scientific curiosities and obsessions on the other. The resulting combination is reflected in the subject matter of some twenty-two published or completed works, written either solo or in collaboration with Mina C. Klein, my best friend and gentlest critic. They include now some seven in more or less straight science, among which is the massive reference/entertainment tome entitled *The World of Measurements* (over 700 fully-packed pages); also a dozen in fine arts, biography, and history; plus several in the areas of aquatic sports—notably, surfing.

"Undoubtedly it is too late for me to concentrate, specialize, or exclude the unusual topics that seem to turn me on, or turn me off from any highroad of predictable preferences.

"I have been much pleased by letters that have arrived, unsolicited and unexpected, from readers of our books—especially the books on Peter Brueghel the Elder and Käthe Kollwitz. Indications of enthusiasm or even perceptive disagreement from chance readers somehow reach out to me more directly than do comments by professional reviewers.

"A special kind of inner excitement has come with the arrival of translations of some of my science books into other langauges—such as the Spanish version of *Masers and Lasers* and the Japanese versions of *The New Gravitation* and *Oceans and Continents in Motion.*

"I cannot honestly urge or encourage others to go in for book writing under present adverse and uncertain conditions. I tell myself also, many a time, that the game isn't worth the candle, and too much is already enough. Yet a few days later I find myself scheming toward another book project. These are inconsistencies that I neither deny nor expect to escape. And however paradoxical, they seem to contribute to making the time fly faster than I'd formerly have deemed possible."

Klein is a collector, with wife, of original graphic works by Käthe Kollwitz. "Deeply interested in poetry of Robinson Jeffers; also of the German poets Berthold Brecht, Christian Morgenstern, Joachim Ringelnatz, and others."

KLEIN, Mina C(ooper)

PERSONAL: Born in England; married H. Arthur Klein (an author); children: Laura, David. *Education:* Attended Schools in Canada, California, New York, and University of Berlin. *Residence:* Malibu, Calif.

CAREER: Author and editor. *Member:* Author's League of America.

WRITINGS—All with husband, H. Arthur Klein: (Translator with others) *Hypocritical Helena, Plus a Plenty of Other Pleasures* (verses based on picture-stories of German artist-satirist, Wilhelm Busch), Dover, 1962; (translator with others) *Max and Moritz, with Many More Mischief-Makers* (verses from Wilhelm Busch), Dover, 1962; (editor) *Surf's Up!: An Anthology of Surfing*, Bobbs-Merrill, 1966; *Peter Bruegel the Elder, Artist of Abundance*, Macmillan, 1968; *Great Structures of the World*, World Publishing, 1968.

As an artist [Käthe Kollwitz] became one of the most effective proponents of peace. Yet she was a native of a part of the world whose history has made it a kind of symbol of incessant warmaking and conquests. ■ (From *Käthe Kollwitz: Life in Art* by Mina C. Klein and H. Arthur Klein.)

MINA C. KLEIN

Temple Beyond Time: The Story of the Site of Solomon's Temple, Van Nostrand, 1970; *Israel, Land of the Jews: A Survey of 43 Centuries*, Bobbs-Merrill, 1972; *Kaethe Kollwitz: Life in Art*, Holt, 1972; *The Kremlin, Citadel of History*, Macmillan, 1973; (editor and translator) B. Traven, *The Kidnapped Saint and Other Stories*, Lawrence Hill & Co., in press; *Hitler's Hang-ups*, Dutton, in press.

SIDELIGHTS: "When not traveling, I have lived and worked with my husband right on the ocean in Malibu for the last seventeen years. We enjoy beach walking, collecting shells, rocks and 'found' things washed up on the sea shore. Our patio beside the sand is filled with a strange collection of sea treasures and 'junk' accumulated on the beach over the years and is the delight of many passing children who love to come and browse.

"We do a great deal of research which I find fascinating. We divide up both the research and the writing of our books, working alone in separate rooms, and then come together to fuse, correct, amalgamate, criticize, discuss and complete the work.

"We have researched much in our travels using many libraries and sources in this and other countries. However, we are fortunate to have available to us only about forty-five minutes drive from Malibu the wonderful U.C.L.A. Research Library and all of the additional libraries of that campus.

"Earlier in life I wrote poetry, later wrote publicity and news stories, but came to writing books after helping my husband edit his science books which he writes solo. Our books are intended not only for the young, but for people of all ages."

KNOWLES, John 1926-

PERSONAL: Born September 16, 1926, in Fairmont, W.Va.; son of James Myron and Mary Beatrice (Shea) Knowles. *Education:* Graduate of Phillips Exeter Academy, 1945; Yale University, B.A., 1949. *Residence:* New York, N.Y.

CAREER: Reporter, *Hartford Courant*, Hartford, Conn., 1950-52; free-lance writer, 1952-56; associate editor, *Holiday*, 1956-60; full-time writer, 1960—. *Awards, honors:* Rosenthal award, National Institute of Arts and Letters, and William Faulkner Foundation award, both 1960, for *A Separate Peace*.

WRITINGS: *A Separate Peace* (novel), Macmillan, 1960; *Morning in Antibes* (novel), Macmillan, 1962; *Double Vision: American Thoughts Abroad*, Macmillan, 1964; *Indian Summer* (novel), Random House, 1966; *Phineas* (short stories), Random House, 1968; *The Paragon* (School Library Journal booklist), Random House, 1972; *Spreading Fires* (novel), 1974.

SIDELIGHTS: "All of my books are based on places, places I know very well and feel very deeply about. I begin with that place and then the characters and the plot emerge from it. *A Separate Peace* began with a playing field at

JOHN KNOWLES

This tree flooded me with a sensation of alarm all the way to my tingling fingers. My head began to feel unnaturally light, and the vague rustling sounds from the nearby woods came to me as though muffled and filtered. I must have been entering a mild state of shock. ▪ (From the movie *A Separate Peace,* copyright © 1972 by Paramount Pictures Corp.)

Exeter Academy, in New Hampshire. *Morning in Antibes* and my new novel, *Spreading Fires*, result from having lived for eight years, off and on, on the French Riviera and coming to love and understand that part of the world very much. My way of increasing my understanding of these places is to set a novel there. *The Paragon* and *Indian Summer* resulted from living in Connecticut for seven years and going to Yale. In my new and as yet untitled novel I at last write about the place where I grew up, West Virginia.

"I do not write with any audience in mind, and I am delighted that I have found one. Now I live in the beautiful eastern end of Long Island, and when I get to know it very much better (I already love it) I will probably set a novel here, too."

The Times Literary Supplement called *A Separate Peace* "a novel of altogether exceptional power and distinction." *The Manchester Guardian* noted that Knowles "draws with tenderness and restraint the pure joy of affection between the boys, their laconic, conscientiously fantastic language, and the extra tension of the summer—1942—when they see their youth curtailed by war."

A Separate Peace was filmed in 1972 by Paramount Pictures.

FOR MORE INFORMATION SEE: Manchester Guardian, May 1, 1959; *Times Literary Supplement*, May 1, 1959; *New Statesman*, May 2, 1959; *New York Times Book Review*, February 7, 1960, August 14, 1966; *Commonweal*, December 9, 1960; *Harper's*, July, 1966; *Book Week*, July 24, 1966; *Life*, August 5, 1966; *Saturday Review*, August 13, 1966.

KOUTS, Anne 1945-

PERSONAL: Surname rhymes with *shouts*; born July 3, 1945, in Washington, D.C.; daughter of Herbert (a physicist) and Hertha (a writer; maiden name Pretorius) Kouts.

ANNE KOUTS

"Can I have—a white rat? Please?" ■ From *Kenny's Rat* by Anne Kouts. Illustrated by Betty Fraser.)

Education: Antioch College, B.A., 1967. *Politics:* "Moderately left-wing." *Religion:* "None." *Home:* 100 East Mosholu Parkway South, Bronx, N.Y. 10458. *Office:* Harper & Row, Publishers, Inc., 156 East 52nd St., New York, N.Y. 10022.

CAREER: Viking Press, Inc., New York, N.Y., began as secretary, became copy editor for Viking Junior Books, 1967-70; Harper & Row, Publishers, Inc., New York, N.Y., editorial assistant for Harper Junior Books, 1971-73, copy editor, 1973-74; District 65, Publishing division, New York, N.Y., organizer for trade union, 1974—. *Member:* SANE (National Committee for a Sane Nuclear Policy), American Museum of Natural History, Common Cause, American Civil Liberties Union, National Organization for Women, New York Zoological Society, Coalition of Labor Union Women.

WRITINGS: Kenny's Rat (juvenile), Viking, 1970.

WORK IN PROGRESS: Several children's books.

SIDELIGHTS: "I'm fascinated by people; love all animals; most respectful of children.

HOBBIES AND OTHER INTERESTS: Anthropology, sociology, psychology, child development, art, Far Eastern cultures, biology, typography, layout and design, wilderness (backpacking), humor and house plants; major interests now: labor law, and organizing book publishing with a trade union.

JANE KRISTOF

KRISTOF, Jane 1932-

PERSONAL: Born May 25, 1932, in Chicago, Ill.; daughter of Donald Saxon (a lawyer) and Mary (Shakespeare) McWilliams; married Ladis K. D. Kristof (a professor of political science), December 29, 1956; children: Nicholas. *Education:* University of Chicago, B.A., 1950, M.A., 1956; graduate study at University of Edinburgh, 1951-52, and Columbia University, 1962-64, Ph.D., 1972. *Politics:* "Ardent Democrat." *Religion:* Presbyterian. *Home:* Rte. 2, Box 430, Gaston, Ore. 97119. *Office:* Department of Art and Architecture, Portland State University, Portland, Ore.

CAREER: Chicago City Junior College, Amundsen-Mayfair Branch, Chicago, Ill., lecturer in art history, 1957-59; University of Waterloo, Waterloo, Ontario, lecturer in art history, 1970-71; Mt. Hood Community College, Portland, Oregon, lecturer in art history, 1972-73; Portland State University, Portland, Ore., lecturer in art history, 1973—.

WRITINGS: Steal Away Home (juvenile), Bobbs, 1969.

SIDELIGHTS: "Some years ago I worked with a tutoring project for children with reading problems, many of whom were black. I looked for a good adventure story based on black history for them and, rather to my surprise, had difficulty finding one. For a couple of years I asked myself 'Why doesn't somebody write an escape story about the Underground Railroad?' Then gradually the question became 'Why don't I?' Finally one day I sat down with a pencil and notebook and started the first chapter without knowing how the story would continue. Characters and plot just seemed to take shape as I went along. Never having written anything before, however, I didn't have much confidence and kept my project a complete secret, even from my husband and son, until the story was accepted.

"I hope to write a sequel to *Steal Away Home* sometime, but as I am a part-time teacher and part-time farmer, as well as a part-time housewife, I don't have much time and don't know when I will get around to it."

FOR MORE INFORMATION SEE: New York Times Book Review, November 9, 1969.

KRÜSS, James 1926-
(Markus Polder)

PERSONAL: Born May 31, 1926, on Helgoland (German-owned island in North Sea); son of Ludwig and Margareta (Friedrichs) Krüss; unmarried. *Education:* Pedagogical High School (teacher training), Luneburg, Germany, graduate, 1948. *Home:* Casa Montaneta, La Calzada, Las Palmas de Grand Canary, Spain. *Agent:* Hein Kohn, Koninginneweg 2A, Hilversum, Netherlands.

CAREER: Started to write for radio and the theater in 1950 while living in Munich, Germany; author, principally of children's books, 1953—. *Military service:* German Luftwaffe (Air Force), 1944-45. *Member:* P.E.N., Deutscher Schriftstellerverband. *Awards, honors:* Deutscher Jugenbuchpreis (German juvenile book award), for *My Great Grandfather and I*, 1960, and *Three by Three*, 1964; Hans

104

Christian Andersen International Children's Book Medal, 1968; *Letters to Pauline* was nominated for Mildred Batchelder Award of American Library Association, 1973, *My Great Grandfather, the Heroes, and I*, 1975.

WRITINGS—More than seventy books in German, with the following titles in English: *Henrietta Chuffertrain* (verses), translation by Marion Koenig, World's Work, 1960, published in America as *Henritte Bimmelbahn*, adaptation by Virginia Shepley and Mary Pat Mullaney, Milliken Publishing, 1966; *My Great-Grandfather and I: Useful and Amusing Occurences and Inspirations from the Lobster Shack on Helgoland*, translation by Edelgard von H. Bruehl, Atheneum, 1964; *The Talking Machine: An Extraordinary Story*, told in English by Oliver Coburn, Universe Books, 1965; *3 x 3: Three by Three*, told in English by Geoffrey Strachan, Macmillan, 1965; *Eagle and Dove*, translation by Edelgard von H. Bruehl, Atheneum, 1965.

Busy, Busy Bettina, adaptation by Mary Pat Mullaney, Milliken Publishing, 1966; *The Jolly Trolley Ride*, adaptation by Mary Pat Mullaney, Milliken Publishing, 1966; *The Blue Bus*, adaptation by Mary Pat Mullaney, Milliken Publishing, 1966; *Seven Frogs Go Travelling*, adaptation by Kerry Quinn, Milliken Publishing, 1966; *Pauline and the Prince in the Wind*, translation by Eldegard von H. Bruehl, Atheneum, 1966; *Ladislaus and Annabella*, adaptation by Nicolete Meredith Stack, Milliken Publishing, 1966; *Rudy*

JAMES KRÜSS

My lower-grandmother lived in a big yellow house with three tremendous chestnut trees in front. She was much more fun than the upper-grandmother. She also had a St. Bernard dog by the name of Urax. ■ (From *My Great-Grandfather and I* by James Krüss. Illustrated by Jochen Bartsch.)

Biplane, the Golden Eagle, adaptation by Nicolete Meredith Stack, Milliken Publishing, 1966 (published in England as *The Little Biplane*, Wheaton & Co., 1969); *The Happy Islands Behind the Winds*, translation by Edelgard von H. Bruehl, Atheneum, 1966; *Florentine*, translation by Marion Koenig, Chatto & Windus, 1967; *Return to the Happy Islands*, translation by Edelgard von H. Bruehl, Atheneum, 1967; *Sally's Red Sash*, Wheaton & Co., 1967; *A Holiday with Henriette*, Wheaton & Co., 1967; *Florentine on Holiday*, translation by Marion Koenig, Chatto & Windus, 1967; *The Animal Parade* (verses), translation by Margaret Fishback, Platt, 1968; *The Lighthouse on the Lobster Cliffs*, translation by Edelgard von H. Bruehl, Atheneum, 1969; (with Eva Johanna Rubin) *The Proud Wooden Drummer*, translation by Jack Prelutsky, Doubleday, 1969; *Said the Hen to the Chick* (verses), translation by Michael C. Kitton, Wheaton & Co., 1969.

Our Favorite Things, adaptation by Rowen Carr, Platt, 1970; *The Zoo That Grew*, adaptation by Sarah Keyser, Platt, 1970; *Coming Home from the War: An Idyll* (autobiographical), translation by Edelgard von H. Bruehl, Doubleday, 1970; *Letters to Pauline*, translation by Edelgard von H. Bruehl, Atheneum, 1971; *The Tailor and the Giant*, adaptation by Valerie Cleve, Platt, 1972; *My Great-Grandfather, the Heroes, and I*, translated by Edelgard von H. Bruehl, Atheneum, 1973; *Winnebago Trickster Cycle*, Octinger Verlag, 1975.

In addition to poems and plays, his publications include articles about linguistic problems.

WORK IN PROGRESS: Tohu Wa-Bohu: Or, the Symbolic Ape, on the genesis of human symbolic systems.

KURELEK, William 1927-

PERSONAL: Surname is pronounced "coo-reh-lehk"; born March 3, 1927; son of Metro and Mary (Huculak) Kurelek; married Jean Andrews, October 8, 1962; children: Catherine, Stephen, Barbara, Thomas. Education: University of Manitoba, B.A., 1949. Religion: Roman Catholic. Home and office: 175 Balsam Ave., Toronto, Ontario M4E 3C2, Canada.

CAREER: Picture framer in Toronto, Ontario, 1959-71; artist in Toronto, Ontario, 1960—. Member: Royal Canadian Academy of Art.

WILLIAM KURELEK

WRITINGS: A Prairie Boy's Winter (self-illustrated), Tundra Books, 1973; O Toronto (self-illustrated), New Press, 1973; Some One With Me (autobiography), Cornell University Press, 1973; The Lumberjack (self-illustrated), Houghton, 1974; A Prairie Boy's Summer (self-illustrated), Houghton Mifflin, 1975; The Passion According to St. Matthew, in press.

WORK IN PROGRESS: Kurelek's Canada.

SIDELIGHTS: William Kurelek is one of the few Canadian artists to paint landscapes and depict historical events in a realistic manner. He is known for the scenes of his pioneer childhood in a Ukrainian farming community in Alberta, and these paintings were included in a film on Kurelek produced by the National Film Board.

In May 1968 William Kurelek spent a period of time as a guest of Terry Ryan, director of the Eskimo Co-operative on Baffin Island, and Justice of the Peace in the Northwest Territories. During that visit, Kurelek recorded his impressions of the Arctic and some of its legends in a series of paintings and also in a diary addressed to his wife Jean. The following excerpts are taken from this dairy:

"May 8, 8 a.m. We saw a moonlit night as we skimmed along the surface of an ocean-like bank of clouds, but at three in the morning, day began to break and below was a wild wilderness broken by ripples of black rock. Emerging from the plane I saw Terry was right—even this early in the morning the only chillness I felt was on my bare legs under my trousers. There certainly was no vicious nip that I recall of prairie winters. The landscape looked almost identical to the denuded area round Sudbury I love to paint (but under snow). What was my surprise on looking out the airport building? I saw all the signs of civilization—a power station on a hillside, a fair sized hospital, a church, telephone and electric powerlines, cars and trucks and taxis, radio station, and so forth.

"11:00 p.m. A long, tiring but eventful day—I proceeded to commence painting while Terry made about 50 phone calls arranging a chartered flight to Dorset. I chose the panoramic scene out the window with an overcast sky and snow flurries. Brian built his house isolated so he'd have peace and quiet—so what happens? The most convenient trail for Ski-Doos fell right back of his house and every once in a while as I work, a hunter or mountie would slide past with a curious glance through the wall window, at me working. So I put them in the picture. The only bright spot of colour in a deliberately restricted palette—naples yellow, black and white. Absolutely no trees but a few blades of yellowed grass showing here and there . . . .

"The inside of the plane reminded me too of the Mexican country buses—all kinds of rough and ready, with seats among the cargo, but of course, no live chickens and goats. The flight took its time it seemed, and I dozed off several times. It was beautifully clear and cold when we made a bumpy ski landing on the frozen bay and found the plane and ourselves surrounded by a large crowd of Eskimos, all ages, with a few whites among them . . . .

"I put on a heavy sheep skin coat and stretched two panels outside the back of the house. The first problem was painting the sun. It's hard to paint the sun, specially here, because if you look at it you get blinded and then when you

At breakfast the table was heaped with plates of flapjacks, mountains of them, big bowls of porridge and tin dishes of fried baloney, bacon, potatoes, beans and stacks of camp-baked bread. ■ (From *Lumberjack* by William Kurelek. Illustrated by the author.)

return your eyes to the painting, there is this dark after-image of the sun dancing around on the board exactly wherever you put your brush down to paint. The glare is so strong, all the landscape—sky, as well as snowhills—are a blinding white and if I look through sun glasses the elements regain their distinction but then the color values are knocked askew. Anyway, I kept slogging as I said with pale blues, whites, and touches of amber, ending up with an overall bomb-sprayed white in the sky. A black raven flying by added a vital touch of interest and below the mountain a Bombardier Tractor truck which I caught as it rolled down the trail . . . .

"Rendering ice is really tricky I discovered because its crystalline structure has so many hues and facets—like a diamond which you turn. But I worked and worked at it . . . until its form began to emerge strong with the help of spatter, wash, scrape, pencil and brush lines. I just managed to complete it by dinnertime, and could relax at last, as I enjoyed the wine and juicy steak.

"May 9. After the hours nap I set off with 2 panels under my arm down to the village (Terry's house is on a hill overlooking Dorset) and sketched in two scenes across the bay, although in between panels I had to flee indoors to the Bay stores to warm my hands for which I'd neglected to take gloves. One panel has a string of husky dogs in the foreground. No sooner had I started down Terry's hill when I became aware of a ruckus in the village which sounded like the damned trapped in hell. A oo-oo-oo-oo-oooo arf arf arf. It was those two strings of dogs chained down, each separately, so they wouldn't fight or get entangled. A young man in the store told me they have to be tied down or they may attack and devour one of the small children. When I squatted down near them to draw, the clamourous wailing and barking increased in volume as if they hoped I'd pity them and cut them loose.

"Back at the house I worked hard on the smaller square panel showing a round-shouldered mountain and bay with a pile of red gasoline drums in the foreground which I just managed to finish after supper before Terry took me to the weekly Eskimo movie. I couldn't miss such a chance to observe an Eskimo community gathering. We walked over and I kept thinking the hall seems on the edge of town but Terry took me over the brow of the hill it sat on and there was the other half of Cape Dorset in another ravine. Terry greeted all his acquaintances, mostly children, in Eskimo language. The hall was long and low. Eskimo families were gathering, the movie would be projected on the back wall which was a dirty off-white. Terry says the distributor keeps sending left-over films to the Eskimos, 20 or 30 years old and they were a series of short slapstick comedies and cowboy films (which these people relish). They started off by running the Kurelek film through. It was a real peculiar feeling. Here was my father's life story being told to primitive people in the far north who'd never seen a tree or a field of grain or heard a Ukrainian folk song. Something about this crowd however reminded me of our Ukrainian gatherings—I believe it's their concerts. Yes, that's it! The children running round at intermission, coke bottles rolling round under the seats, a kind of family affair. I could have spent hours studying the Eskimo types which also much reminded me of Mexico:—boys wrestling and whistling, babies on mothers' backs, either sleeping or feeding themselves from a bottle.

"May 11. Put in a good long day of painting. This is my earthly happiness—my work and good music together. Right now 'Zorba the Greek' themes are on. The devil has the best tunes they say. The first painting literally flew in while we were finishing breakfast; a small plane took advantage of a freak in the snow storm to land on the bay. Terry called me to look and there again was that scene below us like on a map: little figures silhouetted against the white snow scurrying toward the plane as it taxied in. The Bombardier, several ski-doos and even a Honda joining in to present a welcoming party. So I sat down and painted that. It looks skimpy, just a whole lot of little dots in an expanse of white but I guess the art is in the positioning of those dots and the curve of the two shores . . . .

"May 13. First painting I started today at 6 in the morning (that makes it 18 hours I've been painting with short breaks in that time) is of the framework of the Eskimo's Second House which I sketched in yesterday while on a walk toward the wrecked ship. I was fascinated by the gaunt skeleton-like frame standing in the snow and chose it for a subject, even not knowing what it was. In the evening Terry showed me his many slides of this country and there I saw this same structure but covered with canvas and moss. Actually it's no smaller than an igloo would be.

"May 14. Tuesday evening. Terry's gone to bed and I'm sitting in the living room studying *Intellectual Culture of the Iglulik Eskimos*' on the section about Shamans and spirit seances. The wind is blowing in the electric wire, and the night is overcast and I have a creepy feeling, a sense of dread now and then that sets my skin atingle. I just seem to be extra jumpy these last few days. Is it the Arctic doing this to me? Murphy gave a bark when Terry returned from work and I literally leapt up from my chair where I sat painting. I have just finished a painting illustrating an Eskimo myth about the necessity of sharing . . . .

"My over-all concluding view of this trip is not as an inspiring landscape as I'd imagined but well worth this one trip. It was also an eye opener geographically. It filled in a big blank in my concept of Canada to the north. The one big area still waiting there for me as a painter is the Eskimo people themselves but to do it authentically I have to live with them and learn their language; their mythology is fascinating and I might for one thing do a book on it. But what concerns me most is the sociological problem which I saw (and Terry confirmed) similar but different to the Indian problem. Their old way of life has been pretty well completely destroyed by impact of the white man's civilization and as a matter of fact there would be mass starvation waiting for them if they did try to return to the land. Starva-

tion was a thing they accepted in the past but no longer. So they accept government housing in settlements and government relief and they try to carve and make other handicrafts for sale—a lot of it thus comes out as a poor quality because not every Eskimo is a born artist."

KVALE, Velma R(uth) 1898-

PERSONAL: Surname is pronounced Ka-*wah*-lee; born May 12, 1898, in Hastings, Neb.; daughter of Charles Cloke (a farmer) and Margaret (a music teacher; maiden name, Matlock) Mountjoy; married Ora F. Kvale (deceased); children: Kenneth Glenn, Noel Thomas (deceased), Verna Joy. *Education:* Attended University of Washington, Seattle, 1919, Spokane University, 1921-23, and University of Montana, 1924; Eastern Washington College of Education (now Eastern Washington State College), B.S. (with honors), 1954. *Politics:* Republican. *Religion:* Christian. *Home:* 1212 24th St., Ronan, Mont. 59864.

CAREER: Teacher in Montana and Washington, 1918-21, 1923-26, 1954-63, 1964. *Member:* Montana Press Women, International Platform Association, Classroom Teachers of North-Western Montana (director, 1960-63), Northwestern Montana Retired Teachers Association (president, 1968-70), Alaska Crippled Children's Association (charter mem-

VELMA KVALE

CHAPTER TEN

Tobuk Learns About the Sea

Soon the boat landed at Mekoryuk. Tobuk heaved a sigh of relief. "I've firmly decided not to be a sailor. I belong on the tundra," he said shakily. ■ (From *Tobuk, Reindeer Herder* by Velma R. Kvale.)

ber), Delta Kappa Gamma (president, Upsilon chapter, 1968-70), Pi Delta Epsilon, Order of the Eastern Star, Anchorage (Alaska) Garden Club (honorary life member), Ronan Garden Club (president, 1972-73), Ronan Woman's Club (president, 1969-71), Republican Women's Club of Ronan (vice-president, 1967-69). *Awards, honors: Tobuk, Reindeer Herder* took first place in the juvenile book division of Montana Press Women's contest, 1969, and second place in National Federation of Press Women's contest, 1969, also included in the Mamie Eisenhower Library Project.

WRITINGS: Tobuk, Reindeer Herder (juvenile), Denison, 1968.

WORK IN PROGRESS: Pioneer Women of Alaska; (with Margaret Brooke) *History of Early Ronan.*

SIDELIGHTS: "I'm a very average person who lived in Alaska for twenty-five years, and so felt the urge to write about life up there. But I was so busy rearing my family, helping make Anchorage a better place in which to live and of course enjoying the great outdoors of Alaska that I never got around to writing *Tobuk* which was in my head but not

on paper. It is easy to get ideas for books but not so easy to get them down. I finally did.

"I was teaching fifth grade, so I decided to read the story to my pupils and see how they responded. Since I always read to them for ten minutes when they came in from noon play, I just pretended it was a book I was reading to them. They liked it and always asked for more—so I was encouraged.

"I find early morning the best time to write—although, occasionally I write at night. Many times I get ideas while I lie in bed. I have a notebook handy and jot down main ideas then.

"I love children and enjoyed working with them, my own, my pupils and now my grandchildren. Children are the hope of our troubled world. May they demonstrate more wisdom than our generation has."

HOBBIES AND OTHER INTERESTS: "A tiny garden, lots of flowers, being a friend to children and birds, and hiking. I used to ride horseback, ski, swim, snowshoe and climb mountains—but now I'm a grandmother, I take things a little easier."

LAND, Jane
  See SPEICHER, Helen Ross (Smith)

LAND, Ross
  See SPEICHER, Helen Ross (Smith).

LANGNER, Nola 1930-

PERSONAL: Born September 24, 1930, in New York, N.Y.; daughter of Gerald B. (owner of an advertising agency) and Elsie (Feigenbaum) Spiero; married Thomas S. Langner (a research professor of sociology at Columbia University), February 21, 1953; children: Lisa, Josh, Eli, Gretchen and Belinda (twins). *Education:* Vassar College, student, 1948-50; Bennington College, B.A., 1952. *Home and studio:* 271 Central Park W., New York, N.Y. 10024. *Agent:* Marilyn Marlow, Curtis Brown Ltd., 60 East 56th St., New York, N.Y. 10022.

CAREER: After college worked briefly doing paste-ups for movie magazines published by Ideal Publishing Co., New York, N.Y.; illustrator at TV Art Studio, New York, N.Y., 1953-54; writer and illustrator of children's books. *Member:* Authors' Guild. *Awards, honors: Miss Lucy* was named by *New York Times* as one of the outstanding picture books of 1969.

WRITINGS—Self-illustrated juveniles: *Miss Lucy*, Macmillan, 1969; *Go and Shut the Door*, Dial, 1971; *Joseph and the Wonderful Tree*, Addison-Wesley, 1972; (adapter) *Cinderella* (new version), Scholastic Book Services, 1972; *Rafiki*, Viking, in press.

Illustrator: Flora Fifield, *Pictures for the Palace*, Vanguard, 1958; Robert Pack, *The Forgotten Secret*, Macmillan, 1959; Ann McGovern, *Who Has a Secret?*, Houghton, 1963; Robert Pack, *How to Catch a Crocodile*, Knopf, 1964; Sidney Simon, *Henry the Uncatchable Mouse*, Norton, 1964; Ann McGovern, *Little Wolf*, Abelard, 1965; Aileen Olsen, *Bernadine and the Water Bucket*, Abelard, 1966; Charles House, *The Lonesome Egg*, Norton, 1968; Harold Longman, *The Kitchen-Window Squirrel*, Parents' Magazine Press, 1969; *Hi Diddle Diddle*, Scholastic Book Services, 1970; Constance Green, *The Ears of Louis*, Viking, 1974; Ann McGovern, *Scram Kid*, Viking, 1974.

SIDELIGHTS: "I suppose I write and illustrate not so much from memories of childhood, as from childhood feelings and emotions that have never left me. I guess I've never really grown up. And I don't think I ever really want to grow up if it means growing away from these feelings. They bring me close to my own children, to myself and hopefully to the children who read my books. We all tend

"Measles!" said the nurse. ■ (From *Miss Lucy* by Nola Langner. Illustrated by the author.)

to get cynical and less responsive to the world as we grow older and maybe all the words and the pictures take us back to simpler, more direct ways of reacting. I try to put alot of facial and bodily expression into the characters I draw. When children are happy or sad or angry they really show it. I even have a mirror in my workroom and I make faces into it and draw from those sometimes.

"I like writing my own books because pictures can say things that words sometimes can't. Pictures can add humor or mystery. The quietest picture of a table and chair can look human somehow.

"I seem to be getting more specific and more personal in my work. I try to think of specific people or myself when I'm working on a character in a book. I sketch nature in the country and people in New York City. I like to put little stories in the pictures that aren't even mentioned in the text; in *Scram Kid* there's a continuous story of a boy trying to get a cat out of a tree in various ways, in many of the pictures, but not in the text. There are animals that I'm particularly fond of who always seem to get into my pictures—geese, pigs, and of course, cats. Also, my drawings of children always seem to look alot like my own children. In fact, sometimes the animals look like people I know!

NOLA LANGNER

"I was an only child and I spent alot of time alone, drawing and reading. Books were company. I guess I still feel that way. I've always liked reading to my kids—especially the last chapters of marvelous books like all the E. B. White's. In fact, I love dramatic endings of books. Good endings, not necessarily happy endings. The end of the first Pippi Longstockings still knocks me out. And we all, in this family, have sobbed our way through the end of *Charlotte's Web*.

"We travel a lot with our children and places I've seen seem to crop up as background material or story ideas. My children are by now very good travelers and also very good book critics. I test out my writing with them (as well as art) and they keep me from anything which is dishonest, or which doesn't really fit with the story. Children have a good sense of what's true and real. Even in a fantasy story, illogic is quickly spotted."

Langner and her husband built their own summer and week-end house in Connecticut. They have seven Siamese cats, which explains why cats frequent her books.

"My kids always say 'You're so lucky, while we're working and slaving in school every day, you get to stay home and just sit and draw!' And, in a way, I think they're right."

LATHAM, Mavis
See CLARK, Mavis Thorpe

LATHAM, Philip
See RICHARDSON, Robert S(hirley)

LEE, Mary Price   1934-

PERSONAL: Born July 10, 1934, in Philadelphia, Pa.; daughter of Llewellyn and Elise (Mirkil) Price; married Richard Lee (a copywriter), May 12, 1956; children: Richard, Barbara, Monica. *Education:* University of Pennsylvania, B.A., 1956, M.S. in Ed., 1967. *Residence:* Flourtown, Pa.

CAREER: Teacher for short period; employed in public relations department at Westminster Press, Philadelphia, Pa., 1973-74. Has tutored foreign students in English. *Member:* Women in Communications, Children's Reading Roundtable, Phi Beta Kappa, Philadelphia Athenaeum.

WRITINGS: Money and Kids: How to Earn It, Save It, and Spend It (juvenile), Westminster Press, 1973. Columnist, "Chestnut Hill Local" in *Shopper's Column*, 1970-72. Contributing editor, *Today's Girl*, 1972-73. Contributor to *Philadelphia Magazine*.

WORK IN PROGRESS: A book on the veterinarian career.

SIDELIGHTS: "My children provide great incentive to write for their teen age group and serve both as guinea pigs and critics. I am a travel enthusiast and particularly a Francophile."

work of writing. Basically, I think my books are just a process of overspill from a particularly vivid and relentless imagination. When I write I reckon generally that about sixty percent of the story is an inspirational downhill slide, forty percent an uphill slog, though there are exceptions. Mostly my children's books come easily. *The Dragon Hoard*, for example (about 160 pages long), I wrote in two weeks.

"I intend my books for anyone who will enjoy them. Frankly, I write for me, I can't help it. My books are expressions of my private inner world. I love the idea that other people may read and perhaps relish them, but that, if it happens, is a delightful by-product. So I can't say I aim my work at a particular audience. Even the children's books are not really specifically designed for children, which anyway seems a bit patronising. They contain ideas and fantasies and observations like all writing. I hope adults will read them as well as children, and children get a look at the adult stuff, too, if it's their kind of book. Besides which, books find their own friends rather than the other way round, intend all you like.

"I used to maintain that I didn't write from life, but of course all writers do, really, whether they realise it or not. Ten years after you fell down a stone staircase, you find a

LEE, Tanith 1947-

PERSONAL: Born September 19, 1947, in London, England; daughter of Bernard and Hylda (Moore) Lee. *Education:* Attended grammar school in Catford, London, England, and studied art. *Residence:* London, England.

CAREER: Writer.

WRITINGS: The Dragon Hoard (juvenile fantasy novel), Macmillan, 1971, Farrar, Straus, 1971; *Animal Castle* (picture book), Macmillan, 1972, Farrar, Straus, 1972; *Princess Hynchatti*, Macmillan, 1972, Farrar, Straus, 1973; *Companions on the Road*, Macmillan, 1975; *The Birthgrave* (adult fantasy), Daw Books, 1975. Also writer of science fiction and fantasy novels for adults, none as yet published.

WORK IN PROGRESS: Three novels, *The Storm-Lord*, *Unsilent Night* and *Nightshade*.

SIDELIGHTS: "I wrote my first story at the age of nine (an embarrassingly trite thing to do). I don't know how I come to write my books. An idea, or group of ideas, appear suddenly in my mind. They worry and distract me until I begin to work on them, though the pre-writing stimulation and excitement are often more enjoyable than the actual

Jasleth had just seen the town and the palace in the middle of it, on a little rise, down in the valley below him. Beyond the town lay the long white beach and the glittering blue sea. ■ (From *The Dragon Hoard* by Tanith Lee. Illustrated by Graham Oakley.)

character of yours falling down one; or the words of some long-lost acquaintance yelling at you out of a pair of inverted commas. This can be unnerving and amusing. But stranger still are those experiences that seem, as you write about them, to be so familiar and yet are impossible. *The Birthgrave* is a case in point here. When did I ever ride archer in a chariot? Yet that event was so clear in my mind when I wrote about it that it might have happened to me only last month. I do think, actually, that unconscious retention is accountable for a lot—films seen, books read, all stored away and consciously forgotten until some little trigger activates them. On another level, racial memory probably plays a part. I have never, physically, ridden a horse in my life, but I think I know precisely what it feels like, and the burning town at the beginning of *Companions on the Road* is an event I, or some ancestor, has witnessed all too often.

"Although not born under the sign of Gemini, but of Virgo, I am one of those double-sided people half extravert, half introvert, and I think this quality is very clear in my writng. I must admit to a certain element of wish fulfillment, too. I did so enjoy Jasleth's crazy voyage in *The Dragon Hoard*, for where can you find convenient dragons nowadays, when pure wonder is so thin on the ground?"

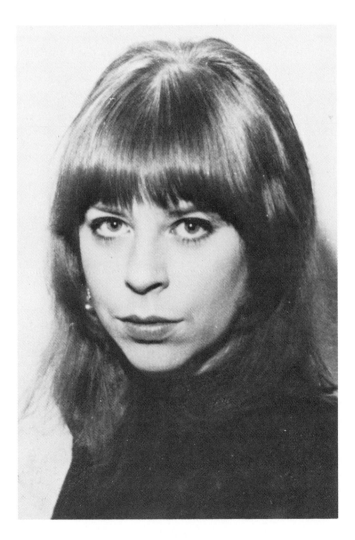

TANITH LEE

HOBBIES AND OTHER INTERESTS: Past civilizations (Egyptian, Roman, Inca), psychic powers (their development, use, and misuse), music, reading.

LINGARD, Joan

PERSONAL: Born in Edinburgh, Scotland; married, with three daughters. *Education:* Moray House Training College, general teaching diploma. *Home:* 31 Scotland St., Edinburgh, Scotland.

CAREER: Teacher and writer.

WRITINGS: Liam's Daughter, Hodder & Stoughton, 1963; *The Prevailing Wind*, Hodder & Stoughton, 1964; *The Tide Comes In*, Hodder & Stoughton, 1966; *The Headmaster*, Hodder & Stoughton, 1967; *A Sort of Freedom*, Hodder & Stoughton, 1969; *The Lord on Our Side*, Hodder & Stoughton, 1970; *The Twelfth Day of July* (Volume I of a trilogy about Ulster for children), Hamish Hamilton, 1970, Nelson, 1972; *Across the Barricades* (Volume II of trilogy), Hamish Hamilton, 1972, Nelson, 1973; *Into Exile* (Volume III of trilogy), Nelson, 1973; *Frying as Usual*, Hamish Hamilton, 1973; *The Clearance* (for children), Hamish Hamilton, 1974; *A Proper Place*, Hamish Hamilton, 1975. Author of television scripts for Scottish television and British Broadcasting Corp. (Scotland).

WORK IN PROGRESS: A children's book; television scripts.

SIDELIGHTS: "I started to write when I was eleven years old, and living in Belfast. I wrote about Devon, the Yorkshire moors, Wester Ross in Scotland, Brazil—all places I had never been to—but not a word about Belfast which I considered dull and uninteresting and totally devoid of action! Years later I came to write about the city, where I ilved until I was eighteen. I wrote an adult novel called *The Lord on Our Side*, and Honor Arundel, the well-known children's writer, suggested to me that I should write a children's book about Ulster. I thought about it, and out of that came *The Twelfth Day of July*.

"I wrote it basically as an appeal for tolerance, to try to show children that they need not accept their parents' prejudices, because I believe that the only hope for peace must come through changing the attitudes of children first. Indoctrination and prejudice begin so young; this is seen very clearly in the Ulster situation. It is pathetic how young some of the children who have been involved are.

"When I wrote *The Twelfth Day of July*, the troubles were not as bad as they later became. When things had changed for the worse, I realized that I must take my characters a stage further, for what had taken place in that first book would no longer be possible. So I wrote *Across the Barricades*. And then it did not seem possible to leave Sadie, the Protestant girl, and Kevin, the Catholic boy: I had to find out how they fared when they went *Into Exile*. I had intended to leave them there, at the end of the trilogy, but now I find I am writing another book about them, which will of course make a quartet.

"As for whom I intend my books, I can only say for whoever wishes to read them, children or adults. And al-

JOAN LINGARD

though of course my intention was to put across a 'message' (normally something I do not like in writing, but this case seemed different) when I began on this sequence of books, it was also equally important to me to tell a story which would grip the reader's attention and entertain. I have now become very interested in writing for children, particularly the older age group. I do not intend to write only about Ulster, and have in fact written a book set in modern Invernesshire called *The Clearance*.

"I always have to write about places I know well so that I understand fully the people who grow out of them. Scotland and Ireland therefore provide me with most of my backgrounds, but I am at present living in Cheshire and this is the setting for the fourth part of the Sadie and Kevin series. Another country I am attached to, and have written about in my adult novels, is France, and I would like to use it as a setting for a children's book sometime."

LIONNI, Leo 1910-

PERSONAL: Born May 5, 1910, in Amsterdam, Holland; came to United States, 1939; naturalized citizen, 1945; son of Louis and Elisabeth (a concert soprano; maiden name, Grossouw) Lionni; married Nora Maffi, December, 1931; children: Louis, Paolo. *Education:* Attended schools in Holland, Belgium, United States, Italy, Switzerland; University of Genoa, Ph.D., 1935. *Politics:* "Sometimes on the left—sometimes beyond." *Religion:* None. *Home:* "Porcignano," Radda in Chianti (Siena), Italy. *Agent:* Agenzia Letteraria Internazionale, Corso Matteotti 3, Milano, Italy.

CAREER: Free-lance writer, designer, and painter, 1930-39; N. W. Ayer & Sons, Inc. (advertising firm), Philadelphia, Pa., art director, 1939-47; Olivetti Corp. of America, San Francisco, Calif., design director, 1949-59; author and illustrator of children's books, 1959—. Head of graphics design department, Parsons School of Design; art director of *Fortune*, 1949-62; has had many one-man shows of his painting and sculpture in galleries, museums, and at universities in U.S. and Europe, including Metropolitan Museum of Modern Art, New York, N.Y. *Member:* Alliance Graphique Internationale, American Institute of Graphic Arts (president), Society of Typographic Arts (honorary member), Bund Deutscher Buchkunstler (honorary member), Authors League of America, Artists Equity. *Awards, honors:* Elected art director of the year by National Society of Art Directors, 1955; Gold Medal for Architecture from Architectural League, 1956; *Inch by Inch* was Caldecott Award runner-up, 1961, and received Lewis Carroll Shelf Award, 1962, and Children's Book Prize in Germany, 1963; *Swimmy* was Caldecott Award runner-up in 1963, as was *Frederick* in 1968; German Government Illustrated Book Award, 1965; Golden Apple Award at Bratislava First Biennial, 1967; five major awards at Teheran Film Festival in 1970 for two animated films; elected to Art Directors Hall of Fame, 1974.

WRITINGS—Self-illustrated children's books: *Little Blue and Little Yellow*, Obolensky, 1959; *Inch by Inch*, Obolensky, 1960; *On My Beach There Are Many Pebbles*, Obolensky, 1961; *Swimmy*, Pantheon, 1963; *Tico and the Golden Wings*, Pantheon, 1964; *Frederick*, Pantheon, 1967; *The Alphabet Tree*, Pantheon, 1968; *The Biggest House in the World*, Pantheon, 1968; *Alexander and the Wind-Up Mouse*, Pantheon, 1969; *Fish Is Fish*, Pantheon, 1970; *Theodore and the Talking Mushroom*, Pantheon, 1971; *Il Taccuino di Leo Lionni*, Electa (Milan), 1972; *The Green-tail Mouse*, Pantheon, 1973; *In the Rabbitgarden*, Pantheon, 1975; *A Color of His Own*, Abelard, 1975; *Pezzettino*, Pantheon, 1975. Contributor to *Casabella, Domus, Print, Fortune, Architecture Plus*. Editor, *Print*, 1955-57, *Panorama* (Italy), 1964-65.

WORK IN PROGRESS: Essays in Parallel Botany for Adelphi.

SIDELIGHTS: Lionni writes: "When I have a story in mind I am not conscious of the average age of my potential readers. I believe, in fact, that a good children's book should appeal to all people who have not completely lost their original joy and wonder in life. When I am asked the embarrassing question of what do I know about children, their psychology, and their needs, I must confess my total ignorance. I know no more about children than the average parent or grandparent. I like to watch them, and when they are exceptionally sweet I like to hold them on my knee. But often I have not much patience for them. This is childish of me, perhaps, since children have very little patience with other children. The fact is that I really don't make books for children at all. I make them for that part of us, of myself and of my friends, which has never changed, which is still a child." Lionni adds that his major regret is "Not to have learned to play a musical instrument, any instrument, well."

FOR MORE INFORMATION SEE: Lee Bennett Hopkins, *Books Are by People*, Citation Press, 1969.

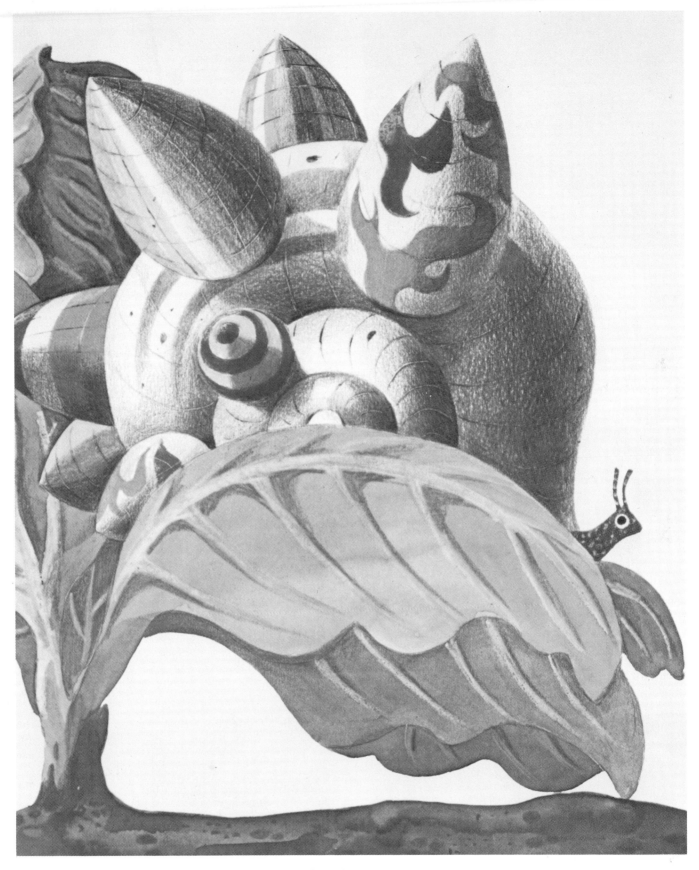

An ordinary little snail with a house like a birthday cake. ■ (From *The Biggest House in the World* by Leo Lionni. Illustrated by the author.)

LEO LIONNI

LIVERSIDGE, (Henry) Douglas 1913-

PERSONAL: Born March 12, 1913, in Swinton, Yorkshire, England; son of Henry and Sarah Ann (Foster) Liversidge; married Cosmina Pistola, September 25, 1954; children: Ann Francesca. *Religion:* Church of England. *Home:* 56 Love Lane, Pinner, Middlesex, England.

CAREER: Left grammar school to study metallurgical chemistry at a steel plant in Sheffield, England, but quit after seven months to go into journalism; worked on various British provincial newspapers, then moved to London, England, as correspondent for *Yorkshire Post*, news editor of *Sunday Chronicle*, assistant leader writer for *Daily Mail*, London correspondent of *Continental Daily Mail* (Paris), correspondent and staff writer for Reuters, and wartime free-lance writer of anti-Nazi propaganda commentaries for British Broadcasting Corp. overseas programs; Central Office of Information, London, England, an editor, now retired. *Military service:* Royal Air Force; invalided out.

WRITINGS: White Horizon, Odhams, 1951; (contributor) D. Monmouth, editor, *The Breath of Life* (anthology), Books 4-5, Allen & Unwin, 1953; *The Last Continent*, Jarrolds, 1958; *The Third Front: The Strange Story of the Secret War in the Arctic*, Souvenir Press, 1960; *The Whale Killers*, Jarrolds, 1963; (contributor) C. V. Glines, *Polar Aviation*, Watts, 1964; *The Arctic*, Watts, 1967; *Saint Francis of Assisi*, Watts, 1968; *Lenin: Genius of Revolution*, Watts, 1969; *Joseph Stalin*, Watts, 1969; *Ignatius of Loyola, the Soldier-Saint*, Watts, 1970; *Arctic Exploration*, Watts, 1970; *British Empire and Commonwealth of Nations*, Watts, 1971; *The Picture Life of Elizabeth II*, Watts, 1971; *The Day the Bastille Fell: The Beginning of the End*

of the French Monarchy, Watts, 1972; *The Luddites*, Watts, 1972; *Crown and People*, Watts, 1972; *Parliament*, Watts, 1973; *The House of Commons*, Watts, 1974; *Queen Elizabeth II*, Arthur Barker, 1974; *Prince Charles*, Arthur Barker, 1974.

SIDELIGHTS: As a Reuter correspondent, Liversidge was the first British journalist to visit both polar regions, in 1949-50. On the Arctic expedition (cold weather tests) he was a "guinea pig" for Dr. G. Pugh, who later joined the party which climbed Mount Everest. He traveled to Antarctica, joining an expedition which went to the relief of Sir Vivian Fuchs and his men, who were imprisoned by icefields. Besides covering news and features, he also served as a photographer. *White Horizon* is the story of the Antarctica expedition.

"I have spent most of my working life in journalism. In that time I have written numerous articles; for instance, as a staff writer at Reuters I wrote articles for newspapers and magazines in over forty countries—the *Toronto Star Weekly* was the most regular recipient. For this newspaper I wrote under three names.

"But it was not until I accompanied a Royal Naval expedition to the Arctic (for Reuters) that I began to write books. The object of this expedition was to glean all manner of data which would be vital in the event of a Third World War (seeing that the north polar region is the shortest distance between the Soviet Union and North America). The expedition covered a great deal of the area which was the setting—that is, East Greenland and the Greenland Sea—of secret Allied and Nazi activity in the Second World War. Because weather guidance was so essential to guide the planning of huge military operations, and because so much of the weather in Europe is born in the Arctic regions, the Allied and Nazi High Commands 'smuggled' secret weather parties into the North. As the Allies grew stronger, it became increasingly more difficult for the Nazis to get parties into the Arctic. My book *The Third Front* explains how the Nazis did this and how they were located in that great wilderness by Norwegian and Danish hunters who formed the Sledge Patrol, the U.S. Ice Patrol, a radio base on Jan Mayen Island in the heart of the Greenland Sea (where my expedition sheltered at times during very fierce storms) which intercepted messages to and from Germany and helped to locate Nazi weather bases, etc.

"*The Third Front* should have been my first book, but soon after returning to London from the Arctic I travelled to the Antarctic. In *The Third Front* I described a non-stop return flight from the Shetlands to Spitzbergen to parachute supplies to Norwegian meteorologists operating among the disused coalmines. This was seen by someone at Franklin Watts, New York, and it was included in a book *Polar Aviation*—an anthology based on extracts from old and recent books—which Watts was preparing. Eventually I received a copy of this well-produced book from Mr. Franklin Watts himself. So far I had written only books for adults and had no intention at that time, although I planned to do so in due course, of writing for younger people. However, while writing to thank Mr. Watts for the book, I asked on the spur of the moment if he would be interested in a book on the Arctic. To my astonishment he said he would. Hence *The Arctic*.

"That might have been my only book for Franklin Watts.

However, I had made a number of visits to Assisi in Italy and, with the aid of a friend, a Franciscan priest, I had visited most of the places associated with St. Francis and became interested in the subject. Again, not thinking that he would accept the idea, I wrote to Mr. Watts asking if he would care to accept a book on St. Francis. It so happened that Watts was then working on their mammoth 'Immortals of Mankind' series. St. Francis had been chosen by an erudite panel of experts but no one as yet had been appointed to write the book. I was commissioned. I was also invited to write about St. Ignatius of Loyola and the Jesuit movement, and because of my interest in Russian history (incidentally, Russian writers are my favourite writers) I was invited to write the biographies of Peter the Great, Lenin and Stalin.

"Although I have a number of subjects for adult books, I have been kept busy writing for younger people (of the older age group); now that I have retired from editing, adult books are receiving attention. Because I have visited both polar regions, I like writing on these subjects. But I have other interests, history and biography. I will not write a book unless the subject appeals to me. I am the type of person who would not do justice to any subject unless I liked it.

"Once having accepted a commission, I immerse myself in the subject. The research in which I involve myself is—perhaps by some people's standards—far more than is necessary. However, I do not think anyone can do justice to any subject unless excessive research is completed. I think that this is certainly essential when writing for younger people because the task of explaining complex issues in a simple manner is far greater.

"As I have explained, I write for older children, even up to the student group, but because of the nature of the subjects the books could be read equally by adults. For instance, in *The Picture Book of Queen Elizabeth II*, I gave not only biographical material but explained in simple terms what British constitutional monarchy really means. Even in Britain so few people, both young and old alike, have an adequate idea. Many adults, therefore, as well as young people, would gain information by reading this book. Incidentally, Queen Elizabeth kindly read this text before it was published.

DOUGLAS LIVERSIDGE

Something about the Author

117

"My books so far have been the outcome of some experience of particular interest. For instance, subjects such as the British monarchy, Parliament and the Commonwealth were the sort of subjects I had to deal with in connection with my daily work at one period. To go to an extreme as regards subject, my book *The Whale Killers* was the result of personal experience. On my way to the Antarctic the expedition ship 'John Biscoe' (a wooden vessel which had been built in America during the Second World War as a mine-layer and was now converted to polar use) had to put into South Georgia for repairs after severe buffeting in a storm and also to leave a small party to found a base. Within a few hours of arriving at this whaling island, I went aboard a little whale catcher at Leith Harbour, the British-owned whaling centre (at that time there were other centres owned by Norwegians and Argentinians and I later visited them). I therefore saw the whaling industry and whale hunters at first hand. Incidentally, most of the personnel were Norwegians, and they formed a very interesting study. What fascinated me was that the names of items and terms had been handed down by whale hunters right from the time of Melville and *Moby Dick*.

"I am a perfectionist by nature (much to my despair because I give myself so much work). Therefore, having gathered my data—and often breaking off to do more research—I write the book in shorthand. I do this because I keep changing my mind; it is easier to cross out shorthand, and I find it less irksome than doing so on a typewriter, apart from the fact that it is easy to insert small shorthand between lines. I then make a typescript from my shorthand and rewrite and generally improve the typescript. The ideal would be to put this revised typescript to one side for some time then read it again to effect further improvements, but so far the final typescript has had to be done immediately. Usually I type myself because—even at this stage—I sometimes alter text. I have no time for authors who start rewriting at the galley proof stage. If this happens I support publishers who charge authors for printers' resetting.

"I prefer to do my own research because I know what sort of book I wish to write. I have no confidence in other people that they will do the work with the same thoroughness as myself; or that they will have grasped what I am really looking for. Also, by doing one's own research one can come across other subjects which will make excellent books. A number of ideas on my list which I planned to do are now already in book form, other people having thought of the same idea. At least it confirms that one's judgment as regards subject matter was right.

"Music is my main recreation. I study piano works as much as possible in the limited time I can devote to it. I am interested only in classical music—by that I also mean the romantics, such as Chopin, Schumann, etc., as well as Mozart, etc. I wanted to be a professional musician. Years ago I studied the organ seriously, but now I have turned to the piano because I do not have access to an organ.

"I am also keen on art but have had to put this to one side. There are only twenty-four hours in a day. But I would like to attempt to produce some picture books one day.

"I am an admirer of the illustrations of Brian Wildsmith whose work is also published by Franklin Watts. Curiously, Brian Wildsmith is a fellow Yorkshireman and was born not many miles from where I was born. But we never met until Franklin Watts held a party to launch *The Picture Book of Queen Elizabeth II*. There is an odd parallel between us. He too wanted to be a musician. And as in my case, his father was also connected with coal-mining. But Brian turned to illustration and I turned to writing."

LIVINGSTON, Richard R(oland) 1922-

PERSONAL: Born September 1, 1922, in South Bend, Ind.; son of Leon Lippman and Irene (Apfelbaum) Livingston; married Myra Cohn (a poet, author, and teacher), April 14, 1952; children: Joshua, Jonas, Jennie. *Education:* Attended University of Pennsylvania, 1941-42, and Southern Methodist University, 1945-46. *Home:* 9308 Readcrest Dr., Beverly Hills, Calif. 90210. *Agent:* McIntosh and Otis, Inc., 18 East 41st St., New York, N.Y. 10017. *Office:* 10889 Wilshire Blvd., Los Angeles, Calif. 90024.

CAREER: Bloch, Livingston & Donohoe (certified public accountants), Dallas, Tex., certified public accountant, 1947-64; Richard R. Livingston, Certified Public Accountant, Los Angeles, Calif., 1965-74; Livingston and Omens, Los Angeles, Calif., certified public accountant, 1974—. *Military service:* U.S. Air Force, navigator, 1942-45; became second lieutenant.

WRITINGS: The Hunkendunkens, Harcourt, 1968.

FOR MORE INFORMATION SEE: New York Times, October 13, 1968; *Commonweal*, November 22, 1968; *Young Readers' Review*, December, 1968.

NORAH LOFTS

118

LOFTS, Norah (Robinson) 1904-
(Peter Curtis)

PERSONAL: Born August 27, 1904, in England; daughter of Isaac and Ethel (Garner) Robinson; married Geoffrey Lofts (died, 1948); married Robert Jorisch, 1949; children: Geoffrey St. Edmund Clive Lofts. *Education:* Norwich Training College, Teaching Diploma, 1925. *Politics:* Conservative. *Home:* North-Gate House, Bury St. Edmund's, Suffolk, England. *Agent:* Curtis Brown, 575 Madison Ave., New York, N.Y.

CAREER: Guildhall Feoffment Girls' School, taught English and history, 1925-36; now an author. Member of Bury St. Edmund's Borough Council, 1957-62; member of Board of Managers for two schools. *Member:* Family Planning Association (president).

WRITINGS: I Met a Gypsy, Knopf, 1935; *Here Was a Man*, Knopf, 1936; *White Hell of Pity*, Knopf, 1937; *Requiem for Idols*, Knopf, 1938; *Out of This Nettle*, Gollancz, 1938; *Blossom Like the Rose*, Knopf, 1939; (under pseudonym Peter Curtis) *Dead March in Three Keys*, P. Davis, 1940; *Hester Roon*, Knopf, 1940, 3rd edition, 1958; *The Road to Revelation*, P. Davies, 1941; *Michael and All Angels*, Joseph, 1943; *The Brittle Glass*, Knopf, 1943; *Jassy*, Methuen, 1944; *The Golden Fleece*, Knopf, 1944; *To See a Fine Lady*, Knopf, 1946; *Silver Nutmeg*, Doubleday, 1947; *A Calf for Venus*, Doubleday, 1949, reissued in paperback as *Letty*, Pyramid, 1968; *Women in the Old Testament*, Macmillan, 1949.

Esther, Macmillan, 1950; *The Lute Player*, Doubleday, 1951; *Bless This House*, Doubleday, 1954; *Winter Harvest*, Doubleday, 1955; *Eleanor the Queen*, Doubleday, 1955; *Afternoon of an Autocrat*, Doubleday, 1956; *Scent of Cloves*, Doubleday, 1957; *Queen in Waiting*, Doubleday, 1958; *Heaven in Your Hand*, Doubleday, 1958; *The Town House*, Doubleday, 1959; (under pseudonym Peter Curtis) *No Question of Murder*, Doubleday, 1959.

(Under pseudonym Peter Curtis) *The Devil's Own*, Doubleday, 1960; *The House at Old Vine*, Doubleday, 1961; *The House at Sunset*, Doubleday, 1962; *The Concubine*, Doubleday, 1963; *How Far to Bethlehem?*, Doubleday, 1965; (with Margery Weiner) *Eternal France*, Doubleday, 1968; *Lost Queen*, Doubleday, 1969; *The King's Pleasure*, Doubleday, 1969; *Out of the Dark*, Doubleday, 1972; *Crown of Aloes*, Doubleday, 1974; *The Maude Reed Tale* (juvenile), Nelson, 1972; *Rupert Hatton's Story* (Junior Literary Guild selection), Nelson, 1973; *Lovers All Untrue*,

The agitation in Summerfield had outlasted that in other places because, in the early days, a farmer had set his dogs on a peaceable crowd of men who had visited him with their request for a consideration. One dog had bitten a labourer, and he had turned and throttled it. The farmer took action, valuing the cur at thirty shillings, and the bitten man had been sent to jail. ■ (From the movie *"Jassy,"* copyright © 1948 by Universal Pictures, Inc.)

Fawcett, 1973; *Catherine of Aragon*, 1975; *Knight's Acre*, 1975; *The Homecoming*, 1975; *Checkmate*, 1975. Contributor to *Ladies' Home Journal, Woman's Journal, Cosmopolitan, Redbook.*

SIDELIGHTS: "About me, what is there to say? You could call me a compulsive writer. It was the one thing I always wanted to do, meant to do. I know it sounds dotty but at no time in my life would I have willingly changed places with the Shah of Persia, or with Greta Garbo, or anybody else you care to name. From the first moment that I remember, and I have almost total recall from the age of three, I have wanted to tell stories, first to myself—this is important, partly because I bore so easily, and anything that bores me is discarded immediately—and then, naturally, to a wider audience.

"That was hard to find. I hawked my first book around for five years. It became known as 'Norah's homing pigeon,' and often when it had homed my kind family would conceal the fact from me when I came in after a hard day—I taught

Before this ceremony I should have taken a bath and spent a night awake and praying in a church . . . but I was "Knighted on the field." ■ (From *The Maude Reed Tale* by Norah Lofts. Illustrated by Anne and Janet Grahame Johnstone.)

school then. It was an awful time, but I clung to my conviction that it was a good story, and I *think* I was right. It was first printed in 1935, and is still in print—a justification of a kind, I like to think.

"For whom do I write? The answer is, Anybody who can read. And from whence do I derive my stories? Anywhere; everywhere. I tend, I know, towards the past, but that is only because the past gives a little more elbow room. I can say that John Bloggs built a house, where and when he chose without bothering about planning permission and all the other hampering things. And there is another aspect, too. The past, although often sorted over and subject to contradictory judgments, has a certain stability. A purely contemporary story attracts a lot of attention, is vastly successful and within a year is out of date. What I hold to, and always shall, is *people*. They don't change much. Love, hatred, ambition, jealousy and all the rest are part of the human condition and will remain so.

"This is something I feel strongly about. I know I could have done better—attracted a wider readership if I'd gone in for red heels and La! Sir Percy, and all the rest of what I call Gad-zooks and Prithee.

"I write good plain English; a fact that has been recognized in a Swiss University, and in India, where a school book contains the best short story I ever wrote. Of course, I try to avoid glaring anachronisms—like the clock in *Julius Caesar*—but at the same time I hold the theory that we can't tell how people in the past *talked*. We know how they wrote and how writers reported their talk. But if civilization broke down tomorrow and all that was left was something written—James Joyce, Dylan Thomas, a pretty false impression would be made.

"Nothing here of myself, I know. Who wants to know that I'm tall, thin, devoted to dogs—indeed to all animals, that I have a son and two grandchildren, all greatly beloved?

"My house is more interesting. Not quite the House at Vine, but not far off it; actually two Tudor Houses put together. One front has a gutter spout with a date 1713, which just makes it Queen Anne. Almost all the inside is panelled, some Tudor, some Georgian and the stairs are inlaid; it seems equally evil to cover them with carpet, or to leave them bare to be worn away.

"I work from nine a.m. to one p.m. and from 4:30 to 7:30 practically every day of the year. When I am not typing I read—omnivorous to the point of being carnivorous.

"I cannot send you a photograph. If I sent you one from the past, when I had some looks, it would be deceptive; if I sent you a present-day one (if I had such a thing) it would be even more deceptive, belying absolutely my *beautiful* nature! I often catch an unexpected glimpse of myself and think—Who is that ferocious looking old woman, and what is she doing in my house?" (Editor's note: photograph was obtained from Doubleday.)

Jassy was filmed in 1947; *You're Best Alone* was filmed as "Guilt is My Shadow"; *The Devil's Own* was filmed as "The Witches."

FOR MORE INFORMATION SEE: Publishers' Weekly, November 11, 1963.

cott, in press. About twenty-five poems have been published in literary magazines, principally in *Shenandoah*, and anthologized in *College Arts Poetry Anthology*, 1968, and *Beyond the Square*, 1972. Writer of weekly humor-food-cooking column, "A Foreign Flavor," in *Roanoke Times*, 1970-74; occasional contributor of reviews and travel articles to newspapers.

WORK IN PROGRESS: Two novels, one for young adults, one for general audience.

SIDELIGHTS: "I have written *something* for about as long as I can remember. I have thought of myself as a writer ever since the first poem I ever wrote was published in *Jack and Jill* when I was eight. It looked to me as if I were a shoo-in, as the poem took maybe five minutes to write, was accepted at once, and then showed up in gorgeous print in a nationwide magazine. The poem, which I imagined everyone reading, I felt pretty bad about—its subject was the recent birth of my twin brother and sister, and the poem said how nice it was to have them. I thought the poem good, but the immensity of my lie lay heavy on my conscience; secretly I thought the twins should return to wherever it was they had come from. My subsequent successes were a long time coming, and not quite so easy as the first. It was eleven prolific years before another poem was accepted, and it was twenty-six years before one of my novels made it.

"I really like teenagers. They may shoot up a foot overnight, act silly about the silliest things and change hairdos, clothes and personalities like characters in dreams; but they are vitally alive, sensitive, interesting people. They are

KATIE LETCHER LYLE

LYLE, Katie Letcher   1938-

PERSONAL: Born May 12, 1938, in Peking, China; daughter of John Seymour (a brigadier general, U.S. Marine Corps) and Elizabeth (an artist; maiden name, Marston) Letcher; married Royster Lyle, Jr. (associate director of George C. Marshall Research Library and Foundation), March 16, 1963; children: Royster Cochran. *Education:* Hollins College, B.A., 1959; Johns Hopkins University, M.A., 1960; Vanderbilt University, further graduate work, 1961-62. *Home address:* P.O. Box 596, Lexington, Va. 24450. *Agent:* Josephine Rogers, Collins-Knowlton-Wing, Inc., 60 East 56th St., New York, N.Y. 10022. *Office:* Division of Liberal Arts, Southern Seminary Junior College, Buena Vista, Va. 24416.

CAREER: Teacher in Baltimore, Md., 1960-61, 1962-63; Southern Seminary Junior College, Buena Vista, Va., member of English faculty, 1963—, chairman of department, 1968—, chairman of Division of Liberal Arts, 1971-73. Staff assistant, Bread Loaf Writers' Conference, summer, 1974. Professional folksinger and occasional actress. *Member:* Modern Language Association of America, College English Association. *Awards, honors:* Bread Loaf Writers' Conference fellowship, 1973.

WRITINGS. (With Maude Rubin and May Miller) *Lyrics of Three Women*, Linden Press, 1964; *I Will Go Barefoot All Summer for You* (teen novel), Lippincott, 1973; *Fair Day, and Another Step Begun* (teen novel), Lippincott, 1974; *The Golden Shoes of Heaven* (teen novel), Lippin-

Summer, bottle-green, wound slowly down to mellow, yellow fall. ■ (From *I Will Go Barefoot all Summer for You* by Katie Letcher Lyle. Illustrated by Paul Bacon.)

often unhappy, and I suspect that most of them are haunted by what they imagine to be their own freakishness. For myself, I can't recall any literature from my teen years that treated people my own age honestly and seriously. Instead it knocked me over with Lessons About Life Writ Large and glossed over those aspects of life that most intensely absorbed and bothered me.

"There is no doubt in my mind that literature's great value is what it shows us about ourselves. I was comforted, and still am, by the constant affirmation that books make to me—that I am indeed a member of the human race.

"In my own books I try to deal fairly and well with the real business of growing without necessarily teaching lessons, talking down to my teenage readers, or assuming that they are too young, stupid or inexperienced to understand good English and the best use I can make of imagery, myth, and symbol. In short, I try to write good literature that has young protagonists."

HOBBIES AND OTHER INTERESTS: Cooking, travel, mycology.

MacCLINTOCK, Dorcas   1932-

PERSONAL: Born July 16, 1932, in New York, N.Y.; daughter of James T. (a businessman) and Helen (Kay) Eason; married Copeland MacClintock (an invertebrate paleontologist), June 30, 1956; children: Margaret, Pamela. *Education:* Smith College, A.B., 1954; University of Wyoming, A.M., 1957. *Politics:* Independent. *Religion:* Episcopalian. *Home:* 33 Rogers Rd., Hamden, Conn. 06517.

DORCAS MacCLINTOCK

The future of giraffes depends upon the efforts of the African governments to conserve . . . at least remnant animal populations within the parks and to increase man's understanding and appreciation of these ambling creatures, full of grace. ∎
(From *A Natural History of Giraffes* by Dorcas MacClintock. Illustrated by Ugo Mochi.)

122

CAREER: American Museum of Natural History, New York, N.Y., student assistant, 1947-53; Yale University, Peabody Museum of Natural History, New Haven, Conn., curator of osteology collection, 1965-67. Research associate, California Academy of Sciences, San Francisco, 1958—. *Member:* American Society of Mammalogists, Society of Vertebrate Paleontology, Ecological Society of America, Sigma Xi. *Awards, honors:* New York Academy of Sciences Award for outstanding 1973 science book in the older category (ages 7-14), for *A Natural History of Giraffes*; the same book was selected by Children's Book Council as one of the outstanding books of the year.

WRITINGS: *Squirrels of North America*, Van Nostrand, 1970; (with Ugo Mochi) *A Natural History of Giraffes* (juvenile), Scribner, 1973. Contributor of articles to *Audubon Magazine, Pacific Discovery*, and other journals.

WORK IN PROGRESS: A book on zebras, for Scribner; research for a book on raccoons.

SIDELIGHTS: "Interest in natural history, especially mammals, stems from childhood. Traveled to East Africa in 1970."

MACRAE, Hawk
See BARKER, Albert W.

MAESTRO, Giulio   1942-

PERSONAL: Given name is pronounced *Jool*-yoh and surname, Ma-*es*-troh; born May 6, 1942, in New York, N.Y.; son of Marcello (a writer) and Edna (Ten Eyck) Maestro; married Betsy Crippen (a kindergarten teacher), 1972. *Education:* Cooper Union, B.F.A., 1964; further study in printmaking at Pratt Graphics Center. *Residence:* Madison, Conn.

CAREER: Design Organization, Inc. (advertising design), New York, N.Y., assistant to art director, 1965-66; Warren A. Kass Graphics, Inc. (advertising design), New York, N.Y., assistant art director, 1966-69; free-lance book illustrator, 1969—. *Member:* American Institute of Graphic Arts. *Awards, honors:* Two books have been included in American Institute of Graphic Arts Children's Book Shows, *The Tortoise's Tug of War* in the 1971-72 show and *Three Kittens* in the 1973-74 show; art work from *The Remarkable Plant in Apartment 4* exhibited in Society of Illustrators' Show, 1974.

WRITINGS—Self-illustrated: *The Tortoise's Tug of War* (animal fable retold), Bradbury, 1971; *The Remarkable Plant in Apartment 4*, Bradbury, 1973; (with Betsy Maestro) *A Wise Monkey Tale*, Crown, 1975.

Illustrator—Picture books: Rudyard Kipling, *The Beginning of the Armadillos*, St. Martin's, 1970; Mirra Ginsburg, *What Kind of Bird Is That?*, Crown, 1973; Mirra Ginsburg, *Three Kittens* (Junior Literary Guild selection), Crown, 1973; Vicki Kimmel Artis, *Gray Duck Catches a Friend*, Putnam, 1974; Tony Johnston, *Fig Tale*, Putnam, 1974; Judy Delton, *Two Good Friends* (Junior Literary Guild selection), Crown, 1974; *One More and One Less* (Junior Literary Guild selection), Crown, 1974; Harry Milgrom, *Egg-Ventures* (Junior Literary Guild selection), Dutton,

1974; Maria Polushkin, *Who Said Meow?* (Junior Literary Guild selection), Crown, 1975.

Illustrator—Readers, math, craft, and other books: Catherine Cutler, *From Petals to Pinecones*, Lothrop, 1969; Catherine Cutler, *Creative Shellcraft*, Lothrop, 1971; Elyse Sommer, *The Bread Dough Craft Book*, Lothrop, 1972; Franklyn Branley, *The Beginning of the Earth*, Crowell, 1972; Jo Phillips, *Right Angles: Paper-Folding Geometry*, Crowell, 1972; Mannis Charosh, *Number Ideas Through Pictures*, Crowell, 1973; Elyse Sommer, *Designing With Cutouts: The Art of Decoupage*, Lothrop, 1973; Elyse Sommer, *Make It With Burlap*, Lothrop, 1973; Roma Gans, *Millions and Millions of Crystals*, Crowell, 1973; Roma Gans, *Oil: The Buried Treasure*, Crowell, 1974; John Trivett, *Building Tables on Tables: A Book About Multiplication*, Crowell, 1974; Carolyn Meyer, *Milk, Butter and Cheese: The Story of Dairy Products*, Morrow, 1974; Sarah Riedman, *Trees Alive*, Lothrop, 1974; Melvin Berger, *The New Air Book*, Crowell, 1974; William R. Gerler, *A Pack of Riddles*, Dutton, 1975.

GIULIO MAESTRO

"No I'm not," said the Tortoise with a smile.
"I know I can beat you at a tug of war."
■ (From *The Tortoise's Tug of War* by Giulio Maestro. Illustrated by the author.)

SIDELIGHTS: "I was born in New York City and lived in Greenwich Village most of my life. My family owned a house on Charlton Street and I attended The Little Red School House from kindergarten through grade six. I started drawing and painting before I even went to school. My parents and teachers were enthusiastic and encouraged me right from the beginning.

"I attended Elisabeth Irwin High School (for seventh and eighth grades) and then was accepted at Music and Art High School, which I attended for the next four years. I completed my education at the Cooper Union Arts School and at Pratt Graphics Center where I pursued my interest in printmaking.

"After graduating, I worked in advertising for a number of years and gained experience in layout, type design, and production, which enables me to do book design as well as illustration. During this period I became interested in the possibility of doing book illustration, and in particular picture books for children. I left advertising, and began to work on a free-lance basis, and soon after I illustrated my first picture book, *The Beginning of the Armadillos*. I find that I am more satisfied with the end results in illustration than I was in advertising, for unlike advertisements, picture books have lasting meaning and importance.

"In addition, free-lancing has allowed me more time for the many other activities I enjoy, in particular reading, painting, and gardening. I also enjoy traveling, and since childhood I have traveled through Europe extensively. At present, my wife and I live in Madison, Connecticut."

FOR MORE INFORMATION SEE: Horn Book, April, 1972; *Junior Literary Guild Catalogue*, September, 1973, March, 1974, September, 1974.

ELIZABETH WINTHROP MAHONY

Something about the Author

MAHONY, Elizabeth Winthrop 1948-
(Elizabeth Winthrop)

PERSONAL: Born September 14, 1948, in Washington, D.C.; daughter of Stewart Johonnot Oliver (a writer and editor) and Patricia (Hankey) Alsop; married Walter B. "Peter" Mahony III (an architect and urban planner), June 13, 1970. *Education:* Miss Porter's School, student, 1963-66; Sarah Lawrence College, B.A., 1970. *Residence:* New York, N.Y.

CAREER: Berkshire Eagle, Pittsfield, Mass., reporter, 1969; Harper & Row Publishers, Inc., New York, N.Y., assistant editor of children's books, 1971-73.

WRITINGS—Under given names, Elizabeth Winthrop: *Bunk Beds* (juvenile), Harper, 1972; *Walking Away* (juvenile), Harper, 1973; *A Little Demonstration of Affection* (young adult), Harper, 1975. Contributor to *New England Review.*

WORK IN PROGRESS: An adult novel dealing with a New England family dominated by a fascinating and sharp-witted grandmother.

Molly pressed her feet against the mattress springs and threw him up with a bounce. ■ (From *Bunk Beds* by Elizabeth Winthrop. Illustrated by Ronald Himler.)

MATSUI, Tadashi 1926-

PERSONAL: Born October 5, 1926, in Kyoto, Japan; son of Yoshifumi and Sumi Matsui; married Mikiko Sato (a crafts artist), May 5, 1952; children: Tomo (son), Kazu (son), Sachi (daughter). *Education:* Dohshisha University, LL.D., 1951. *Home:* 1-5 Kugayama 1-chome, Suginami-ku, Tokyo 167, Japan. *Office:* Fukuinkan Shoten Publishers, 1-9 Misaki-cho 1-chome, Chiyoda-ku, Tokyo 101, Japan.

CAREER: Fukuinkan Shoten Publishers, Tokyo, Japan, president, 1947—. Biennale of Illustrations Bratislava, member of international committee; Tokyo Book Development Centre, member of council. *Member:* Japan Book Publishers' Association (member of board, 1969—).

WRITINGS—Mostly Japanese folktales retold, for children: *Yama no Kikansha* (title means "The Train in the Mountain"), Fukuinkan, 1958; *Daiku to Oniroku*, Fukuinkan, 1962, translation by Masako Matsuno published as *Oniroku and the Carpenter*, Prentice-Hall, 1963; *Kobu Ji-isama* (title means "The Old Men and Their Wens"), Fukuinkan, 1964; *Momotaro*, Fukuinkan, 1965; *Pika-kun Me o Mawasu*, Fukuinkan, 1965, translation by M. Weatherby published as *Peeka, the Traffic Light*, Walker/Weatherhill, 1970; *What is a Picture Book?*, Japan Editor School, 1973. Editor of several reference books on children's literature published by Fukuinkan.

Peeka is working just as hard as before, helping both people and cars to get home quickly and safely. ■ (From *Peeka, the Traffic Light* by Tadasha Matsui. Illustrated by Shinta Cho.)

TADASHI MATSUI

McCAFFREY, Anne 1926-

PERSONAL: Born April 1, 1926, in Cambridge, Mass.; daughter of George Herbert (a city administrator and colonel, U.S. Army) and Anne D. (McElroy) McCaffrey; married H. Wright Johnson (in public relations), January 14, 1950 (divorced, 1970); children: Alec, Todd, Georgeanne. *Education:* Radcliffe College, B.A. (cum laude), 1947; postgraduate work in meteorology, University of City of Dublin; also studied voice for nine years. *Politics:* Democrat. *Religion:* Presbyterian. *Agent:* Bill Berger Associates, Inc., 535 East 72nd St., New York, N.Y. 10021.

CAREER: Liberty Music Shops, New York, N.Y., copywriter, 1948-50; Helena Rubinstein, New York, N.Y., copywriter and secretary, 1950-52; author. Was professional stage director for several groups in Wilmington, Del. *Member:* Science Fiction Writers of America, Mystery Writers of America, Authors' Guild, P.E.N. (Ireland). *Awards, honors:* Hugo Science-Fiction Award, 1967, for *Dragon Flight*; Science Fiction Writers of American Nebula Award, 1968.

WRITINGS: Restoree, Ballantine, 1967; *Dragonflight*, Ballantine, 1968, hardcover edition, Walker, 1969; *Decision at Doona*, Ballantine, 1969; *The Ship Who Sang*, Walker, 1969; *Dragonquest*, Ballantine, 1971; *To Ride Pegasus*, Ballantine, 1973; (editor) *Alchemy and Academe*, Doubleday, 1970; *The Mark of Merlin*, Dell, 1971; *Ring of Fear*, Dell, 1971; *I'll Love You in the Morning*, Dell, 1972; (editor) *Cooking Out of This World* (nonfiction), Ballantine, 1973; (contributor) *Continuum*, Berkley-Putnam, in press. Contributor of short stories to *Science Fiction, Galaxy, Fantasy and Science Fiction, Analog*, and assorted anthologies.

SIDELIGHTS: "When I was a very young girl, I promised myself fervently (usually after I'd lost another battle with one of my brothers) that I would become a famous author and I'd own my own horse. Since my books are now trans-

lated into five foreign languages, I have achieved a degree of fame. Since I moved to Ireland, I have owned my own horse: a big 16.1 hand-high dapple grey Irish hunter, named by a previous owner Mister Ed. I call him 'Horseface' to which he answers with a neigh and a head toss. He's part Connemara pony and part Irish draught horse and a superb hunter. I've hunted him and my daughter, Georgeanne, rides him to hunt (we've never caught a fox yet, so not to worry) and occasionally my son, Todd does, too, though Todd much prefers motorbikes.

"How do I write stories? First I find interesting people to write about (I have written an anthology series, *Crystal Singer*, because I wanted to name a feminine character 'Killeshandra') and then I find something for them to argue about or fight for or against. Or, I think about an interesting concept—the dragons of Pern—telepathic, huge, flame-throwing, dragons who fly because they 'think' they can. Aerodynamically, they can't. I like to write better than anything else, including riding Horseface. And I write because I can't always get the kind of story I like to read on library shelves.

"When I run into a science problem for which I am not equipped, I find myself an expert in that specialty: (Not as easy here in Ireland as it was in the good Ol' U.S. of A.) and I make him tell what I need to know to make my story convincing. I learn a great deal about science that way and not all of it gets into the stories. It would be easier if I were a scientist myself but when I was growing up, girls were not encouraged to be scientists. I'm glad that that notion has changed. You never know what you'll need to know when you grow up: and every bit of information you learn will be useful to you at one time in your life. Being a writer is a constant learning process—learning, reading and then writing."

McCOY, J(oseph) J(erome) 1917-

PERSONAL: Born January 4, 1917, in Philadelphia, Pa.; son of Joseph J. (a civil engineer) and Clara (Tinaro) McCoy; married Barbara Kocyan (an actress and teacher), April 13, 1948; children: Tara Irene, Liza Marie. *Education:* Studied at The Pennsylvania State University, 1938-42. *Agent:* Bertha Klausner, International Literary Agency, 71 Park Avenue, New York, N.Y.

CAREER: Radio producer-director in Philadelphia, Pa., 1946-47; Children's Aid Society, New York, N.Y., instructor in agriculture and nature, 1947-48; farm manager in Connecticut, 1948-50; New York (N.Y.) Humane Society, manager, 1950-56; Gaines Dog Research Center, New York, N.Y., assistant to director, 1956-60; full-time writer, 1960—. *Military service:* U.S. Army, Veterinary Service, 1942-46; became technical sergeant. *Member:* National Audubon Society, American Medical Writers' Association, Comstock Society, Hawk Mountain Sanctuary. *Awards, honors:* New York Herald Tribune Spring Book Festival honor book, 1966, for *The Hunt for the Whooping Cranes*; National Association of Independent Schools Award for one of ten best books for pre-college reader, 1966, for *The Hunt for the Whooping Cranes; New York Times* notable book, 1970, for *Shadows Over the Land*.

WRITINGS: (With H. J. Deutsch) *How to Care for Your Cat*, Cornerstone, 1961; *The Complete Book of Dog*

J. J. McCOY

Training and Care, Coward, 1962; *Lords of the Sky* (juvenile), Bobbs, 1963; *Animal Servants of Man* (juvenile), Lothrop, 1963; *The World of the Veterinarian* (juvenile), Lothrop, 1964; *The Hunt for the Whooping Cranes* (juvenile), Lothrop, 1966; *The Complete Book of Cat Care and Health* (adult), Putnam, 1968; *Swans* (juvenile), Lothrop, 1967; *House Sparrows: Ragamuffins of the City* (juvenile), Seabury, 1968; *The Nature Sleuths* (juvenile), Lothrop, 1969; *Shadows over the Land* (ALA Notable Book), Seabury, 1970; *Saving Our Wildlife*, Macmillan, 1970; *To Feed a Nation* (juvenile), Nelson, 1971; *Our Captive Animals* (juvenile), Seabury, 1972; *Wild Enemies* (Junior Literary Guild selection), Hawthorn, 1974. Contributor to *Grolier Encyclopedia International*.

SIDELIGHTS: "First, all of my books—juvenile and adult—stem from my background, experience, and knowledge in the fields of nature study, ecology, conservation, agriculture, and pet care. I have been involved in these fields—as an activist—ever since I earned the Eagle Scout badge thirty-eight years ago. Incidentally, it was my work in Scouting, particularly the exposure to the fields of nature, conservation, and animals while studying for the various merit badges which led me into these fields as an adult.

"I am still involved in Scouting, serving as a merit badge counselor for the nature, conservation, and agricultural merit badges. I also engage actively in ecology and conservation through some national and local conservation organizations: National Wildlife Federation, Wilderness Society, Hawk Mountain Sanctuary Association, Zoological Society of Philadelphia, Smithsonian Institute. I make an annual pilgrimage to Hawk Mountain in Pennsylvania to witness the thrilling Fall migration of hawks, eagles, and falcons—and have been doing this for more than twenty years. Whenever possible, I take some young people along to introduce them to the fascinating world of the hawks—the lords of the sky, as I call them (and the title of one of my books for young people).

"I prefer to write my nature and conservation books for young people because I firmly believe that young people are more interested in these areas—and that they have the task of undoing the damage to the environment which was done by past generations. I usually try to pick an area of natural history or conservation which needs pointing up. For example, I wrote *The Hunt For the Whooping Cranes* because the plight of the cranes was desperate and needed to be brought before more people—few people knew (at the time I wrote the book) that there were less than fifty of these big cranes in the world—or that it took ten years to locate their secret nesting grounds in Northwest Canada. Today, thanks to the publicity given the cranes through my book and other media, there are more than seventy of the cranes.

"The illegal taking of game birds and mammals by poachers and unsportsmanlike sportsmen disturbed me—I felt that Americans were being robbed of an important part of their natural heritage and that more people ought to know who was doing it—and how they did it. So I decided to write a book about the problem, which became *The Nature Sleuths*, a book that tells about the poachers—how they operate—what kind of game they take—and the work of the federal and state game protectors and conservation officers—the nature sleuths—who have to collect evidence, present the case in court, etc. I went into the field with both federal and state wildlife agents to see just how they went about apprehending violators and collecting the evidence.

"As one who has long been engaged in conservation, I saw the ravages of environmental pollution—and thought that a simple survey of the problems should be written up for young people. I believed that we had to re-evaluate our concept of conservation—changing from one of resource preservation and management to one of protecting and improving the total environment, which included the preservation of natural resources, but added other factors, such as noise pollution, air and water pollution, pesticides, etc. Also, I believed that young people needed to know what they could do to improve and protect the environment and I spelled these out in my book, *Shadows Over the Land*. I believed that young people needed to know what they were really protesting about—that environmental protection and conservation of natural resources were not just hollow slogans to be scrawled on a wall or waved on a street banner.

"When I write about a particular bird or mammal, I try to give it another dimension. Of course, it's important to know the natural history, but equally important to know how the bird or mammal has affected man's social and artistic life—and so I include these aspects in my books about swans, cranes, sparrows, and other wildlife. (See *Swans, House Sparrows, Whooping Cranes*, etc.)

"As for my adult books on cats and dogs, etc., these, too, stem from my background and experience as an army veterinary technician (where I helped to take care of the medical problems of horses, dogs and mules), my tenure as a manager of a humane society animal shelter, my work with the Gaines Dog Research Center in New York and my present capacities as chairman of several Boards of Animal Regulation in Pennsylvania and as a dog and cat owner.

"The other writing that I do—dramatic—is not so far afield as it may seem, since I have written radio and television, as well as children's plays and musical libretti for a number of years. My wife, Barbara, is a professional actress and together we have produced some children's theater in the Philadelphia area. I have written story lines for two children's ballets ('Persephone,' based on the Greek myth, and 'The Sultan's Daughter,' an original story), three children's plays and one children's musical, 'The Puppeteers.' I like to write dramatic material because it gives me a chance to exercise my imagination—which, of course, I cannot do with the factual books on nature and conservation. But, I usually manage to put nature and conservation in the plays and musicals—somewhere—someway.

"I write at home—have dogs, cats, birds, fish and in the summer, manage to collect various small mammals and reptiles. I treat my writing as a regular job, working at it every day, seven days a week. I do a lot of reading—limit myself to a few hours of television a day—go on field trips—and keep my eyes on nature around me.

"When my wife is in a play, I usually become involved with her . . . attending rehearsals, etc. My oldest daughter, Tara, is a young student at the Pennsylvania Ballet and when she is doing something, I get involved with that.

Pet sparrows frequently escaped from their cages or pens. Most of them became semiwild birds, living in the cities and suburbs. ■ (From *House Sparrows* by J. J. McCoy. Illustrated by Jean Zallinger.)

Similarly, my youngest daughter, Dyza, is an aspiring actress and when she is in a school play, I get involved in that.

"In general, I try to keep in close contact with the world of young people, either through my own endeavors or those of my daughters. I find that knowing about young people, about how they feel, act and what they want to do, helps me a great deal in writing books for them. Also, when I am asked to speak to children in schools or at library gatherings, the contact is invaluable to me as a writer. I usually conduct a panel discussion rather than deliver a straight lecture, because this gives the children a chance to participate. I think it imperative that a juvenile writer keep in contact with his reader group.

"A self-appraisal is difficult, of course, but here goes. I consider myself a disciplined artist, one who seeks universal truth through knowledge and creation. I am not a slick writer, but one who takes great pains with his work—digging deeper than the surface—learning at the same time that I am teaching through my writings. I am impatient with those who want shortcuts, those who seek the easy way rather than the more difficult way that might lead them closer to the truth of something. I am never satisfied with what I write but am constantly changing and revising, trying not so much for perfect literary style but the best way to say something—to say what I mean—and in a way that the reader can grasp. For, after all, a book is a communication and if it fails to communicate, then the writer has failed as an artist and craftsman. When people say to me, 'You write so simply yet give a lot of information', then I feel that I have succeeded and that all the work, the effort, the strain have been justified.

"One doesn't write down to children today; one is lucky to be able to keep up with them. Children want their intelligence to be respected and demand accuracy and clarity. My two daughters are my most severe critics. The criticism of juvenile readers is blunt, unadorned, and pragmatic—and I would like to see juvenile books reviewed by children!"

HOBBIES AND OTHER INTERESTS: Natural history, especially birds of prey and whooping cranes; gardening, scouting, theater, hiking.

McCULLOUGH, Frances Monson 1938-

PERSONAL: Born October 23, 1938, in Quantico, Va.; daughter of George Edward (a career officer in the Marine Corps; retired as a colonel) and Frances (Fouche) Monson; married David McCullough (a book critic), November 20, 1965; children: Benjamin, Katy. *Education:* Stanford University, B.A., 1960; Brandeis University, graduate study, 1960-61. *Politics:* Democrat. *Residence:* Brooklyn, N.Y. *Office:* Harper & Row Publishers, Inc., 10 East 53rd St., New York, N.Y. 10016.

CAREER: Harper & Row Publishers, Inc., New York, N.Y., editor, 1963—. *Awards, honors:* Roger Klein Award for creative writing, 1971.

WRITINGS: (Editor) *Earth, Air, Fire and Water* (poetry anthology for young people), Coward, 1971.

SIDELIGHTS: "My editor *willed* me to write this book; I did not want to do it. As an editor myself, I am very conscious of the great overkill in books, especially anthologies, but he convinced me (by showing me the competition) that there was a need for a non-cute, accessible, fresh anthology for young people. I understand that the book is now being used on the college level and in a number of other unexpected places. My own idea in assembling the book was that I hoped to make a collection that would have excited me when I was in high school, that would help me get into poetry instead of treating it like a math problem that defied solution."

FOR MORE INFORMATION SEE: *Horn Book*, June, 1971.

McGOVERN, Ann

PERSONAL: Born in New York, N.Y.; daughter of Arthur (a bacteriologist) and Kate (Malatsky) Weinberger; married Martin L. Scheiner (an engineer), June 6, 1970; children: Peter McGovern; (second marriage): Charles, Ann, Jim. *Education:* Attended University of New Mexico. *Residence:* Pleasantville, N.Y.

CAREER: Scholastic Book Services, New York, N.Y., associate editor of Arrow Book Club, 1958-65, editor and founder of See Saw Book Club, 1965-67, presently member of editorial board of See Saw Book Club. *Member:* International P.E.N., Authors Guild. *Awards, honors:* Named author of the year, 1974, by Scholastic Book Services' Lucky Book Club.

WRITINGS—For children: *Why It's a Holiday*, Random House, 1960; *Story of Christopher Columbus*, Random House, 1962; *Aesop's Fables*, Scholastic Book Services, 1963; *If You Lived in Colonial Times*, Four Winds, 1964;

ANN McGOVERN

Who Has a Secret?, Houghton, 1964; *Zoo, Where Are You?*, Harper, 1964; *Little Wolf*, Abelard, 1965; *Arrow Book of Poetry*, Scholastic Book Services, 1965; *Questions and Answers About the Human Body*, Random House, 1965; *Runaway Slave: The Story of Harriet Tubman*, Four Winds, 1965; *If You Grew Up with Abraham Lincoln*, Four Winds, 1966; *Too Much Noise*, Houghton, 1967; *Robin Hood of Sherwood Forest*, Crowell, 1968; *Stone Soup*, Scholastic Book Services, 1968; *Black Is Beautiful*, Four Winds, 1969; *Hee-Haw*, Houghton, 1969; *If You Sailed on the Mayflower*, Four Winds, 1969; *Shakespearean Sallies, Sullies, and Slanders*, Crowell, 1969.

The Defenders, Scholastic Book Services, 1970; *Ghostly Fun*, Scholastic Book Services, 1970; *If You Lived with the Circus*, Four Winds, 1971; *Ghostly Giggles*, Scholastic Book Services, 1972; *Squeals and Squiggles and Ghostly Giggles*, Four Winds, 1973; *The Pilgrims' First Thanksgiving*, Scholastic Book Services, 1973; *If You Lived with the Sioux Indians*, Four Winds, 1974; *Scram, Kid*, Viking, 1974; *Sharks!*, Scholastic Book Services, 1975.

Contributor to *Newsday*, *WomenSports*, and *Saturday Review*. Reviewer of children's books for *New York Times*, 1960-66.

WORK IN PROGRESS: *Underwater World of the Coral Reef*; *Secret Soldier: The Story of Deborah Sampson*.

SIDELIGHTS: "Looking backward (and forward) to my books, I realize that they reflect my life in three parts: 1) ideas I strongly believe in; 2) desire for knowledge (I never finished college); 3) exciting personal experiences—scuba diving, for example, or exploring Mayan ruins or camping out in Africa, and photographing everywhere.

"*Black is Beautiful* was written right after Martin Luther King's murder. I went to a rally in the city and heard a young man say in anger and grief: 'Black is beautiful, baby. Know it. Feel it.' I knew it and felt it but I also knew that the word 'black' had held negative images for far too long. The next two days I wrote pages of positive images about blackness and it became a kind of poem. Because I was strongly against the Vietnam war, I wrote *Little Wolf* to show how one person rejected violence even though the world around him condemned pacifism. In *Runaway Slave: The Story of Harriet Tubman*, I chose a woman in history whom black and white girls could admire. There are still too few heroines for today's society, and my book is about a young woman who was denied adventure because of her sex and poverty during Revolutionary times. In my historical books I try to ferret out the truth, even though the truth may not be popular. I think it important to tell it like it was; to show for example, that the Pilgrims got seasick on the Mayflower and threw up, like ordinary folk.

"Trying to dispel damaging stereotypes, I emphasized the Sioux nation's peaceable nature in *If You Lived With the Sioux Indians*.

"For my future writings, I plan to concentrate on events in our history long ignored, and books that reinforce humanistic values such as love, individuality, and honesty to each other."

HOBBIES AND OTHER INTERESTS: Travel. "With my husband, Martin Scheiner, toured Morocco, watched a

McGREGOR, Craig 1933-

PERSONAL: Born October 12, 1933, in Jamberoo, Australia; son of Alister Stephen Charles (a clerk) and Jean (Craig) McGregor; married Jane Watson, June 10, 1962; children: Robert, Kate, Sarah Alison, Clare. *Education:* Attended Cranbrook School, Sydney, Australia, 1945-50; University of Sydney, B.A., 1955. *Home and office:* 20 Moncur St., Wollahra, Sydney, Australia. *Agent:* Innes Rose, John Farquharson Ltd., 15 Red Lion Sq., London W.C. 1, England.

CAREER: Journalist in Sydney, Australia, 1950-58; journalist and teacher, London, England, 1958-62, writer, Sydney, Australia, 1962—. *Member:* Australian Society of Authors, Australian Journalists' Association, Australian Writer's Guild. *Awards, honors:* Xavier Society Prize for Literature, 1969.

WRITINGS: (With Midget Farrelly) *This Surfing Life*, Rigby, 1965 (published in America as *The Surfing Life*, Arco, 1967); *Profile of Australia*, Hodder & Stoughton, 1966, Regnery, 1967, revised edition, Penguin, 1968; *People, Politics and Pop: Australians in the 'Sixties* (essays, reviews, articles, short stories), Ure Smith, 1967; (editor with David Beal) *Life in Australia* (photographs and text), Southern Cross International, 1967; (with Helmut Gritscher) *The High Country* (photographs and text), Angus & Robertson, 1967; *To Sydney with Love*, Thomas Nelson, 1968; *In the Making*, Thomas Nelson, 1969; *Don't Talk to Me about Love* (novel), Ure Smith, 1971, Penguin, 1972; *Bob Dylan: A Retrospective*, Morrow, 1972; *Up*

"What manner of man art thou . . . to win our master's favor and then help thyself to his food and drink? Whereupon he dealt Little John three bold strokes with his staff. ■ (From *Robin Hood of Sherwood Forest* by Ann McGovern. Illustrated by Arnold Spilka.)

sunrise over the Himalayas in Nepal, explored ancient temples in Burma, visited opium-smoking villages in Thailand, traveled thorugh Hong Kong, Japan and India.

"In 1970, 1972 and 1973 we journeyed to the total eclipse of the sun—a farmer's field in South Carolina, to Nova Scotia by ship, and in '73 to northern Kenya's remote Lake Rudolf. In 1974 we returned to Japan and India, explored Ethiopia, lived in tents in the jungles of East Africa and toured Nigeria.

"With our four children we make trips for scuba diving and underwater photography. We have dived in Granada, Barbados, Martinique, and Quintana Roo. My scuba adventures include diving with sharks and sea lions, diving a coral reef at night, running out of air, exploring ancient shipwrecks. Our interest in archeology has taken us to the Yucatan Peninsula, Chichen Itza, Tolum and Copan, Honduras.

"An enthusiasm for scuba-diving is shared by the whole family and has been the focus of many family vacations."

FOR MORE INFORMATION SEE: Lee Bennett Hopkins, *Books Are by People*, Citation Press, 1969.

CRAIG McGREGOR

Against the Wall, America, Angus & Robertson, 1973; *The Great Barrier Reef*, Time-Life, 1974. Story anthologized in *Pick of Today's Short Stories*, Putnam, 1962.

WORK IN PROGRESS: A novel, *Anywhere but Somewhere Else*.

SIDELIGHTS: McGregor told *Contemporary Authors* that he has a "sociological bias." According to a *Times Literary Supplement* critic, McGregor is a "portraitist, with the appearance and attitudes of people at large and young people in particular. . . . He writes more vividly and with the breathlessness of a guide who is not only bent on covering more ground than anyone else, but who is convinced it is well worth covering."

HOBBIES AND OTHER INTERESTS: Popular culture, jazz, folk music, and the cinema.

FOR MORE INFORMATION SEE: Times Literary Supplement, March 30, 1967.

MEE, Charles L., Jr. 1938-

PERSONAL: Born September 15, 1938, in Evanston, Ill. *Education:* Harvard University, B.A., 1960. *Office: Horizon*, 1221 Avenue of the Americas, New York, N.Y.

CAREER: Horizon Magazine, New York, N.Y., editor, 1961—.

WRITINGS: (With editors of *Horizon* Magazine) *Lorenzo de Medici and the Renaissance*, American Heritage Press, 1968; (with Edward L. Greenfield) *Dear Prince: The Unexpurgated Counsels of N. Machiavelli to Richard Milhous Nixon*, American Heritage Press, 1969; (editor) *Horizon Bedside Reader*, American Heritage Press, 1971; *White Robe, Black Robe*, Putnam, 1972; *Erasmus*, Coward, 1974. Plays: "Constantinople Smith," one-act, first produced Off-Broadway at the Playbox Studio, July, 1968; "Anyone! Anyone!," and "Players' Repertoire," first produced off-Broadway at Writers' Stage Company, 1964; "God Bless Us Everyone," published in *Tulane Drama Review*, 1965; "The Life of the Party."

FOR MORE INFORMATION SEE: Village Voice, July 4, 1968; *Show Business*, May 22, 1969; *Best Sellers*, June 1, 1969; *Saturday Review*, July 19, 1969; *Horn Book*, August, 1969, April, 1974; *Book World*, October 12, 1969; *New York Times Book Review*, November 9, 1969.

MEHDEVI, Anne (Marie) Sinclair

PERSONAL: Born in Manila, Philippine Islands; daughter of Solomon Sanford (a lawyer) and Ida (Lowry) Sinclair; married Mohamed Mehdevi (now an author and management analyst), June 5, 1945; children: Rafael, Alexander, Florence. *Education:* University of Rochester, B.A. (magna cum laude). *Home:* Puerto de Alcudia, Majorca, Spain. *Address:* c/o Alfred A. Knopf, 501 Madison Ave., New York 22, N.Y.

CAREER: Collier's, New York, N.Y., assistant editor (distaff), 1942-43; *Dayton Herald*, Dayton, Ohio, reporter, 1943; *Newsweek*, New York, N.Y., researcher, 1943-46. *Member:* Phi Beta Kappa.

. . . with his sharp teeth, he gnawed the carrot into a perfect little ladder with twenty steps. ■ (From *Persian* by Anne Sinclair Mehdevi. Illustrated by Paul E. Kennedy.)

WRITINGS: Persian Adventure, Knopf, 1953; *From Pillar to Post*, Knopf, 1956; *Don Chato*, Knopf, 1959; (contributor) *Over the Horizon*, Duell, Sloan & Pearce, 1960; *The Leather Hand*, Knopf, 1961; *Rubies of the Red Sea*, Knopf, 1963; *Persia Revisited*, Knopf, 1964; *Persian Folk and Fairy Tales*, Knopf, 1965; *Parveen*, Knopf, 1969. Articles in *New Yorker, Harper's, Mademoiselle, Collier's, Newsweek, Omnibook, New York Times Magazine*.

WORK IN PROGRESS: Persian Epic Tales (retold).

SIDELIGHTS: Books translated into German, Italian, Japanese; all but one also published in England. Competent in Spanish, German, French; speaks "a little Farsi."

MILES, Betty 1928-

PERSONAL: Born 1928, in Chicago, Ill.; daughter of David D. and Helen (Otte) Baker; married Matthew B. Miles, 1949; children: Sara, David Baker, Ellen. *Education:* Antioch College, B.A., 1950. *Home:* 94 Sparkill Ave., Tappan, N.Y. 10983.

CAREER: Bank Street College of Education, New York, N.Y., publications associate, 1958-65. Now self-employed free-lance writer.

WRITINGS: *A House for Everyone*, 1958, *What Is the World?*, 1958, *The Cooking Book*, 1959, *Having a Friend*, 1959, *A Day of Summer*, 1960, *Mr. Turtle's Mystery*, 1961, *A Day of Winter*, 1961, *The Feast on Sullivan Street*, 1963, *A Day of Autumn*, 1967, *A Day of Spring*, 1970, (with Joan Blos) *Just Think!*, 1971, *Save the Earth!*, 1974, *The Real Me*, 1974, (contributor of "Atalanta") *Free to Be You and Me*, McGraw-Hill, 1974, *Around and Around-Love*, 1975 (all published by Knopf, except where otherwise noted). Associate editor, *The Bank Street Readers*, Macmillan, 1965. Articles in numerous magazines. Also writes for film and television.

SIDELIGHTS: "I write about the things I care about, hoping that I can get other people to care about them too. I wrote *Save the Earth!* to explain ecological concepts, and to help people understand environmental problems. But I wanted to show, also, how knowledge, foreward planning and hard work can lead to useful solutions. I do believe that, though it will be complicated and difficult, people can cooperate to save the earth.

[*The Real Me* is, as its title suggests, about me—although I am forty-seven and Barbara Fisher, the heroine, is eleven. Many of my thoughts about justice and fairness, and about the importance of the women's liberation movement for everyone—men and women, girls and boys—are reflected in the things Barbara Fisher says. Barbara Fisher makes the kind of jokes I like to make. And her deep wish for a dog, which doesn't come true by the time the book ends, is a kind of apology to my daughter, who doesn't have a dog, either.

"I can only write about things I know about and care about very much. I like putting my ideas and feelings on paper so that people who read my books will understand and perhaps share them."

Here is a house with two aunts and some plants. ■ (From *A House for Everyone* by Betty Miles. Illustrated by Jo Lowrey.)

BETTY MILES

MILITANT
See SANDBURG, Carl (August)

MILLER, Eddie
See MILLER, Edward

MILLER, Edward   1905-1974
(Eddie Miller)

PERSONAL: Born September 5, 1905, in De Soto, Mo.; son of Edward (a barber) and Louise Ann (Craig) Miller; married Lucille A. Kaufman, September 24, 1934. *Education:* Central Methodist College, student, 1926; studied art in night classes at Art Institute of Chicago and St. Louis School of Fine Arts. *Politics:* Liberal. *Religion:* Protestant. *Home address:* Route 2, Peter Moore Lane, De Soto, Mo. 63020. *Agent:* Bertha Klausner, International Literary Agency, Inc., 71 Park Ave., New York, N.Y. 10016.

CAREER: Architectural Decorating Co. (general displays and exhibits), Chicago, Ill., designer and art director, 1931-40; Sears, Roebuck & Co., Chicago, Ill., art director of headquarters display department, 1940-42; free-lance artist in De Soto, Mo., 1942-74, doing advertising agency commissions, painting in water colors, and illustrating books. Did whimsical paper sculpture and more conventional advertising designs for Ford Motor Co., United Airlines, U.S. Steel, Purina Mills, and other corporations; also drew a comic strip for six years for Falls City Brewing Co.; designer of television slides and film strips for TV Arts, Inc., St. Louis, Mo., 1958-59; when illness forced him to give up advertising art in 1960, he formed Storybook Associates to create ideas for children's picture books. Member of De Soto Public Library Board, 1952-61, and former secretary of the board. *Member:* State Historical Society of Missouri. *Awards, honors:* Awards for water colors at various art exhibitions

EDWARD MILLER

WRITINGS—"Halls of Greatness" series for young people; author and illustrator with Betty Jean Mueller; *The Franklin Delano Roosevelt Home and Library*, 1967, *The Harry S. Truman Library*, 1967, *The Dwight D. Eisenhower Library*, 1967, *The Halls of Lincoln's Greatness*, 1968, *Mount Vernon*, 1968 (all published by Meredith).

Illustrator of more than thirty books and texts, including a twelve-book animal adventure series for Benefic Press, three books, *Jerry Goes Riding, Apron Strings and Rowdy*, and *Carlos of Mexico* for Beckley-Cardy, and science, language, spelling, and history books for Webster Division of McGraw-Hill; also illustrator of magazine articles for *This Day*, Concordia Publishing House. Under the byline Eddie Miller, writer and illustrator of a weekly historical feature, "As you Were," for *De Soto Press-Dispatch*, 1967-74.

WORK IN PROGRESS: Gettysburg Today and *Kennedy Memorial at Arlington*, for "Halls of Greatness" series; a light-hearted book about the art game, tentatively titled *Is It True About Artists?*

FOR MORE INFORMATION SEE: Illustrator, spring, 1959, summer, 1969; *American Artist*, May, 1962; *Chicago Tribune*, May 7, 1967.

(Died February 14, 1974)

MIRSKY, Jeannette   1903-

PERSONAL: Born September 3, 1903, in Bradley Beach, N.J.; daughter of Michael David (a businessman) and Frieda (Ittleson) Mirsky; married Edward Bellamy Ginsburg, February 14, 1942 (deceased). *Education:* Columbia University, B.A., 1924, graduate study in anthropology, 1935-38. *Home and office:* 230 Nassau St., Princeton, N.J. 08540.

CAREER: Author. Princeton University, Princeton, N.J., visiting fellow, department of Oriental studies, 1964-67, East Asian studies, 1973-74. Lecturer for U.S. Department of State and on radio and television. *Member:* Society of Woman Geographers, Society for the History of Discoveries, Royal Central Asian Society, P.E.N., Phi Beta Kappa. *Awards, honors:* Guggenheim fellowship; Rockefeller Foundation grant; National Endowment for the Humanities, Lucius N. Littover Foundation grant.

WRITINGS: To the North!, Viking, 1934, revised edition published as *To the Arctic!*, Knopf, 1946, reissued, University of Chicago Press, 1970; *The Westward Crossings: Balboa, Mackenzie, Lewis and Clark*, Knopf, 1944, reissued, University of Chicago Press, 1970; (with Allan Nevins) *The World of Eli Whitney*, Macmillan, 1952; *Elisha Kent Kane and the Seafaring Frontier*, Little, 1954; *Balboa, Discoverer of the Pacific*, Harper, 1964; (editor and compiler) *The Great Chinese Travelers* (anthology), Pantheon, 1964; (author of introduction) M. Aurel Stein, *On Ancient Central Asian Tracks*, Pantheon, 1964; *Houses of God*, Viking, 1965; *The Gentle Conquistadors*, Pantheon, 1969; (introduction) Emily James Putnam, *The Lady*, University of Chicago, 1970.

JEANNETTE MIRSKY

WORK IN PROGRESS: Research for a critical biography of Sir M. Aurel Stein.

SIDELIGHTS: Jeanette Mirsky has pursued her interest in historical geography and cultural anthropology in Middle East, Central America, Europe, the U.S.S.R., and India. *To the North!* was published in England, and in German and Spanish editions, and *The Westward Crossings*, in England; Arabic and French editions of *The World of Eli Whitney* were distributed overseas by U.S. Information Agency.

He had . . . walked out on a plank which jutted twenty feet out of the tower of the Cathedral of Seville. ■ (From *Balboa* by Jeanette Mirsky. Illustrated by Hans Guggenheim.)

MOFFETT, Martha (Leatherwood) 1934-

PERSONAL: Born January 3, 1934, in Pell City, Ala.; daughter of William E. (a teacher) and Martha (Funderburk) Leatherwood; married Robert Knight Moffett (an editor and writer), January 31, 1955; children: Cameron, Tyler, Kirsten. *Education:* University of Alabama, B.S., 1954; Columbia University, M.S., 1972. *Home:* 201 West 94th St., New York, N.Y. 10025. *Agent:* Charles Neighbors, 36 Waverly Pl., New York, N.Y.

CAREER: New Book of Knowledge, New York, N.Y., head of proof department, 1964-66; *American Heritage Dictionary*, New York, N.Y., senior copy editor, 1966-68; *Ladies' Home Journal*, New York, N.Y., editorial staff, 1974—. Active in the peace movement and local co-operative and school organizations. *Member:* Forum of Writers for Young People.

WRITINGS: (With husband, Robert Knight Moffett) *The Whale in Fact & Fiction*, Quist, 1967; (with R. Moffett) *First Book of Dolphins*, Watts, 1971; (editor) *Great Love Poems*, 5 volumes, World Publishing, 1971; *A Flower Pot is Not a Hat*, Dutton, 1972; *Great Women Athletes*, Platt & Munk, 1974.

WORK IN PROGRESS: A children's book exploring a child's basic fears; an adult novel; poetry.

SIDELIGHTS: "Everything in the small, isolated, raw mining town in the mountains of northeast Alabama is removed by more than time from the life I lead now—it is all a world away. I grew up dreaming of escape, of life in a great city; reading books that I hoped would lead me there."

FOR MORE INFORMATION SEE: New York Times Book Review, September 24, 1967.

MARTHA MOFFETT

Baby Brother is not a chair. ■ (From *A Flower Pot is Not a Hat* by Martha Moffett. Illustrated by Susan Perl.)

Something about the Author

MOHN, Viola Kohl 1914-

PERSONAL: Born February 18, 1914, in Myerstown, Pa.; daughter of Ervin E. (a well drilling contractor) and Carrie Kohn; married Harold F. Mohn (a businessman and writer of patriotic poetry), November 28, 1940. *Education:* Lebanon Business College, graduate, 1933; Wyomissing Institute of Fine Art, graduate, 1943; Famous Artists Schools, graduate, 1950. *Politics:* Republican. *Religion:* Protestant. *Home and studio:* Box 144, R.D. 1, Myerstown, Pa. 17067.

CAREER: Kohl Bros. (well drilling contractor), Myerstown, Pa., bookkeeper and secretary, 1933-46; member of board and part owner of Harrisburg's Kohl Bros., Inc., Harrisburg, Pa., 1964—. Conducted Mohn Studio of Dance, Myerstown, 1940-45; free-lance artist, 1970—, with paintings exhibited in annual shows at Reading Museum and elsewhere in Pennsylvania. Member of board, Historic Preservation Trust of Lebanon County, 1968—; active in Girl Scouts as leader, camp director, and council consultant, 1931—. *Member:* Pennsylvania German Society, Lebanon County Historical Society (member of board, 1971—), Tulpehocken Settlement Society, Myerstown Community Library (president, 1975—), Myerstown Federated Woman's Clubs (president, 1961-63). *Awards, honors:* First in awards and best of show in exhibitions of Lebanon Valley Art Association four years.

ILLUSTRATOR: Christine Ruth Grier, *Kathy's New World*, Manthorne & Burack, 1939; Helen Ross Russell, *Winter Search Party: A Guide to Insects and Other Invertebrate* (Child Study Association book list), Thomas Nelson, 1971. Author and illustrator of *Shadows of the Rhine Along the Tulpehocken*, Book I, Lebanon County Historical Society, 1972, Book 2, 1975, and editor and co-author of Myerstown Centennial volume, 1968.

WORK IN PROGRESS: Further volume in *Shadows of the Rhine Along the Tulpehocken*, for Lebanon County Historical Society; a book of poems.

MOHR, Nicholasa 1935-

PERSONAL: Born November 1, 1935, in New York, N.Y.; daughter of Pedro and Nicolasa (Rivera) Golpe; married Irwin Mohr (a child psychologist), October 5, 1957; children: David, Jason. *Education:* Studied at Art Students' League of New York, 1953-56, Brooklyn Museum Art School, 1959-66, and Pratt Center for Contemporary Printmaking, 1966-69. *Politics:* Independent. *Religion:* None. *Residence:* Teaneck, N.J. *Agent:* Joan Daves, 515 Madison Ave., New York, N.Y. 10022.

CAREER: Painter, 1952-62, working in New York, California, Mexico, and Puerto Rico; printmaker, 1963—. Teacher in art schools in New York and New Jersey, 1967—; Board of trustees, Young Filmakers, Inc. Work has been shown in several one-woman exhibitions and in group shows. *Awards, honors:* MacDowell Colony writing fellowship, summer, 1974; Jane Addams Children's Book Award of U.S. Section of Women's International League for Peace and Freedom, 1974, for *Nilda*; Citation of Merit at Society of Illustrators annual exhibition, 1974, for book jacket of *Nilda*.

WRITINGS: (Author, illustrator, and designer of book jacket) *Nilda* (juvenile novel), Harper, 1973; *El Bronx Remembered* (short stories), Harper, in press.

WORK IN PROGRESS: A set of plays concerned with the Puerto Rican woman; working under a grant with Young Filmaker's, Inc. as creative writer and production designer for ten half-hour T.V. programs on Caribbean Hispanic Americans in the Northeastern United States.

SIDELIGHTS: "My work as a writer is expressed through the creative medium of fiction with the intent of reaching all people. It incorporates a strong social statement; the plight and constant struggle of the Puerto Ricans on the mainland, to receive their basic human rights. Using art, the universal language of humanity, I bring forth the point of view of a sub-culture in America, the Puerto Rican people with all their variety and complexity."

FOR MORE INFORMATION SEE: Horn Book, April, 1974.

NICHOLASA MOHR

Summers in New York City's Barrio were unbearable. Even when there was a cool spell, it seemed a long time before the dry fresh air could find a way past the concrete and asphalt, into the crowded buildings which had become blazing furnaces. ■ (From *Nilda* by Nicholasa Mohr. Illustrated by the author.)

MORGAN, Lenore 1908-

PERSONAL: Born October 3, 1908, in Princeton, N.J.; daughter of David (a law professor and college president) and Laura (Mooney) Hutchison; married David H. Morgan (a director, Dow Chemical Co.), December 30, 1933; children: Ann (Mrs. Charles D. Dever), Dale (Mrs. Sandford T. Waddell). *Education:* State University of New York, B.A., 1929; Vanderbilt University, M.A., 1930; University of Paris, Dr. en Droit, 1932; Academy of International Law, The Hague, Netherlands, Certificat, 1932; Colorado State University, M.S., 1949; additional graduate study at Columbia University, London School of Economics and Political Science, and University of California. *Politics:* Republican. *Religion:* Presbyterian. *Home:* 612 North Saginaw Rd., Midland, Mich. 48640.

CAREER: Has worked for station KRE, Berkeley, Calif., as a program director, U.S. Office of War Information, San Francisco, Calif., as a staff member, Radio Station WOKO, Albany, N.Y., as a programmer, and has worked in special children's health radio programming in New York; Writer's Conference, Judson, N.Y., teacher of writing for children, 1966-69. Actress with little theaters and stock companies in New York, Tennessee, London, England, and Paris, France; holder of U.S. patents for toy designs. *Member:* Authors League of America, Midland Women's Club, Kings Daughters, Phi Beta Kappa.

WRITINGS—Juveniles: *The Mouse Who Was Stirring*, Baker Book, 1961; *The Shepherds Brought a Song*, Baker Book, 1962; *Peter's Pockets*, Oddo, 1965; *Dragons and Stuff*, Oddo, 1970. Contributor of short stories to "SRA Reading Series." Contributor of more than 125 stories and articles to national magazines. Writer-producer of Midland Centennial Pageant, 1968.

WORK IN PROGRESS: A juvenile novel on the Revolution; a humorous personal-essay type novel on the life of a college president and his wife.

HOBBIES AND OTHER INTERESTS: Designing toys; theatre; golf.

FOR MORE INFORMATION SEE: Library Journal, October 15, 1970.

MORRISS, James E(dward) 1932-

PERSONAL: Born February 9, 1932, in Oklahoma City, Okla.; son of William Jacob (a farmer) and Anna Ellen Morriss. *Education:* John Brown University, B.A. and B.S., 1952; City University of New York Graduate School of Education, M.A., 1963; further graduate study at New School for Social Research and New York University, 1968. *Home:* Oak Beach, N.Y. 11702. *Office:* Division Avenue High School, Levittown, N.Y. 11756.

JAMES E. MORRISS

CAREER: High school teacher of life sciences in public schools of Levittown, N.Y., 1958—, presently teaching courses he designed in ecology, human behavior, animal behavior, and parapsychology, at Division Avenue High School. Member of environmental advisory board, Town of Babylon, N.Y. *Member:* National Audubon Society, New York Zoological Society, American Society for Psychical Research, American Museum of Natural History. *Awards, honors: The Brains of Animals and Man* was named one of the five best nonfiction books of the year by *School Library Journal*, 1972.

WRITINGS—With Russell Freedman: *How Animals Learn*, Holiday House, 1969; *Animal Instincts*, Holiday House, 1970; *The Brains of Animals and Man* (Junior Literary Guild selection), Holiday House, 1972. Collaborator (research) on National Broadcasting Co. television series, "Animal Secrets," 1966-67.

WORK IN PROGRESS: A book for young adults, *Man's Mysterious Mind*; developing a teaching module on parapsychology for the Human Behavior Curriculum Project, which is funded by National Science Foundation.

SIDELIGHTS: "Growing up in the country (Ozark Mountains) gave me a special reverence for nature. To sustain this sacred communion with the out-of-doors I divide my time between a cabin in the wooded hills of New England and my home on an almost deserted stretch of beach on the Atlantic Coast. I find these sanctuaries conducive to writing.... My present focus of attention is on describing the advances being made by scientists in understanding the dimensions of consciousness, and the potential of the human mind."

Morriss has tamed and trained a variety of animals. He and his high school students even taught a pet chicken to play baseball.

MULVIHILL, William Patrick   1923-

PERSONAL: Born June 25, 1923, in Sag Harbor, Long Island, N.Y.; son of Daniel Frances and Anna (McDonough) Mulvihill, married Mary Marceau, 1946; children: Nancy Jeanne, Mary Ann. *Education:* Cornell University, B.A., 1948; Columbia University, M.A., 1951. *Home:* 70 Dosoris Way, Glen Cove, N.Y.

CAREER: Public high school, Glen Cove, N.Y., teacher of history, 1953—. *Military service:* U.S. Army, 1943-46, corporal. *Member:* Sigma Nu. *Awards, honors:* Putnam $10,000 award for *The Sands of Kalahari*, 1960.

He was a hunter and they did not understand him; they did not know what hunting was, the waiting, the planning, the thinking. They did not know . . . ■ (From the movie *"The Sands of the Kalahari,"* copyright © 1965 by Paramount Pictures Corp. and Embassy Pictures Corp.)

WILLIAM PATRICK MULVIHILL

WRITINGS: Fire Mission, Ballantine, 1957; *The Mantrackers*, New American Library, 1960; *The Sands of Kalahari*, Putnam, 1960; *Night of the Axe* (*School Library Journal* book list), Houghton, 1972; *I've Got Viktor Schalkenburg*, Berkley, 1974.

SIDELIGHTS: "My novels are personal explorations into the dual nature of the human species. The soldiers in *Fire Mission* enjoy war and combat; John Thrushwood, the old hunter in *The Mantrackers*, is motivated by a great sense of guilt for having been an agent in the slaughter of African wildlife. O'Brien in *The Sands of the Kalahari* survives by regressing to animal status. *Night of the Axe* is concerned with man's dark urge to destroy beauty—as well as his ability to preserve it. *I've Got Viktor Schalkenburg* deals with man's capacity for mass murder and his capacity to transcend it."

The Sands of the Kalahari was made into a motion picture in 1965.

NAVARRA, John Gabriel   1927-

PERSONAL: Born July 3, 1927, in Bayonne, N.J.; son of Salvatore Anthony (a chemist) and Yolanda (Scala) Navarra; married Celeste Scala, September 12, 1947; children: John Gabriel, Jr., Elisa (Mrs. L. Michael Treadwell). *Education:* Columbia University, A.B., 1949, M.A., 1950, Ed.D., 1954. *Office:* P.O. Box 647, Farmingdale, N.J. 07727.

CAREER: East Carolina College (now East Carolina University), Greenville, N.C., associate professor of science, 1954-58; Jersey City State College, Jersey City, N.J., professor of geoscience and science education, 1958—, chairman of Division of Science, 1958-68. Visiting professor or lecturer at University of Washington, Seattle University, University of Virginia, University of Hawaii, University of California (Los Angeles), Fordham University, Columbia University, and other institutions; visiting scientist to high schools under auspices of American Institute of Physics, 1960-63. Director of Learning Resources Laboratories, Farmingdale, N.J., 1967—; editorial director of Harper & Row-RCA Instructional Systems development program in computer-assisted instructional materials, 1967-69. Consultant in science education for Arabian American Oil Co., 1963; consultant to California Test Bureau, Coronet Films, Essex International Corp., Cascade Productions of California, and school systems; member of advisory committee, Scientific Products Corp. President, Council for Elementary Science International, 1958-60. *Military service:* U.S. Army Air Forces, 1944-45.

MEMBER: American Association for Advancement of Science, National Association of Geology Teachers, American Geological Institute, American Educational Research Association, American Institute of Physics, National Association for Research in Science Teaching, Kappa Delta Pi, Iota Mu Pi. *Awards, honors:* Science Recognition Award of *Science Education*, 1961.

WRITINGS: The Development of Scientific Concepts in a Young Child, Teachers College Press, 1955, Greenwood Press, 1973; *Experimenting in Science* and *Teachers' Manual*, Ginn, 1955, 3rd edition, 1961; (senior author) *Science*

JOHN GABRIEL NAVARRA

The passenger should keep his feet on the footrests at all times, especially when you stop.
■ (From *Wheels for Kids* by John Gabriel Navarra. Photographs by Celeste Scala Navarra.)

Today for the Elementary School Teacher, Harper, 1960; (with F. L. Fitzpatrick and others) *Policies for Science Education*, Teachers College Press, 1960; (contributor) Theodore Harris and Wilson Schwahn, editors, *Selected Readings on the Learning Process*, Oxford University Press, 1961; (member of editorial committee) *Research in the Teaching of Science*, U.S. Department of Health, Education, and Welfare, 1965; *Fundamentals of Optics*, Essex International, 1966; *Clocks, Calendars, and Carrousels: A Book About Time*, Doubleday, 1967; *A Turtle in the House*, Doubleday, 1968; *Wide-World Weather*, Doubleday, 1968; *Our Noisy World*, Doubleday, 1969.

From Generation to Generation, Natural History Press, 1970; *The World You Inherit: A Story of Pollution*, Natural History Press, 1970; *Earth Science*, Wiley, 1971; *Nature Strikes Back*, Natural History Press, 1971; *Flying Today and Tomorrow*, Doubleday, 1972; *Drugs and Man*, Doubleday, 1973; *Wheels for Kids*, Doubleday, 1973; *Safe Motorboating for Kids*, Doubleday, 1974; *Supercars*, Doubleday, 1975; *Science in the Elementary School: Content and Methods*, Charles E. Merrill, 1975; *Supertrains*, Doubleday and Chicago Museum of Science and Industry, 1975.

Series: (Senior author) "Today's Basic Science," nine books and nine manuals, Harper, 1963, revised edition, six books and six manuals, 1967; (senior author) "Junior High School Science Program," three books and three manuals, Harper, 1967; "InvestiGuide," seven books and three guides, Harper, 1967-68; "InvestiVision," twelve books, Harper, 1967-69; (senior author) "Young Scientist," six books and six manuals, Harper, 1971; (senior author) "Junior High Science Program," three books and three manuals, Harper, 1973.

Writer of instructional manuals, *Elements of Electricity* and *Elements of Mechanics*, Essex International, 1962, and achievement tests. Contributor of more than fifty articles to professional journals; book reviewer, *Educational Forum*. Editor and contributor, *Classroom Science Bulletin*, 1958-67; assistant editor and regional editor, *American Biology Teacher*, 1960—; contributing editor, *Instructor*, 1962-64; science editor, two newsletters of Croft Educational Services, 1964-68.

FOR MORE INFORMATION SEE: Science Education, February, 1961; Hillel Black, *The American Schoolbook*, Morrow, 1967; *Saturday Evening Post*, October 7, 1967.

NIXON, Joan Lowery 1927-

PERSONAL: Born February 3, 1927, in Los Angeles, California; daughter of Joseph Michael and Margaret (Meyer) Lowery; married Hershell H. Nixon (a petroleum geologist), August 6, 1949; children: Kathleen Mary (Mrs. Kirkland Brush), Maureen Louise, Joseph Michael, Eileen Marie. *Education:* University of Southern California, A.B. journalism, 1947; California State College, elementary education certificate, 1949. *Religion:* Roman Catholic. *Home:* 8602 Shadowcrest, Houston, Texas 77036.

CAREER: Elementary teacher in Los Angeles, California, 1947-50; instructor in creative writing at Midland College, Midland, Texas, 1971-73; creative writing instructor at the University of Houston Continuing Education Department, 1974—; teacher of writing classes for adults in Houston and Pasadena, Texas; volunteer teacher of writing classes for children in Corpus Christi, Houston, and Midland, Texas; lectured to writing groups in Corpus Christi, Amarillo, Abilene, Lubbock and Odessa, Texas; participated as instructor in writers' conferences at the University of Houston, Hardin-Simmons University, and the Kerrville Arts Center. *Member:* Authors Guild, Authors League, Mystery Writers of America, Associated Authors of Children's Literature, (Houston), Society of Children's Book Writers (charter member), Houston Writers' Workshop, Midland Writers Association (founder), Kappa Delta Alumnae Association. *Awards, honors:* Texas Institute of Letters award for best children's book, 1974, for *The Alligator under the Bed.*

*WRITINGS—*All published by Criterion: *Mystery of Hurricane Castle*, 1964, *Mystery of the Grinning Idol*, 1965, *Mystery of the Hidden Cockatoo*, 1966, *Mystery of the Haunted Woods*, 1967, *Mystery of the Secret Stowaway*,

1968, *Delbert, the Plainclothes Detective*, 1971; *The Alligator under the Bed*, Putnam, 1971; *The Mysterious Red Tape Gang*, Putnam, 1971; *The Secret Box Mystery* (Junior Literary Guild selection), Putnam, 1974; *The Mysterious Prowler*, Harcourt, 1976. Contributor of fiction and non-fiction to juvenile and adult magazines. Columnist, *Houston Post.*

WORK IN PROGRESS: A juvenile mystery novel; easy to read fiction and non-fiction for the primary grades.

SIDELIGHTS: "Two of my children are responsible for my entry into writing books for young people. Kathy and Maureen, who were in the fifth and first grades, begged, "Write us a mystery story! And put us in it!" This is how

JOAN LOWERY NIXON

The Mystery of Hurricane Castle was born. I enjoyed writing the book so much I continued to write juvenile mysteries. Two of the most current: *The Secret Box Mystery* and *The Mysterious Prowler*, are 'easy to read' books for the primary grades, and came about because my editor, Barbara Lucas, asked me if I'd like to try writing mysteries for this younger group.

"I wrote stories and poetry for my own pleasure when I was a child, and hoped that some day I would be a professional writer. My parents encouraged their three daughters in creative activities, at one time building a portable theatre for fist puppets and helping us to make and dress our own puppets. Under my mother's direction, we wrote our scripts, based on some of the classic fairy tales, such as 'Peter Rabbit' and the traditional 'Punch and Judy', and took our shows—on a volunteer basis—to children's hospitals and orphanages and schools for many years. One moment I shall always remember: when we put on our puppet show for a group of very young Japanese children, none of whom spoke English. I realized that day the power of 'story telling' and laughter and friendship, as these little ones, unable to understand the dialogue, still responded to the puppets with as much enthusiasm as any audience we had ever met.

"I always hope I can capture some of this same enthusiasm with young readers when I communicate with them through books. As an author of books for children, I try to remember my own childhood—how I felt, how I reacted, how I responded to the emotions of happiness, sorrow, excitement, fear . . . so I can understand how a child of today would feel, how he would approach his problems, and how he would identify with the character in a book, who perhaps had the same problems to solve. Even though most of my books are mystery stories, the main characters in each also have personal problems to resolve.

"I like to use humor in my books. Perhaps I am an optimist, but I think there is much to look forward to in life, and many daily troubles and frustrations can disappear if they're handled with a sense of humor.

"Because I enjoy writing for children, I also enjoy writing *with* children. For many years I have conducted classes as a volunteer teacher with students of junior high and high school age, helping them to learn to write creatively. Although a teacher certainly cannot bestow talent upon her students, she is able to give them certain basic rules of writing to follow which will help them develop their talents and writing skills. The three most important techniques which I stress to my students are these: description utilizing the five senses, use of strong action verbs which present a visual image in themselves, and opening sentences which are so interesting they reach out and firmly grasp a reader's attention.

"Material for my books is derived from places I have lived or visited, people I have known, and interesting things I have seen—yet through all of it runs the deeper, underlying thoughts which make up me, as a person: my beliefs, my approach to life, my goals, even my own sense of what is humorous, right or good. And I hope that some of the children who read my books will say, 'Yes. I feel that way too. I liked reading that book.' Then I will consider that I have successfully communicated with them, author to reader."

OAKLEY, Don(ald G.) 1927-

PERSONAL: Born November 3, 1927, in Pittsburgh, Pa.; son of William Hageman (an accountant) and Mildred (Koerner) Oakley; married Gertrude Acklin, 1958; children: Glenn William. *Education:* Carnegie Institute of Technology, student, 1945-46; Western Reserve University, B.A., 1951; University of Chicago, M.A., 1955. *Home:* 258 Parkview Dr., Aurora, Ohio 44202.

CAREER: Newspaper Enterprise Association, Cleveland, Ohio, and New York, N.Y., chief editorial writer, 1957—. *Military service:* U.S. Army, Paratroops, 1946-47. *Awards, honors:* Meeman Award for newspaper series on conservation, 1964; Friends of American Writers Award, 1972, for *Two Muskets for Washington.*

WRITINGS: Two Muskets for Washington (juvenile novel), Bobbs, 1970.

WORK IN PROGRESS: Another juvenile novel based on the true story of Christian Fast, a boy captured and adopted by Delaware Indians in the Ohio country during the Revolutionary War.

DON OAKLEY

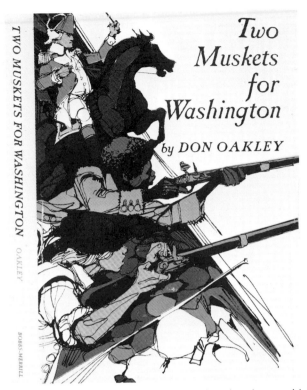

Dang-dratted-double-damned musket! Oh, what he wouldn't give for a rifle. . . . Feverishly, he bit the top off another cartridge, shook powder into the pan and shoved ball and paper wadding into the muzzle. ■ (From *Two Muskets for Washington* by Don Oakley. Jacket designed by John R. Lane.)

PARKS, Gordon (Alexander Buchanan) 1912-

PERSONAL: Born November 30, 1912, near Fort Scott, Kan.; son of Andrew Jackson (a dirt farmer) and Sarah (Ross) Parks; married Sally Alvis, 1933 (divorced, 1961); married Elizabeth Campbell, 1962 (divorced, 1973); married Genevieve Young (a book editor), August 26, 1973; children: (first marriage) Gordon, Jr., Toni (Mrs. Jean-Luc Brouillaud), David; (second marriage) Leslie. *Education:* Attended public high schools in Minneapolis, Minn., three-and one-half years. *Politics:* Democrat. *Religion:* Methodist. *Home:* 860 United Nations Plaza, New York, N.Y. 10017. *Agent:* (Film) Ben Benjamin, Creative Management Associates, 9255 Sunset Blvd., Los Angeles, Calif. 90069.

CAREER: Photographer, writer, film director, songwriter, and composer. Held varied jobs before 1937, when he focused on photography; photographer with Farm Security Administration, 1942-43, Office of War Information, 1944, and Standard Oil Co. of New Jersey, 1945-48; photo-journalist for *Life*, New York, N.Y., 1948-72; editorial director of *Essence* (magazine), New York, N.Y., 1970-73; film director, 1968—, directing productions for Warner Brothers-Seven Arts, Metro-Goldwyn-Mayer, and Paramount Pictures. President of Winger Enterprises, Inc. Composer of concertos and sonatas performed by symphony orchestras in United States and Europe. Motion pictures directed include "The Learning Tree," Warner, 1968, "Shaft," M.G.M., 1972, "Shaft's Big Score," M.G.M., 1972, "The Super Cops," M.G.M., 1974, and "Leadbelly," Paramount, 1975 and documentaries.

MEMBER: Directors Guild of America (member of national board, 1973-76), Authors Guild (member of board, 1973-74), Black Academy of Arts and Letters (fellow), American Federation of Television and Radio Artists, American Society of Magazine Photographers (past member of board), American Society of Composers, Authors and Publishers, National Association for the Advancement of Colored People, Urban League, The Players (New York).

AWARDS, HONORS: Rosenwald Foundation fellow, 1942; two Mass Media Awards of National Conference of Christians and Jews, 1964, for outstanding contributions to better human relations; named photographer-writer who had done the most to promote understanding among nations of the world in an international vote conducted by makers of Nikon cameras, 1967; Litt.D., Kansas State University, 1970; Carr Van Anda Journalism Award of Ohio University, 1970; Spingarn Medal of National Association for the Advancement of Colored People (awarded annually to one black American for distinguished achievement), 1972; H.H.D., St. Olaf College, 1973; other honors include awards from Syracuse University School of Journalism, 1963, Philadelphia Museum of Art, 1964, Art Directors Club, 1964, and University of Miami, Coral Gables, 1964.

WRITINGS: The Learning Tree (autobiographical novel), Harper, 1963, adapted by the author for motion picture of same name, produced by Warner Brothers-Seven Arts, 1968; *A Choice of Weapons* (autobiography), Harper, 1966; (self-illustrated with photographs) *A Poet and His Camera* (poems), Viking, 1968; (self-illustrated with photographs) *Born Black* (essays commissioned by *Life* plus new material), Lippincott, 1971; (self-illustrated with photographs) *Gordon Parks: Whispers of Intimate Things* (poems), Viking, 1971; (self-illustrated) *In Love* (poems), Lippincott, 1971; (self-illustrated) *Moments Without Proper Names* (retrospective exhibition of photographs with verse), Viking, 1975.

Television documentaries produced by National Educational Television: "Flavio"; Piri Thomas', "Mean Streets."

Contributor to *Show, Vogue, Venture,* and other magazines.

SIDELIGHTS: "F. Scott Fitzgerald once wrote that 'we have two or three great and moving experiences in our lives—experiences so great and moving that it doesn't seem at the time that anyone else has been caught up and pounded and dazzled and astonished and beaten and broken and rescued and illuminated and rewarded and humbled in just that way ever before.

"' Then we learn our trade, well or less well, and we tell our two or three stories—each time in a new disguise—Maybe ten times, maybe a hundred, as long as people will listen. . . . Whether it's something that happened twenty years ago or only yesterday, I must start out with an emotion—one that's close to me and that I can understand.'

"I would like to push Fitzgerald's philosophy further, to the need of man simply to dream. To dream remarkable and impossible dreams and to have the desire to fulfill those dreams.

Newt, feeling it useless to run any more, stopped—the stick clutched tightly in his hand. He stood against a tree; will shattered; body tensed; wanting to cry out for mercy; for help; ready to fall whenever the bullet came ripping through. ■ (From the movie "The Learning Tree," copyright © 1968 by Warner Bros.-Seven Arts.)

Something about the Author

"I am often asked why I do so many different things. I used to wonder about this myself, and for a long time I passed it off as a sort of professional restlessness. But, in retrospect, I know that it was a desperate search for security within a society that held me inferior simply because I was black. It was a constant inner rebellion against failure. I was a poor black boy who wanted to be somebody. So I created desires until I was drowning neck deep in them, before I would attempt to swim my way out. It was all the more difficult because I was not technically prepared. Two months before I was to be graduated from high school, the great depression of the thirties, plus a physical breakdown, forced me to quit school. Penniless, and without a place to live, I struck out, unprepared and frightened, praying to God for help in one breath, questioning and damning Him in the very next, feeling that He alone was responsible for my predicament.

"From then on, everything I touched was used for survival. Basketball, football, and photography—simple pleasures for other boys of my age, had to make money for me. In my fright, I set up all sorts of hypothetical tragedies for myself, then I would contemplate an alternative to offset whatever tragedy I felt might strike. For instance, I would imagine I had lost my legs in an accident. Then, just as quickly I would daydream myself into a situation whereby I would play music or perhaps compose for a living. Or if I lost my sight or hearing I could learn Braille and somehow

The house that J.T. built was strangely beautiful. He had fitted the windowpane to the back of the stove, and when the door at the front was closed the cat was protected from the wind.
■ (From C.B.S. Children's Hour production of "J.T." Photograph copyright © 1969 by Gordon Parks, Jr.)

survive by writing. To top it all I had become quite skilled as a cook and dishwasher. So with all the tragic possibilities considered, and all the alternatives accounted for, I could push on with a little less fear.

"Perhaps if I had been fortunate enough to have gone on to college, to study medicine, engineering or whatever, I would not have become involved in so many other things. More than likely I would have given all my time to one chosen avocation. As it happened I tried several fields. In case one failed me I could turn to another one. Finally, it means that I was forced to rid myself of the insecurities that the lack of education brought me. But, in retrospect, I honestly say that I enjoyed the uncertainty of the broader and more precarious adventure.

"So, in Fitzgerald's terms, I go on attempting to reveal my experiences, each time in a different way, through a different medium, hoping that, in some small way, they might make a dent—some mark—on our times. If only I could feel that a photograph, a piece of music or a film of mine could help put an end to hatred, poverty, bigotry or war, the pain of those early years would have been worth while."

The range of Parks' talents was indicated in the filming of "The Learning Tree," shot in the vicinity of Fort Scott,

GORDON PARKS

Kan., where he grew up in poverty, the youngest of fifteen children. Parks scripted his novel for the film, composed the musical score, and directed the production—as the first black man to be signed as director by a major Hollywood studio.

FOR MORE INFORMATION SEE: Publishers' Weekly, April 29, 1968; *Newsweek*, April 29, 1968; *Variety*, November 6, 1968, June 25, 1969; *Show Business*, August 2, 1969; *Cue*, August 9, 1969; John D. Roslansky, editor, *Creativity*, North-Holland Publishing, 1970; Midge Turk, *Gordon Parks*, Crowell, 1971; *Horn Book*, April, 1971, August, 1971; Terry Harnan, *Gordon Parks: Black Photographer and Film Maker*, Garrard, 1972.

PENNAGE, E. M.
See FINKEL, George (Irvine)

In a red-and-white striped
Home-a-rolla
that never stopped going
lived Josette with her father and mother.
■ (From *The Endless Pavement* by Jacqueline Jackson and William Perlmutter. Illustrated by Richard Cuffari.)

Something about the Author

PERLMUTTER, O(scar) William 1920-1975

PERSONAL: Born July 5, 1920; son of Julius B. and Hermina (Langer) Perlmutter; married Eila Helen Siren (a professor), September 10, 1945; children: William, Charles, Francis Xavier, Josette-Marie, Gregory. *Education:* Studied at Yeshiva University, 1938-42, and University of Wyoming, 1943-44; University of Chicago, M.A., 1949, Ph.D., 1959. *Politics:* Independent. *Religion:* Jewish. *Home:* Big Watab Lake, Route 2, St. Joseph, Minn. 56374. *Agent:* Curtis Brown Ltd., 60 East 56th St., New York, N.Y. 10022. *Office:* St. John's University, Collegeville, Minn. 56321.

CAREER: University of Chicago, Chicago, Ill., lecturer in political science, 1948-51; St. Xavier College, Chicago, Ill., instructor, 1948-51, assistant professor, 1951-54, professor of social sciences and chairman of division, 1954-59, vice-president of college, 1956-59; academic adviser from Institute of European Studies at Universities of Vienna, Freiburg, and Paris, 1959-62; University of Minnesota, Minneapolis, visiting professor of political science, 1962-63; University of Santa Clara, Santa Clara, Calif., honors professor, 1963-64; Kent State University, Kent, Ohio, professor of political science and dean of College of Fine and Professional Arts, 1964-66; State University of New York at Albany, professor of political science and dean of College of Arts and Sciences, 1966-72; St. John's University, Collegeville, Minn., professor of government and academic vice-president, 1972-75. Consultant to U.S. Office of Education and U.S. Office of Economic Opportunity. Executive director, New York State Commission to Review Compensation of Judges and Legislators, 1970. *Military service:* U.S. Army and U.S. Army Air Forces, 1942-46; served in European and Pacific theaters; received Air Medal and five battle stars.

MEMBER: American Association of School Administrators, National Education Association, American Political Science Association, American Sociological Association; other academic organizations. *Awards, honors:* Ford Foundation faculty fellow at Yale University, 1952-53; Palmes Academique (France), 1969.

WRITINGS: (With Jacqueline Jackson) *The Endless Pavement* (Junior Literary Guild selection), Seabury, 1973. Contributor of articles to education and political science journals.

HOBBIES AND OTHER INTERESTS: Camping and outdoor life in Minnesota's north woods and lakes, traveling abroad, "love of languages."

(Died March 5, 1975)

WILLIAM O. PERLMUTTER

PETERSON, Hans 1922-

PERSONAL: Born October 26, 1922, in Varing, Sweden; son of Emil G. (an electrician) and Hilda (Peterson) Peterson; married Anne Marie Nordstrand (a photographer), June 17, 1958; children: Lena, Jan. *Education:* Attended public schools in Sweden. *Home:* Marstrandsgatan 21, Gothenburg, Sweden 41724.

CAREER: Has worked at various jobs, including lift-boy, factory worker, and electrician; author, 1947—. *Awards, honors:* Nils Holgersson prize, 1958, for *Magnus and the Van Horse*; German young-books prize, 1959, for *Magnus and the Squirrel*; *Liselott and the Goloff* included in Hans Christian Andersen Honor List, 1964; several Swedish State and Gothenburg town prizes for collected work.

WRITINGS: Den uppdaemda ravinen: Roman (novel), Bonnier (Stockholm), 1949; *Flicken och sommaren* (title means "The Girl and the Summer"), Tidens forlag (Stockholm), 1950; *Laerkorna* (title means "The Larks"), Tidens forlag, 1952; *Hejda solnedgaangen* (title means "Stop the Sunset"), Tidens forlag, 1955; *Kvinnors Kaerlek: Noveller* (novel; title means "Women's Love"), Norstedt (Stockholm), 1956; *Skaadespelaren* (title means "The Actor"), Norstedt, 1957; *Aelskarinnan* (title means "The Mistress"), Norstedt, 1959; *Resebidrag* (title means "Traveling Letters"), Norstedt, 1961; *Kvinnorna: Tre beraettelser* (short stories; title means "The Women: Three Stories"), Norstedt, 1962; *Historien om en by: Roman* (novel; title means "A Story about a Village"), Norstedt, 1963.

Children's books; all Swedish editions published by Raben & Sjoegren (Stockholm), except as indicated: *Magnus och ekorrungen*, 1956, translation by Madeleine Hamilton published as *Magnus and the Squirrel*, Viking, 1959; *Magnus, Mattias och Mari*, 1958, translation by Marianne Turner

His mind was not on the St. Lucy's Day Celebration. ■ (From *Erik and the Christmas Horse* by Hans Peterson. Illustrated by Ilon Wikland.)

published in England as *Magnus and the Van Horse*, Burke, 1961, published as *Magnus and the Wagon Horse*, Pantheon, 1966; *Magnus i hamn*, 1958, translation by Turner published as *Magnus in the Harbor*, Pantheon, 1966; *Naer vi snoeade inne*, 1959, translation by Irene Morris published as *The Day It Snowed*, Burke, 1969; *Magnus i fara*, 1959, translation by Turner published as *Magnus in Danger*, Pantheon, 1967; *Petter Joensson hade en gitarr*, 1959, adaptation by Kay Ware and Lucille Sutherland published as *Peter Johnson and His Guitar*, Webster, 1961, stage adaptation by Turner, Burke, 1965.

Naer vi regnade inne (title means "The Day It Rained"), 1960; *Gubben och Kanariefaageln*, 1960, adaptation by Ware and Sutherland published as *The Old Man and the Bird*, Webster, 1964, stage adaptation by Marianne Helweg, Burke, 1966; *Maens och mia*, 1960, translation published as *Tom and Tabby*, Lothrop, 1965; *Magnus och skeppshunden Jack*, 1961, translation by Turner published as *Magnus and the Ship's Mascot*, Burke, 1964; *Lille-Olle och sommardagen*, 1962, adaptation by Ware and Sutherland published as *Benjamin Has a Birthday*, Webster, 1964; *Liselott och Garaffen*, 1962, translation by Annabelle

Macmillan published as *Liselott and the Goloff*, Coward, 1964; *Det nya huset*, 1962, adaptation by Ware and Sutherland published as *The New House*, Webster, 1964, stage adaptation by Helweg, Burke, 1966; *Mick och Malin*, 1962, translation published as *Mickey and Molly*, Lothrop, 1964; *Boken om Magnus* (title means "A Book about Magnus"; includes *Magnus och ekorrungen*, *Magnus, Mattias och Mari*, *Magnus i hamn*, *Magnus i fara*), 1963; *Haer kommer Petter*, 1963, translation by Turner published as *Here Comes Peter*, Burke, 1965; *Hunden Buster*, 1963, translation published as *Brownie*, Lothrop, 1965; *Stina och Lars rymmer*, 1964, translation by Patricia Crampton published as *Stina and Lars in the Mountains*, Burke, 1970; *Petter kommer igen*, 1964, translation by Turner published as *Peter Comes Back*, Burke, 1966; *Naer hoensen blaaste bort*, 1964, translation by Morris published as *The Day the Chickens Blew Away*, Burke, 1970; *Liselott och de andra*, 1965, translation by Morris published as *Lisa Settles In*, Burke, 1967; *Den nya vaegen*, 1965, translation by Morris published as *The New Road*, Burke, 1967; *Petter klarar allt*, 1966, translation by Evelyn Ramsden published as *Peter Makes His Way*, Burke, 1968; *Bara Liselott*, 1967, translation by Morris published as *Just Lisa*, Burke, 1969;

150

Den nya bron, 1967, translation by Morris published as *The New Bridge*, Burke, 1969; *Sara och sommerhuset*, 1967, translation by Morris published as *Sara in Summer-time*, Burke, 1973; *Expedition Snoestorm* (title means "Expedition Snowstorm"), 1968; *Jag vill inte, sa Sara*, 1968, translation by Morris published as *I Don't Want to, Said Sara*, Burke, 1969; *Lill-Anna, Johan och den vilda bjoernen* (title means "Lill-Anna, Johan and the Wild Bear"), Geber (Stockholm), 1968; *Magnus Lindberg och haesten Mari*, 1968, adaptation by Christine Hyatt published as *Eric and the Christmas Horse*, Burke, 1969, Lothrop, 1970; (with Harald Wiberg) *Naer Per gick vilse i skogen*, 1969, translation published as *When Peter Was Lost in the Forrest*, Coward, 1970.

Franssonsbarna i Faagelhult (title means "These Children in Bird-Cottage"), Geber, 1970; *Aake gaar till sjoess* (title means "Aake Goes on Board"), Geber, 1970; *Ett lejon i huset* (title means "A Lion in the House"), 1970; *Pelle*

HANS PETERSON, with wife Anne Marie

Jansson, en kille med tur, 1970, translation by Hanne Barnes published as *Pelle Jansson*, Burke, 1974; *Sara och Lillebror*, 1970, translation by Morris published as *Sara and Her Brother*, Burke, 1973.

Also author of novels, "Elise and Richard," 1971; "Elise Alone," 1972; "Elise and the Others," 1973; "The Tale about Elin," 1973; "Helge and Annie," 1974.

WORK IN PROGRESS: Novels, short stories, picture-books, children's books.

SIDELIGHTS: Peterson has written novels for adults with seeing and hearing difficulties and intends to write more.

HOBBIES AND OTHER INTERESTS: Traveling, working at his summer house, meeting friends, living.

PETERSON, Harold L(eslie)   1922-

PERSONAL: Born May 22, 1922, in Peekskill, N.Y.; son of Leslie Chauncey and Mildred (Croft) Peterson; married Dorothy Parker, 1945; children: Harold L., Jr., Kristin Dorothy. *Education:* Drew University, A.B., 1945; University of Wisconsin, M.A., 1947. *Religion:* Methodist. *Home:* 5113 8th Rd., North, Arlington, Va. 22205. *Agent:* Lurton Blassingame, 10 East 43rd St., New York, N.Y. 10017. *Office:* Branch of Reference Services, National Park Service, 5256 Port Royal Rd., Springfield, Va. 22151.

CAREER: U.S. Department of Interior, National Park Service, Washington, D.C., curator, 1946-47, historian, 1947-48, chief of historical investigations, 1951-55, staff historian, 1955-64, chief curator, 1964—. Advisor on military matters, Colonial Williamsburg, 1949-50, Plimoth, Plantation, 1949—; consultant on weapons to Henry Ford Museum, 1953-59; associate curator, U.S. Artillery and Guided Missile Center Museum, 1959—. *Military service:* U.S. Army, 1942-43.

MEMBER: Company of Military Historians (founder, governor, 1951—, president, 1960-63, fellow), National Rifle Association of America (director, 1960-66), Wisconsin Gun Collectors Association (founder), American Society of Arms Collectors (honorary), Society of American Sword Collectors, Potomac Arms Collectors (director, 1955—), Armor and Arms Club, Arms and Armor Society (Great Britain), Vaabenhistorisk Selskab (Denmark), Massachusetts Arms Collectors (honorary), Texas Gun Collectors Association, International Institute for Conservation of Historic and Artistic Works, International Association of Museums of Arms and Military History (executive council). *Awards, honors:* U.S. Department of Interior Distinguished Service Medal, 1958, for contribution in historical research and museum planning; U.S. Artillery, Order of Saint Barbara, 1959, Ancient Order of Artillerists, 1963; Alumni Achievement Award, Drew University, 1966.

WRITINGS: The American Sword, 1775-1945, River House, 1954; *American Silver Mounted Swords*, privately printed, 1955; *Arms and Armor in Colonial America*, Stackpole, 1956; *Arms and Armor of the Pilgrims*, Plimoth Plantation, Inc., 1957; *American Knives*, Scribner, 1958; *Notes on Ordnance of American Civil War*, American Ordnance Association, 1959.

A History of Firearms, Scribner, 1961; *The Treasury of the Gun*, Ridge Press, Golden Press, 1962; *Encyclopedia of Firearms*, Dutton, 1963; *Forts in America*, Scribner, 1964; *American Indian Tomahawks*, Museum of the American Indian, 1965; *A History of Knives*, Scribner, 1966; *Pageant of the Gun*, Doubleday, 1967; *The Fuller Collection of American Firearms*, Eastern National Park & Monument Association, 1967; *The Book of the Continental Soldier*, Stackpole, 1968; *Daggers and Fighting Knives of the Western World*, Jenkins, 1968; *A History of Armor*, Scribner, 1968; *Round Shot and Rammers*, Stackpole, 1969; *Americans at Home*, Scribner, 1971; (with Peter Copeland) *America's Fighting Men*, New York Graphic Society, 1971; (with Robert Elman) *The Great Guns*, Grosset, 1971; *How Do You Know It's Old?*, Scribner, 1975. Consulting editor, *Military Collector and Historian*, 1952—; technical editor, *Artillery Through the Ages*, 1949. Contributor of articles on arms and armor to encyclopedias and magazines.

SIDELIGHTS: "A writer is probably the least qualified person in the world to describe himself. When pressed, I think I would classify myself as gregarious with a deep interest in people of all ages and a delight in talking with them. If I were to choose the adjective I would most like to have someone apply to me, it would be 'kind.' Despite the fact that I have been a professional military historian for almost thirty years and served in World War II, I deplore violence of all kinds, including verbal violence, and would never willingly injure any living creature in the name of sport.

"My interests are very wide; some would call them undisciplined. I greatly enjoy travel and am interested in all forms of art as well as the lesser cultural objects of everyday life. My interest in people includes the study of the way they have lived, their pleasures and their working techniques through the years, a field that would now be called social or cultural history although there was no such recognized specialization when I was a graduate student. Since the National Park Service now administers more than sixty furnished historic structures and has become active in 'living history' demonstrations, this former avocation has now become a significant part of my work.

"Most of my books have been intended for adults, but those that I have written for young readers stem from my own experiences as a child. One of my happiest memories of my own childhood relates to the nightly periods when my parents would read to me. I continued this practice with my own children, and I was disappointed to note that many of the books on technical subjects were written by non-specialists and contained an unfortunate number of errors. I feel strongly that a book that will not stand the critical review of a professional in the field is not good enough for a child who will often gain his first—and most lasting impressions—from it. Thus I thought I would try my hand in the field, and I am glad that I did. It has been a most rewarding experience.

"The materials for my writing come from research in archival sources plus the study of objects and discussions with colleagues here and abroad. In the past my writing has been largely confined to arms and armor or military history, but in the future I hope to get more into the field of social history. *Americans at Home* was the first venture in this direction. *How Do You Know It's Old?* is the second. I have also been thinking of a compilation of the ghost stories which one encounters in an agency like the National Park Service which administers many historic sites, a light-hearted approach such as *Visit Your National Historical Ghost*."

HOBBIES AND OTHER INTERESTS: Interested in fencing, music, and athletics. Collects arms and armor, and general antiques since 1932. Also produced a series of records of historical military music in America.

HAROLD L. PETERSON

PETERSON, Helen Stone 1910-

PERSONAL: Born May 12, 1910, in Binghamton, N.Y.; daughter of George Fordyce and May (Cox) Stone; married Arthur Howard Peterson (treasurer of Cornell University), July 7, 1934; children: George E., Arthur H., Jr. *Education:* Oberlin College, A.B., 1932; Smith College, M.S.S., 1933. *Politics:* Independent. *Home:* 223 Highgate Rd., Ithaca, N.Y. 14850.

CAREER: Community Service Society, New York, N.Y., social worker, 1934-36; Connecticut State Department of Health, Hartford, mental hygienist, 1936-39. *Member:* National Association of Social Workers.

WRITINGS—Children's books: *Henry Clay*, Garrard, 1964; *Jane Addams*, Garrard, 1965; *Abigail Adams*, Garrard, 1967; *Roger Williams*, Garrard, 1968; *Electing Our Presidents*, Garrard, 1970; *Susan B. Anthony*, Garrard, 1971; *Sojourner Truth*, Garrard, 1972; *Give Us Liberty: The Story of the Declaration of Independence*, Garrard, 1973; *The Making of the United States Constitution*, Garrard, 1974. Contributor to *Jack and Jill, Children's Activities*, and to education journals.

SIDELIGHTS: "I grew up in a story-telling home. When my sister, two brothers and I were little, our father began creating and telling us wonderful stories at bedtime. For me, this was the beginning of a lifelong interest in stories for children.

"With my own two sons, we started early enjoying books together. They loved having their own shelves of books, as well as choosing still others on our regular visits to the library.

HELEN STONE PETERSON

"That man over there says that women need to be helped into carriages and lifted over ditches and to have the best place everywhere. Nobody ever helps me into carriages or over mud puddles or gives me any best place." ■ (From *Sojourner Truth* by Helen Stone Peterson. Illustrated by Victor Mays.)

"The boys and I also enjoyed taking walks together through our fields and woods. They played along the creek and looked down upon Cayuga Lake. 'Who were the first children who played here?' asked our older son, five-year-old George, later a Rhodes Scholar. To answer him I wrote my first stories *Indian Boy on Cayuga Lake*. They were presented as a series in the magazine 'Children's Activities.'

"After that, I kept writing in response to my sons' interests. And in response also to the interests of their friends, for I had quite a number of boys in my Cub Scout Den where I was den mother for four years.

"Since I loved writing for that age group—grade school children—I have continued to do it. And I have continued writing about people and events in American history, again because I love to do so. I am fortunate to be able to do my research at Cornell University, where my husband is treasurer. In the splendid library there, I have access to a vast amount of rich, detailed, and exciting material."

PETROVSKAYA, Kyra
See WAYNE, Kyra Petrovskaya

PEVSNER, Stella

PERSONAL: Born in Lincoln, Ill.; married; children: (four). *Education:* Attended Illinois University. *Home:* Palatine, Ill.

CAREER: "I was taking art courses that first summer in Chicago when one evening, in an amiable mood, I registered for a course in advertising at Northwestern University to keep a friend company. She went on to become a reporter but I landed a job in advertising. From the lowly assignment of writing ads for a drug chain I advanced to the pots and pans division of a State Street store's ad department. After about a year I managed to land a job in an advertising agency writing high fashion copy, and from then on went to various other agencies and finally to Dana Perfumes, where I was promotion director. After marriage I wrote free-lance articles until, at the suggestion of one of my children, I turned to juvenile novels." *Member:* Authors Guild. *Awards, honors:* Chicago Women Publishing first annual fiction award for children's literature, 1973, for *Call Me Heller, That's My Name.*

WRITINGS: The Young Brontes (a one-act play for young adults), Baker, 1967; *Break a Leg!,* Crown, 1969; *Footsteps on the Stairs,* Crown, 1970; *Call Me Heller, That's My Name,* Seabury, 1973; *A Smart Kid Like You* (Junior Literary Guild selection), Seabury, 1975. Writes advertising copy, promotion, publicity, free-lance articles, commercial film strips.

SIDELIGHTS: "Being raised with three brothers near my own age and two older sisters, I was both shoved around and spoiled. After school I'd play football or baseball with my brothers but after the dishes were washed at night I'd make them play store, boarding house, school, or best yet, theatre. With a rolled-up rug as footlights I'd sing, tapdance or do impersonations to the infinite boredom and disgust of my captive audience. My eldest sister, however, thought I was adorable, and coaxed me into doing a comedy song routine for a PTA meeting while she hammered out the melody on the piano. This happened in first grade. My sister, I believe, wanted me to follow the lead of my name and become a star. I stubbornly . . . and sensibly . . . refused, but did develop an interest in theatre which led to backstage work in various community groups.

"It was natural, therefore, that when one of my children suggested that since I spent so much time at the typewriter (robbing her of my precious company) I might at least write something she could enjoy. I turned to the theatre for inspiration. *Break a Leg!* describes how the participation in a play not only helps a young girl overcome her shyness but also makes her aware of the fact that off-beat kids have something to offer. *Footsteps on the Stairs,* deals with the young brother of the first book, his fear, and how he learns to overcome it.

"Once, as a respite, I took a course in collage and found that this art form bears a close relationship to writing. In each . . . a collage or novel . . . the artist/author takes bits of this and that, scraps and dreams and memories and weaves them into a design which is new and strange and yet somehow familiar.

"In *Call Me Heller, That's My Name,* there are traces of my relationship with my older sisters and their boyfriends 'way back when, contrasted with my combatative attitude towards my eldest brother. The town is imaginary, the railroad is real, the trestle is from a newspaper clipping of a real tragedy. While for plot (and just plain fun) purposes the story is set in the Roaring Twenties, the theme, I hope, is a relevant one: There is a time for letting go and for moving on.

"*A Smart Kid Like You* is a contemporary novel about a junior high girl who solves the problem of having Dad's new wife as a math teacher, but then finds her real need is to establish rapport with her own mother.

"But while the teacher and mother parts of me try to inject something positive into each book, my main purpose in writing is to entertain. I would like to lead at least some children into the pleasant path of reading with the hope that they will go on and on to other books for the rest of their lives."

STELLA PEVSNER

Something about the Author

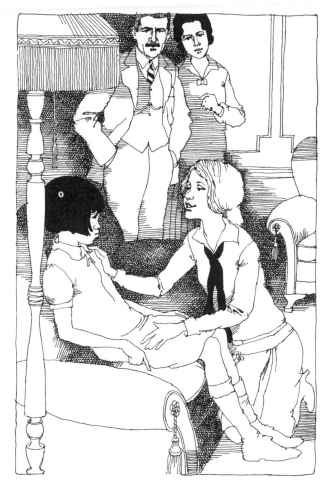

She flopped back on the davenport and ran her fingers along the line where the cushions divided. "Everyone seems to know it. I'm just the last." ■ (From *Call Me Heller, That's My Name* by Stella Pevsner. Illustrated by Richard Cuffari.)

PHILLIPS, Jack
See SANDBURG, Carl (August)

PHILLIPS, Louis 1942-

PERSONAL: Born June 15, 1942, in Lowell, Mass.; son of Louis James and Dorothy (Perkins) Phillips; married Patricia Ranard (chairman of English department at Spence School), August 23, 1972. *Education:* Stetson University, B.A., 1964; University of North Carolina, M.A. (radio, television, and motion pictures), 1967; City University of New York, M.A. (English and comparative literature), 1968. *Home:* 324 East 34th St., Apt. E-2, New York, N.Y. 10016. *Agent:* Barbara Rhodes, Kahn, Lifflander & Rhodes Agency, 853 Seventh Ave., New York, N.Y. 10019. *Office:* State University of New York, Maritime College, Bronx, N.Y. 10465.

CAREER: State University of New York, Maritime College, Bronx, assistant professor of English, 1967—. *Member:* Dramatists' Guild, Society of American Magicians, International Brotherhood of Magicians.

WRITINGS: The Man Who Stole the Atlantic Ocean, Prentice-Hall, 1972; *The Emancipation of the Encyclo-*

pedia Salesman, Prologue Press, 1972; *Theodore Jonathan Wainwright Is Going to Bomb the Pentagon,* Prentice-Hall, 1973; *The Film Buff's Calendar,* Drake Publishers, 1973; *A Catalogue of Earthly Pleasures* (poems), Prologue Press, 1973; *It Takes a Lot of Paper to Gift Wrap an Elephant,* Prologue Press, 1973; *Octopus Applause,* Prologue Press, 1973; *How Do You Dial a Crocodile,* Prologue Press, 1974; *The Animated Thumb-Tack Railroad Dollhouse and All Round Surprise Book* (juvenile), Lippincott, in press. Author of play "The Last of the Marx Brothers' Writers," first performed at Brandeis University, April, 1973; author of libretto with Robert Karmon of "Gulliver," first produced at Guthrie Theatre, 1975. Contributor to *Dramatists' Guild Quarterly, Learning, Playbill, McCall's, Family Circle, Rotarian, Grit, Humpty Dumpty,* and *Modern International Drama.*

WORK IN PROGRESS: Fist, a collection of poems.

SIDELIGHTS: "I began writing children's books for a number of reasons. First, I find that most books for children are simply banal and unimaginative, insulting the intelligence of the child and his parents. A child who has been

LOUIS PHILLIPS

exposed to the world via television and motion pictures is certainly not the same child of a hundred years ago, and yet editors of children's books and librarians for children's reading are, for the most part, terribly conservative in their tastes, buying and publishing what pretty much has already been bought and published a thousand times over.

"A good children's book should appeal to the child in the adult and to the adult possibilities in the child. *Alice in Wonderland* does that magnificently. Hence I write children's books because it allows me a form where I can allow my imagination to go unfettered. I would hope that adults would find some measure of joy in reading or retelling my books to their children.

"I also think that children love verse and poetry, but unfortunately their natural joy with playing with language is often discouraged by our schools and by adults who have been taught to dislike poetry because they can't read it with any degree of understanding."

PINKWATER, Manus 1941-

PERSONAL: Born November 15, 1941, in Memphis, Tenn.; son of Philip (a ragman) and Fay (Hoffman) Pinkwater; married Jill Schutz (illustrator and author), October 12, 1969. *Education:* Bard College, B.A., 1964; also studied at Art Institute of Chicago, Harvard University, University of Liverpool, University College, Nairobi, Kenya. *Politics:* Republican. *Religion:* Taoist. *Home:* 22 Hudson Pl., Hoboken, N.J. 07030.

MANUS PINKWATER (self-portrait)

When the wizard woke up he was not unhappy any more. He was not a wizard any more either. He was a frog. ■ (From *Wizard Crystal* by Manus Pinkwater. Illustrated by the author.)

CAREER: Children's Aid Society, New York, N.Y., art instructor, 1967-69; Lower West Side Visual Arts Center, New York, N.Y., art instructor, 1969; Henry Street Settlement, New York, N.Y., art instructor, 1969; Bonnie Brae Farm for Boys, Millington, N.J., art instructor, 1969. Inner City Summer Arts Program, Hoboken, N.J., assistant project director, 1970. Exhibitions at Brooklyn Museum, St. John's University, State University of New York at Potsdam, Carleton College, First Zen Institute, and the First Hawaii National Print Exhibition.

WRITINGS—All juveniles; all self-illustrated: *The Terrible Roar*, Knopf, 1970; *Bear's Picture*, Holt, 1972; *Wizard Crystal*, Dodd, 1973; *Magic Camera*, Dodd, 1974; *Fat Elliot and the Gorilla*, Four Winds, 1974; *Wingman*, Dodd, 1975; *Three Big Hogs*, Seabury, 1975. Contributor of illustrations and articles to *Zen Notes, Island Review, Gnomon, Liberation*, and other little magazines.

WORK IN PROGRESS: A children's book about lizards, hamburgers, and an old man with a chicken on his head.

SIDELIGHTS: "I have abandoned fine art as a field having, for the most part, an unworthy audience, in favor of writing and drawing for children exclusively. This came about as the indirect result of hanging out in a museum and eavesdropping on the comments of adults as they viewed a work of mine.

"All my books so far have been written to please a kid named Manus Pinkwater who is nominally thirty-two years old at this writing.

"My method and theory of art: I have this desk. When I spend a number of hours per day seated at it, I usually wind up having written or drawn something. When I don't sit, I don't write or draw, because when the writing or drawing comes around I am fooling with the dogs, talking on the phone, or fixing the stairs. My artistic production is of a higher quality than my imagination, skill, or intelligence would suggest, which leads me to believe that those faculties have very little to do with it. I would not take $1,-000,000 for my desk."

HOBBIES AND OTHER INTERESTS: African landscape, people, and wildlife; hiking and climbing of mountains; oriental art, philosophy, and cuisine; "I spend much time training dogs. One of my students has received an associate diploma from a two-year college in New Jersey, and is planning a career in some federal agency."

FOR MORE INFORMATION SEE: Graphis 155, Volume 27, 1971-72; *Washington Post* (Children's Book World), November 5, 1972; *Christian Science Monitor,* May 1, 1974.

POHLMANN, Lillian (Grenfell) 1902-

PERSONAL: Born March 31, 1902, in Grass Valley, Calif.; daughter of William Albert and Myrtle (Massie) Grenfell; married second husband, George Russell Pohlmann, May 16, 1947; children. (previous marriage) Iris

LILLIAN POHLMANN

Twigg MacInnes, Hal Grenfell Twigg. *Education:* Special courses at Universities of California, Colorado, and Mexico, and at Free University, Amsterdam, Netherlands. *Home:* 15 Mesa Ave., Mill Valley, Calif. 94941.

WRITINGS: Myrtle Albertina's Secret, Coward, 1956; *Myrtle Albertina's Song,* Coward, 1958; *Calypso Holiday,* Coward, 1959; *Owls and Answers* (Junior Literary Guild selection), Westminster, 1964; *The Summer of the White Reindeer,* Westminster, 1965; *Love Can Say No,* Westminster, 1966; *Wolfskin,* Norton, 1968; *Sing Loose,* Westminster, 1968; *The Bethlehem Mouse,* Stone Educational Publications, 1970; *Tall, Skinny, Towheaded and Miserable,* Westminster, 1975.

FOR MORE INFORMATION SEE: Book World, November 3, 1968.

POLDER, Markus
See KRÜSS, James

PRICE, Olive 1903-
(Anne Cherryholmes, Barbara West)

PERSONAL: Born September 21, 1903, in Pittsburgh, Pa.; daughter of Harry Wilson (a police sergeant) and Lydia (Barchfeld) Price; married R. M. Cherryholmes, June 30, 1927. *Education:* Attended University of Pittsburgh, 1922-23. *Religion:* Baptist. *Residence:* Asbury, N.J. *Agent:* McIntosh & Otis, Inc., 18 East 41st St., New York, N.Y. 10017.

CAREER: Writer of books and plays for children and young people. Copywriter for department stores in Pittsburgh, Pa., 1923-28. *Member:* Kappa Delta (Xi chapter).

WRITINGS—For children and young people, except as noted: *A Donkey for the King,* McGraw, 1945; *Miracle by the Sea,* McGraw, 1947; *Three Golden Rivers* (Catholic Book Club selection), Bobbs-Merrill, 1948; *The Valley of the Dragon,* Bobbs-Merrill, 1951; *The Story of Marco Polo* (selection of *Parents' Magazine* Book Club, People's Book Club, Boy's Club of America Book Club, and Sear's Book Club), Grosset, 1953; *The Story of Clara Barton* (Boy's Club of America Book Club selection), Grosset, 1954; *The Glass Mountain,* Washburn, 1954; *The Blue Harbor,* Washburn, 1956; *Snifty,* Westminster, 1957; *The Golden Wheel,* Westminster, 1958; *River Boy,* Westminster, 1959.

Reindeer Island, Westminster, 1960; *The Phantom Reindeer,* Coward, 1961; *Mystery of the Sunken City,* Westminster, 1962; *The Donkey with Diamond Ears,* Coward, 1962; *The Boy with One Shoe,* Coward, 1963; (under pseudonym Anne Cherryholmes) *The Island of the Silver Spoon,* Coward, 1963; (under pseudonym Anne Cherryholmes) *The Island of the Voyageurs,* Coward, 1964; *The Dog that Watched the Mountain,* Coward, 1967; *Kim Walk-in-My-Shoes* (Books for Brotherhood Book Club selection), Coward, 1968; *Rosa Bonheur: Painter of Animals,* Garrard, 1972.

Picture books adapted for children from literary classics; all published by Grosset: Alfred Ollivant, *Bob, Son of Battle,* 1960; Jack London, *Call of the Wild,* 1961; Margaret Sydney, *Five Little Peppers and How They Grew,* 1963.

Books of plays: *Short Plays from American History and Literature for Classroom Use: Grade Schools*, Samuel French, Volume I, 1925, Volume II, 1928, Volume III, 1929, Volume IV, 1935; *Plays for Schools*, Baker's Plays, 1927; *American History in Masque and Wig for Classroom Use*, Baker's Plays, 1931; *Plays for Young Children*, U.S. Bicentennial Commission to Celebrate the Bicentennial of George Washington's Birthday, 1932; *Plays of Far Places*, Baker's Plays, 1936; *Debutante Plays for Girls Twelve to Twenty*, Samuel French, 1936; *Plays of Belles and Beaux: Seven Short Plays for High School and Junior High*, Samuel French, 1937.

Plays published singly: *Lantern Light*, Samuel French, 1925; *The Gateway of Tomorrow* (an Americanization play), Scott Mitchell, 1929; *Washington Marches On*, U.S. Bicentennial Celebration, 1931; *Angelica, Inc.*, Samuel French, 1937; *The Young May Moon*, Samuel French, 1939; *Star Eternal*, Dramatists Play Service, 1939; *Holiday Hill*, Row, Peterson, 1940; *When the Bough Breaks*, Eldridge Entertainment House, 1940; *Freshman Bill*, Eldridge Entertainment House, 1941; *Announcing Antonia*, Samuel French, 1941; *Ask for the Moon*, Row, Peterson, 1942; *Sub-Deb Sue*, Dramatists Play Service, 1942; *Family Tree*, Row, Peterson, 1943; (under pseudonym Barbara West) *Belles in Waiting*, Row, Peterson, 1943; *Out of the Mist*, Eldridge Entertainment House, 1943; *Magic on Main Street* (for women), Row, Peterson, 1945; *Stage Struck*, Row, Peterson, 1946; *Rummage Sale* (for women), Row, Peterson, 1946; *Sparkling Sixteen*, Northwestern Press, 1947. Also author of plays published in anthologies compiled by Robert Haven Schauffler, by Dodd Mead.

Radio scripts: "Twelve Municipal Plays," "Sixteen and Six Fashion Programs," "Story Hour Books," all produced.

WORK IN PROGRESS: Research on Greece, Lebanon, and Israel, with a historical novel expected to result.

SIDELIGHTS: "I was born in Pittsburgh, Pa. The house I grew up in faced a park which all the children loved. It was beautiful with growing things, grassy hills and trees and flowers, winding paths through dark, sweet-smelling woods. There was a cool-flowing spring, three dusky interconnected caves in which we played 'pirate,' and most magical of all, a waterfall! High white waters splashed down over boulders below and sang and sang and sang with a child's special kind of music. I knew where the violets grew, when the forsythias brought their gold, where the weeping willows were that I could hide under. I had so many secret places! My joy was to run down a green hillside, a book in my hand, and my beloved collie, Judy, racing beside me.

"Above the park was a stretch of uninterrupted sky. I came to know the sunsets and the evening star and a certain star to wish on. I was always grateful to my father for finding that modest childhood home fronting on such loveliness. In his gentle way he said: 'I want things to be beautiful for you. There are greater things than money.'

"I was to discover that. One was a big old-fashioned Morris chair in which I sat to read, lost to the whole world. I always went to the library where I was introduced to the Wonderland of books. It was up on Mount Washington with a fantastic view of Pittsburgh, the city far below at the point of three rivers, the Monongahela, the Allegheny, and the Ohio. It was an inspiration then and many years later when I was to write *Three Golden Rivers* which inspired a fifteen-year-old boy in the 1850's to put them on glass.

"'Books,' I was told at the library, 'can become your best friends.' The first time I saw hundreds of them arranged on the shelves I felt a hush come over me as though I were in a cathedral. Beginning with the fairy tales of Hans Christian Andersen and the Brothers' Grimm, I read on through *The Green Fairy Book, The Red Fairy Book, The Blue Fairy Book*, and *The Arabian Nights*. With *King Arthur* and the poets I entered the most rewarding world on earth, 'the country of the mind.'

"Then came the great day. I was a little girl, nine years old, sitting at the kitchen table. I was writing my first novel. It was set on a Southern plantation, even grander to my mind than 'Tara' in *Gone with the Wind*. My heroine, wearing a cloudy white dress, was sitting in a rose garden. Of course she was rich, very rich! I could tell about her house and how she learned to ride high-bred horses, but somehow or

OLIVE PRICE

"Let's pretend that big oak tree is a castle tower where a princess is imprisoned. We'll all be knights, some of us guarding the princess, the rest coming to rescue her. I'll lead the charge."
■ (From *Rosa Bonheur* by Olive Price. Illustrated by Cary.)

other, I never knew how to end a chapter. Thinking that no matter how lovely things were with her, she would really have to eat, gave me an idea to end every chapter with the line, 'And so the dinner bell rang (and who among us ever had a dinner bell?) and Belinda Bentley Bennington walked gracefully into the dining room.'

"But that, I suppose, is part of the actress-syndrome in every girl's dreams. And if one thought of being an actress (talented or not!) one would have to have plays. Undaunted I proceeded to write them. But that was after high school and attendance at college while I was still writing advertising copy for Pittsburgh department stores—copy for everything from fashions to Oriental rugs and Venetian glass. All that was Business. More than anything else I wanted to do creative writing for children and young people, especially those still in the school room who had few plays to choose from in those days when 'dramatics' were just beginning to flourish as part of the course in public schools.

"By this time I had become what is now known as a 'History Buff.' My plays were drawn from American history and literature. The touching part of the experience was the fact that I bought a mimeograph and reproduced the plays for distribution to the schools. These were produced on elementary and high school stages. Neighborhood kids became American Indian princesses and princes in 'The Prince of the Golden Arrow,' Sons of Liberty in 'The Green Dragon,' charming little Salem witches in 'The Witch with Golden Hair.'

"Then came my dream of New York, the mecca of every writer, where stood the shining towers of the glittering publishing world. I was nineteen years old. Armed with the scripts of twelve 'produced plays' I set forth. My trek began with Macmillan's who *almost* published the plays and ended with Samuel French, renowned publisher of Broadway plays and other theatrical offerings for over a hundred years with roots in Shakespeare's London. The book was published under the title *Short Plays from American History and Literature* and became a series of four volumes. It was a great day!

"Thus I grew up with Samuel French, writing school and Little Theatre plays for the next fifteen years. During this time I also wrote plays for other publishers, radio, and television.

"Meanwhile I became interested in the magical world of young people's books. Remembering my days in the old Morris chair, I began with *A Donkey for the King*, the story of what may have happened to the little donkey Christ rode into Jerusalem. Then came books of adventure in which I roamed the world from thirteenth-century China in *The Valley of the Dragon* to the Korean War in *Kim Walk-in-My-Shoes*. I traveled with Marco Polo in wondrous Cathay and the Far East and walked with Clara Barton on the battlefields of the Civil War. I looked at paintings in the Louvre with Rosa Bonheur and watched her paint 'The Horse Fair.' An author must live with his or her characters. Meanwhile there were picture-book adaptations of the classics for younger children.

"Many of my books speak for my love of animals. The little donkey Christ rode, Wandering Star, the young snow-white mare stolen from Kublai Khan's royal meadows, Snifty, the little black bear cub found by Cherokee chil-

dren. There were, too, the phantom reindeer of Finland, the donkey with diamond ears who worked in the jewel mines of Brazil, and the moody St. Bernard, the dog that watched the mountain on the ski slopes of Switzerland.

"It is good that children's books by American authors find their way across the seas. It is like building a bridge for Brotherhood. School children in England read my books published in London, others read translations of those published in Denmark, Norway, Portugal, Italy, and Israel. Children's literature is a field of enchantment. Many have helped along the way, including the editors, who like writers dream dreams that books can become 'best friends.'"

Debutante Plays for Girls Twelve to Twenty have been produced on television; *Snifty*, has been broadcast on radio. "The Valley of the Dragon," a science-fiction film by Paramount Pictures, used that title only, and was not otherwise related to Olive Price's book, the story of which is set in the year 1280. *American History in Masque and Wig for Classroom Use* has been published in Braille.

HOBBIES AND OTHER INTERESTS: Travel (Europe, Canada, and the Caribbean).

PRIETO, Mariana B(eeching) 1912-

PERSONAL: Born August 6, 1912, in Cincinnati, Ohio; daughter of Charles Train (an engineer) and Sylvia (Beck) Beeching; married Martin Prieto, August 22, 1936; chil-

In all his seven years he had never seen snow. ■ (From *Johnny Lost* by Mariana Prieto. Illustrated by Catherine Hanley.)

dren: Nita. *Education:* Attended Colegio Sagrada Corazon, Havana, Cuba, University of Miami, Coral Gables, Fla., and University of Florida. *Home and office:* 2499 Southwest 34th Ave., Miami, Fla. 33145.

CAREER: Radio Station WIOD, Miami, Fla., dual language (Spanish-English) broadcasting, 1937; Pan American Library and Research Center, Miami, Fla., librarian, 1937; taught Spanish to Air Force officers, World War II, at Miami, Fla., and Orlando, Fla.; University of Miami, Coral Gables, Fla., evening division, teacher of creative writing, 1960-62; Miami (Fla.) Public Schools, currently teacher of creative writing classes in evening division. *Member:* Friendly Visitors Club, Grove House, Florida Education Association. *Awards, honors:* Award for a play in a Samuel French contest.

WRITINGS: Spanish and How, Taylor Press, 1944; *Pattern for Beauty*, Glade House, 1945; *His Cuban Wife* (novel), College Publishing Co., 1954; *The Wise Rooster, El Gallo Sabio* (English-Spanish, for children), John Day, 1962; *Ah Ucu and Itzo* (English-Spanish, for children), John Day, 1964; *A Kite for Carlos* (English-Spanish, for children), John Day, 1965; *Tomato Boy* (English-Spanish, for children), John Day, 1966; *Johnny Lost*, John Day, 1969; *When the Monkeys Wore Sombreros*, Harvey, 1969; *Raimundo*, Harvey, 1971; (with Grizella Hopper) *The Birdmen of Papantla*, Ritchie, 1972; *Pablo's Petunias*, Oddo, 1972; (editor) *Play It in Spanish*, John Day, 1973; *Peter Pelican*, 1973; *Fun Jewelry*, Sam Har Press, 1973; *Beautiful You*, 1974; *The Hu Tu Bird*, 1975. Also author of

filmstrip, "Mayan Warrior." Contributor of more than six hundred articles and short stories to periodicals including *Mademoiselle, New York Times.* Writes under pseudonym for men's magazines.

SIDELIGHTS: "I write because I enjoy it. I love to travel and many of my books are the result of ideas I got while on my travels. Most of my backgrounds are Latin American as I have lived and studied in many Latin American countries and Spain. I am interested in archeology, art and history, especially Mayan ruins."

HOBBIES AND OTHER INTERESTS: Painting, research (especially folklore), people, cooking, exotic clothes, animals.

FOR MORE INFORMATION SEE: Miami Herald, December 9, 1962; *Horn Book*, April, 1968; Hoffman and Samuels, *Authors and Illustrators of Chidren's Books*, Bowker, 1972.

PURDY, Susan Gold 1939-

PERSONAL: Born May 17, 1939, in New York, N.Y.; daughter of Harold A. (a dentist) and Frances (Joslin) Gold; married Geoffrey Hale Purdy (now a computer programmer), September 29, 1963. *Education:* Vassar College, student, 1957-59; Ecole des Beaux Arts and Sorbonne, University of Paris, student, 1959-60; New York University, B.S., 1962. *Home:* Wilton, Conn.

SUSAN PURDY

A yeoman of the Guard or Beefeater, wears a colorful red costume with yellow and black striped trim, military medals on his chest, a black top hat, and a white neck ruffle. ■ (From *Festivals for You to Celebrate* by Susan Purdy. Illustrated by the author.)

CAREER: Wamsutta Mills, New York, N.Y., textile designer, 1962-63; now full-time writer, mainly for children, and illustrator. Wilton Music and Art Day Camp (for girls six to twelve), co-director, summers, 1964, 1965. Has demonstrated various craft techniques on local and national television; teaches cooking on children's TV show, "Patchwork Family," on C.B.S. in New York, 1969—.

WRITINGS—Author and illustrator: *My Little Cabbage*, Lippincott, 1965; *Christmas Decorations for You to Make*, Lippincott, 1965; *If You Have a Yellow Lion*, Lippincott, 1966; *Holiday Cards for You to Make*, Lippincott, 1967; *Be My Valentine*, Lippincott, 1969; *Festivals for you to Celebrate*, Lippincott, 1969; *Jewish Holidays*, Lippincott, 1969; *Costumes for You to Make*, Lippincott, 1971; *Books for You to Make*, Lippincott, 1973. Contributor of articles to *Family Circle, Ladies' Home Journal, Good Housekeeping*.

Illustrator: Lydia A. Duggins, *Developing Children's Perceptual Skills in Reading*, Mediax, 1968; Irene Bowen, *Suddenly a Witch!*, Lippincott, 1970.

SIDELIGHTS: Speaks French, Italian. *Hobbies and other interests:* Painting.

FOR MORE INFORMATION SEE: Illustrators of Children's Books: 1957-66, Horn Book, 1968; *Horn Book*, August, 1969.

RAUCHER, Herman 1928-

PERSONAL: Surname is pronounced *Row*-sher; born April 13, 1928, in New York, N.Y.; son of Benjamin Brooks and Sophie (Weinshank) Raucher; married Mary Kathryn Martinet, April 20, 1960; children: Jacqueline Leigh, Jennifer Brooke. *Education:* New York University, B.S., 1949. *Religion:* Hebrew. *Residence:* Greenwich, Conn. *Agent:* Owen Laster, William Morris Agency, 1350 Avenue of the Americas, New York, N.Y. 10019.

CAREER: Advertising writer in Hollywood, Calif., for 20th Century-Fox, 1950-54, and Walt Disney, 1954-55; worked at Calkins & Holden (advertising), New York, N.Y., 1956-57; Reach, McCluton (advertising), New York, N.Y., vice-president, creative director, member of board of directors, 1957-63; Maxon (advertising), New York, N.Y.,

HERMAN RAUCHER

Something about the Author

They called themselves the Terrible Trio but for no real reason known to man, mostly to just bolster their own egos, to sort of establish themselves on the planet. ■ (From the movie *"Summer of 42,"* copyright © 1971 by Warner Bros.)

vice-president, creative director, 1963-64; Gardner (advertising), New York, N.Y., vice-president, creative director, 1964-65; consultant, Benton & Bowles (advertising), New York, N.Y., 1965-67. *Military service:* U.S. Army, 1950-52; became second lieutenant. *Member;* Writers Guild of America, Dramatists Guild of Authors League of America.

Screenplays: "Sweet November," Warner Brothers, 1968; "Can Heironymus Merkin Ever Forget Mercy Humppe and Find True Happiness?," Regional Film Distributors, 1969; "Watermelon Man," Columbia, 1970; "Summer of '42," Warner Bros, 1971; "Class of '44," Warner Bros., 1973. Writer of original television dramas for "Studio One," "Alcoa Hour," and "Goodyear Playhouse," 1956-58, also "Remember When" for N.B.C., 1974.

Novelizations of screenplays: *Watermelon Man*, Ace Books, 1970; *Summer of '42 (School Library Journal* book list), Putnam, 1971; *A Glimpse of Tiger*, Putnam, 1971.

HOBBIES AND OTHER INTERESTS: "Amorphic and everchanging."

FOR MORE INFORMATION SEE: Punch, July 29, 1970; *Best Sellers*, March 1, 1971; *Commonweal*, May 21, 1971.

RAY, Deborah 1940-

PERSONAL: Born August 31, 1940, in Philadelphia, Pa.; daughter of Louis X. and Hildegarde (Wimenitz) Cohen; married Christopher Ray (a sculptor), July 8, 1960; children: Karen, Nicole. *Education:* Studied at Philadelphia College of Art, 1958-59, University of Pennsylvania, 1959-61, Pennsylvania Academy of the Fine Arts, 1959-62, and Albert C. Barnes Foundation, 1962-64. *Residence:* Philadelphia, Pa.

CAREER: Artist. Paintings have been shown in six solo exhibitions, mostly in Philadelphia, and in group shows at Philadelphia Art Alliance, Pennsylvania Academy of the Fine Arts, Philadelphia Museum of Arts, Rutgers University, American Institute of Graphic Arts, and elsewhere; represented in collections of Chase Manhattan Bank (graphic mural), Free Library of Philadelphia, University of Minnesota, Library of Congress, Drexel University, and Fidelity Bank. *Member:* Artist Equity Association. *Awards, honors:* Louis Comfort Tiffany Foundation fellowship in painting, 1968; Mabel Rush Homer Award, 1968; Philadelphia Art Directors Award for design and book illustration, 1970; other awards from American Institute of Graphic Arts, 1970, and Woodmere Art Gallery, 1973.

Her mother was silent. ■ (From *The Train* by Robert Welber. Illustrated by Deborah Ray.)

WRITINGS—Reteller for children and illustrator: *The Fair at Sorochintsi: A Nikolai Gogol Story Retold*, Macrae Smith, 1969; *Abdul Abul-Bul Amir and Ivan Skavinsky Skavar*, Macrae Smith, 1969.

Illustrator: Robert Welber, *The Winter Picnic*, Pantheon, 1970; Robert Welber, *Frog, Frog, Frog*, Pantheon, 1971; Robert Welber, *The Train*, Pantheon, 1972; Robert Welber, *Song of the Seasons*, Pantheon, 1973; Robert Welber, *The Winter Wedding*, Pantheon, in press.

SIDELIGHTS: "In illustrating children's books I have found another audience to communicate with. My basic aim is to create a good art for children in books—that children respond to the nuance and look beyond what many adults miss. My first books were in a created or fantasy world. The books I have most recently done must speak directly to the world children are most familiar with in their day to day lives. To create real people they might know from words."

FOR MORE INFORMATION SEE: Donnarae MacCann and Olga Richard, *The Child's First Books*, Wilson, 1973.

RICHARDSON, Grace Lee
See DICKSON, Naida

RICHARDSON, Robert S(hirley) 1902-
(Philip Latham)

PERSONAL: Born April 22, 1902, in Kokomo, Ind.; son of Joel Howard (a salesman) and Arlene (Moore) Richardson; married Delia Shull, August 19, 1929 (died January 2, 1940); married Marjorie Helen Engstead; children: (second marriage) Rae (daughter). *Education:* University of California at Los Angeles, B.A., 1926; University of California at Berkeley, Ph.D., 1931. *Religion:* None. *Home and office:* 1533 East Altadena Dr., Altadena, Calif. 91001. *Agent:* Scott Meredith, 580 Fifth Ave., New York, N.Y. 10036.

CAREER: Hale Observatory (formerly Mt. Wilson and Palomar Observatory), Pasadena, Calif., staff astronomer, 1931-58; Griffith Observatory, Los Angeles, Calif., associate director, 1958-64; writer, 1964—. *Member:* American Astronomical Society, Astronomical Society of the Pacific, Los Angeles Astronomical Society (life member), Excelsior Telescope Club (honorary life member), Pasadena Art Museum, Friends of Altadena Library. *Awards, honors:* New York Academy of Sciences Children's Science Book Award, 1971, for *The Stars & Serendipity*.

WRITINGS: (With William T. Skilling) *Astronomy*, Holt, 1947; (with Skilling) *A Brief Text in Astronomy*, Holt, 1954, revised edition, 1959; *Exploring Mars*, McGraw, 1954; *Second Satellite* (juvenile fiction), Whittlesey House, 1956; (with Skilling) *Sun, Moon and Stars*, McGraw, 1959, revised edition, 1964; *The Fascinating World of Astronomy*, McGraw, 1960; *Man and the Moon*, World Publishing, 1961; *Astronomy in Action*, McGraw, 1962; (with Chesley Bonestell) *Mars*, Harcourt, 1964; *Getting Acquainted with Comets*, McGraw, 1967; *The Star Lovers*, Macmillan, 1967; *The Stars & Serendipity*, Pantheon, 1971.

Under pseudonym Philip Latham; novels: *Five Against Venus* (juvenile), Winston, 1952; *Missing Men of Saturn* (juvenile), Winston, 1953.

Contributor of articles and short stories to *Analog, Magazine of Fantasy and Science Fiction, Galaxy, Colliers.*

WORK IN PROGRESS: Short stories; book on metric system; novel for older juveniles entitled *Dial-a-Ghost*.

SIDELIGHTS: "I started serious writing in 1939, because I have always liked to write AND needed the money. My second article, published in 'Astounding S.F.' (later 'Analog'), entitled 'Luna Observatory No. 1,' was the first serious scientific article ever written about establishing an observatory on the moon.

"I majored in mathematics at U.C.L.A. and was also active in athletics, particularly boxing and track. I was the first trackman at U.C.L.A. to break ten seconds in the 100-yard dash (but wouldn't be able to make the third team now). I still keep fit shadow boxing which is excellent exercise.

"I much prefer writing fiction than fact articles. Fiction is more challenging and more demanding on imagination and inventive ability. As in the case of every writer, I have blank spells and periods of depression when I feel I will never write again. But then an idea always comes along, often from some trivial and unexpected incident. It is my experience that ideas cannot be forced. It is useless trying desperately to think up an idea.

"I consider my best story is 'Kid Anderson' published in 1949 in the old 'Astounding' magazine. It is also available in a couple of anthologies. The story is about a prize fighter, and has nothing to do with science.

"I have done very little writing that I would call easy. For me there is no such thing as 'hack' writing. You always try to give your best, regardless of the publisher and pay. And I don't sell all my stuff by any means.

"To people who ask me 'How to write?' I tell them, 'Write it the way it sounds the best to you.' Don't follow trends. Don't try to imitate some popular writer of the moment. You've got to write the way you feel you *must* write."

HOBBIES AND OTHER INTERESTS: Science—tending toward the supernatural, but "because I write about the occult does not mean I believe it. (I DO NOT.)"

ROBERTSON, Don 1929-

PERSONAL: Born March 21, 1929, in Cleveland, Ohio; son of Carl Trowbridge (associate editor, *Cleveland Plain Dealer*) and Josephine (Wuebben) Robertson; married Shari Kah, August 31, 1963. *Education:* Attended Harvard University, 1948-49, Western Reserve University, 1953-57. *Politics:* Democrat. *Agent:* Max Gartenberg, 331 Madison Ave., New York, N.Y. 10017. *Office:* Cleveland Press, Cleveland, Ohio 44114.

CAREER: Cleveland Plain Dealer, Cleveland, Ohio, reporter, 1949-52, 1953-55, copy editor, 1955-57; *Cleveland News*, Cleveland, Ohio, reporter, 1957-59; executive assistant to the Attorney General of Ohio, 1959-60; *Cleveland Plain Dealer*, Cleveland, Ohio, reporter, 1963-66; *Cleveland Press*, Cleveland, Ohio, columnist, 1968—. WVIZ-TV and WKBF-TV, Cleveland, Ohio, talkshow host, 1967-70; WKYC-TV, Cleveland, Ohio, movie and play reviewer, 1969, 1971—. *Military service:* U.S. Army, 1946-48. *Member:* American Newspaper Guild. *Awards, honors:* Putnam Award ($10,000), 1964, for *A Flag Full of Stars*; Cleveland Arts Prize, 1966.

WRITINGS: The Three Days, Prentice-Hall, 1959; *By Antietam Creek*, Prentice-Hall, 1960; *The River and the Wilderness*, Doubleday, 1962; *A Flag Full of Stars*, Putnam, 1964; *The Greatest Thing Since Sliced Bread*, Putnam, 1965; *The Sum and Total of Now*, Putnam, 1966; *Paradise Falls*, Putnam, 1968; *The Greatest Thing that Almost Happened*, Putnam, 1970; *Praise the Human Season*, Fields, 1974.

SIDELIGHTS: "I like model trains, John O'Hara, the Democratic Party, baseball, bridge, books, and most newspapermen below the rank of city editor. I also like cats and pro basketball."

ROBINSON, Adjai 1932-

PERSONAL: Born February 2, 1932, in Freetown, Sierra Leone; son of Ephraim Jonathan and Lavretta (Elliot) Robinson; married Shola Odedeyi (a teacher), August 5, 1965; children: Olamide, Olukemi, Ajibola, Kehinde Soyinka (a foster child). *Education:* Fourah Bay College, B.A., 1961, diploma in education, 1962; Columbia University, M.A., 1970, M.Ed., 1972, further study, 1972—. *Religion:* Christian. *Home:* 4 Ranger St., Freetown, Sierra Leone. *Agent:*

DON ROBERTSON

ADJAI ROBINSON

His knees almost gave way as he stood before the giant. ■ (From *Singing Tales of Africa* by Adjai Robinson. Illustrated by Christine Price.)

Russell & Volkening, Inc., 551 Fifth Ave., New York, N.Y. 10017. *Office:* United Nations Development Programme, 485 Lexington Ave., New York, N.Y. 10027.

CAREER: Teacher and head of Latin and religion department at Methodist high school for boys in Freetown, Sierra Leone, 1962-64; St. Joseph's Teachers College, Lagos, Nigeria, head of department of English, 1965-67; Kings College, Lagos, head of department of religion, 1967-69; teacher of elementary education at Marymount Manhattan College and Hunter College of the City University of New York, New York, N.Y., 1970-71; United Nations Development Programme, New York, N.Y., programmer, 1972—. Has given poetry readings on Sierra Leone radio programs and acted in plays. *Member:* Kappa Delta Pi.

WRITINGS: Femi and Old Grandaddie, Coward, 1972; *Kasho and the Twin Flutes*, Coward, 1973; *Singing Tales of Africa*, Scribner, in press.

WORK IN PROGRESS: A Race for Devil Eyes, about illicit diamond mining in Africa; *A Freshman's Dilemma*; research on performance-based teacher education in the principles and practices of education in the teacher training colleges in Lagos, Nigeria.

ROBINSON, Barbara (Webb)   1927-

PERSONAL: Born October 24, 1927, in Portsmouth, Ohio; daughter of Theodore L. and Grace (Mooney) Webb; married John F. Robinson, 1949; children: Carolyn, Marjorie. *Education:* Allegheny College, B.A., 1948. *Home:* 2063 Fox Creek Rd., Berwyn, Pa. 19312. *Agent:* Peggy Caulfield, 77 Park Ave., New York, N.Y. 10016.

CAREER: Free-lance writer. *Awards, honors:* Breadloaf Fellow, 1962.

WRITINGS: Across From Indian Shore, Lothrop, 1962; *Trace Through the Forest*, Lothrop, 1965; *The Fattest Bear in the First Grade*, Random House, 1969; *The Best Christmas Pageant Ever*, Harper, 1972. Contributor of short stories to *McCall's, Good Housekeeping, Redbook, Ladies' Home Journal, Toronto Star Weekly.*

SIDELIGHTS: "Each book that I have written for boys and girls is also a book I have written for myself. . . . since, if I don't find the story exciting or interesting or funny; if I don't enjoy the characters or care what happens to them, I don't think boys and girls will either.

"As with most authors I tend to write about the things which interest me—American Indians, the adventure of our country's past—and I especially enjoy doing the research which must be done for this kind of book. I usually start

BARBARA ROBINSON

The Herdmans were absolutely the worst kids in the history of the world. They lied and stole and smoked cigars (even the girls) and talked dirty and hit little kids and cussed their teachers and took the name of the Lord in vain and set fire to Fred Shoemaker's old broken-down toolhouse. ▪ (From *The Best Christmas Pageant Ever* by Barbara Robinson. Illustrated by Judith Gwyn Brown.)

with a broad idea—the first road ever built across the wilderness of the Ohio territory; the last living descendant of a famous Indian chief—and since I don't plan my books in outline form I am often in the position of the reader, asking 'what's going to happen next?'

"When I'm not writing I cook supper and make cookies and sweep the floor and let the dog out and let the dog in and fuss at my daughters to pick up their rooms. My favorite place to be is at the ocean, on Cape Cod, and my own all-time favorite book is *Treasure Island*."

RODGERS, Mary   1931-

PERSONAL: Born January 11, 1931, in New York, N.Y.; daughter of Richard (composer) and Dorothy (Feiner) Rodgers; married Julian B. Beaty, Jr., December 7, 1951 (divorced, 1957); married Henry Guettel (a vice-president of a motion picture company), October 14, 1961; children: (first marriage) Richard R., Linda M., Constance P.; (second marriage) Adam, Alexander. *Education:* Attended Wellesley College, 1948-51. *Politics:* Liberal. *Religion:* Jewish. *Home:* 115 Central Park West, New York, N.Y. 10023. *Agent:* Shirley Bernstein, Paramuse Artists, Inc., 1414 Avenue of the Americas, New York, N.Y. 10019.

CAREER: Composer and lyric writer. Assistant producer of New York Philharmonic's Young People's Concerts, 1957-71. Member of board of trustees, Brearley School, 1973—. *Member:* Dramatists Guild (member of council), American Federation of Television and Radio Artists (AFTRA), Screen Actors Guild, Cosmopolitan Club. *Awards, honors: Book World* Spring Book Festival Award, 1972, and Christopher Award, 1973, both for *Freaky Friday.*

WRITINGS: The Rotten Book, Harper, 1969; (with mother, Dorothy Rodgers) *A Word to the Wives*, Knopf, 1970; *Freaky Friday* (ALA Notable Book), Harper, 1972; *A Billion for Boris*, Harper, 1974.

Musical plays: (Composer of music and author of book and lyrics) "Three to Make Music," first produced in New York, N.Y., at Hunter College of the City University of New York, 1959; (composer of music) "Once Upon a Mattress," first produced on Broadway at Phoenix Theatre, 1959; (composer of music) "Hot Spot," first produced on Broadway at Majestic Theatre, 1963; (composer of music) "Mad Show," first produced Off-Broadway at New Theatre, 1966.

Also composer of numerous children's musicals, including "Davy Jones' Locker," performed with Bill Baird Marionettes, 1959; "Young Mark Twain," 1964; "Pinocchio," performed with Baird Marionettes, 1973.

Co-author, with mother Dorothy Rodgers, of monthly column, "Of Two Minds," *McCall's*, 1971—.

SIDELIGHTS: "Since I had nothing to do but take care of five children, a nine-room apartment, an eleven-room house in the country, and show up once a month at the Professional Children's School Board of Trustees meeting, once a month at the Dramatist Guild Council meeting, and eight times a month at the A&P, I thought I'd be delighted to

MARY RODGERS

You are not going to believe me, nobody in their right minds could *possibly* believe me, but it's true, really it is! *When I woke up this morning, I found I'd turned into my mother.* ■ (From *Freaky Friday* by Mary Rodgers. Book jacket illustrated by Edward Gorey.)

write a children's book, because I had all this extra time on my hands. (Between the hours of two and five a.m., I just loll around the house wondering how to amuse myself.)"

FOR MORE INFORMATION SEE: Horn Book, August, 1972.

ROLERSON, Darrell A(llen) 1946-

PERSONAL: Born February 21, 1946, in Camden, Me.; son of Clyde Andros (a farmer) and Lydia (Coombs) Rolerson. *Education:* Graduated from high school in Islesboro, Me., 1964. *Politics:* "My politics and my religion are one. I am a free thinker . . . one who has a lot to learn." *Home:* 743 Cole St., San Francisco, Calif. *Agent:* Rosemary Casey, 79 Madison Ave., New York, N.Y.

CAREER: "I am a farmer first and only incidentally a writer." *Military service:* U.S. Navy, 1965-67.

WRITINGS—For children: A Boy and a Deer, Dodd, 1970; *Mister Big Britches*, Dodd, 1971; *In Sheep's Clothing*, Dodd, 1972; *A Boy Called Plum*, Dodd, 1974. Regular contributor to adult magazines, *Down East, Organic Farming, Yankee*, and *Maine Farmstead.*

WORK IN PROGRESS: A novel, *The River Song*, about life and death as it is experienced in a folk culture, for publication by Dodd; a farm book, a new age approach to self-sufficient homesteading.

SIDELIGHTS: "The three things I enjoy most in life are writing, travelling, and farming. I think that any day I shall

[The barn] was a forlorn-looking thing, just a hollow place that gaped out at the world. It was empty. It offered nothing except more despair. ■ (From *In Sheep's Clothing* by Darrell A. Rolerson. Illustrated by Ted Lewin.)

add sailing, for I come from a family with a long sea-faring tradition. I have travelled extensively in the U.S. I have lived in Scotland and London, and visited the major cities of Europe, which means I have only begun. I have a good ten books in outline. At the same time I am gathering stones to build a house and perfecting a scheme I have for a concept of gardening which goes beyond the vegetable patch to include the environment as a whole, taking into account man and his relationship to nature."

ROSE, Anne

PERSONAL: Born in Antwerp, Belgium; naturalized U.S. citizen; daughter of Chaim H. and Tyla (Kolber) Kaufman; married Gilbert J. Rose (a physician); children: Renee, Dan, Cecily, Ron. *Education:* Hunter College (of City University of New York), B.A.; graduate work at Columbia. *Politics:* Democrat. *Office:* Gallery Imago, Becket, Mass.

CAREER: Five Mile River Gallery, Rowayton, Conn., director, 1961-62; Gallery Imago, Becket, Mass., director, 1973—. *Member:* American Field Service (chairman of Brien McMahon chapter, 1969-70), Planned Parenthood.

WRITINGS: Samson and Delilah, Lothrop, 1968; *How Does a Czar Eat Potatoes?*, Lothrop, 1973; *Sand and Dreams: An Oriental Fantasy*, Harcourt, in press; *Akimba and the Magic Cow*, Scholastic, in press; *As Right As Right Can Be*, Dial, in press. Contributor to *Cricket.*

WORK IN PROGRESS: A story of adolescents in World War II; stories for children.

Child, child, but your father,
How does he cry?
■ (From *How Does a Czar Eat Potatoes?* by Anne Rose. Illustrated by Janosch.)

ANNE ROSE

SIDELIGHTS: Anne Rose is interested in anthropology, myths, and folktales of primitive peoples. She has travelled extensively in Central and South America, Europe, the Near East, Ethiopia, Russia, Japan, the Galapagos, and India. She has also been on a dugout canoe trip in Surinam and a whaling trip in Iceland. The languages she speaks include French, Flemish, German, Yiddish, and Spanish.

ROSEN, Winifred   1943-

PERSONAL: Born October 16, 1943, in Columbia, S.C.; daughter of Victor H. (a psychoanalyst) and Elizabeth (Ruskay) Rosen (a modern dancer and dance therapist). *Education:* New York University, B.A., 1964, M.A., 1966. *Home:* 259 East 2nd Ave., Eugene, Ore. 97401. *Agent:* Betty Ann Clarke, International Famous Agency, Inc., 1301 Avenue of the Americas, New York, N.Y. 10019.

CAREER: High school teacher in New York, N.Y., 1965-68; Dial Press, Inc., New York, N.Y., editorial assistant, 1970. *Member:* Phi Beta Kappa.

WRITINGS—All juvenile: *Marvin's Manhole*, Dial, 1970; *Ralph Proves the Pudding*, Doubleday, 1972; *Hiram Makes Friends*, Four Winds Press, 1974; *The Golden Book of Hippos*, Golden Press, 1975; *Henrietta: The Wild Woman of Borneo*, Four Winds Press, 1975; *A Sand Story*, Cricket, in press. Contributor to *Harper's Magazine*.

. . . then all of a sudden everyone was jumping or bouncing, squeaking or howling like crazy. I didn't know what to do. It was awful. ■ (From *Hiram Makes Friends* by Winifred Rosen Casey. Illustrated by J. Winslow Higginbottom.)

WINIFRED ROSEN

WORK IN PROGRESS: *Confessions of a Head-Shrinker's Daughter*, an autobiographical novel.

SIDELIGHTS: "I think it is always difficult for writers to pin point the source of the inspiration for most of their work. I have sometimes sat down with what I thought was a completely empty mind, and found that a story was spontaneously born, almost through no apparent effort of my own. That is a wonderful experience, worth months of waiting for. Books like *The Golden Book of Hippos*, which I was asked to do, require much more conscious and deliberate labor.

"The hardest times for me, as I think for most writers, are not when I am working, but when I am not. There are always fallow periods between projects, and one must learn to bear with the apparent inactivity. This is when I turn to making jewelry, writing letters, embroidering, playing music—non-verbal activities for the most part. Writing, I have noticed, comes out of silence. Too much conversation makes writing impossible. Writers therefore need to spend a lot of time alone, and since lots of us are very social people, this requires some self-control.

"Recently I have been drawing more on autobiographical material for my books. That is, I think all books that come out of the author's imagination (rather than research) are autobiographical at some deep level. However *Henrietta: The Wild Woman of Borneo* is consciously autobiographical. My mother actually used to tell me that I looked like the wild woman of Borneo, and that was my inspiration. Henrietta's fantasies are probably not the fantasies I had as an eight year old because of course they are literature and not life. But I think they reflect something very real about my attitude about myself at that time, and that most eight year olds will be able, therefore, to relate to and even identify with the character."

HOBBIES AND OTHER INTERESTS: Silver-smithing, embroidery, music, and yoga.

170

ROSENBERG, Sharon 1942-

PERSONAL: Born December 14, 1942, in New York, N.Y.; daughter of Louis (a salesman) and Mildred (Feder-bush) Rosenberg. *Education:* Harpur College, student, 1960-63. *Home:* 3917 18th St., San Francisco, Calif. 94114. *Agent:* Oscar Collier.

CAREER: Modern dancer in New York, N.Y., 1963-67, worked with Martha Graham, Erick Hawkins, and Rod Rodgers, among others; artist and designer with Electric Lotus Co. (designers of environments and multi-media shows), New York, N.Y., 1967; cook in small vegetarian restaurant, and then in macrobiotic restaurant, London, England, 1968-69; designer and seamstress in Formentera and Ibiza, Spain, 1969-70; free-lance work, 1970—, as cook, caterer, costume designer for dance and theater, clothing designer, dancer, seamstress, and model for artist.

WRITINGS: (With Joan Wiener) *The Illustrated Hassle-Free Make Your Own Clothes Book* (for young adults), Straight Arrow, 1971; (with Wiener) *Son of Hassle-Free Sewing: Further Adventures in Homemade Clothes* (for young adults), Straight Arrow, 1972. Magazine columnist with Joan Wiener, writing on sewing in *Rags* and on food in *Sundance.*

SHARON ROSENBERG

WORK IN PROGRESS: A vegetable cookbook; a sewing book for young children.

SIDELIGHTS: "I must admit the thought of being a writer, much less an author, was about the furthest thing from my mind. My friend, Joan Wiener, who had, herself, already written two or three books, was looking for a new project.... She suggested we work together on a sewing book, and I agreed, but didn't actually take it very seriously, until I realized that there was an interested publisher.

"As to how I actually got to the position of knowing enough about sewing to write a book—I have to say simply that I've stood near, watched over the shoulder of, and asked a lot of questions of, some of the most talented and creative people around. I've learned gourmet cooking and European tailoring this way but mostly I learned about courage. Jump right in, 'cause otherwise you'll never make those mistakes that teach more than the best books. Keep your eyes open, be daring, and mostly work from your heart."

ROUNDS, Glen (Harold) 1906-

PERSONAL: Born April 4, 1906, in Near Wall, S.D.; son of William E. (a rancher) and Janet I. (Barber) Rounds; married Margaret Olmsted, January, 1938 (died December, 1968); children: William E. II. *Education:* Attended Kansas City Art Institute, 1926-27, and Art Student's League, New York, N.Y., evenings, 1930-31. *Residence:* Southern Pines, N.C. 28387.

CAREER: Traveled throughout United States, holding a variety of jobs, including those of muleskinner, cowboy, sign painter, railroad section hand, baker, carnival medicine man, and textile designer; began experimenting with etching and painting, then wrote stories to accompany his drawings; full-time author and illustrator of adult and children's books, 1936—. *Military service:* U.S. Army, Coast Artillery and Infantry, 1942-45; became staff sergeant. *Member:* Authors Guild. *Awards, honors:* Lewis Carroll Shelf award, 1969, for *Wild Horses of the Red Desert.*

WRITINGS—All self-illustrated; all published by Holiday House, except as indicated: *Ol' Paul, the Mighty Logger*, 1936; *Lumbercamp*, 1937, reissued as *Whistle Punk*, 1959; *Paydirt*, 1938; *The Blind Colt* (Junior Literary Guild selection), 1941; *Whitey's Sunday Horse* (excerpted from *The Blind Colt*), 1943; *Whitey's First Roundup* (Junior Literary Guild selection), Grosset, 1942; *Whitey Looks for a Job*, Grosset, 1944; *Whitey and Jinglebob*, Grosset, 1946; *Stolen Pony* (sequel to *The Blind Colt*), 1948, revised edition, 1969; *Rodeo*, 1949.

Whitey and the Rustlers, 1951; *Hunted Horses*, 1951; *Whitey and the Blizzard*, 1952; *Buffalo Harvest*, 1952; *Lone Muskrat*, 1953; *Whitey Takes a Trip*, 1954; *Whitey Ropes and Rides*, 1956; *Swamp Life: An Almanac*, Prentice-Hall, 1957; *Whitey and the Wild Horse*, 1958; *Wildlife at Your Doorstep*, Prentice-Hall, 1958, new edition, Holiday House, 1974.

Whitey's New Saddle (contains *Whitey and the Rustlers* and *Whitey and the Blizzard*), 1960; *Beaver Business*, Prentice-Hall, 1960; *Wild Orphan*, 1961; *Whitey and the*

GLEN ROUNDS

Colt Killer, 1962; *Rain in the Woods*, World Publishing, 1964; (editor) Andy Adams, *Trail Drive* (originally published as *Log of a Cowboy*, 1903), 1965; (editor) George F. Ruxton, *Mountain Men*, 1966; *The Snake Tree*, World Publishing, 1967; (compiler) *Boll Weevil*, Golden Gate, 1967; *The Treeless Plains*, 1967; *The Prairie Schooners*, 1968; (compiler) *Casey Jones*, Golden Gate, 1968; *Wild Horses of the Red Desert*, 1969.

Strawberry Roan, Golden Gate, 1970; *The Cowboy Trade*, 1971; *Once We Had a Horse*, 1971; *Sweet Betsy from Pike*, Golden Gate, 1973; *The Day the Circus Came to Lonetree*, 1973.

Illustrator: Irma S. Black, *Flipper, a Sea Lion*, Holiday House, 1940; Walter Blair, *Tale America*, Coward, 1944; Frank O'Rourke, *"E" Company*, Simon & Schuster, 1945; Martha Hardy, *Tatoosh*, Macmillan, 1947; Wheaton P. Webb, *Uncle Swithin's Inventions*, Holiday House, 1947; *Aesop's Fables*, Lippincott, 1949.

Vance Randolph, *We Always Lie to Strangers*, Columbia University Press, 1951; Randolph, *Who Blowed Up the Church House?*, Columbia University Press, 1952; Sarah R. Riedman, *Grass, Our Greatest Crop*, Thomas Nelson, 1952; Jim Kjelgaard, *Haunt Fox*, Holiday House, 1954; Paul Hyde Bonner, *Those Glorious Mornings*, Scribner,

1954; Randolph, *The Devil's Pretty Daughter*, Columbia University Press, 1955; Paul M. Sears, *Firefly*, Holiday House, 1956; Randolph, *The Talking Turtle*, Columbia University Press, 1957; Randolph, *Sticks in the Knapsack*, Columbia University Press, 1958.

Elizabeth Seeman, *In the Arms of the Mountain*, Crown, 1961; Wilson Gage, *A Wild Goose Tale*, World Publishing, 1961; Gage, *Dan and the Miranda*, World Publishing, 1962; Gage, *Big Blue Island*, World Publishing, 1964; Adrien Stoutenburg, *The Crocodile's Mouth*, Viking, 1966; Richard Chase, *Billy Boy*, Golden Gate, 1966; Maria Leach, *How the People Sang the Mountains Up*, Viking, 1967; Rebecca Caudill and James Ayars, *Contrary Jenkins*, Holt, 1968; Gladys Conklin, *Lucky Lady Bug*, Holiday House, 1968; Stoutenburg, *American Tall Tale Animals*, Viking, 1968; John Greenway, *Folklore of the Great West*, American West, 1969.

Austin Fife and Alta Fife, *Ballads of the Great West*, American West, 1970; Wilson Gage, *Mike's Toads*, World Publishing, 1970; Alexander L. Crosby, *Go Find Hanka*, Golden Gate, 1970; Ida Chittum, *Farmer Hoo and the Baboons*, Delacorte, 1971; Alvin Schwartz, *A Twister of Twists, a Tangler of Tongues*, Lippincott, 1972; Gladys Conklin, *Tarantula, the Giant Spider*, Holiday House, 1972; Sandra S. Sivulich, *I'm Going on a Bear Hunt*, Dutton, 1973; Schwartz, *Tomfoolery*, Lippincott, 1973; Schwartz, *Witcracks*, Lippincott, 1973; Schwartz, *Cross Your Fingers, Spit in Your Hat*, Lippincott, 1974; Mark Taylor, *Jennie Jenkins*, Little, Brown, 1975; Schwartz, *Whoppers, Tall Tales, and Other Lies*, Lippincott, 1975; Betty Baker, *3 Fools and a Horse*, Macmillan, 1975; Berniece Freschet, *Lizard in the Sun*, Scribner, 1975.

Author of scripts for "School of the Air," CBS, 1938-39. Work is represented in school readers and anthologies, including *Treasury of American Folklore*, edited by Benjamin Botkin, Crown, 1944, and *Subtreasury of American Humor*, edited by E. B. White and Katherine S. White, Coward, 1941. Contributor to *Story Parade, Scholastic Magazines*.

SIDELIGHTS: "I'm an artist who has written for a living—learned the trade freehand. I'm listed as a juvenile writer but I don't write for children. All I'm interested in at the time is the tale itself, and the drawings that will go with it—or that came before the story itself.

"I sort of drift, doing mostly only what pleases me. Lately that has been illustrating rather than writing. Now I'm stirring around some old sketch books of speakeasy days, people I knew among the grifters, soldiers, travelling sign painters and the like at one time or another. I seem to have known more than my share of slightly peculiar people—and most of them had mighty peculiar stories to tell, or told about them.

"I got to New York in 1935 and I used to sleep among the other homeless men—there were a lot of them in those days—in Madison Square Park. I'd go around to various publications, trying to sell drawings. I'd call on editors near lunchtime; start spinning yarns and mostly they'd take a bottle out of a drawer and we'd have a couple while I spieled and they listened. If I spun it out right, they'd say 'Why not have lunch, and you can finish the story.' I didn't

One by one they rolled their beds, threw them on the wagon, and headed for the creek to wash. ■ (From *Whitey's First Round-up* by Glen Rounds. Illustrated by the author.)

sell much; they usually wanted something more slick and mannered than my work—but I ate pretty regular.

"Frank Crowninshield at the old *Vanity Fair* looked at my stuff and said he'd like to buy some of it before I got a chance to launch into a story! I didn't know how much to ask for the pictures so I said would he excuse me while I went to the men's room and went out and asked a friend of mine what Mr. Crowninshield would pay. He told me $40 and I made up my mind I would get that $40. When I got back to Frank's office, he says, 'I know $100 isn't much but it's all I can offer.' I turned white and he saw my face and said, "Well, I *can* go as high as $125.' I was smart enough not to say anything, but just waited for the money. Then he told me the magazine paid on the 1st and the 15th so I leveled with him, told him I was broke and needed the money, so he gave me his personal check.

"First thing I did was open a checking account. The men in the park used to beg me to show them my checkbook. Whenever I would go to the bank to take out $1.50 or $1.75 for a pair of shoes, a long line of park people would go with me. They would stand in awe as I wrote my name on a piece of paper and got money for it."

Rounds' books have been published in Denmark, Spain, and Germany. *Whitey's First Round-Up* was adapted for broadcast by the BBC in 1960; several of his books have been recorded for the blind. *Hobbies and other interests:* Woodcut print-making.

FOR MORE INFORMATION SEE: Illustrators of Children's Books: 1744-1945, Horn Book, 1947; *Junior Book of Authors*, edited by Kunitz & Haycraft, H. W. Wilson, 1951; *Illustrators of Children's Books: 1946-1956*, Horn Book, 1958; *Illustrators of Children's Books: 1957-1966*, Horn Book, 1968; *New York Times Book Review*, May 7, 1972, April 8, 1973; *Horn Book*, August, 1972; *Publishers' Weekly*, July 15, 1974.

ROWLAND, Florence Wightman 1900-

PERSONAL: Born January 2, 1900, in Newark, N.J.; daughter of William Henderson and Florence (Fairbanks) Wightman; married L. Vernon Rowland (now an electrician), March 8, 1924; children: Madge Wightman Essayan, Jayne Fairbanks Word, Joyce Marian Toy. *Education:* University of Southern California, A.B., 1923; University of California, Los Angeles, general secondary teaching certificate, 1938. *Politics:* Democrat. *Religion:* Episcopalian. *Mailing address:* P.O. Box 848, Nice, Calif. 95464.

FLORENCE WIGHTMAN ROWLAND

MEMBER: Southern California Women's Press Club (honorary).

WRITINGS: Austrian Colt, Macrae Smith, 1950; *Jade Dragons*, Oxford University Press, 1954; *Juddie*, Oxford University Press, 1958; *Eo of the Caves*, Walck, 1959; *Pasquala of Santa Ynez Mission*, Walck, 1961; *The Singing Leaf*, Putnam, 1965; *Let's Go to a Hospital*, Putnam, 1968; *School for Julio*, Putnam, 1969; *Little Sponge Fisherman*, Putnam, 1969; *Amish Boy*, Putnam, 1970; *Amish Wedding*, Putnam, 1971; *Robbie of the Kirkhaven Team*, Ginn, 1973. More than 350 short stories, poems, and articles in magazines, including *McCall's, Good Housekeeping, Everywoman's*, and in juvenile publications.

SIDELIGHTS: "In the elementary grades and in high school, I always enjoyed the English courses and frequently I received praise from instructors on my compositions and essays. I did not know then that I was going to be a writer until after college graduation, marriage to my childhood sweetheart, and becoming the mother of three little girls.

"When my children began to say cute things and wise sayings, I put them into verse, hoping they would sell. Since the depression wiped out my husband's business, I wanted to earn money at home to help out. I also wrote poems, stories, and articles that sold to good markets right from the start. It was easier then than now. In fact, my first check for $7.75 from the *Christian Science Monitor* for a manuscript titled, 'Vacationing at Home,' bought enough groceries in 1934 to feed our family of five for more than a week.

"Years ago, a radio show for children in our area needed another writer to produce an occasional story for their 'Story Hour.' This non-paying job gave me invaluable experience and eventually developed into many sales. My radio scripts the show aired, later sold as stories to magazines for boys and girls.

"One summer the director decided to take our listeners to a foreign land each Sunday. I did an Austrian story about horses. Its idea came from a newspaper item. The tale about China was inspired by an illustration and its caption that I saw in a *National Geographic Magazine*. Both of these eventually became my first and second books after I lengthened them with the help of intensive research and from information supplied by a sister who taught English at a Chinese University.

"In the very beginning I attended a night school class in creative writing, two nights a week for eight semesters. Our instructor encouraged me after reading some of my verses and articles to her students. She predicted that I would become a well-known writer. Years later, I dedicated one of my books to her.

"The most difficult part of writing is selling what you write. I have had a book published after twenty years of trying that included three complete rewrites of the manuscript. I mailed it out sixty-seven times before the Henry Walck Company, who had seen the three rewrites, finally liked it enough to send me a contract. I learned *how* to write a book by reworking that story: *Pasquala of Santa Ynez Mission.*

"I often sold articles and short stories after they went to more than thirty markets. If I am convinced that what I have written should be published, *I never give up!*"

RUSHMORE, Robert (William) 1926-

PERSONAL: Born July 7, 1926, in Tuxedo Park, N.Y.; son of George Mead (a businessman) and Virginia (Odom) Rushmore; married Marion Von Saldern, November 2, 1957; married second wife, Alfreda Huntington, April 2, 1963; children: Thomas, Katharine, Robert Urquhart. *Education:* Attended St. Mark's School, Southboro, Mass., 1940-44, and Mannes College of Music. *Politics:* Democrat. *Home:* Sage House, Sandisfield, Mass. 01255. *Agent:* Philip Spitzer, 111-27 76th Ave., Forest Hills, N.Y. 11375; and Shaw, MacLean, 11 Rumbold Rd., London S.W.6, England.

CAREER: U.S. Information Agency, Publications Branch, Washington, D.C., writer, primarily for Russian-language magazine, *Amerika*, 1950-60, originally on a full-time basis, later as a free-lance contributor; author, now living part of the year in England. *Military service:* U.S. Navy, 1944-46.

WRITINGS: Life of George Gershwin, Crowell-Collier, 1966; *A Passion for Meddling* (novella), Alan Ross, 1966; *Who'll Burn the House Down* (novel), Longmans, Green, 1966, World Publishing, 1967; *The Unsubstantial Castle* (novel), Dodd, 1969; *Fanny Kemble*, Crowell-Collier, 1970;

ROBERT RUSHMORE

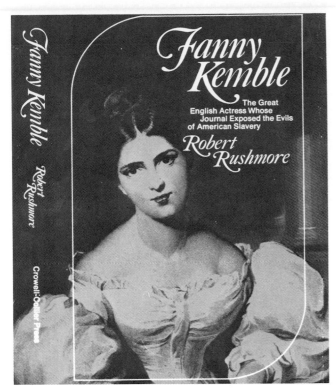

A pretty, dark-haired child clever—also willful—Fanny Kemble grew up almost literally in the lap of the theater. ■ (From *Fanny Kemble* by Robert Rushmore.)

Singing Voice, Dodd, 1970; *A Life in the Closet* (novella and short stories), Bobbs, 1973; *If My Love Leaves Me* (novel), Bobbs, 1975. Short story anthologized in *Winter's Tales*, Macmillan, 1969. Contributor of articles and stories to magazines, including *Collier's, Coronet, Saturday Review, Reporter*, and *Opera News*.

WORK IN PROGRESS: The Procession to Frigerio, a novel; *If My Love Leaves Me*.

SIDELIGHTS: "My books about George Gershwin and Fanny Kemble were intended for so-called 'young people' of high school age but I have found that adults ranging up to the elderly have read them with absorption.

"Though I love the music of George Gershwin it was not easy to write about him as a man and make it interesting. This is because nothing very dramatic happened to him. He was a success almost from the beginning until his tragically early death.

"Fanny Kemble was another story. She wrote copius journals and memoirs putting down the story of her incredibly varied life. My mother was from the South, my father a Yankee. The split in Fanny Kemble's family life was somewhat a part of my heritage as well. And her comments on the black situation seemed as apt today as they were when she wrote them in 1837. That's how I came to write about her.

"To young people I would say if you're interested in becoming an author, the test is to ask yourself: can I not *not* write. If the answer is, No, I can not not write—then you're hooked!"

RUSSELL, Helen Ross 1915-

PERSONAL: Born February 21, 1915, in Myerstown, Pa.; daughter of George Smith and Helen (Boyd) Ross; married Robert S. Russell (an art professor), September 24, 1960. *Education:* West Chester State College, teaching certificate, 1934; Lebanon Valley College, B.A., 1943; Cornell University, M.A., 1947, Ph.D., 1949. *Politics:* Independent. *Religion:* Christian. *Home:* 44 College Dr., Jersey City, N.J. 07305. *Agent:* Curtis Brown, Ltd., 60 East 56th St., New York, N.Y. 10022.

CAREER: Teacher, in one-room rural school, Lebanon County, Pa., 1934-35, of 3rd grade, Bethel Township, Pa., 1935-42, of art and science, Lebanon City Schools, Lebanon, Pa., 1942-46; Massachusetts State College at Fitchburg, professor of biology, 1949-66, chairman of science department, 1951-56, dean of studies, 1956-66; part-time science consultant to Wave Hill Center for Environmental Studies, New York, N.Y., 1966-70, Manhattan Country School, New York, N.Y., 1970—. *Member:* American Association for the Advancement of Science (fellow), American Nature Study Society (secretary, 1954-58; president, 1974), Conservation Education Association (life), New York Academy of Sciences, Women's Society of Christ United Methodist Church (Jersey City; president).

WRITINGS: City Critters, Hawthorn, 1969; *The True Book of Buds*, Childrens Press, 1970; *Clarion, the Killdeer*, Hawthorn, 1970; *Winter Search Party: A Guide to Insects and Other Invertebrates*, Nelson, 1971; *The True Book of Springtime Seeds*, Childrens Press, 1972; *Winter: A Field Trip Guide*, Little, Brown, 1972; *Soil: A Field Trip Guide*, Little, Brown, 1972; *Small Worlds: A Field Trip Guide*, Little, Brown, 1972; *Ten Minute Field Trips: Using the School Grounds for Environmental Studies*, J. G. Ferguson, 1972; *Water: A Field Trip Guide*, Little, Brown, 1972; *Earth the Great Recycler*, Nelson, 1973; *Foraging for Dinner*, Nelson, 1974. Contributor of over 60 articles to magazines, more than 60 articles to *Junior Encyclopedia Britannica*. Author of 15 video tapes and one filmstrip; science editor, Junior Encyclopedia Britannica, 1955—.

SIDELIGHTS: "My books come out of a lifetime of exploration. I was born on a farm and my first memories include collecting insects, watching earthworms, setting up experiments with horse hairs to see if they really would turn into horse-hair snakes, nibbling wild foods with my father, gardening with my mother. Very soon I began recording observations and writing stories about them for my dolls and my grandmother.

"As a teenager I started leading groups of young people on exploring trips and I learned with them. And I'm still doing it. Exploring—learning—teaching.

"I have had some wonderful teachers starting with my parents and including college professors who took us outside the classroom and challenged us to observe and to think as well as youngsters who asked questions that were best answered with 'Let's Find Out Together.'

"All of my books contain some things that young people and I have done together. Even books like *City Critters* that document the travels of animals like house sparrows, rats and clothing moths through the centuries are supplemented with first-hand observations of these animals on street corners, homes and parks of the world."

HOBBIES AND OTHER INTERESTS: Kids, the natural world, social justice and responsibility, writing, wild foods, skiing, "travelling with my husband to learn about pre-Columbian art at original sites."

RYDEN, Hope

PERSONAL: Born in St. Paul, Minn.; daughter of Ernest E. (a minister) and Agnes (Johnson) Ryden. *Education:* Attended Augustana College, Rock Island, Ill.; University of Iowa, B.A. *Home:* 345 East 81st St., New York, N.Y. 10028. *Agent:* N. S. Bienstock, 850 7th Ave., New York, N.Y. 10019.

HOPE RYDEN

The wild colt was the color of pale sand. His mane and tail were as black as a crow's wing. ■ (From *The Wild Colt* by Hope Ryden. Photographs by the author.)

CAREER: Drew Associates (affiliate of Time-Life Broadcast), New York, N.Y., film producer, 1960-64; Hope Ryden Productions, New York, N.Y., film producer, writer and director, 1965; American Broadcasting Corp., New York, N.Y., feature producer for ABC-TV evening news, 1966-68; free-lance documentary film producer, 1968—. Free-lance still photographer. *Awards, honors:* "Oppie" award for best book in Americana category, 1970, and *Library Journal* citation as one of 100 best sci-tech titles, 1970, for *America's Last Wild Horses;* Screen Writers Guild nomination for best film documentary, 1970, for "Missing in Randolph."

WRITINGS: America's Last Wild Horses, Dutton, 1970; *The Wild Colt,* Coward, 1972; *Mustangs: A Return to the Wild,* Viking, 1972; *God's Dog,* Coward, 1975; *The Wild Pups,* Putnam, 1975.

Documentary films—writer, producer, and director: "Susan Starr," produced by Drew Associates/Time-Life Films, 1962; "Jane," produced by Drew Associates/Time-Life Films, 1963; "Mission to Malaya," produced by Drew Associates/ABC-TV Network News, 1964; "Operation Gwamba," produced by Hope Ryden Productions and CBS-TV, 1965; "To Love A Child," produced by ABC-TV News, 1969; "Missing in Randolph," produced by ABC-TV news, 1970; "Strangers in Their Own Land: The Chicanos," produced by ABC-TV News, 1971.

Contributor of articles to *Look, Children's Day, National Geographic, Reader's Digest, National Parks, Conservation Magazine,* and *New York Times Magazine*; contributor of photographs to *National Geographic, Time, New York Times, Reader's Digest, Children's Day,* and other periodicals.

SIDELIGHTS: "I feel very little attention has been paid to North American wildlife. Most people are more concerned with animals on other continents whose fate is beyond our control. Our own animals are exploited by commercial interests or removed if they have little or no commercial value and stand in the way of fuller exploitation of some other facet of nature. Though many people are enlightened regarding the balance of nature, the concept is not practised in wildlife management. I wish to make this understood."

SANDBURG, Carl (August) 1878-1967
(Charles A. Sandburg; pseudonyms:
Militant, Jack Phillips)

PERSONAL: Born January 6, 1878, in Galesburg, Ill.; son of August (a railroad blacksmith; original surname Johnson) and Clara (Anderson) Sandburg; married Lillian ("Paula") Steichen (sister of photographer Edward Steichen), June 15, 1908; children: Margaret, Janet, Helga (originally named Mary Ellen; Mrs. George Crile). *Education:* Attended Lombard College, 1898-1902. *Politics:* Formerly Social-Democrat, later Democrat. *Home and office:* Connemara Farm, Flat Rock, N.C.

CAREER: Held many odd jobs, including work as milk delivery boy, barber shop porter, fireman, truck operator, and apprentice house painter; sold films for Underwood and Underwood; helped to organize Wisconsin Socialist Democratic Party; worked for *Milwaukee Sentinel,* and *Milwaukee Daily News;* city hall reporter for *Milwaukee Journal;* secretary to Milwaukee Mayor Emil Seidel, 1910-12; worked for *Milwaukee Leader* and *Chicago World,* 1912; worked for *Day Book* (daily), Chicago, 1912-17; *System: The Magazine of Business,* Chicago, associate editor, February to early fall, 1913 (returned to *Day Book*); worked for *Chicago Evening American* for three weeks in 1917; Newspaper Enterprise Association (390 newspapers), Stockholm correspondent, 1918, ran Chicago office, 1919; *Chicago Daily News,* 1917-30, served as reporter (covered Chicago race riots), editorial writer, and motion picture editor, later continued as columnist until 1932; wrote weekly column syndicated by *Chicago Daily Times,* beginning in 1941. Lecturer, University of Hawaii, 1934; Walgreen Foundation Lecturer, University of Chicago, 1940. Contributed newspaper columns and radio broadcasts for Office of War Information during World War II. Lectured and sang folk songs to his own guitar accompaniment. *Military service:* Sixth Illinois Volunteers, 1898; served in Puerto Rico during Spanish-American War.

MEMBER: American Academy of Arts and Letters, National Institute of Arts and Letters, Phi Beta Kappa (honorary); honorary member of Chicago's Tavern Club and Swedish Club (Chicago). *Awards, honors:* Litt. D., Lombard College, 1928, Knox College, 1929, Northwestern University, 1931, Harvard University, 1940, Yale University, 1940, New York University, 1940, Wesleyan University, 1940, Lafayette College, 1940, Syracuse University, 1941, Dartmouth College, 1941, University of North Carolina, 1955; LL.D., Rollins College, 1941, Augustana College, 1948, University of Illinois, 1953; Ph.D., Uppsala University, 1948, Levinson Prize, *Poetry* Magazine, 1914; shared Poetry Society of America prize, 1919, 1921; Friend of American Writers award; Phi Beta Kappa poet, Harvard University, 1928, William & Mary College, 1943; Friends of Literature award, 1934, for *Lincoln: The Prairie Years;* Theodore Roosevelt distinguished service medal, 1939; Pulitzer Prize in History, 1939, for *Abraham Lincoln: The War Years;* Pulitzer Prize for poetry, 1951; American Academy of Arts and Letters gold medal for history, 1952, 1953; Poetry Society of America gold medal for poetry, 1953; Taminent Institution award, 1953, for *Always the Young Strangers;* honored by Sweden's Commander Order of the North Star on his seventy-fifth birthday, January 6, 1953; New York Civil War Round Table silver medal, 1954; University of Louisville award of merit, 1955; Albert Einstein award, Yeshiva College, 1956; Roanoke-Chowan Poetry Cup, 1960, for *Harvest Poems, 1910-1960,* and 1961, for *Wind Song;* National Association for the Advancement of Colored People award, 1965, acclaiming Sandburg as "a major prophet of civil rights in our time."

WRITINGS: (As Charles A. Sandburg) *In Reckless Ecstasy,* Asgard Press, 1904; (as Charles A. Sandburg) *The Plaint of a Rose,* Asgard Press, 1905; (as Charles A. Sandburg) *Incidentals,* Asgard Press, 1905; (as Charles A. Sandburg) *You and Your Job,* [Chicago], ca. 1906; *Chicago Poems,* Holt, 1916; *Cornhuskers,* Holt, 1918; *The Chicago Race Riots, July, 1919,* Harcourt, 1919; *Smoke and Steel,*

CARL SANDBURG

Harcourt, 1920; *Rootabaga Stories*, Harcourt, 1922, new edition, 1973; *Slabs of the Sunburnt West*, Harcourt, 1922; *Rootabaga Pigeons*, Harcourt, 1923; *Selected Poems of Carl Sandburg*, edited by Rebecca West, Harcourt, 1926; *Songs of America*, Harcourt, 1926; (editor) *The American Songbag*, Harcourt, 1927; *Abraham Lincoln: The Prairie Years*, Harcourt, 1927; *Abe Lincoln Grows Up*, Harcourt, 1928; *Good Morning, America*, Harcourt, 1928; *Rootabaga Country: Selections from Rootabaga Stories and Rootabaga Pigeons*, Harcourt, 1929; *Steichen, the Photographer*, Harcourt, 1929.

Early Moon, Harcourt, 1930; *Potato Face*, Harcourt, 1930; *Mary Lincoln, Wife and Widow*, Harcourt, 1932; *The People, Yes*, Harcourt, 1936; *Smoke and Steel [and] Slabs of the Sunburnt West*, Harcourt, 1938; *A Lincoln and Whitman Miscellany*, Holiday Press, 1938; *Abraham Lincoln: The War Years*, four volumes, Harcourt, 1939.

Abraham Lincoln: The Sangamon Edition, six volumes, Scribner, 1940; *Bronze Wood*, Grabhorn Press, 1941; *Storm Over the Land*, Harcourt, 1942; *Smoke and Steel, Slabs of the Sunburnt West [and] Good Morning, America* (omnibus volume), Harcourt, 1942; *Home Front Memo*, Harcourt, 1943; (with Frederick Meserve) *Photographs of*

Lincoln saw one auction in New Orleans where an octoroon girl was sold, after being pinched, trotted up and down, and handled so the buyer could be satisfied she was sound of wind and limb. ■ (From *Abe Lincoln Grows Up* by Carl Sandburg. Illustrated by James Daugherty.)

Abraham Lincoln, Harcourt, 1944; *Poems of the Midwest*, two volumes, World Publishing, 1946; *The Lincoln Reader: An Appreciation*, privately printed, 1947; *Remembrance Rock* (novel), Harcourt, 1948; *Lincoln Collector: The Story of Oliver R. Barrett's Great Private Collection*, Harcourt, 1949.

(Editor) *Carl Sandburg's New American Songbag*, Broadcast Music, Inc., 1950; *Complete Poems*, Harcourt, 1950; *Always the Young Strangers* (autobiography), Harcourt, 1952; *A Lincoln Preface*, Harcourt, 1953; *Prairie-Town Boy*, Harcourt, 1955; *The Sandburg Range*, Harcourt, 1957; *The Fiery Trial*, Dell, 1959; *Address Before a Joint Session of Congress, February 12, 1959*, Harcourt, 1959 (also appeared as *Carl Sandburg on Abraham Lincoln*, [Cedar Rapids], 1959, and as *Abraham Lincoln, 1809-1959*, J. St. Onge, 1959); *Abraham Lincoln*, three volume condensation of earlier work, Dell, 1959.

Harvest Poems, 1910-1960, Harcourt, 1960; *Wind Song*, Harcourt, 1960; *Six New Poems and a Parable*, privately printed, 1960; *Address Upon the Occasion of Abraham Lincoln's One Hundredth Inaugural Anniversary*, Black Cat Books, 1961; *Honey and Salt*, Harcourt, 1963; *The Wedding Procession of the Rag Doll and the Broom Handle and Who Was in It* (chapter of Rootabaga stories), Harcourt, 1967; *The Letters of Carl Sandburg*, edited by Herbert Mitgang, Harcourt, 1968; *The Sandburg Treasury: Prose and Poetry for Young People*, Harcourt, 1971.

Wrote commentary for U.S. Government film "Bomber." Did captions for "Road to Victory" mural photograph show, 1942. *The World of Carl Sandburg*, a stage presentation by Norman Corwin, was published by Harcourt in 1961. Sandburg recorded excerpts from *Always the Young Strangers*, Caedmon, 1966; also recorded "The People, Yes," "Poems for Children," "A Lincoln Album," "Carl Sandburg Sings His American Songbag," and "The Poetry of Carl Sandburg," for Caedmon.

Contributor to *International Socialist Review, Tomorrow, Poetry, Saturday Evening Post, Masses, Little Review, New Leader, Nation*, and *Playboy*.

SIDELIGHTS: Carl Sandburg was born to Swedish immigrant parents in Galesburg, Illinois. He worked before and after school from the time he was eleven; when he finished grammar school at fourteen, his first full-time job was driving a milk wagon, often in prairie blizzards. After that came jobs in a barber shop, a tinsmith shop, a pottery, a bottling works, harvesting ice in Illinois zero weather and wheat in Western Kansas, washing dishes in Kansas City, Denver, and Omaha. These early jobs in the cities and in the open spaces of America equipped him, as no amount of learning could have done, to be the poet of industrial America.

He saw active service during the Spanish-American War as a member of Company C, Sixth Infantry Regiment of Illinois Volunteers. On his return from the campaign in Puerto Rico, Sandburg entered Lombard College in Galesburg, working his way through, but finding time also to edit the college paper and captain the basketball team. After leaving college, he did all manner of things to earn a living. He was a stereograph salesman from door to door and farm to farm, a fireman, advertising manager for a department store, secretary to the Mayor of Milwaukee, a pamphleteer, a news-

It was a grand wedding with one of the grandest processions ever seen at a rag doll wedding. And we are sure no broom handle ever had a grander wedding procession when he got married. ■ (From *The Wedding Procession of the Rag Doll and the Broom Handle and Who Was in It* by Carl Sandburg. Illustrated by Harriet Pincus.)

paperman. In 1908 he married Lillian Paula Steichen, sister of Edward Steichen the photographer.

Until he was thirty-six years old, Sandburg was totally unknown to the literary world. In 1914 a group of his poems appeared in *Poetry*, and during the same year one of the group—the now famous "Chicago"—was awarded the Levinson Prize. A little more than a year later, *Chicago Poems*, his first book, was published, and Sandburg had "arrived."

His second volume of poems, *Cornhuskers*, followed in 1918 and shared the Poetry Society Prize that year. Since then more than forty books by Sandburg have been published, each adding to his stature. They cover a wide range—from the humorous Rootabaga stories for children, and an appreciation of the photographic genius of his brother-in-law, *Steichen the Photographer*, to his great poetic work, *The People, Yes*, and to the six volumes of his classic biography of Lincoln, *The Prairie Years* and *The War Years*.

Sandburg's account of the life of Abraham Lincoln is one of the monumental works of the century. *The War Years* alone exceeds the collected writings of Shakespeare by some 150,000 words. Though Sandburg did deny the story that in preparation he read everything ever published on Lincoln, he did collect and classify Lincoln material for thirty years, moving himself into a garret, storing his extra material in a barn, and for nearly fifteen years writing on a cracker-box typewriter. His intent was to separate Lincoln the man from Lincoln the myth, to avoid hero-worship, to relate with graphic detail and humanness the man both he and Whitman so admired. The Pulitzer Prize committee prohibited from awarding the biography prize for any work on Washington or Lincoln, circumvented the rules by placing the book in the category of history. As a result of this work Sandburg was the first private citizen to deliver an address before a joint session of Congress (on February 12, 1959, the 150th anniversary of Lincoln's birth).

With their three daughters the Sandburgs lived in the Midwest until 1945, when they moved to Flat Rock, North Carolina, to get away from the rigorous Lake Michigan winters.

Seldom was a living author given recognition in so many fields as Carl Sandburg. The little Galesburg cottage in which he was born, was dedicated in 1946 as a literary shrine. His photograph was featured on front covers of the important literary media, as well as *Time*, *Life*, and *Newsweek*. Lecture audiences throughout the country knew him for readings of his poetry and for his inimitable guitar-playing and ballad singing. In 1959 Mr. Sandburg's poetry was adapted for the stage by Norman Corwin, and Bette Davis and Gary Merrill presented "The World of Carl Sandburg" to audiences throughout the country. And there is still another facet to the Sandburg fame: his goat farm was among the best known throughout the country, and Mrs. Sandburg was long recognized as a leading authority on breeding and raising blooded dairy goats. In 1966, Carl Sandburg was the subject of a picture biography *Sandburg: Photographers View Carl Sandburg*, edited by his brother-in-law Edward Steichen, which contains the work of more than thirty-seven photographers.

A self-styled hobo, Sandburg received numerous honorary degrees, had six high schools and five elementary schools named for him, and held news conferences with Presidents at the White House. "My father couldn't sign his name," wrote Sandburg; "[he] made his 'mark' on the CB&Q payroll sheet. My mother was able to read the Scriptures in her native language, but she could not write, and I wrote to Abraham Lincoln whose own mother could not read or write! I guess that somewhere along in this you'll find a story of America."

A Sandburg archives is maintained in the Sandburg Room at the University of Illinois. Ralph G. Newman, who is known primarily as a Lincoln scholar but who also is the possessor of what is perhaps the largest and most important collection of Sandburgiana, has said that a complete bibliography of Sandburg's works, including contributions to periodicals and anthologies, forewords, introductions, and foreign editions would number more than four hundred pages. Sandburg received 200-400 letters each week. Though, to a friend who asked how he managed to look ten years younger than he appeared on his last visit, he replied: "From NOT answering my correspondence," he reportedly filed his mail under "F" (friendly and fan letters). "No reply needed," and "Hi fi" (to be read and answered).

For all this fame, he remained unassuming. What he wanted from life was "to be out of jail, . . . to eat regular, . . . to get what I write printed, . . . a little love at home and a little nice affection hither and yon over the American landscape, . . . [and] to sing every day." He wrote with a pencil, a fountain pen, or a typewriter, "but I draw the line at dictating 'em," he said. He kept his home as it was, refusing, for example, to rearrange his vast library in some orderly fashion; he knew where everything was. Furthermore, he said, "I want Emerson in every room."

On September 17, 1967, there was a National Memorial Service at the Lincoln Memorial in Washington, D.C., at which Archibald MacLeish and Mark Van Doren read from Sandburg's poetry. A Carl Sandburg Exhibition of memorabilia was held at the Hallmark Gallery, New York City, January-February, 1968. His home is under consideration as a National Historical site.

HOBBIES AND OTHER INTERESTS: Walking. "Like Thoreau," writes Golden, "Carl had a genius for walking." He outwalked Edward R. Murrow, Robert Sherwood, and Arlene Francis.

FOR MORE INFORMATION SEE: Carl Sandburg, by Karl William Detzer, Harcourt, 1941; *New York Herald Tribune Book Review*, October 8, 1950; *New York Times Book Review*, June 1, 1952, January 2, 1966; *Tribute to Carl Sandburg at Seventy-Five*, special edition of the *Journal of the Illinois State Historical Society*, Abraham Lincoln Book Shop, 1953; *Look*, July 10, 1956; *Life*, December 1, 1961; *Carl Sandburg*, by Harry Golden, World Publishing, 1961; *Picture Book of American Authors*, Sterling, 1962; *New York Public Library Bulletin*, March, 1962; *Publishers' Weekly*, January 28, 1963; *Carl Sandburg, Poet and Patriot*, by Gladys Zehnpfennig, Denison, 1963; *Saturday Evening Post*, June 6, 1964; Richard Crowder, *Carl Sandburg*, Twayne, 1964; *Detroit Free Press*, November 30, 1965; Hazel Durnell, *America of Carl Sandburg*, University Press of Washington, 1965; *Redbook*, February, 1966; Edward Steichen, editor, *Sandburg: Photographers View Carl Sandburg*, Harcourt, 1966; *New York Times*, July 23, 1967, January 10, 1968; *Time*, July 28, 1967; *Books*, August, 1967; *Horn Book*, February, 1971; Carolyn Riley, *Contemporary Literary Criticism/1*, Gale, 1973.

(Died July 22, 1967)

SANDBURG, Charles A.
See SANDBURG, Carl (August)

MARJORY BARTLETT SANGER

SANGER, Marjory Bartlett 1920-

PERSONAL: Born February 11, 1920, in Baltimore, Md.; daughter of J. Kemp, Jr. (a lawyer) and Katharine Kendall (Simons) Bartlett. *Education:* Wellesley College, B.A., 1942. *Address:* Box 957, Winter Park, Fla. 32789.

CAREER: Massachusetts Audubon Society, Boston, chairman of public relations and assistant editor of *Bulletin*, 1954-57, administrative assistant at nature camp in Barre, Mass., 1955-57. U.S. representative at International Council for Bird Preservation and International Ornithological Congress in England, 1966. Member of advisory board, Rollins College Annual Writers' Conference, 1968-75. *Member:* International Council for Bird Preservation, American Ornithologists' Union, Wilson Ornithological Society, John Bartram Association, Florida Historical Society, Cooper Ornithological Society. *Awards, honors:* Charlton W. Tebean Book Award, 1973, for the "best book published about Florida for the young adult reader," *Billy Bartram and His Green World*; Certificate of Commendation of the National Awards Committee of the American Association for State and Local History, 1973, also for *Billy Bartram*.

WRITINGS: The Bird Watchers (juvenile), Dutton, 1957; *Greenwood Summer* (juvenile), Dutton, 1958; *Mangrove Island*, World Publishing, 1963; *Cypress Country*, World Publishing, 1965; *World of the Great White Heron*, Devin-Adair, 1967; *Checkerback's Journey: The Migration of the Ruddy Turnstone* (juvenile), World Publishing, 1969; *Billy Bartram and His Green World* (juvenile), Farrar, Straus, 1972. Contributor to *Audubon, Florida Magazine*, and *Florida Naturalist*.

WORK IN PROGRESS: A biography of Georges Auguste Escoffier.

SIDELIGHTS: "As for my writing, as a trained scientist I realize the value of research in the field, and therefore it is in the environment itself that I do most of my studies. I also use libraries and archives, and for my historical works: court houses, cemeteries, battlefields, and, of course, historical societies and the aid of descendants.

"I should say that in the preparation of my manuscripts, one half of the time is spent in the field, one quarter in libraries or similar research, and one quarter at my typewriter. I might also add that the writing of nonfiction for young adults is a highly rewarding occupation, and I would urge anyone with talent and ambition in that direction to join us."

HOBBIES AND OTHER INTERESTS: "I travel as much as I can, and am particularly interested in the French Caribbean islands, the west coast of Italy, Greece, and the Highlands of Scotland . . . quite a bit of diversity here!"

FOR MORE INFORMATION SEE: New York Times Book Review, December 24, 1967.

SAVITT, Sam

PERSONAL: Born March 22, in Wilkes-Barre, Pa.; son of Hyman (salesman) and Rose (Eskowitz) Savitt; married Bette Orkin, March 28, 1946; children: Dara Vickery, Roger Scott. *Education:* Pratt Institute, graduated 1941; Art Students League, student, 1950-51. *Home:* One-Horse Farm, North Salem, N.Y.

CAREER: Free-lance illustrator; official artist for United States equestrian team. *Military service:* U.S. Army, China-Burma-India Theater, 1942-46, became first lieutenant. *Member:* Society of Illustrators, Authors Guild, Graphic Artists Guild. *Awards, honors:* Boys' Clubs of America junior book award for *Midnight*, 1958.

WRITINGS: Step-A-Bit, Dutton, 1956; *Midnight*, Dutton, 1958; *There Was a Horse*, Dial, 1960; *Around the World with Horses*, Dial, 1962; *Rodeo: Cowboys, Bulls, and Broncos*, Doubleday, 1963; *Sam Savitt Guide to Horses* (chart), Black Horse Press, 1963; *Vicki and the Black Horse*, Doubleday, 1964; *Day at the LBJ Ranch*, Random, 1965; *America's Horses*, Doubleday, 1966; *Equestrian Olympic Sketchbook*, A. S. Barnes, 1968; *Sam Savitt's True Horse Stories*, Dodd, 1971; *Wild Horse Running* (Junior Literary Guild selection), Dodd, 1973; (with Suzanne Wilding) *Ups and Downs*, St. Martin's Press, 1973. Series of articles, "Draw Horses with Sam Savitt," ran in *Western Horseman* (magazine), 1966.

Illustrator: *Bold Passage*, Simon & Schuster, 1950; *Learning to Ride Hunt and Show*, Doubleday, 1950; *Tiger*

The stately Ward's heron waits to spear a killifish near the rookery of the ancient-looking, colonial white ibis. ▪ (From *World of the Great White Heron* by Marjory Bartlett Sanger. Illustrated by John Henry Dick.)

There were several wolves in the area and they shadowed the band constantly. Before the winter was over, the predators managed to bring two foals, as well as some old horses that were weak from age and exhaustion. ■ (From *Wild Horse Running* by Sam Savitt. Illustrated by the author.)

Roan, Pocket Books, 1950; *Trailing Trouble*, Holiday House, 1952; *Desert Dog*, Holiday House, 1956; *Wildlife Cameraman*, Holiday House, 1957; *Horsemanship*, 1958; *A Saddlebag of Tales*, Dodd, 1959; *Blizzard Rescue*, Watts, 1959; *Born to Race*, St. Martin's Press, 1959; *Challenger*, Coward, 1959; *Pets at the White House*, Dutton, 1959; *Silver Brumby*, Dutton, 1959; *The Torch Bearer*, Watts, 1959.

Up and Away, Harcourt, 1960; *The Top Hand of Lone Tree Ranch*, Crowell, 1960; *Johnny's Island Ark*, Watts, 1960; *Diving Horse*, Coward, 1960; *Fury and the Mustangs*, Holt, 1960; *Horse in Her Heart*, Coward, 1960; *Horseback Riding*, Lippincott, 1960; *Little Smoke*, Coward, 1961; *Loco the Bronc*, Coward, 1961; *The Snow Filly*, Dutton, 1961; *Thudding Hoofs*, St. Martin's Press, 1961; *Wilderness Renegade*, Watts, 1962; *The Horse Trap*, Coward, 1962; *Teddy Koala*, Dodd, 1962; *Lad, a Dog*, Dutton, 1962; *Fawn in the Forest*, Dodd, 1962; *Dream Pony for Robin*, St. Martin's Press, 1962; *Dinny and Dreamdust*, Doubleday, 1962; *Cavalry Manual of Horsemanship*, Doubleday, 1962; *Buffalo Bill*, Garrard, 1962; *American Girl Book of Horse Stories*, Random House, 1963; *Boy's Life Book of Horse Stories*, Random House, 1963; *Care and Training of Dogs*, Random House, 1963; *Forever the Wild Mare*, Dodd, 1963; *Horse of Your Own*, Doubleday, 1963; *Hit Parade of Horse Stories*, Scholastic Books, 1963; *No Love for Schnitzle*, St. Martin's Press, 1963; *Patrick Visits the Zoo*, Dodd, 1963; *Show Ring Rouge*, Coward, 1963; *Wild Heart*, Doubleday, 1963; *Two Dogs and a Horse*, Dodd, 1964; *Old Quarry Fox Hunt*, Ives Washburn, 1964; *Horse in the House*, Coward, 1964; *Big Book of Favorite Horse Stories*, Platt & Munk, 1965; *Big Jump for Robin*, St. Martin's Press, 1965; *Ghost Hound of Thunder Valley*, Dodd, 1965; *Redhead and the Roan*, Van Nostrand, 1965; *If You Want a Horse*, Coward, 1966; *Dave and His Dog Mulligan*, Dodd, 1966; *Star, the Sea Horse*, Norton, 1968; *Golden Book of Horses*, Golden Press, 1968; *Great Stories for Young Readers*, Reader's Digest, 1969; *Harlequin Horse*, Van Nostrand, 1969; *Horses*, Golden Press, 1969; *Ride, Gaucho*, World Publishing, 1969.

Sky Rocket, Dodd, 1970; *Horses, Horses, Horses*, Van Nostrand, 1970; *Elementary Dressage*, A. S. Barnes, 1970; *Horseman's Almanac*, Agway, 1971; *Wild Animal Rescue*, Dodd, 1971; *Hundred Horse Farm*, St. Martin's Press, 1972; *Horses in Action*, St. Martin's Press, 1972; *How to Bring Up Your Pet Dog*, Dodd, 1973; *Gift of Gold*, Dodd, 1973; *Summer Pony*, Macmillan, 1973; *The Art of Painting Horses*, Grumbacher Library, 1973; *A Boy and A Pig, But Mostly Horses*, Dodd, 1974; *Gallant Grey Trotter*, Dodd, 1974; *Grand Prix Jumping*, Aberdeen Press, 1974; *Backyard Pony*, Watts, 1975; *Horses: A First Book*, Watts, 1975; *Riding Teachers Manual*, Doubleday, 1975.

WORK IN PROGRESS: What to do for Your Horse Before the Vet Comes.

SIDELIGHTS: "I have had a 'thing' for horses as far back as I can remember. As a child I actually wanted to be a horse. I watched horses wherever and whenever I could and tried to imitate them. I learned a great deal about them at that time with my one track observations that were uncluttered by the reality of living.

"I began my career strictly as an illustrator in the magazine and book field. I illustrated all animals in outdoor adventure stories but my first love was horses.

"I schooled and trained horses for many years (I still do) and know a great deal about them. The first horse I ever trained, War Bride, went on to become a member of the United States Equestrian Team.

"I often illustrated horse stories by authors who did not know their subject. They humanized the animal which was a source of irritation to me and I felt I could do better. My first venture into writing came after I had kept a record in drawings of a foal from the time she was born until she was weaned. Dutton published these drawings in my first book, *Step-a-Bit*. I wrote a commentary kind of text and I was on my way.

SAM SAVITT

"In the books that have followed, my horses think like horses and act like horses. Books that depict horses with human characteristics are not only untrue but they are misleading and can be dangerous.

"I write my books to any age group that is interested in my subject. I write as an artist. By that I mean I visualize an incident as if I were painting it and then describe in words the picture I have created."

HOBBIES AND OTHER INTERESTS: Sculpture, fox hunting with Golden Bridge hounds, swimming and hiking.

FOR MORE INFORMATION SEE: Polo Magazine, XXVI, 7, 1960; *Sunday Independence*, Wilkes Barre, Pa., January 17, 1960; *The Sun*, Baltimore, Md., July 17, 1962; *Junior Literary Guild Catalogue*, April, 1973; *Western Horseman Magazine*, April, 1973; *Palm Beach Daily News*, February 7, 1974; *Sun Sentinel* (Pompano Beach), February 14, 1974; *The Reporter Dispatch* (White Plains, N.Y.), April 1, 1974; *Horse Play Magazine*, April, 1974.

SCHEER, Julian (Weisel) 1926-

PERSONAL: Born February 20, 1926, in Richmond, Va.; son of George Fabian and Hilda (Knopf) Scheer; married Virginia W. Williams, 1947; married Suzanne Huggan, October 9, 1965; children: (first marriage) Susan, Scott, Grey; (second marriage) Hilary. *Education:* Attended Richmond Professional Institute, 1946; University of North Carolina at Chapel Hill, A.B., 1950. *Politics:* Democrat. *Religion:* Jewish. *Home address:* R.D. 2 Box 24, Catlett,

Va. 22019. *Agent:* G. F. Scheer, P.O. Box 807, Chapel Hill, N.C. *Office:* Sullivan, Murray & Scheer, 1120 Connecticut Ave. Washington, D.C.

CAREER: Mid-Virginia Publications, Richmond, reporter, 1939-43; Scheer Syndicate, Chapel Hill, N.C., president, 1947-53; *Charlotte News*, Charlotte, N.C., columnist-reporter, 1953-62; National Aeronautics and Space Administration (NASA), Washington, D.C., assistant administrator of public affairs, 1962-71; Sullivan, Murray & Scheer (communications firm), Washington, D.C., partner, 1971—. Free-lance writer, 1945-62; sports publicist, University of North Carolina, 1949-53. *Wartime and military service:* U.S. Merchant Marine, 1943-46. U.S. Naval Reserve, 1946-53. *Member:* Algonquin Society, Sigma Delta Chi, Pi Lambda Phi. *Awards, honors:* Caldecott Award runner-up, 1965, for *Rain Makes Applesauce*; numerous press association awards.

WRITINGS: (With Robert Quincy) *Choo Choo: Charlie Justice Story*, Colonial Press, 1958; (with Elizabeth Black) *Tweetsie: The Blue Ridge Stemwinder*, Heritage House, 1958; (with Theodore J. Gordon) *First into Outer Space*,

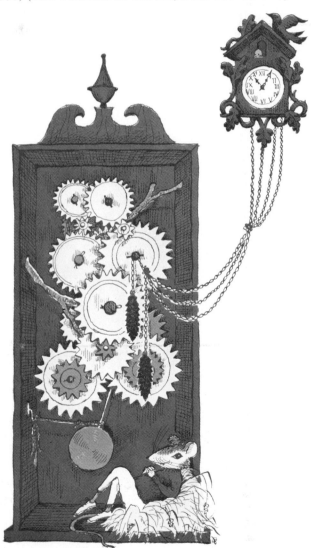

[On an Upside Down Day] clocks won't tick. ■ (From *Upside Down Day* by Julian Scheer. Illustrated by Kelly Oechsli.)

JULIAN SCHEER

St. Martin's, 1959; *Rain Makes Applesauce* (juvenile), Holiday House, 1964; *Upside Down Day* (juvenile), Holiday House, 1968.

SIDELIGHTS: Of *Upside Down Day*, Jerome Beatty, Jr. wrote in the *New York Times Book Review*: " 'Water won't trickle. Feathers won't tickle. Rain won't drop. Balloons won't pop.' That's Mr. Scheer's plot. . . . As most youngsters are fond of the notion of things not happening the way adults insist they do, they should be pleased with 'Upside Down Day' and its whimsy."

SCHWARTZ, Charles W(alsh)   1914-

PERSONAL: Born June 2, 1914, in St. Louis, Mo.; son of Frederick O. (a physician) and Clara E. (Walsh) Schwartz; married Elizabeth Reeder (now a biologist with Missouri Conservation Commission), December 22, 1938; children: Barbara (Mrs. Michael Miller), Carl Bruce, John Curtis. *Education:* University of Missouri, A.B., 1938, A.M., 1940. *Home:* Route 1, Jefferson City, Mo. 65101.

CAREER: Missouri Conservation Commission, Jefferson City, biologist and wildlife photographer, 1940-45; Board of Agriculture and Forestry, Hawaii, biologist, 1946-47; Missouri Conservation Commission, biologist and wildlife photographer, 1948—. *Member:* American Ornithologists' Union, Wilson Ornithological Society, American Society of

Mammalogists, Wildlife Society, Phi Beta Kappa. *Awards, honors:* Citations from Wildlife Society for *The Game Birds of Hawaii* as best publication in wildlife management and ecology, 1949-50, and from American Association for Conservation Information for *The Wild Mammals of Missouri* as outstanding wildlife book of 1959; awards for motion pictures include CONI Grand Medal at International Sports Film Festival, Cortina d'Ampezzo, Italy, for "Bobwhite Through the Year," and American Association for Conservation Information award for "The Story of the Mourning Dove" as best North American wildlife movie, 1959.

WRITINGS: The Prairie Chicken in Missouri, Missouri Conservation Commission, 1945; (with wife E. R. Schwartz) *The Game Birds of Hawaii* [Honolulu], 1949; (with E. R. Schwartz) *Cottontail Rabbit*, Holiday House, 1957; (with E. R. Schwartz) *Bobwhite*, Holiday House, 1959; (with E. R. Schwartz) *The Wild Mammals of Missouri*, Missouri Conservation Commission and University of Missouri Press, 1959; (with E. R. Schwartz) *Bobwhite From Egg to Chick to Egg*, Holiday House, 1959; (with E. R. Schwartz) *When Animal Are Babies*, Holiday House, 1964; (with E. R. Schwartz) *When Water Animals Are Babies* (Junior Literary Guild selection), Holiday House, 1970; (with E. R. Schwartz) *When Flying Animals Are Babies*, Holiday House, 1973. Contributor of articles to periodicals. Writer and producer of wildlife films, including "Bobwhite Through the Year," "The Story of the Mourning Dove," and "This is the Mallard."

SCHWARTZ, Elizabeth Reeder   1912-

PERSONAL: Born September 13, 1912, in Columbus,

When a turkey is a baby
there are many other babies
in the family—
▪ (From *When Animals Are Babies* by Elizabeth and Charles Schwartz. Illustrated by Charles Schwartz.)

ELIZABETH and CHARLES SCHWARTZ

Ohio; daughter of Charles Wells (a professor) and Lydia (Morrow) Reeder; married Charles Walsh Schwartz (now a biologist), December 22, 1938; children: Barbara Reeder (Mrs. Michael L. Miller), Carl Bruce, John Curtis. *Education:* The Ohio State University, A.B., 1933; Columbia University, A.M., 1934; University of Missouri, Ph.D., 1938. *Home:* Route 1, Jefferson City, Mo. 65101.

CAREER: University of Missouri, Columbia, instructor in zoology, 1934-38; Sweet Briar College, Sweet Briar, Va., instructor in zoology, 1938-39; Stephens College, Columbia, Mo., instructor in biology, 1939-40; Board of Agriculture and Forestry, Honolulu, Hawaii, biologist, 1946-48; Missouri Conservation Commission, Jefferson City, biologist, 1950—. Wildlife photographer, and producer with husband of films on wildlife. *Member:* Phi Beta Kappa, Sigma Xi, Mortar Board, Alpha Phi. *Awards, honors:* North American Wildlife Society award, 1949-50; co-winner of

American Association for Conservation Information award for outstanding wildlife book of the year, for *The Wild Mammals of Missouri*, 1960; other awards for motion pictures produced in collaboration with husband, including "Cottontail," "The Story of the Mourning Dove," "This is the Mallard," and "Wild Chorus;" University of Missouri, Doctor of Science, 1975.

WRITINGS—With husband, Charles W. Schwartz: *Cottontail Rabbit*, Holiday House, 1957; *The Wild Mammals of Missouri*, University of Missouri Press, 1959; *Bobwhite from Egg to Chick to Egg*, Holiday House, 1959; *When Animals Are Babies*, Holiday House, 1964; *When Water Animals Are Babies* (Junior Literary Guild selection) Holiday House, 1970; *When Flying Animals Are Babies*, Holiday House, 1973. Contributor to popular magazines and scientific journals.

SEED, Jenny   1930-

PERSONAL: Born May 18, 1930, in Cape Town, South Africa; daughter of Ivan Washington (a draftsman) and Bessie (Dickerson) Booysen; married Edward Robert Seed (now a railway employee), October 30, 1953; children: Anne, Dick, Alan, Robbie. *Education:* Educated in Cape Town, South Africa. *Home:* 10 Pioneer Crescent, Northdene, Queensburgh, Natal, South Africa.

JENNY SEED

CAREER: Draftsman in Roads Department and Town Planning Department, Pietarmaritzburg, South Africa, before marriage; free-lance writer, mainly for children.

WRITINGS: *The Dancing Mule*, Thomas Nelson, 1964; *The Always-late Train*, Nasionale Boekhandel, 1965; *Small House, Big Garden*, Hamish Hamilton, 1965; *Peter the Gardener*, Hamish Hamilton, 1966; *Tombi's Song*, Hamish Hamilton, 1966, Rand McNally, 1968; *To the Rescue*, Hamish Hamilton, 1966; *Stop Those Children*, Hamish Hamilton, 1966; *Timothy and Tinker*, Hamish Hamilton, 1967; *The Red Dust Soldiers*, Heinemann, 1968; *The River Man*, Hamish Hamilton, 1968; *The Voice of the Great Elephant*, Hamish Hamilton, 1968, Pantheon, 1969; *Canvas City*, Hamish Hamilton, 1968; *Prince of the Bay*, Hamish Hamilton, 1970, Pantheon, 1971; *Kulumi the Brave*, Hamish Hamilton, 1970, World, 1970; *Vengeance of the Zulu King*, Pantheon, 1971; *The Great Thirst*, Hamish Hamilton, 1971, Bradbury, 1971; *The Broken Spear*, Hamish Hamilton, 1972; *The Sly Green Lizard*, Hamish Hamilton, 1973.

SIDELIGHTS: "I was born and educated in Cape Town, South Africa, and I think that my interest in writing must have been partly inherited. My father was a writer when he was younger and as a small child I can remember rummaging through his cupboard drawers when I was allowed to play in his room, sorting through piles of his old manuscripts. And then, too, my mother was an excellent reader of stories. My sister Jewel and I would keep her busy with stories until her poor voice was reduced to a croak. It was not surprising then that from the age of about eight I too became interested in the written word and used to enjoy trying to compose little verses.

"After I was married and had children of my own (four to be exact) I turned to tales for young people. Oh what joy when my first short story was accepted for publication in a little local paper in 1960!

"Then as my children grew older they used to ask me to hear their history homework. It sounded so dull—all those facts and dates. I began to delve into old books in our reference library in Durban and the past became real to me. I found that it was not boring at all but tremendously exciting and filled with real and interesting people just waiting to be put into books." Jenny Seed's children's stories have been republished and broadcast in Canada, England, Rhodesia, New Zealand, and Australia.

SEJIMA, Yoshimasa   1913-

PERSONAL: Born August 29, 1913, in Hokkaido, Japan; son of Shimpei (headman of his town) and Yana Sejima; married Yae Shimoda, December 14, 1943; children: Yoshie, Momoko. *Education:* Attended Rikkyo University. *Home:* 5-6-12 Tsujido-Motomachi, Fujisawa-shi, Kanagawa-ken, Japan.

CAREER: Tama Art University, Tokyo, Japan, professor of oil painting, 1953—.

WRITINGS—Illustrator: Yasoo Takeichi, *Okorinbo No Tonosama*, Shikosha, 1970, published in the United States as *The Mighty Prince*, Crown, 1971.

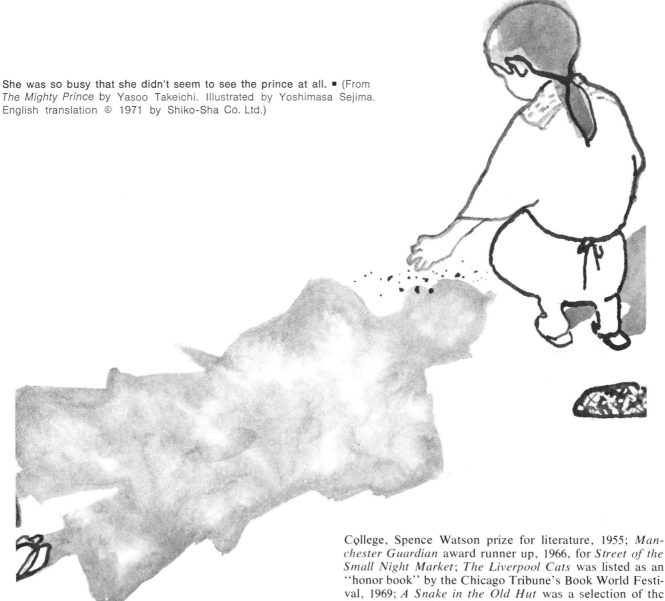

She was so busy that she didn't seem to see the prince at all. ■ (From *The Mighty Prince* by Yasoo Takeichi. Illustrated by Yoshimasa Sejima. English translation © 1971 by Shiko-Sha Co. Ltd.)

SHERRY, (Dulcie) Sylvia   1932-

PERSONAL: Born April 20, 1932, in Newcastle-upon-Tyne, England; daughter of Samuel William and Evelyn (Forster) Brunt; married Norman Sherry (a professor and author), June, 1955. *Education:* Attended Kenton Lodge College of Education, Newcastle-upon-Tyne, 1948-50; Kings College, University of Durham, B.A. (with honors), 1955. *Home:* 6 Gillison Close, Melling, near Carnforth, Lancashire, England.

CAREER: Kenton Lodge College of Education, Newcastle-upon-Tyne, England, teacher and lecturer in English, 1955-60; Federal Publications Ltd., Singapore, part-time editor, 1960-64; full-time writer, 1964—. Has also taught at a primary school in Newcastle-on-Tyne, Church High School in Newcastle-on-Tyne, and Constantine Technical College, Middlesborough. *Awards, honors:* Kings

College, Spence Watson prize for literature, 1955; *Manchester Guardian* award runner up, 1966, for *Street of the Small Night Market*; *The Liverpool Cats* was listed as an "honor book" by the Chicago Tribune's Book World Festival, 1969; *A Snake in the Old Hut* was a selection of the Foyles Children's Book Club, 1974.

WRITINGS—Juvenile fiction: *Street of the Small Night Market*, Cape, 1966, published as *Secret of the Jade Pavilion*, Lippincott, 1967; *Frog in a Coconut Shell*, Lippincott, 1968; *The Liverpool Cats*, Lippincott, 1969 (published in England as *A Pair of Jesus Boots*, Cape, 1969); *The Haven-Screamers*, Lippincott, 1970 (published in England as *The Loss of the Night Wind*, Cape, 1970); *A Snake in the Old Hut*, Cape, 1972, Nelson, 1974; *Dark River, Dark Mountain*, Cape, 1975.

Contributor: Edward Blishen, editor, *Miscellany Five*, Oxford University Press, 1968; John Foster, editor, *In Love, out of Love*, Macmillan Topliner, 1974. Aidan Chambers, editor, *Eleventh Ghost Book*, Barrie & Jenkins, 1975.

WORK IN PROGRESS: Runaway, a book for children, aged seven to nine, for Abelard's "Red Grasshopper" series; a Macmillan Topliner; an adult novel set in the Far East.

"I suppose I began writing through the encouragement of my father (who has always written poetry—unpublished—and who bought me my first typewriter as a Christmas present when I was ten) and through telling stories to my younger sister. He helped us to make a puppet theatre (with a lighting system and curtains that worked) and we created plays round that, and wrote our own 'books' and 'magazines' in which our parents always took an interest. I sold my first short story when I was twelve and a small paper-backed collection when I was fourteen and later short stories to the BBC Children's Hour. My husband and I share literary interests, and read and comment on mutual work in progress. We share a study with a desk at each end, and two typewriters going.

"A novel for me begins with a place—a village, town, or particular area—and I do a lot of work finding out about the place and the people who live there—the work they do, the way they live, the way they speak and their attitudes to life. I hope to find there the people I will write about, though no character is based entirely on one real person. For example, Ah Wong, hero of my first novel, derived from a boy I saw working for a foodstall in a street in Singapore at midnight. He was about twelve years old and was walking along the street tapping two pieces of bamboo together to make a particular rhythm which told people that the noodle dish at his stall was ready and that he would take orders for it.

"I hope the story will also come out of the setting and will be an adventure that could only happen there. For example, *The Loss of the Night Wind* was based on the loss of an actual fishing boat off the coast of Northumberland—her loss was a mystery that had never been solved.

"I take about a year over a novel, which includes research and at least three drafts. I don't make many notes, but have a good visual imagination which enables me to recall places and people that are important for the novel, and I also take photographs. I write straight on to a type-writer—very inaccurately.

"I try to keep in touch with the children I write for by giving lectures (illustrated with slides of the countries I've written about) to groups of children at libraries and book shows, etc., and talking to them about my work, and through my nephews and nieces, but I don't consciously write for an age group.

"I like to travel. Apart from Singapore, I've been to Malaya, Hong Kong, Taiwan, Cambodia, Kenya, Poland, and Barbados—not simply to find inspiration for a novel, but because I like seeing new countries and meeting people there. I like reading, I swim (not very well), play tennis (not very well), and I cook a fairly good curry."

A Pair of Jesus Boots will be dramatized by the BBC-TV Children's Programme.

FOR MORE INFORMATION SEE: Horn Book, August, 1969, October, 1970; Sheila G. Ray, *Children's Fiction*, Brockhampton, 1972.

SYLVIA SHERRY

SILVERSTEIN, Alvin   1933- ("Dr. A")

PERSONAL: Born December 30, 1933, in New York, N.Y.; son of Edward (a carpenter) and Fannie (Wittlin) Silverstein; married Virginia B. Opshelor (a translator and writer), August 29, 1958; children: Robert Alan, Glenn Evan, Carrie Lee, Sharon Leslie, Laura Donna, Kevin Andrew. *Education:* Brooklyn College (now Brooklyn College of the City University of New York), B.A., 1955; University of Pennsylvania, M.S., 1959; New York University, Ph.D., 1962. *Home address:* R.D. 2, Lebanon, N.J. 08833. *Office:* Staten Island Community College of the City University of New York, 715 Ocean Ter., Staten Island, N.Y. 10301.

CAREER: Staten Island Community College of the City University of New York, Staten Island, N.Y., instructor, 1959-63, assistant professor, 1963-66, associate professor, 1966-70, professor of biology, 1970—. *Member:* Authors Guild, American Association for the Advancement of Science, American Chemical Society, American Institute of Biological Sciences, National Collegiate Association for the Conquest of Cancer (national chairman, 1968-70).

WRITINGS: The Biological Sciences (textbook), Holt, 1974.

Juvenile books, with wife, Virginia B. Silverstein: *Life in the Universe*, Van Nostrand, 1967; *Rats and Mice: Friends and Foes of Mankind*, Lothrop, 1968; *Unusual Partners*, McGraw, 1968; *The Origin of Life*, Van Nostrand, 1968; *The Respiratory System*, Prentice-Hall, 1969; *A Star in the Sea*, Warne, 1969; *A World in a Drop of Water*, Atheneum,

1969; *Cells: Building Blocks of Life*, Prentice-Hall, 1969; *Carl Linnaeus*, John Day, 1969; *Frederick Sanger*, John Day, 1969.

Germfree Life: A New Field in Biological Research, Lothrop, 1970; *Living Lights*, Golden Gate, 1970; *Circulatory Systems*, Prentice-Hall, 1970; *The Digestive System*, Prentice-Hall, 1970; *Bionics*, McCall Publishing, 1970; *Harold Urey*, John Day, 1971; *Metamorphosis: The Magic Change*, Atheneum, 1971; *Mammals of the Sea*, Golden Gate, 1971; *The Nervous System*, Prentice-Hall, 1971; *The Sense Organs*, Prentice-Hall, 1971; *The Endocrine System*; Prentice-Hall, 1971; *The Reproductive System*, Prentice-Hall, 1971; *The Code of Life*, Atheneum, 1972; *Guinea Pigs*, Lothrop, 1972; *The Long Voyage*, Warne, 1972; *The Muscular System*, Prentice-Hall, 1972; *The Skeletal System*, Prentice-Hall, 1972; *Cancer*, John Day, 1972; *The Skin*, Prentice-Hall, 1972; *The Excretory System*, Prentice-Hall, 1972; *Exploring the Brain*, Prentice-Hall, 1973; *The Chemicals We Eat and Drink*, Follett, 1973; *Rabbits*, Lothrop, 1973; *Sleep and Dreams*, Lippincott, 1974; *Animal Invaders*, Atheneum, 1974; *Hamsters*, Lothrop, 1974; *Epilepsy*, Lippincott, 1975; *Beans*, Prentice-Hall, 1975; *Oranges*, Prentice-Hall, 1975.

Author, under pseudonym, of syndicated juvenile fiction column, "Tales from Dr. A," which appeared in about 250 American and Canadian newspapers, 1972-74.

SIDELIGHTS: "I was fortunate to find two professions

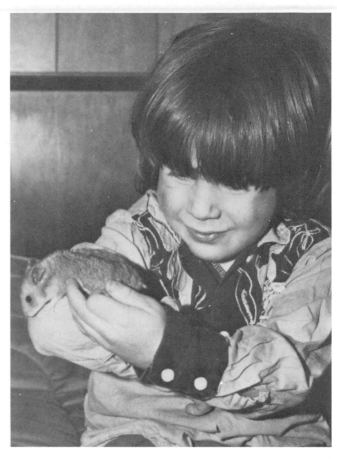

Are you looking for a pet who is tame and friendly, clean and easy to care for, and doesn't take much room? ■ (From *Hamsters* by Alvin and Virginia Silverstein. Photograph by the author.)

that I enjoy, college teaching and writing, and a marriage that has been both emotionally satisfying and a successful professional partnership. My reading preferences are mainly nonfiction, and thus I combine pleasure with the necessary task of keeping up with the literature in my field. (We subscribe to some fifty-odd magazines and journals.)"

Various of the Silversteins' juvenile books have been described as "stimulating," "cogent," "a concise, accurate treatment." A reviewer in *Christian Education Findings* wrote: "In *A Star in the Sea*, the life cycle of the starfish is told simply but in an interesting way, with superb illustrations. This is science as it should be presented." A number of the books are of a more technical nature, however; Zena Sutherland notes that in *Germfree Life*, which treats a relatively new research approach called gnotobiology, "the straightforward, brisk writing is lucid, the material neatly organized, the subject one of the most intriguing on the biological frontier."

HOBBIES AND OTHER INTERESTS: Vegetable gardening and sports.

FOR MORE INFORMATION SEE: New York Times Book Review, May 4, 1969, July 28, 1974; *Library Journal*, July, 1969, October 15, 1969, September 15, 1969, November 15, 1970; *Saturday Review*, August 22, 1970; *Horn Book*, October, 1970, December, 1970, April, 1974.

ALVIN and VIRGINIA B. SILVERSTEIN

SILVERSTEIN, Virginia B(arbara Opshelor) 1937-

PERSONAL: Born April 3, 1937, in Philadelphia, Pa.; daughter of Samuel W. (an insurance agent) and Gertrude (Bresch) Opshelor; married Alvin Silverstein (a professor of biology and writer), August 29, 1958; children: Robert Alan, Glenn Evan, Carrie Lee, Sharon Leslie, Laura Donna, Kevin Andrew. *Education:* University of Pennsylvania, A.B., 1958; also studied at McGill University, summer, 1955. *Home address:* R.D. 2, Lebanon, N.J. 08833.

CAREER: American Sugar Co., Brooklyn, N.Y., chemist, 1958-59; free-lance translator of scientific Russian, 1960—. *Member:* Authors Guild, American Translators Association.

WRITINGS—Juvenile books, with husband, Alvin Silverstein: *Life in the Universe*, Van Nostrand, 1967; *Rats and Mice: Friends and Foes of Mankind*, Lothrop, 1968; *Unusual Partners*, McGraw, 1968; *The Origins of Life*, Van Nostrand, 1968; *The Respiratory System*, Prentice-Hall, 1969; *A Star in the Sea*, Warne, 1969; *A World in a Drop of Water*, Atheneum, 1969; *Cells: Building Blocks of Life*, Prentice-Hall, 1969; *Carl Linnaeus*, John Day, 1969; *Frederick Sanger*, John Day, 1969.

Germfree Life: A New Field in Biological Research, Lothrop, 1970; *Living Lights*, Golden Gate, 1970; *Circulatory Systems*, Prentice-Hall, 1970; *The Digestive System*, Prentice-Hall, 1970; *Bionics*, McCall Publishing, 1970; *Harold Urey*, John Day, 1971; *Metamorphosis: The Magic Change*, Atheneum, 1971; *Mammals of the Sea*, Golden Gate, 1971; *The Nervous System*, Prentice-Hall, 1971; *The Sense Organs*, Prentice-Hall, 1971; *The Endocrine System*, Prentice-Hall, 1971; *The Reproductive System*, Prentice-Hall, 1971; *The Code of Life*, Atheneum, 1972; *Guinea Pigs*, Lothrop, 1972; *The Long Voyage*, Warne, 1972; *The Muscular System*, Prentice-Hall, 1972; *The Skeletal System*, Prentice-Hall, 1972; *Cancer*, John Day, 1972; *The Skin*, Prentice-Hall, 1972; *The Excretory System*, Prentice-Hall, 1972; *Exploring the Brain*, Prentice-Hall, 1973; *The Chemicals We Eat and Drink*, Follett, 1973; *Rabbits*, Lothrop, 1973; *Sleep and Dreams*, Lippincott, 1974; *Animal Invaders*, Atheneum, 1974; *Hamsters*, Lothrop, 1974; *Epilepsy*, Lippincott, 1975; *Beans*, Prentice-Hall, 1975; *Oranges*, Prentice-Hall, 1975.

Translator from Russian of numerous books, including: V. N. Kondratev, *Kinetics of Chemical Gas Reactions*, Atomic Energy Commission, 1960; M. A. Elyashevich, *Spectra of the Rare Earths*, Atomic Energy Commission, 1960; L. K. Blinov, *Hydrochemistry of the Aral Sea*, Office of Technical Services, 1961; R. A. Belyaev, *Beryllium Oxide*, Atomic Energy Commission, 1963; G. V. Samsonov, *High-Temperature Compounds of Rare Earth Metals with Nonmetals*, Plenum, 1965; M. B. Neiman, *Aging and Stabilization of Polymers*, Plenum, 1965. Regular contributor of translations to about twenty scientific journals; translator of bi-monthly journal, *Radiobiologiya*.

SIDELIGHTS: "I slipped into my professions (translating and writing) somewhat accidentally, but was ideally prepared for both by my strong school background in both sciences (chemistry major) and languages (formal studies in French, Latin, and German, plus Spanish and Russian self-taught). Writing is done in collaboration with my husband, with whom I (nearly always) have an almost perfect meshing of minds. So far we've averaged one major shift of career emphasis every three years or so; if the past is any guide, the future should be interesting—and probably unexpected." The author adds that "two professions, six children, and a seventeen-acre farm don't leave much time for either travel or avocations, but I do read voraciously, and enjoy listening to classical music and doing various handcrafts."

SKURZYNSKI, Gloria (Joan)   1930-

PERSONAL: Born July 6, 1930, in Duquesne, Pa.; daughter of Aylmer Kearney and Serena (Decker) Flister; married Edward Joseph Skurzynski (an aerospace engineer), December 1, 1951; children: Serena, Janine, Joan, Alane, Lauren. *Education:* Mt. Mercy College, Pittsburgh, Pa., student, 1948-50. *Religion:* Roman Catholic. *Home:* 2559 Spring Haven Dr., Salt Lake City, Utah 84109.

CAREER: U.S. Steel Corp., Pittsburgh, Pa., statistical clerk, 1950-52.

WRITINGS: The Magic Pumpkin (juvenile), Four Winds,

GLORIA SKURZYNSKI

Blue lifted off smoothly from the dandelion blossom and began to circle. The buzzing of the fly in flight was much louder than Gustavus had expected, and it began to make his ears ring. ■ (From *The Remarkable Journey of Gustavus Bell* by Gloria Skurzynski. Illustrated by Tim and Greg Hildebrandt.)

1971; *The Remarkable Journey of Gustavus Bell* (juvenile), Abingdon, 1973; *The Poltergeist of Jason Morey*, Todd, 1975. Contributor of three dozen short stories and articles to magazines.

WORK IN PROGRESS: The Wolf of Krol Forest, a novel for young adults.

SIDELIGHTS: "Born in the steel town of Duquesne, Pennsylvania, I considered smoke and soot in the air the natural order of things, and rather pleasant. In 1951 I married Ed Skurzynski, an aerospace engineer, and during the rest of that decade we became the parents of five daughters. When the youngest started first grade, I looked around for something to keep me occupied, but at home. I began free-lance writing, learning the craft slowly and painstakingly on my own. This is something like learning to play the piano by ear—not the easiest way to learn, but still possible. Even today, when every craft from the simplest to the most sophisticated is being taught in universities, a writer can learn to write very privately, by himself, at home."

FOR MORE INFORMATION SEE: Horn Book, December, 1971.

SLOTE, Alfred 1926-

PERSONAL: Born September 11, 1926, in Brooklyn, N.Y.; son of Oscar and Sallie Slote; married Henrietta Howell (a senior editor at University of Michigan Graduate

ALFRED SLOTE

Juki peered over the side of the well, and he smiled, for far down there in the dark water was Mare herself, white and peerless, looking up at them. ■ (From *The Moon in Fact and Fancy* by Alfred Slote. Illustrated by John Kaufmann.)

School of Business Administration), August 23, 1951; children: John, Elizabeth, Ben. *Education:* University of Michigan, B.A., 1949, M.A., 1950; University of Grenoble, further study, 1950. *Residence:* Ann Arbor, Mich. *Agent:* Curtis Brown Ltd., 60 East 56th St., New York, N.Y. 10022. *Office:* Television Center, University of Michigan, Ann Arbor, Mich. 48104.

CAREER: Williams College, Williamstown, Mass., instructor in English, 1953-56; University of Michigan Television Center, Ann Arbor, 1956—, started as producer-writer, associate director, 1968-73, executive producer, 1973—. Lecturer on children's literature at University of Michigan and University of California, Davis. *Military service:* U.S. Navy, 1944-46. *Member:* American Civil Liberties Union, Phi Beta Kappa. *Awards, honors:* Avery and Jules Hopwood Award in creative writing, University of Michigan, 1949; Fulbright scholar in France, 1950; Friends of American Writers Award, 1971, for *Jake*.

WRITINGS—Adult novels, except as noted: *Denham Proper*, Putnam, 1953; *Lazarus in Vienna*, McGraw, 1956; *Strangers and Comrades*, Simon & Schuster, 1964; *Termination: The Closing at Baker Plant* (nonfiction), Bobbs, 1969.

Children's books: *The Princess Who Wouldn't Talk*, Bobbs, 1964; *The Moon in Fact and Fancy*, World Publishing, 1967, revised edition, 1971; *Air in Fact and Fancy*, World Publishing, 1968; *Stranger on the Ball Club*, Lippincott, 1970; *Jake*, Lippincott, 1971; *The Biggest Victory*, Lippincott, 1972; *My Father, the Coach*, Lippincott, 1972; *Hang Tough, Paul Mather*, Lippincott, 1973; *Tony and Me*, Lippincott, 1974; *Matt Gargan's Boy*, Lippincott, 1975.

Writer of scripts for films and educational television programs.

hate traveling. I like talking and listening to kids. I like driveway basketball and lose to all my kids except my daughter."

"I don't think of my books as baseball books specifically. Of course, they have a baseball background, but I think of them as books about young people and what happens to them. Here I am writing about the things I know and love best.

"I played a lot of baseball when I was young. My position was third. I had a big chest, given to me to knock ground balls down. Later on, coaching Little League baseball gave me insights into kids, baseball and mostly myself."

SNEVE, Virginia Driving Hawk 1933-
(Virginia Driving Hawk)

PERSONAL: Surname rhymes with "navy"; born February 21, 1933, in Rosebud, S.D.; daughter of James H. (an Episcopal priest) and Rose (Ross) Driving Hawk; married Vance M. Sneve (a teacher of industrial arts), July 14, 1955; children: Shirley Kay, Paul Marshall, Alan Edward. *Education:* South Dakota State University, B.S., 1954, M.Ed., 1969. *Politics:* Republican. *Religion:* Episcopal. *Residence:* Flandreau, S.D.

Joe was excited now. As he dug he could see a raw-hide bundle, old and rotten, that had been painstakingly tied with leather thongs. ■ (From *High Elk's Treasure* by Virginia Driving Hawk Sneve. Illustrated by Oren Lyons.)

CAREER: Teacher of English in the public schools of White, S.D., 1954-55, and Pierre, S.D., 1955-56; Flandreau Indian School, Flandreau, S.D., teacher of English and speech, 1965-66, guidance counselor, 1966-70; Brevet Press, Sioux Falls, S.D., editor, 1972—. Member of Rosebud Sioux Tribe; member of board of directors of United Sioux Tribes Cultural Arts, 1972-73. *Member:* National League of American Pen Women, South Dakota Press Women. *Awards, honors:* Manuscript award in American Indian category from Interracial Council for Minority Books for Children, 1971, for *Jimmy Yellow Hawk.*

WRITINGS: Jimmy Yellow Hawk (juvenile), Holiday House, 1972; *High Elk's Treasure* (juvenile), Holiday House, 1972; (editor) *South Dakota Geographic Names*, Brevet Press, 1973; *The Dakota's Heritage*, Brevet Press, 1973; *When Thunders Spoke* (juvenile), Holiday House, 1974; *Betrayed* (juvenile), Holiday House, 1974. Contributor to educational units on American Indians, and to journals.

WORK IN PROGRESS: Fool Soldier Society of Teton Sioux; editing a history of the Episcopal Church in South Dakota.

SIDELIGHTS: "In my writing, both fiction and nonfiction, I try to present an accurate portrayal of American Indian life as I have known it. I also attempt to interpret history from the viewpoint of the American Indian and in

VIRGINIA DRIVING HAWK SNEVE

so doing I hope to correct the many misconceptions and untruths which have been too long perpetrated by non-Indian authors who have written about us."

FOR MORE INFORMATION SEE: Horn Book, August, 1972; *Sioux Falls Argus-Leader*, August 5, 1973.

SPEICHER, Helen Ross (Smith) 1915-
(Alice Abbott; Jane and Ross Land, a joint pseudonym)

PERSONAL: Born September 14, 1915, in Indianapolis, Ind.; daughter of Orren E. (a physician) and Nellie Jane (Schrock) Smith; married Kenneth E. Speicher (now an attorney), June 7, 1941; children: David Ross, Stephen Lee, John Allan, Susan Jane. *Education:* Butler University, B.S in Journalism (magna cum laude), 1937. *Politics:* Republican. *Religion:* Protestant. *Home:* 9620 Willow View Dr., Indianapolis, Ind. 46250.

CAREER: International Typographical Union, Indianapolis, Ind., reviser of correspondence course for apprentice printers, 1937-41; International Harvester, Indianapolis, Ind., editor of plant magazine, 1942-44. *Member:* Daughters of American Revolution (president of Golden Wheel, junior women's group, 1942-43), Theta Sigma Phi, Kappa Alpha Theta.

HELEN ROSS SPEICHER

WRITINGS—With Kathryn Kilby Borland: *Southern Yankees*, Bobbs, 1960; *Allan Pinkerton, Young Detective*, Bobbs, 1962; *Eugene Field: Young Poet*, Bobbs, 1964; *Phyllis Wheatley: Young Colonial Poet*, Bobbs, 1968; *Harry Houdini: Boy Magician*, Bobbs, 1969; *Clocks*, Follett, 1969; (under pseudonym Alice Abbott) *The Third Tower*, Ace, 1974; *Julie Scott*, Ace, 1975; *Goodby to Stony Crick*, McGraw, 1975.

With K. K. Borland under pseudonym Jane and Ross Land: *Miles and the Big Black Hat*, E. C. Seele, 1963; *Everybody Laughed and Laughed*, E. C. Seele, 1964; *The Stranger in the Mirror*, Ballantine, 1974; *Come Walk the Night*, Ballantine, 1975. Co-authored fourteen Bible story programs for children presented by WLW-I-TV, Indianapolis.

SIDELIGHTS: "My life has been uneventful if you disregard the almost daily crises that are quite normal to a family which includes four active children. I have always read to them from the age of six months on, and this has been reflected in their comprehensive vocabularies and excellent scholastic records.

"My co-author, Kathryn Borland, has the same attitude toward reading (we are both compulsive readers ourselves, even to the extent of recipes and advertisements if nothing better presents itself), and while I still had pre-school children, we both decided we could write something that, while it would be entertaining, could also make history seem interesting. *Southern Yankees* was accepted by the first publisher to whom we offered it. If it hadn't been, we might not have had the courage to do other books, although since then we have had several manuscripts that have never found a home.

"Generally we find that research (and we do much of this in order to understand the period about which we are writing) leads us into topics which we find fascinating enough to trigger another book.

"Many people have asked us how two authors can write together. We have been close friends through church, high school and college and frequently seem to have a special kind of ESP when we are writing—even to coining similar phrases. We usually outline the book chapter by chapter, then later in more detail, until we feel we are well-acquainted with our characters and the way they would act. We read aloud what we have written, finding that frequently the ear will catch a rough sentence that the eye has passed over."

STARKEY, Marion L(ena) 1901-

PERSONAL: Born April 13, 1901, in Worcester, Mass.; daughter of Arthur Eugene (a printer and publisher) and Alice Thorne (Gray) Starkey. *Education:* Boston University, B.S., 1922, M.A., 1936; Harvard University, further study, 1946. *Politics:* Independent. *Religion:* Unitarian Universalist. *Home:* 7 Stocker St., Saugus, Mass. 01906. *Agent:* Collins-Knowlton-Wing, Inc., 60 East 56th St., New York, N.Y. 10022.

CAREER: Saugus Herald, Saugus, Mass., editor, 1924-29; Hampton Institute, Hampton, Va., associate professor of English, 1930-43; University of Connecticut Extension, assistant professor of English at New London, 1946-50, and Hartford, 1950-51; full-time writer, 1951—. *Military service:* Women's Army Corps, 1943-45; translator for Office of Strategic Services in Algiers, Bari, Caserta, and Paris. *Member:* League of Women Voters, Phi Beta Kappa. *Awards, honors:* Guggenheim fellowships, 1953-54, 1958; Honorary Phi Beta Kappa, Boston University, College of Liberal Arts, 1950.

WRITINGS: The First Plantation: A History of Hampton and Elizabeth City County, Va. 1607-1887, privately printed, 1936; *The Cherokee Nation,* Knopf, 1946, reprinted, Russell, 1972; *The Devil in Massachusetts: A Modern Enquiry into the Salem Witch Trials,* Knopf, 1949; *A Little Rebellion,* Knopf, 1955; *Land Where Our Fathers Died: The Settling of the Eastern Shores 1607-1735,* Doubleday, 1962; *Striving to Make It My Home: The Story of Americans from Africa,* Norton, 1964; *The Congregational Way: The Role of the Pilgrims and Their Heirs in Shaping America,* Doubleday, 1966; *Lace Cuffs and Leather Aprons: Popular Struggles in the Federalist Era (1738-1800),* Knopf, 1972; *The Visionary Girls: Witchcraft in Salem Village* (juvenile novel), Little, Brown, 1973. Contributor to encyclopedias, magazines, and newspapers, most recently to *New England Galaxy.*

WORK IN PROGRESS: A children's book, tentatively titled *The Tall Man from Boston.*

MARION L. STARKEY

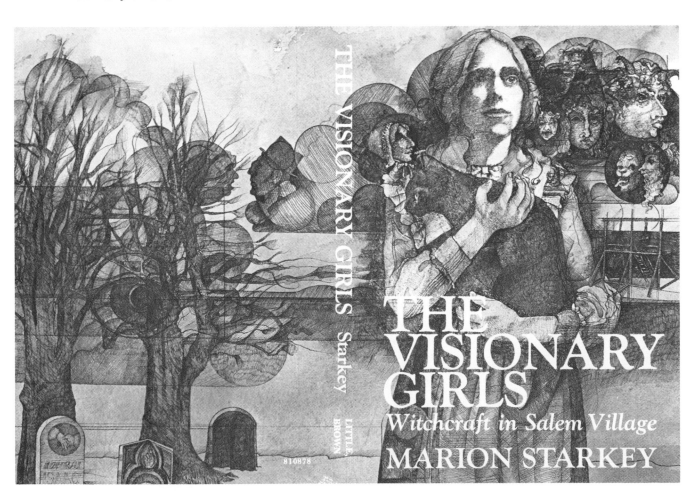

For six months in 1692 a pack of young girls, mostly teenagers, were all-powerful in Massachusetts. ■ (From *The Visionary Girls* by Marion Starkey. Jacket illustrated by Chris Duke.)

SIDELIGHTS: Now that she has left the teaching field, Starkey finds that she misses her students but "not the grading of papers." She terms herself a maverick in the academic field, explaining that "while I taught English, what I wrote was history. I'm also interested in psychology, approached the theme of *The Devil in Massachusetts* from that viewpoint, and was proud that the Library of Congress classified it as psychology." Her recent travels include West Africa and sundry trips to the West Indies, Peru, Greece, and Israel. She likes to explore the Saugus marshes with her cats.

The Devil in Massachusetts has been reprinted in two American editions, published in England (two editions) and Argentina, and included in reading programs.

FOR MORE INFORMATION SEE: *Horn Book*, October, 1973.

STEPHENS, Mary Jo 1935-

PERSONAL: Born March 10, 1935, in Harlan, Ky.; daughter of H. M. and Edith (Baker) Campbell; married Roger S. Stephens (a teacher), August 1, 1955; children: Amy. *Education:* Eastern Kentucky State College, B.A. (with highest honors), 1955. *Politics:* Democrat. *Religion:* Protestant. *Home:* 994 Avondale Ave., Cincinnati, Ohio 45229.

MARY JO STEPHENS

Pudd'nhead [the dog] had discovered the glider at the end of the porch . . . and exerted himself enough to climb into it. He had to be dragged away bodily at night. ■ (From *Zoe's Zodiac* by Mary Jo Stephens. Illustrated by Leonard Shortall.)

CAREER: Teacher of English, 1960-65; Cincinnati, Ohio Public Schools, Cincinnati, librarian, 1965-74. *Member:* American Civil Liberties Union, Independent Voters of Ohio, Council of the Southern Mountains, American Library Association, Ohio Association of School Librarians.

WRITINGS: *Zoe's Zodiac* (juvenile), Houghton, 1971; *Witch of the Cumberlands* (juvenile), Houghton, 1974.

WORK IN PROGRESS: A novel for children tentatively titled *Up the Road to Xanadu*.

SIDELIGHTS: "My first book, *Zoe's Zodiac*, was done just as an exercise—really to see if I could do it. But the second, *Witch of the Cumberlands*, came as a result of a good deal of research done for a junior high school course in Appalachian culture. I am an Appalachian and I found, in selecting and reviewing books on Appalachian culture that I knew, from my childhood in the Kentucky hills, so much about herbs, flora and fauna, moonshining, snake-handling, and the effects of the coal industry, especially, that I wanted to do a book of my own."

FOR MORE INFORMATION SEE: *Horn Book*, April, 1972, August, 1974.

One day my momma told me, "You know you're gonna have a little friend come stay with you?"
And I said, "Who is it?" ▪ (From *Stevie* by John Steptoe. Illustrated by the author.)

JOHN STEPTOE

STEPTOE, John (Lewis)   1950-

PERSONAL: Born September 14, 1950, in Brooklyn, N.Y.; son of John Oliver (a transit worker) and Elesteen (Hill) Steptoe; children: Bweela (daughter), Javaka (son). *Education:* Attended New York School of Art and Design, 1964-67. *Home and office:* 66 Grove St., Peterborough, N.H. 03458. *Agent:* Alice Bach, 222 East 75th St., New York, N.Y.

CAREER: Painter and writer of children's books. Teacher at Brooklyn Music School, summer, 1970. *Member:* Amnesty International. *Awards, honors:* Gold Medal from Society of Illustrators, 1970, for *Stevie.*

WRITINGS—For children; all self-illustrated: *Stevie,*

Harper, 1969; *Uptown*, Harper, 1970; *Train Ride*, Harper, 1971; *Birthday*, Holt, 1972.

Illustrator: Lucille B. Clifton, *All Us Come cross the Water*, Holt, 1972; Eloise Greenfield, *She Come Bringing Me That Little Baby Girl*, Lippincott, 1975.

WORK IN PROGRESS: My Special Best Words, for Viking, and *Marcia*, both books for children.

SIDELIGHTS: "One of my incentives for getting into writing children's books was the great and disastrous need for books that black children could honestly relate to. I ignorantly created precedents by writing such a book. I was amazed to find that no one had successfully written a book in the dialogue which black children speak." *Stevie* was written when Steptoe was sixteen.

FOR MORE INFORMATION SEE: Life, August, 29, 1969; *Horn Book*, December, 1969, October, 1971, August, 1972; *Interracial Books for Children*, Autumn, 1971; Selma G. Lanes, *Down the Rabbit Hole*, Atheneum, 1971; *Washington Post* "Children's Book World," November 5, 1972; *New York Times Book Review*, November 6, 1974.

STERLING, Philip   1907-

PERSONAL: Surname originally Shatz; legally changed to Sterling, 1937; born July 12, 1907, in New Rochelle, N.Y.; son of William (a house painter) and Helen (Levine) Shatz; married Dorothy Dannenberg (a writer under name Dorothy Sterling), May 14, 1937; children: Peter, Anne (Mrs. Nelson Fausto). *Education:* Attended high school in Cleveland, Ohio, 1922-25. *Residence:* Wellfleet, Mass. *Address:* Box 626, South Wellfleet, Mass. 02663.

CAREER: Reporter, writer, or copy editor for *Cleveland Press, Omaha World Herald*, and then for suburban New York newspapers, 1926-31; New York Emergency Home Relief Bureau, New York, N.Y., clerk, later caseworker, 1933-35; Federal Writers Project (under Works Progress Administration), New York, N.Y., associate editor of *Film Index*, 1936-39; Columbia Broadcasting System, New York, N.Y., writer with radio and television press information departments, 1945-65, assistant director of radio press information, 1960-63. *Awards, honors:* Christopher Book Award, 1971, for *Sea and Earth: The Life of Rachel Carson.*

WRITINGS—For young readers, except as noted: (With wife, Dorothy Sterling) *Polio Pioneers*, Doubleday, 1955; (with Bella Rodman) *Fiorello LaGuardia*, Hill & Wang, 1962; (editor) *Laughing on the Outside* (anthology of Negro humor for adults), Grosset, 1965; (with Rayford W. Logan) *Four Took Freedom: The Lives of Harriet Tubman, Frederick Douglass, Robert Smalls and Blanche K. Bruce*, Doubleday, 1967; (with Maria Brau) *The Quiet Rebels: Four Puerto Rican Leaders*, Doubleday, 1968; *Sea and Earth: The Life of Rachel Carson*, Crowell, 1970; *The Real Teachers: Conversations After the Bell* (adult nonfiction), Random House, 1972; *The Question of Color*, Scholastic Book Services, 1973.

WORK IN PROGRESS: Collaborating with his son, Dr. Peter Sterling, on a book about the physical treatment of mental disorder, for Beacon Press.

In his free time there were places to go that gave a boy's spirit some stretching room. And there were things to see that had more life and beauty in them than he could find on a blackboard. ■ (From *The Quiet Rebels* by Philip Sterling and Maria Brau. Illustrated by Tracy Sugarmen.)

STEVENSON, Janet   1913-

PERSONAL: Born February 4, 1913, in Chicago, Ill.; daughter of John C. (an investment banker) and Atlantis (McClendon) Marshall; married second husband, Benson Rotstein (an educator), 1964; children: (previous marriage) Joseph Stevenson, Edward Stevenson. *Education:* Bryn Mawr College, B.A. (magna cum laude), 1933; Yale University, M.F.A., 1937. *Religion:* Unitarian Universalist.

CAREER: University of Southern California, Los Angeles, lecturer in drama, 1951-53. Free-lance writer. *Member:* Authors League, P.E.N. *Awards, honors:* Friends of American Writers awards for *Weep No More* and *The Ardent Years*; National Arts of the Theatre Award for "Weep No More," dramatic version of book; John Golden fellowship in playwriting.

WRITINGS: Weep No More, Viking, 1957; *The Ardent Years*, Viking, 1960; *Painting America's Wildlife* (biography of John James Audubon), Encyclopaedia Britannica, 1961; *Singing for the World* (biography of Marian Anderson), Encyclopaedia Britannica, 1963; *Sisters and Brothers*, Crown, 1966; *Woman Aboard*, Crown, 1969; *Spokesman for Freedom* (biography of Archibald Grinké), Crowell-Collier, 1969; *Pioneers in Freedom* (juvenile), Reilly & Lee, 1969; *Soldiers in the Civil Rights War* (juvenile), Reilly & Lee, 1971; *The Montgomery Bus Boycott* (juvenile), Watts, 1971; *First Book of Women's Rights* (juvenile), Watts, 1972; *The School Segregation Cases* (juvenile), Watts, 1973. Author of plays, "Declaration" and "Counter-attack," in collaboration with Philip Stevenson,

JANET STEVENSON

If the boys were carrying water, they had no hands left to defend themselves, for each carried one pail in his outside hand, and they shared the third pail between them. ■ (From *Spokesman for Freedom: The Life of Archibald Grimke* by Janet Stevenson. Illustrated by John Wagner.)

and "Weep No More." Contributor to *American Heritage* and *Atlantic Monthly*. Also author of motion picture scripts, short stories, and reading texts.

WORK IN PROGRESS: An adult historical novel entitled, *Right Ascension*, which deals with a woman navigator on a sea voyage in the Pacific in 1851.

SIDELIGHTS: "I have had a particular interest in sailing, since I spent six months as part of a crew of four on a small vessel in the South Pacific (the material from which *Woman Aboard* is excerpted). The story of a real woman who had to learn some of the mysterious mathematical skills necessary to figure out where you are on the watery face of the world and how to get where you want to go—and in the days of square-riggers, no radios, or other 'aids to navigation'—was irresistible when I ran across it in an old history book. Since there was little hard fact available about this anonymous heroine, I have spent two years reconstructing something 'like it was'—and hope to have produced a novel which will also work as a film. Thus, after a long hard struggle, finding a way to serve both masters at the same time. *Right Ascension* is, of course, intended for adult readers.

"In the field of writing for young readers, I seem to have ridden two horses only: stories that concerned the long American struggle for equal rights—black and white, men and women; and stories about women in roles where they are not usually expected to appear. Maybe, after all, it is the same horse."

SUHL, Yuri   1908-

PERSONAL: Born July 30, 1908, in Podhajce, Poland; came to United States, 1923; son of Sam and Miriam (Fox) Suhl; married Isabelle H. Shugars (a high school librarian), June 24, 1950. *Education:* Studied at Brooklyn Centre (now Brooklyn College) of City College, New York, 1928-29, and New York University, 1929-30, 1949-53. *Home and office:* 232 East Sixth St., New York, N.Y. 10003. *Agent:* Cyrilly Abels, 119 West 57th St., New York, N.Y. 10019.

CAREER: During depression years of the 1930's worked as fruit peddler, ditch digger, teacher of Yiddish, and writer on Federal Writers' Project; four books of his Yiddish poetry were published between 1935 and 1952, and in 1942 he became a bilingual writer—continuing to write verse in Yiddish but prose in English; since publication of his first novel, Suhl has been a full-time writer and lecturer. Teacher of course on Jewish resistance to Nazism at New School for Social Research, 1971—. *Military service:* U.S. Army, 1942-44. *Member:* Authors Guild. *Awards, honors:* Lewis Carroll Shelf Award of Wisconsin Book Conference, 1972, for *Simon Boom Gives a Wedding*; National Jewish Book Award, 1974, for *Uncle Misha's Partisans*.

YURI SUHL

200

By midnight the guests were so full of water that they couldn't even keep their eyes open, and they fell asleep at the table. ■ (From *Simon Boom Gives a Wedding* by Yuri Suhl. Illustrated by Margot Zemach.)

WRITINGS—In Yiddish: *Dos Licht oif Mein Gas* (title means "The Light on My Street"; poems), Signal, 1935; *Dem Tog Antkegen* (title means "Toward the Day"; poems), Signal, 1938; *Yisroel Partisan* (title means "Israel the Partisan"; novel in verse), Signal, 1942; *Der Alter Fun Lompaduni* (title means "The Old Man of Lompaduni"; collection of children's stories), Nidershlesie (Poland), 1948; *A Vort fun Traist* (title means "A Word of Consolation"; poems), Ykuf (Mexico), 1952.

In English: *One Foot in America* (novel), Macmillan, 1950; *Cowboy on a Wooden Horse* (novel), Macmillan, 1953; *Ernestine Rose and the Battle for Human Rights* (adult biography), Reynal, 1959; (editor, translator, and author of six original chapters) *They Fought Back: The Story of Jewish Resistance in Nazi Europe* (documentary anthol-

ogy), Crown, 1967; *Eloquent Crusader: Ernestine Rose* (juvenile biography), Messner, 1970; *Simon Boom Gives a Wedding* (juvenile), Four Winds, 1972; *An Album of Jews in America* (juvenile pictorial history), Watts, 1972; *Uncle Misha's Partisans* (young adult), Four Winds Press, 1973; *The Man Who Made Everyone Late* (juvenile), Four Winds, 1974; *On the Other Side of the Gate* (young adult novel), Watts, 1975; *The Merrymaker*, Four Winds Press, 1975.

Other works: Book and lyrics for "Benyomen der Dritter" (title means "Benjamin the Third"; choral and dance), first produced in New York at Carnegie Hall, 1938; "Gedenk Mein Folk" (title means "Remember My People"; cantata), first produced in New York at Town Hall, 1963; "To a Jew" (play in English), as yet unproduced and unpublished.

WORK IN PROGRESS: A novel, *To Run with the Dead*, about a Jew who escapes from the Warsaw Ghetto and seeks shelter with a Polish family; a novel, as yet untitled, based on Suhl's experiences in the U.S. Army during World War II.

SIDELIGHTS: Suhl returned to Poland in 1948 for the first time since he left the country as an immigrant at age fifteen. "After attending the unveiling ceremonies of the Warsaw Ghetto Monument, I visited the surviving Jewish communities in Lower Silesia and other parts of Poland on a poetry reading tour sponsored by Jewish communal leaders. This experience marked the beginning of my deep interest in the Holocaust theme. When I returned to Poland a second time, in 1959, it was to do research at the Jewish Historical Institute of Warsaw and interview surviving resistance leaders for *They Fought Back*.

"In the early 1960's I became interested in found-object sculpture. I have since had several exhibits of my work on Martha's Vineyard where I am a summer resident."

FOR MORE INFORMATION SEE: Book Week, May 14, 1967; *New York Review of Books*, June 1, 1967; *Punch*, March 20, 1968; *Library Journal*, October 15, 1970; Wayne Miller, *A Gathering of Ghetto Writers*, New York University Press, 1972; *Horn Book*, February, 1974.

SWIGER, Elinor Porter 1927-

PERSONAL: Born August 1, 1927, in Cleveland, Ohio; daughter of Louis Charles (a farmer) and Mary (Shank) Porter; married Quentin G. Swiger (an attorney), February 5, 1955; children: Andrew, Calvin, Charles. *Education:* Ohio State University, B.A., 1949, LL.B., 1951. *Religion:* Protestant. *Home:* 1933 Burr Oak Dr., Glenview, Ill. 60025. *Agent:* Russell & Volkening, Inc., 551 Fifth Ave., New York, N.Y. 10017.

CAREER: Internal Revenue Service, Office of Chief Counsel, Washington, D.C., attorney, 1951-56. Active in Legal Aid and other volunteer work, including lecturing to special classes in social studies and community groups. *Member:* American Bar Association, National League of American Pen Women, Ohio Bar Association, Children's Reading Round Table (Chicago), Off-Campus Writers Workshop, Lyric Opera Guild.

WRITINGS: Mexico for Kids, Bobbs, 1971; *Europe for Young Travelers*, Bobbs, 1972; *The Law and You: A Handbook for Young People* (Junior Literary Guild selection), Bobbs, 1973, revised edition, 1975. Contributor to magazines and newspapers.

WORK IN PROGRESS: Four books for juveniles.

SIDELIGHTS: "Writing *The Law and You* was a highly satisfying experience because in its preparation three abiding interests—in young people, in community work, and in the law—converged and the contribution of each proved vital, not unlike the underpinnings of a three-legged stool.

"As my children developed, I became aware of the multitude of ways in which the law touches young people. They encounter health, safety, and nuisance laws as they acquire

ELEANOR PORTER SWIGER

pets and mini-bikes, take minor jobs, and make their first steps toward the adult world. They are involved with property of all kinds, and in many different ways: they may trespass upon it, damage it, inherit it, find it, or purchase it. Diverse legal proceedings—accident cases, custody suits, shoplifting arrests—bring them before authorities and into the courts.

"Volunteering in the schools, I was impressed during Law Day programs in recent years by the barrage of student questions. There are probably several reasons for this upsurge in interest in the law. The most obvious one is that the sheer number of laws has increased in a more crowded world. A second reason is the attention directed to specific laws and courts, and to the legal process in general, by the wide publicity of certain recent trials and by the large number of television shows replete with references to law, particularly criminal law. Today's young people are clearly interested in learning the true facts about the law, having been nurtured in a 'tell it like it is' educational atmosphere. I've tried to focus on key facts about American law as it relates to their contemporary concerns. The thrust of the book is to provide a wide-screen view. The law embodies responsibilities as well as rights and I tried to convey this balanced image."

HOBBIES AND OTHER INTERESTS: Art, opera, and golf.

THOMAS, J. F.
See FLEMING, Thomas J(ames)

MARTHA TOLLES

TOLLES, Martha   1921-

PERSONAL: Born September 7, 1921, in Oklahoma City, Okla.; daughter of Willis and Mary Natalie (Dunbar) Gregory; married Edwin Leroy Tolles (an attorney), June 21, 1944; children: Stephen, Henry, Cynthia, Roy, James, Thomas. *Education:* Smith College, B.A., 1943. *Religion:* Presbyterian. *Home:* 860 Oxford Rd., San Marino, Calif. 91108.

CAREER: Port Chester Daily Item, Port Chester, N.Y., reporter, 1943-44; *Publishers' Weekly*, New York, N.Y., member of editorial staff, 1945. *Member:* California Writers Guild, Southern California Council on Literature for Children and Young People.

WRITINGS: Too Many Boys, Thomas Nelson, 1965, reissued as *Katie and Those Boys*, Scholastic Arrow Book Club, 1974; *Katie*, Scholastic Arrow Book Club, 1975. Contributor to children's magazines.

WORK IN PROGRESS: A juvenile novel and short stories.

SIDELIGHTS: "When I decided to write my first book I cast about for an idea and soon realized I had one right before me. In our family we had a problem, created by the fact that there were five boys and only one girl. Our daughter, with two older brothers and three younger ones, con-

stantly wanted another girl to play with and there were none at all in our neighborhood, only boys. Much of her time was spent on the front lawn, or in our playroom or eating lunch with perhaps a dozen boys . . . all her brothers and their many friends. And so her life was indeed filled with too many boys.

"I took the problem and some of the characters from real life but the incidents were mainly make-believe. I wrote the book one summer after persuading the older children to mind the younger ones for an hour each day . . . then read each chapter to them for their comments.

"I have received letters from girls since, some saying they sympathize with Katie because they have the same problem, others saying they wish they had it too!"

TOYE, William E(ldred)   1926-

PERSONAL: Born June 19, 1926, in Toronto, Ontario, Canada; son of Eldred Dalston and Clarenda (Steenson) Toye. *Education:* Victoria College, University of Toronto, B.A., 1948. *Home:* 139 Collier St., Toronto 5, Ontario, Canada. *Office:* Oxford University Press, 70 Wynford Dr., Don Mills 403, Toronto, Ontario, Canada.

CAREER: Oxford University Press, Toronto, Ontario, Canada, production manager, editor of children's books,

W. E. TOYE

He went to the beautiful place where Winter lived. ■ (From *How Summer Came to Canada* by William Toye. Illustrated by Elizabeth Cleaver.)

1950—, editorial director. *Member:* Society of Typographic Designers of Canada (president, 1962). *Awards, honors:* Award for best-designed book of 1959, for *The St. Lawrence*, Society of Typographic Designers of Canada; book-of-the-year medal, 1961, 1970, Canadian Association of Children's Librarians; three awards for typographic design in the national typography exhibition, "Typography 58."

WRITINGS: (With Ivon Owen) *A Picture History of Canada*, Watts, 1956; *The St. Lawrence*, Walck, 1959; (editor) *A Book of Canada*, Collins, 1962; *The Mountain Goats of Temlaham*, Walck, 1969; *How Summer Came to Canada*, Walck, 1969; *Cartier Discovers the St. Lawrence*, Walck, 1970; (with Robert Weaver) *The Oxford Anthology of Canadian Literature*, Oxford University Press, 1973; *Supplement to the Oxford Companion to Canadian History and Literature*, Oxford University Press, 1973. Associate editor, *The Tamarack Review*.

TRIPP, Paul

PERSONAL: Born February 20, in New York, N.Y.; son of Benjamin (a singer and actor) and Esther (Stelzer) Tripp; married Ruth Enders (an actress), August 8, 1943; children: Suzanne (Mrs. Richard Jurmain), David. *Education:* City College, New York, N.Y., student, 1927-31. *Politics:* Independent. *Home:* 2 Fifth Ave., New York, N.Y. 10011. *Agent:* Mrs. Carolyn Willyoung Stagg, 156 East 52nd St., New York, N.Y. 10022.

CAREER: Editor of *Ridgefield Park Bulletin* (weekly newspaper), Ridgefield Park, N.J., 1946-47; specialist in entertainment for children, 1949—, producing and acting in television series, narrating films, and writing songs. Creator, director, and star of "Mr. I. Magination," 1949-52, and producer and star of "On the Carousel," 1954-59, both CBS-TV series; star of "Birthday House," NBC-TV series, 1963-67; narrator of fourteen films produced by Childhood Productions, Rome, Italy, 1965-68, and co-star of one, "The Christmas That Almost Wasn't," 1966. President of Fantasy Music Publishing, Inc., New York, N.Y., 1960-63, director, 1960—. Member of New York City Youth Board, 1955-57. *Military service:* U.S. Army, 1942-45; served in China-Burma-India Theater; became staff sergeant.

MEMBER: American Society of Composers, Authors and Publishers (ASCAP), Screen Writers Guild, National Academy of Television Arts and Sciences (board of governors, 1958—; trustee, 1960-61), The Players (New York). *Awards, honors:* *Look* Award, George Foster Peabody Award, and Ohio State Television Award, all for "Mr. I. Magination"; Emmy Award of National Academy of Television Arts and Sciences and four Ohio State Television awards for "On the Carousel"; "Tubby the Tuba," a film short, was nominated for an Oscar by Academy of Motion Picture Arts and Sciences; Grammy Award for recording of "The Christmas That Almost Wasn't."

WRITINGS: The Strawman Who Smiled by Mistake (illustrated by Wendy Watson), Doubleday, 1967; *The Little Red Flower* (*Junior Literary Guild* selection), Doubleday, 1968; *Minnie the Mump*, Ross Lab, 1969; *The Tail That Went Looking*, Doubleday, 1970. Writer of script and lyrics for film, "The Christmas That Almost Wasn't"; has also written more than thirty record albums for children, including "Tubby the Tuba," "Story of Celeste," "Mr. I. Magination," and "Birthday House." He has written and published about 600 songs. Contributor to *Television* (quarterly); columnist, "Don't Kid Me," in *Rockland Independent* (published in Rockland County, N.Y.). Recently completed commissioned dramatic work "A Sackful of Dreams" with wife, Ruth Enders Tripp.

WORK IN PROGRESS: An animated full-length film based on "Tubby the Tuba," completion expected in 1975; autobiography, tentatively titled "Who's Scared of Kids?"

SIDELIGHTS: "I consider myself a 'storyteller' in the real old-fashioned sense of the word. In my early years as a social worker, it was a 'must' for me to invent stories I could tell children gathered around a camp-fire. Later on, I mounted some of these same original stories and they became plays performed by underprivileged children of the Lower East Side settlement—then called Christodora House. There was no money to pay for royalties, nothing for scenery or props, so I developed a skill for 'imagining' first a story, then a play, then using imagination for whatever necessities could not be afforded. Thus a broomstick became a tree and a kitchen pot, a treasure chest of gold. My skill at imagination became a contagion—cast and audience BELIEVED.

"From the storyteller to the young amateur playwright, I employed my talents for writing for the 'EAR.' Writers and readers often fail to realize that writing for the 'EAR' is a totally different technique than writing for the 'EYE.' It was a tough struggle. I had to practically *translate* all the ideas in my mind to properly suit the printed page. The imagination I used in staging a dramatic work, I had to reshape into ideas for an artist or illustrator to draw and paint. It took me hours of rewriting to design a story in terms of 'print and pictures' to be housed and confined between two covers.

"My transitional problems were twofold. First, my initial success, *Tubby the Tuba*, was a *musical* story—since hailed as a classic in its field—that began a trend in my career where I used *music* to 'illustrate' my stories instead of pictures. I developed a new style of weaving *voice and music* into a story which would capture the listener. Therefore the 'listener,' NOT the 'reader' became my goal. To switch from a composer to an illustrator necessitated a violent wrench in my story-telling process.

"Secondly, as a professional actor with years of experience, I could easily disguise flaws in my own stories by making them *sound* better than they really were. In order to write for the 'EYE,' I had to relinquish the artful trickery of my voice. Now the book was in the hands of a 'reader' and I felt vulnerable. I had to stand by, helplessly, while the merciless 'EYE' of a *reader* examined the precious little story. Words that sounded 'good' did not necessarily read 'good.' I had to learn to write again.

"Encouraged and criticized by my wife, an actress and journalist, I eventually emerged from the sea of blue-penciled editing, to bring forth my first children's story between-two-covers. My own children were delighted. Their father was now not only a writer, actor and lyricist—but an AUTHOR.

"I'm not an author who isolates himself in a small closet—or on a mountaintop. I am capable of concentrating (and actually do better) when I am surrounded by people, activity, noise and confusion—and frequently the pursuit of other creative projects. I have enjoyed the laughter of my children at a witty phrase; the tears of my wife at a poignant section—and the criticism, pro and con—of a very tightly knit family group. I'm a very merry person.

"Both of my children are art historians and writers. David, with a thesis soon to be published, and Suzanne following in her father's footsteps, and on the verge of her first children's work. My wife, Ruth, is private and personal typist and editor for the family output of the written word.

"Basically a writer of fantasy, I do not dare 'manufacture,' or piece together, a story. Fantasy must spring 'whole cloth' from the author's brain. Fantasy has to be more

PAUL TRIPP

logical than Fact. It has to make sense to the reader. I try to achieve this by making my characters seem real and 'full of character.' Dialogue is my strong suit. Here again it was necessary for me to learn that 'spoken' dialogue will not always 'read' well. The 'eye' sounds words differently than the 'ear.'

"When an idea springs into my mind, it becomes compulsive. It must LEAP into the world and make itself known. Until the IDEA translates itself into words, I am inwardly the most miserable man in the world. There's a glassiness in my eyes which blocks out my surroundings while I 'write' the story in my mind. Once seated at the typewriter, the language flows in a torrent. The brain dictates more rapidly than the machine can spell. After the months of 'brain agony,' the story can unfold sometimes in a day.

"Of course, being obsessed with an IDEA doesn't necessarily result in instant publication. As I have to cheerfully but ruefully admit, I have written some of the best UNpublished stories. But, I like them and believe in them and that makes me feel happy and fulfilled.

"I just like to create and write. Furthermore, You 'never-can-tell.' I have written stories which were not immediately publishable; only to find that five years later, styles had changed! PRESTO! Out of the dusty files emerges a manuscript which—at last—reaches that lovely heaven Between-Two-Covers."

VAVRA, Robert James 1935-

PERSONAL: Born March 9, 1935, in Los Angeles, Calif.; son of William John and Mable (Hamilton) Vavra. *Educa-*

ROBERT VAVRA

Again he called to the bull. And again the sharp horns brushed his legs, and the spectators' shouts of "olé" rose all round him. ■ (From *Felipe the Bullfighter* by Robert Vavra. Photograph by the author.)

tion: University of Southern California, B.A. *Home:* Villa Santa Cecilia, Avenida Manuel Siurot, Seville, Spain.

CAREER: Writer-photographer. *Military service:* U.S. Air Force.

WRITINGS—Juvenile books, except as noted, the majority illustrated with his own photographs: (With John Fulton) *Lament for the Death of a Matador* (adult), [Spain], 1964; *Little Egret and Toro*, Collins, 1966, Lion, 1967; *Anna and Dula*, Harcourt, 1966; *Felipe the Bullfighter*, Harcourt, 1967; *Tiger Flower* (paintings by Fleur Cowles; preface by Yehudi Menuhin), Collins, 1968, Harcourt, 1969; *Pizorro*, Harcourt, 1968; *The Story of Taou*, Dial, 1968; *Milane: The Story of a Hungarian Gypsy Boy*, Harcourt, 1969; *Lion and Blue*, Morrow, 1974. Illustrator of James A. Michener's *Iberia: Spanish Travels and Reflections*, Random House, 1968.

WORK IN PROGRESS: Curro, a book on a novice bullfighter.

SIDELIGHTS: "I have always written and photographed all of my books—juvenile and adult—for myself." United Artists has made an animated color film of *Tiger Flower*, with a musical score by Mitch Leigh.

FOR MORE INFORMATION SEE: New Statesman, November, 1968; *Punch*, December 11, 1968; *Horn Book*, December, 1969.

VENABLE, Alan (Hudson) 1944-

PERSONAL: Surname is accented on first syllable; born October 26, 1944, in Pittsburgh, Pa., son of Emerson (a chemist) and Regis Alva (Illston) Venable; married Gail

Portnuff, January 11, 1970. *Education:* Harvard University, B.A., 1966; University of Pennsylvania, graduate study, 1968-69. *Agent:* John Meyer, 141 East 55th St., New York, N.Y. 10022.

CAREER: Writer. *Wartime service:* Civilian Public Service, 1970-71.

WRITINGS: The Checker Players (picture story), Lippincott, 1973; *Hurry the Crossing*, Lippincott, 1974; *The Bed* (picture story), Lippincott, 1975.

SIDELIGHTS: "I wrote *Hurry the Crossing* on the basis of my experience teaching sociology in Tanzania, East Africa. I was greatly impressed with the socialist, egalitarian direction of development in that country and wanted to convey this hopefulness to young Americans. But I wrote the stories mainly for myself, rather than 'for children,' in the process of discovering how to write fiction.

"I think that children's literature should be more honest in recognizing the existence of injustice at all levels of our society. It should help them understand the forces which dominate their parents and which dictate the training which they themselves are forced to undergo. It should deal with the racism, sexism, big money and imperialism. There should be books appealing to children about the meaning of private property, about labor unions, about racial tension, about sexual experience—and even about love!

"We need books that will cause children to ask questions, of themselves and of their parents. We need books that will make us, as parents, squirm."

ALAN VENABLE

So they built their boat, a beautiful one, and spent many days on the river together.

(From *The Checker Players* by Alan Venable. Illustrated by Byron Barton.)

VOIGHT, Virginia Frances 1909-

PERSONAL: Born March 30, 1909, in New Britain, Conn.; daughter of Henry G. (an engineer and inventor) and Drusilla (Kelly) Voight. *Education:* Attended Yale School of the Fine Arts and a commercial art school for two years each. *Home:* 205 Helen St., Hamden, Conn. 06514. *Agent:* Muriel Fuller, P.O. Box 193, Grand Central Station, New York, N.Y. 10017.

CAREER: Writer.

WRITINGS: Apple Tree Cottage, Holiday, 1949; *The House in Robin Lane*, Holiday, 1951; *Zeke and the Fishercat*, Holiday, 1953; *Lions in the Barn*, Holiday, 1955; *Rolling Show*, Holiday, 1956; *Mystery at Deer Hill*, Funk, 1958; *Black Elephant*, Prentice-Hall, 1959.

The Missing $10,000 Bill, Funk, 1960; *The Girl from Johnnycake Hill*, Prentice-Hall, 1961; *Treasure of Hemlock Mountain*, Funk, 1961; *Uncas, Sachem of the Wolf People*, Funk, 1963; *Picta, the Painted Turtle*, Putnam, 1963; *A Book for Abe*, Prentice-Hall, 1963; *Mystery in the Museum*, Funk, 1964; *Nathan Hale*, Putnam, 1965; *Mohegan Chief*, Funk, 1965; *Patch, a Baby Mink*, Putnam, 1965; *I Know a Librarian*, Putnam, 1967; *Sacajawea*, Putnam, 1967; *The Hidden Pearls*, Macrae Smith, 1967; *Catamount*, Macrae Smith, 1968; *Little Brown Bat*, Putnam, 1969; *Adventures of Hiawatha*, Garrard, 1969; *Patriot's Gold*, Macrae Smith, 1969; *Cuff a Baby Bear*, Putnam, 1969.

VIRGINIA F. VOIGHT

Stagecoach Days and Stagecoach Kings, Garrard, 1970; *Brave Little Humming Bird*, Putnam, 1970; *Massasoit Friend of the Pilgrims*, Garrard, 1971; *Close to the Rising Son*, Garrard, 1972; *Red Blade and the Black Bear*, Dodd, 1973; *Red Cloud: War Chief of the Sioux*, Garrard, 1975. Contributor of articles and short stories to *American Girl, Boys' Life, Trails for Juniors, Child Life, Story Parade*, and other young people's publications.

SIDELIGHTS: "I cannot remember when I first decided that I wanted to be a writer. Books have always been an important part of my life. We were a reading family and our house was crammed with all kinds of books. It seemed a natural step from being a reader to the adventure of writing stories of my own. Before I learned to read, my mother and my two grandmothers read to me and told me stories. One grandmother told delightful and often exciting stories of life on a Virginia farm before and during the Civil War. The other grandmother had equally interesting tales to tell of life in Germany. These glimpses into the history and folklore of different people started me on a lifelong interest in history.

"It was my father who first drew my attention to conservation. Our family walked, picnicked, birdwatched, and fished for trout and bass in the beauty spots of Connecticut. I remember my father telling me never to pick wildflowers but to leave them for others to enjoy. I used to rob the squirrels, though, by going forth with a sack to gather black walnuts in the fall. My mouth still waters when I remember the nut cake and walnut fudge that were the results of my labors.... My dog Pete was a constant companion in my girlhood. Pete, a big Gordon setter, and Tinkerbell, one of my cats, live again as characters in my book *Mystery at Deer Hill*. Into that book also went some of my girlhood camping experiences with my best friend.

"When I grew older, I spent most of my vacations in the Maine woods, where I had all kinds of wildlife from chipmunks to moose for neighbors. I thought of them as friends and wrote about many of them. The family den of the young mink who was the hero of my book *Patch* was quite close to our cabin and I witnessed many of the mink antics that go on in the book. My nature material is usually gathered firsthand, but I always back it up with sound book research in order to be very sure of my facts.

"My study of history finally concentrated on the history and lore of Eastern Woodland Indians. When I discovered what rich and interesting lives these First Americans led, I wanted to tell others about it. This ambition led to my biography of Uncas, the great sachem of the Mohegan, who lived in the Connecticut woodlands that I know so well. In his story I could combine Indian lore with nature lore and I can truly say that writing it was a labor of love. Uncas has been followed by several other books on Indians and Indian folklore.

"One of the nicest things that can happen to an author is to receive a letter from some reader telling her that her books have been enjoyed. One such letter came from a boy who wrote that he had just finished reading *Catamount*. Then he wrote 'WOW!' Just 'WOW!' I took this to mean that he liked the book, and needless to say, it made me feel very good."

HOBBIES AND OTHER INTERESTS: Gardening, nature study, book collecting.

Polar bears, walruses, and white arctic foxes stared in wonder at the red giant who had escaped the charmed grip of Old Man Winter. ■ (From *Close to the Rising Sun* by Virginia Frances Voight. Illustrated by Gordon Laite.)

In everything else Dad usually got Ben to obey him however long it took, and sometimes it took very long. Ben's size made you forget that he was still only a puppy eight months old.
■ (From *Big Ben* by David Walker. Illustrated by Victor Ambrus.)

WALKER, David Harry   1911-

PERSONAL: Born February 9, 1911, in Dundee, Scotland; son of Harry Giles and Elizabeth Bewley (Newsom) Walker; married Willa Magee, 1939; children: Allan Giles, Barclay James, David Clibborn, Julian Harry. *Education:* Attended Shrewsbury School, 1924-29, Royal Military College at Sandhurst, 1929-30. *Religion:* Presbyterian. *Home:* Strathcroix, St. Andrews, New Brunswick, Canada. *Agent:* Russell & Volkening, Inc., 551 Fifth Ave., New York, N.Y. 10017.

CAREER: British Army, the Black Watch, 1931-47; served in India, 1932-36, Sudan, 1936-38; aide-de-camp to Governor General of Canada, 1938-39; captured in France with Highland Division in 1940 and held prisoner of war until 1945; instructor at Staff College, Camberley, 1945-46; comptroller to Viceroy of India, 1946-47; retired with rank of major, 1947. Professional writer, 1947—. Canada Council, member, 1957-61. *Member:* Royal Society of Literature (fellow), Royal and Ancient Golf Club, St. Andrews (Scotland). *Awards, honors:* Member of the Order of the British Empire (military), 1946; D.Litt., University of New Brunswick; Governor General's prize, 1952, for *The Pillar*, and 1953, for *Digby*.

WRITINGS: The Storm and the Silence, 1949, *Geordie*, 1950, *The Pillar*, 1952, *Digby*, 1953, *Harry Black*, 1956, *Sandy was a Soldier's Boy*, 1957, *Where the High Winds Blow*, 1960, *Storms of Our Journey, and Other Stories*,

DAVID HARRY WALKER

"But I dinna' want to wear the kilt, Mum." He was an awful simple lump of clay in a woman's hands, was Geordie. ■ (From the movie *"Wee Geordie,"* copyright © 1956 by George K. Arthur-Times Film Corp.)

1962, *Winter of Madness*, 1964, *Mallabec*, 1965, *Come Back, Geordie*, 1966, *Cob-Intersec*, 1968, *The Lord's Pink Ocean*, 1972, *Black Dougal*, 1974 (all published by Houghton). Contributor to *Saturday Evening Post*, *Atlantic*, other magazines.

Books for young people: *Dragon Hill*, Houghton, 1962; *Big Ben*, Houghton, 1969; *Pirate Rock*, Houghton, 1969.

SIDELIGHTS: All of his books have been published in Canada and England and translated into twelve languages. *Geordie* was filmed with title "Wee Geordie," by George K. Arthur in 1956; *Harry Black* was made into film with title, "Harry Black and the Tiger," by Twentieth Century-Fox in 1958.

HOBBIES AND OTHER INTERESTS: Skiing, bird-watching.

WALKER, (Addison) Mort 1923-

PERSONAL: Born September 3, 1923, in El Dorado, Kan.; son of Robin A. (an architect) and Carolyn (a designer-illustrator; maiden name, Richards) Walker; married Jean Suffill, March 12, 1949; children: Greg, Brian, Polly, Morgan, Marjorie, Neal, Roger. *Education:* University of Missouri, B.A., 1948. *Residence:* Greenwich, Conn.

CAREER: Hallmark Greeting Cards, Kansas City, Mo., designer, 1942-43; Dell Publishing Co., New York, N.Y., editor, 1948-50; King Features Syndicate, New York, N.Y., creator of comic strips "Beetle Bailey," 1950—, "Hi and Lois," 1954—, "Sam's Strip," 1961-63, and "Boner's Ark," 1969—. Former member of President's Committee for Employing the Handicapped; has given public lectures. *Military service:* U.S. Army, 1943-46; served in Europe; became first lieutenant. *Member:* National Cartoonists Society (past president), Artists and Writers Association, Newspaper Comic Council, Museum of Cartoon Art (Greenwich, Conn.; president). *Awards, honors:* Reuben Award for best cartoonist, 1954; Banshee Award, 1955; best comic strip award from National Cartoonists Society, 1966, 1969; El Secolo XIX, 1972.

WRITINGS: *Beetle Bailey and Sarge* (cartoons), Dell, 1958; *Trixie* (cartoons), Avon, 1960; *Beetle Bailey* (cartoons), Grosset, 1968; *Fall Out Laughing, Beetle Bailey* (cartoons), Grosset, 1969; *At Ease, Beetle Bailey* (cartoons), Grosset, 1970; (with Dik Browne) *Hi and Lois* (cartoons), Grosset, 1970; *I Don't Want to Be Out Here Any*

It was a happy Booney who flew back over Lonely Lake that night with Tad dangling in the basket beneath the plane. For the first time he realized how much he loved him.

(From *The Land of Lost Things* by Mort Walker and Dik Browne. Illustrated by Dik Browne.)

More Than You Do, Beetle Bailey (cartoons), Grosset, 1970; *Most* (juvenile fiction; illustrated by Browne), Windmill Books, 1971; *What is it Now, Beetle Bailey?*, Grosset, 1971; *Beetle Bailey on Parade*, Grosset, 1972; *Land of Lost Things* (juvenile fiction; illustrated by Browne), Windmill Books, 1972; *We're All in the Same Boat, Beetle Bailey*, Grosset, 1973; *I'll Throw the Book at You, Beetle Bailey*, Grosset, 1974; *Shape Up and Ship Out, Beetle Bailey*, Grosset, 1974; *Take Ten, Beetle Bailey*, Grosset, 1975; *You're On My List, Beetle Bailey*, Grosset, 1975.

Work is widely anthologized in the United States and abroad. Contributor of cartoons to popular magazines, including *New Yorker* and *Saturday Evening Post*. Former editor of *National Cartoonists Society Album*.

SIDELIGHTS: "I try to make people laugh, and keep my own views out of it. People don't want ideas pressed on them. They get plenty of that on the editorial page. I wouldn't want a clown in a circus to deliver an ecology speech. I wouldn't want to find anti-war messages on my golf balls. The papers are full enough of tragedy. The comic pages should be a relief from that other stuff." Walker

began selling his cartoons at the age of twelve. "Beetle Bailey" now appears in some twelve hundred publications, including those of thirty-seven foreign countries.

FOR MORE INFORMATION SEE: Greenwich Review, October 12, 1972; *Christian Science Monitor*, May 2, 1973.

WAYNE, Kyra Petrovskaya 1918-
(Kyra Petrovskaya)

PERSONAL: Born December 31, 1918, in Crimea, Union of Soviet Socialist Republics; daughter of Prince Vassily S. (an Army colonel) and Zinaida (Von Haffenberg) Obolensky; married George J. Wayne (a doctor); children: Ronald George. *Education:* Leningrad Institute of Theatre Arts, M.A. *Politics:* Independent.

CAREER: Actress and singer in Soviet Union, performing with Leningrad Drama Theatre, Leningrad, 1939-41, with

MORT WALKER

Moscow Satire Theatre, Moscow, 1943-46, and in films. Since coming to the United States has appeared on television, as singer with own show, "An Interlude with Kyra," and as guest on other shows, including Jack Paar, Art Linkletter, and Mike Wallace programs; lecturer. Founder and president, Clean Air Program of Los Angeles County Lung Association, 1971-73. *Military service:* U.S.S.R. Red Army, 1941-43, sniper; became second lieutenant; received Red Star, Defence of Leningrad medal. *Member:* California Children's Theatre Association, South California Council on Literature for Children and Young Adults, Blue Ribbon 400 of the Music Center, International Platform Association, Academy of Television Arts and Sciences. *Awards, honors:* Medal for excellence in the theater, Moscow, 1946; Crusade for Freedom award, 1956; award of TB and Health Association, 1964-65, 1966, 1967, 1968, 1969, 1970; *Shurik* was nominated for the Dorothy Canfield Fisher Prize.

WRITINGS—under name Kyra Petrovskaya, unless otherwise noted: *Kyra*, Prentice-Hall, 1959; *Kyra's Secrets of Russian Cooking*, Prentice-Hall, 1961 (under title *Secrets of Russian Cooking*, Heinemann, 1962); *The Quest for the Golden Fleece* (juvenile), Lothrop, 1962; (under name Kyra Petrovskaya Wayne) *Shurik*, Grosset, 1970; (under name

But they stubbornly dragged their ship forward, day after day, until they lost all idea of time. Their feet and hands were bleeding, their lips were parched by thirst and heat, and their minds began to wander. ■ (From *The Quest for the Golden Fleece* by Kyra Petrovskaya. Illustrated by W. T. Mars.)

Kyra Wayne) *The Awakening*, Grosset, 1972. Contributor to *Grolier Encyclopedia, Ford Times*, and *This Week*.

WORK IN PROGRESS: Sequel to *Shurik: The Dogs of San Miguel.*

SIDELIGHTS: Because she was the daughter of Prince Vassily Obolensky, the author faced execution by a Red firing squad when she was less than a year old—but she and her mother were rescued by her father's former orderly, and traveled across Russia in a cattle car to safety. Raised under an assumed name by her impoverished mother and grandmother, the girl did not learn of her aristocratic origin until she was twenty years old.

At the age of eight, she won admission to a school for musically gifted children. One of a handful of talented students graduated from Leningrad's Institute of Theatrical Arts, she joined the Leningrad Drama Theatre at nineteen as one of the company's highest-paid principals, and within three years she was also being chosen for important film roles.

KYRA PETROVSKAYA WAYNE

Her screen career was interrupted by World War II.

214

Trained as a 'druzhinniza,' a field nurse, she served with entertainment units at the front lines, spent grueling months as a hospital worker, and endured the horrors of the siege of Leningrad. She was commissioned as a lieutenant in the infantry and was twice wounded in action. She received three medals for heroism.

In 1946, while playing at Moscow's renowned Satire Theater, she gave three command performances at the Kremlin, and became quite friendly with Vassily Stalin. It was only through his intervention that she was able to embark for the United States. Speaks Russian, French, Spanish, Italian, Bulgarian, and a little German.

FOR MORE INFORMATION SEE: Horn Book, February, 1971, December, 1972.

WEBER, Alfons 1921-

PERSONAL: Born July 26, 1921, in Zurich, Switzerland; son of Leo and Ida (Buergisser) Weber; married Margrit Ritschel, October 17, 1953; children: Elizabeth, Dagmar, Bernhard, Beda. *Education:* Studied at University of Zurich, University of Basel, and University of Vienna; University of Basel, M.D., 1949, advanced study in pediatrics and child psychiatry, 1949-58. *Politics:* None. *Religion:* Roman Catholic. *Home:* 1m Rotel Aga, 6300 Zug, Switzerland. *Office:* Children's Hospital, 8032 Zurich, Switzerland.

CAREER: Physician specializing in pediatrics, Zug, Switzerland, 1958-65; Children's Hospital, Zurich, Switzerland, chief of department of child psychiatry, 1965—; University of Zurich, Faculty of Medicine, Zurich, Switzerland, assistant professor of child psychiatry, 1970—. *Military service:* Swiss Army, Sanitary Troops, with rank of major. *Member:* Swiss Society for Paediatry, Swiss Society for Child Psychiatry, Swiss Society for Psychosomatic Medicine, International Society for Psycho-Endocrinology.

WRITINGS: Elisabeth wird gesund (juvenile), Ex Libris Verlag, 1969, published in America as *Elizabeth Gets Well*, Crowell, 1970, and in England as *Lisa Goes to Hospital*, Blackie & Son, 1970.

WORK IN PROGRESS: A textbook on child psychiatry;

Visiting hours were over much too soon, but Mother promised to come again. ■ (From *Elizabeth Gets Well* by Alfons Weber, M.D. Illustrated by Jacqueline Blass.)

ALFONS WEBER

research on the effects of television in childhood, on problems of hospitalization in childhood, and in psychoendocrinology.

SIDELIGHTS: "I am not a professional book writer. I have written a single book, *Elizabeth Goes to Hospital*, and it has been translated into English, Swedish, French, and the Romansh (the fourth language spoken in Switzerland). I conceived the idea of the book while working as a physician at the Children's Hospital in Zurich. Almost daily I witnessed the great anguish of children who had to enter hospital and had not been prepared for it. They lost their fear when I sat down on their beds and explained everything to them. Hence, I thought that if one explained it to them before they had to go to hospital they would be less scared. I carried the idea with me for several weeks and then sat down and wrote it all on a single Sunday. A mother of one of our chronically ill children illustrated it. She was very well acquainted with our hospital and knew what could happen in it. This is why she was able to depict everything to the last detail. The book was an immediate success.

"For seven years I practiced pediatrics in a small town situated in central Switzerland. In 1965 I took a position as chief child psychiatrist at the Children's Hospital in Zurich.

I am still living in Zug with my wife, my two boys and two girls. I spend most of my leisure time at home, reading, gardening, listening to music, to my wife and my children. A German sheep dog makes up the full crew; we hike a lot together in the mountains."

HOBBIES AND OTHER INTERESTS: Painting, literature.

FOR MORE INFORMATION SEE: Horn Book, February, 1971.

WEST, Barbara
See PRICE, Olive

WILLIAMS, Charles
See COLLIER, James Lincoln

WILLIAMS, Clyde C. 1881-
(Slim Williams)

PERSONAL: Born January 14, 1881, in Fresno, Calif.; son of Charles (a rancher) and Alverta (Bigelow) Williams; married Gladys Pennington (conductor of a travel agency). *Education:* Attended public grade schools in California. *Residence:* Chicago, Ill. *Mailing address:* The Redpath Bureau, Western Department, 1713 North Park St., Chicago, Ill. 60614.

CAREER: Spent a quarter century in Alaska, working as trader, trapper, prospector, farmer, and mail carrier; lecturer on Alaskan experiences, 1934-59. *Member:* Adventurers Club of Chicago.

WRITINGS: (Under name Slim Williams, with E. C. Foster) *The Friend of the Singing One* (juvenile), Atheneum, 1967; (with E. C. Foster) *The Long Hungry Night*, Atheneum, 1973.

SIDELIGHTS: "My grandparents left Virginia in 1844, crossed the plains and settled in Visalia, California in 1848. I was born in the foothills of the Sierra Nevada mountains on a little cattle range in Fresno, California in 1881. The first thing I remember was three little Indian kids coming to play with me from an Indian village three miles away. Later when I went to visit them, they knew I was coming and met me half way. This puzzled me and so I asked father how they knew I was coming and he answered, 'instinct like an animal.' Grandmother said instinct was something God took away from the white man for being mean to the Indians, putting them on a Reservation. Since I grew up I believe grandmother was half Indian and this may be the reason I am Indian to Indians and Eskimos from Mexico to Siberia. They all believe in reincarnation and that everything that lives has a spirit and everything but a white man has a dual spirit.

"When I was 18 I found a map of Alaska and two-thirds of it was marked unexplored. I wanted to know about nature and wild life more than anything else, so I headed for Alaska. An old Indian friend adopted me, taught me how to find my way, how to get directions by a light breeze and how to live with nature when I was alone in this wild country. Now if I have a dual spirit I don't know it, but the

CLYDE C. WILLIAMS

first Indian I met in Alaska, decided I was a 'States' Indian and I was a 'States' Indian while there to all Indians and Eskimos.

"I soon found I could trap and trade with the Indians or Eskimos, make enough for three months out of the year and have the rest of the year to myself. I chose the Eskimo for

he hadn't been spoiled by the white man. I liked to trap for it was a lesson in nature and my old Indian friend had taught me the secrets of the trapline, so I spent two or three months getting an outfit together. The Eskimos are the finest, kindest, and happiest people on earth to be with. No stealing, no lying, no divorces, and if an old couple was in need and their son supported them, he was a hero of the village.

"I'd trade in their village, then leave for the trading post not knowing when I would be back—if ever. The next winter I would decide to go to the same village, traveling miles and miles through wild country—no one knew I was coming. Yet when I came in sight of the village, most of them would be outside watching for me. I asked one of them how they knew. The answer was always the same: 'Little man talk and what little man no talk you just think.' So I was puzzled again. But now with two or three months hard work the rest of the time I would board my dogs with the Inn. I would take a .22 calibre rifle with me and a fish hook and head for some wild place. When I got hungry, I would catch a fish or shoot a rabbit or grouse and cook it on a stick. When tired, I would get under a spruce tree and sleep. If a storm came up, lightning won't strike a spruce tree. Sometimes I would build a log cabin and live three or four years and raise pets. I have had every type of Alaskan animal as a pet.

"Then off to some out of the way place to watch the wild things. I was the first man they had ever seen. In 1932, the waste and destruction of fish and wildlife was so bad I hooked up my dogs and drove from Alaska to Washington, D.C. to see President Roosevelt to get some protection. The trip took thirteen months, I spent 1933 and 1934 driving to the White House. Six times F.D.R. promised to give me funds but the delegate from Alaska said it would take an Act of Congress to make it work so I wound up the summer of '34 at the Century of Progress in Alaska.

"I met Gladys, my wife, and then signed up with Red Path Lecture Bureau and the next twenty years lectured in every state in the U.S., at the biggest universities to kindergartens. Then I got hit with a car, busted up, and had to exit. Gladys owns the Red Path Bureau now, so if I lecture I

Slim Williams, at Century of Progress in Alaska

won't have to pay a commission. I don't travel much. Met Bettie (E. C.) Foster by accident, got to talking about books and wound up writing them.''

FOR MORE INFORMATION SEE: Richard Morenus, *Alaska Sourdough: The Story of Slim Williams*, Rand McNally, 1956; *Chicago Sun-Times*, May 2, 1973.

WILLIAMS, Slim
See WILLIAMS, Clyde C.

WILSON, Beth P(ierre)

PERSONAL: Born in Tacoma, Wash.; daughter of Samuel Deal (a tailor) and Mae (Conna) Pierre; married William Douglas Wilson (a dentist); children: Diane M. Wilson Thomas. *Education:* University of Puget Sound, B.A.; graduate study at University of California, Los Angeles. *Residence:* Berkeley, Calif. 94707.

CAREER: Oakland Public Schools, Oakland, Calif., elementary teacher, 1936-44, elementary assistant, 1945-60. Member of Links, Inc. *Member:* National Association for the Advancement of Colored People, Alpha Kappa Alpha. *Awards, honors:* Senior citizens award, 1971, and Cate award from California Association of Teachers of English, 1972, both for *Martin Luther King, Jr.*; Delta Sigma Theta Award, 1975.

WRITINGS: Martin Luther King, Jr., Putnam, 1971; *Muhammed Ali*, Putnam, 1974; *The Great Minu*, Follett, 1974.

The woman just smiled and went on washing her clothes.
■ (From *The Great Minu* by Beth P. Wilson. Illustrated by Jerry Pinkney)

Something about the Author

BETH P. WILSON

SIDELIGHTS: "When a child, my sisters and brothers would join me in writing to our favorite aunt, who lived in another part of the state. She once told my father that she eagerly looked forward to receiving my letters because I painted such a clear picture. She always knew how everyone looked and what they were doing. I remember that this inspired me to write more and better letters.

"The author's responsibility to society is to write books, for children or adults, that will help various peoples to understand one another better and bring all people closer together. Most age restrictions on books should be lifted because many books for children are books for all ages."

Beth Wilson has travelled throughout Europe, Canada, Hawaii, Mexico, Scandinavia, and western Africa.

HOBBIES AND OTHER INTERESTS: Music, traveling, and community work.

FOR MORE INFORMATION SEE: The Post (Berkeley, Calif.), January 20, 1972.

WINTHROP, Elizabeth
  See MAHONY, Elizabeth Winthrop

WOLFE, Louis 1905-

PERSONAL: Born June 29, 1905, in Bound Brook, N.J.; son of William (a merchant) and Charlotte (Kasnetz) Wolfe; married, 1958 (wife, Adele, is a teacher). *Education:* Rutgers, The State University, B.Litt.; graduate work at Columbia University, New York University, New School for Social Research, College of City of New York, Colorado University. *Home and office:* 160 East 89th St., New York, N.Y. 10028.

CAREER: Teacher and radio broadcaster in New York, N.Y.; professional storyteller at camps, recreation centers, and on the air. Board of Education, New York, N.Y., editor, Bureau of Curriculum Research; G. P. Putnam's Sons, New York, N.Y., editor. *Member:* Authors Guild.

WRITINGS: Clear the Track, Lippincott, 1951; *Adventures on Horseback*, Dodd, 1952; *Indians Courageous*, Dodd, 1953; *Stories of Our American Past*, Globe, 1954; *Let's Go to a Planetarium*, Putnam, 1958; *Let's Go to a City Hall*, Putnam, 1958; *Let's Go to a Weather Station*, Putnam, 1959.

Probing the Atmosphere, Putnam, 1961; *Wonders of the*

LOUIS WOLFE

Atmosphere, Putnam, 1962; *Let's Go to the Louisiana Purchase*, Putnam, 1963; *The Deepest Hole in the World*, Putnam, 1963; *Let's Go with Paul Revere*, Putnam, 1964; *Let's Go on the Klondike Gold Rush*, Putnam, 1964; *Let's Go with Drake to Discover Oil*, Putnam, 1966; *United States History: A Simplified Outline*, American R.O.M. Corp., 1967; *Journey of the Oceanauts: Across the Bottom of the Atlantic Ocean on Foot*, Norton, 1968.

Ships That Explore the Deep, Putnam, 1971; *Aqua-Culture: Farming in Water*, Putnam, 1972. Contributor to *Reader's Digest, Woman's Home Companion, Coronet, Pageant, True, Children's Digest, Parade*, and other magazines; writer of radio scripts and of stories for comics.

SIDELIGHTS: Speaks French, some Italian.

HOBBIES AND OTHER INTERESTS: Fishing, golf, travel.

WORTH, Valerie 1933-

PERSONAL: Born October 29, 1933, in Philadelphia, Pa.; daughter of Charles Brooke (a biologist) and Merida (Grey) Worth; married George W. Bahlke (a professor of English literature), December 28, 1955; children: Conrad, Catherine, Margaret. *Education:* Swarthmore College, B.A., 1955. *Residence:* Clinton, N.Y.

CAREER: Poet. Yale University Press, New Haven, Conn., secretary/assistant in promotion department, 1956-58.

VALERIE WORTH

The watering can
Rusts among friends.
■ (From *Small Poems* by Valerie Worth. Illustrated by Natalie Babbitt.)

WRITINGS: The Crone's Book of Words, Llewellyn, 1971; *Small Poems*, Farrar, Straus, 1972. Work is anthologized in *New World Writing, No. 7*, New American Library, 1955, and *Best Poems of 1961-1963* (Borestone Mountain Poetry Awards, 1962-64), edited by Lionel Stevenson and others, three volumes, Pacific Books, 1962-64. Contributor of poems to *Harper's, Burning Deck*, and *Gnostica*.

WORK IN PROGRESS: A sequel to *Small Poems*; a prose fable for children; a volume of poems written between 1962 and 1975.

SIDELIGHTS: "That which changes slowly (the earth's crust, the stars, the diverse species of living things, those aspects of Man which are constant in his progress from embryo to bone to dust) has always seemed to me the stuff of poetry *par excellence*; perhaps because poetry itself does not change, once it is written, and therefore asks its concerns to be as durable as possible." Valerie Worth's many interests have provided subject matter for her poetry—astronomy, gardening, and witchcraft, among others.

WRIGHTSON, Patricia 1921-

PERSONAL: Born June 19. 1921, in Lismore, New South Wales, Australia; daughter of Charles Radcliff and Alice (Dyer) Furlonger; married, 1943 (divorced, 1953); children: Jennifer Mary (Mrs. Donald Ireland), Peter Radcliff. *Education:* Attended St. Catherine's College, 1932, and State Correspondence School, 1933-34. *Residence:* Turramurra, New South Wales, Australia. *Office:* Department of Education, Box 33, G.P.O., Sydney, New South Wales, Australia.

CAREER: Hospital administrator; *School Magazine*, Sydney, New South Wales, editor, 1970—. *Member:* Australian Society of Authors, Authors Guild of America. *Awards, honors:* Book of the year award from Australian Children's Book Council, 1956, for *The Crooked Snake*; Notable Books of the Year award from American Library

PATRICIA WRIGHTSON

Lindy climbed down into the shallow water, where, with muddy sand squishing between her toes, she found a small stone and began smashing and scraping at the oysters on the sides of the barge. ■ (From *The Feather Star* by Patricia Wrightson. Illustrated by Noela Young.)

Association, 1963, for *The Feather Star*; Spring Award from *Book World*, 1968, and Hans Christian Andersen Honors List, 1970, for *A Racecourse for Andy*; Book of the Year from Children's Book Council of Australia, 1974, for *The Nargun and the Stars*.

WRITINGS: The Crooked Snake, Angus & Robertson, 1955, Hutchinson, 1972; *The Bunyip Hole*, Angus & Robertson, 1957, Hutchinson, 1973; *The Rocks of Honey*, Angus & Robertson, 1960, Puffin Books, 1966; *The Feather Star*, Harcourt, 1962; *Down to Earth*, Harcourt, 1965; *I Own the Racecourse*, Hutchinson, 1968, published in the United States as *A Racecourse for Andy* (*Horn Book* Honor List), Harcourt, 1968; *An Older Kind of Magic*, Harcourt, 1972; *The Nargun and the Stars* (Margaret McElderry book), Atheneum, 1974.

SIDELIGHTS: "I was born at Lismore in New South Wales, the daughter of a country solicitor and the third of a family of six. I attended several state schools including the State Correspondence School for isolated children. I also spent a year as a boarder in a private school but couldn't take the homesickness. All of my schools supposed I was a potential writer, but my courage to attempt this diminished as my appreciation of literature increased. I only ventured on the attempt when I had two children of my own and realized that their lives would be rather arid if I really had nothing worth saying to children.

"Having spent some twenty years as a hospital administrator, I am now the editor of the New South Wales Department of Education's *School Magazine*, which has a monthly circulation of half a million."

FOR MORE INFORMATION SEE: Book World, May 5, 1968; *Books and Bookmen*, July, 1968; *National Observer*, July 1, 1968; *Young Readers' Review*, September, 1968; *School Librarian*, March, 1969; *Newsletter*, May, 1970; H. M. Saxby, *A History of Australian Children's Literature*, Volume 2, Wentworth Books, 1971; John Rowe Townsend, *A Sense of Story*, Lippincott, 1971; *Horn Book*, October, 1972, August, 1974; *Washington Post* "Children's Book World," November 5, 1972; *Author's Choice/2*, Crowell, 1974; *Children's Literature in Education/15*, APS Publications, 1974.

SOMETHING ABOUT THE AUTHOR

CUMULATIVE INDEXES, VOLUMES 1-8

Authors and Illustrators

ILLUSTRATIONS INDEX

(In the following index, the number of the volume in which an illustrator's work appears is given *before* the colon, and the page on which it appears is given *after* the colon. For example, a drawing by Adams, Adrienne appears in Volume 2 on page 6, and another drawing by her appears in Volume 3 on page 80.)

Aas, Ulf, *5:* 174
Abel, Raymond, *6:* 122; *7:* 195
Adams, Adrienne, *2:* 6; *3:* 80; *8:* 1
Adkins, Jan, *8:* 3
Aichinger, Helga, *4:* 5, 45
Akino, Fuku, *6:* 144
Alajalov, *2:* 226
Albright, Donn, *1:* 91
Alcorn, John, *3:* 159; *7:* 165
Alexander, Martha, *3:* 206
Aliki, *See* Brandenberg, Aliki
Aloise, Frank, *5:* 38
Ambrus, Victor G., *1:* 6-7, 194; *3:* 69; *5:* 15; *6:* 44; *7:* 36; *8:* 210
Ames, Lee J., *3:* 12
Amoss, Berthe, *5:* 5
Amundsen, Dick, *7:* 77
Amundsen, Richard E., *5:* 10
Anderson, Carl, *7:* 4
Anglund, Joan Walsh, *2:* 7, 250-251
Anno, Mitsumasa, *5:* 7
Antal, Andrew, *1:* 124
Appleyard, Dev, *2:* 192
Ardizzone, Edward, *1:* 11, 12; *2:* 105; *3:* 258; *4:* 78; *7:* 79
Armitage, Eileen, *4:* 16
Arno, Enrico, *1:* 217, *2:* 22, 210; *4:* 9; *5:* 43; *6:* 52
Aruego, Ariane, *6:* 4
   See also Dewey, Ariane
Aruego, Jose, *4:* 140; *6:* 4; *7:* 64
Asch, Frank, *5:* 9
Ashmead, Hal, *8:* 70
Austin, Robert, *3:* 44
Averill, Esther, *1:* 17
Axeman, Lois, *2:* 32

Babbitt, Natalie, *6:* 6; *8:* 220
Bacon, Bruce, *4:* 74

Bacon, Paul, *7:* 155; *8:* 121
Bacon, Peggy, *2:* 11, 228
Baker, Charlotte, *2:* 12
Bannon, Laura, *6:* 10
Barkley, James, *4:* 13; *6:* 11
Barnett, Moneta, *1:* 157; *3:* 86
Barron, John N., *3:* 261; *5:* 101
Barry, Katharina, *2:* 159; *4:* 22
Barry, Robert E., *6:* 12
Barth, Ernest Kurt, *2:* 172; *3:* 160; *8:* 26
Barton, Byron, *8:* 207
Bartsch, Jochen, *8:* 105
Bate, Norman, *5:* 16
Baum, Willi, *4:* 24-25; *7:* 173
Baynes, Pauline, *2:* 244; *3:* 149
Beckhof, Harry, *1:* 78; *5:* 163
Behrens, Hans, *5:* 97
Bell, Corydon, *3:* 20
Bendick, Jeanne, *2:* 24
Bennett, Susan, *5:* 55
Benton, Thomas Hart, *2:* 99
Berelson, Howard, *5:* 20
Berg, Joan, *1:* 115; *3:* 156; *6:* 26, 58
Berkowitz, Jeanette, *3:* 249
Bernadette, *See* Watts, Bernadette
Berry, Erick. *See* Best, Allena.
Berry, William A., *6:* 219
Berson, Harold, *2:* 17, 18; *4:* 28-29, 220
Best, Allena, *2:* 26
Bethers, Ray, *6:* 22
Bettina. *See* Ehrlich, Bettina
Biggers, John, *2:* 123
Bileck, Marvin, *3:* 102
Bimen, Levent, *5:* 179
Bird, Esther Brock, *1:* 36
Biro, Val, *1:* 26
Bjorklund, Lorence, *3:* 188, 252; *7:* 100
Blaisdell, Elinore, *1:* 121; *3:* 134

Blake, Quentin, *3:* 170
Blass, Jacqueline, *8:* 215
Blegvad, Erik, *2:* 59; *3:* 98; *5:* 117; *7:* 131
Bock, Vera, *1:* 187
Bock, William Sauts, *8:* 7
Bodecker, N. M., *8:* 13
Bolian, Polly, *3:* 270; *4:* 30
Bolognese, Don, *2:* 147, 231; *4:* 176; *7:* 146
Borten, Helen, *3:* 54; *5:* 24
Bozzo, Frank, *4:* 154
Bradford, Ron, *7:* 157
Bradley, William, *5:* 164
Brady, Irene, *4:* 31
Bramley, Peter, *4:* 3
Brandenberg, Aliki, *2:* 36-37
Bridwell, Norman, *4:* 37
Brock, Emma, *7:* 21
Bromhall, Winifred, *5:* 11
Brotman, Adolph E., *5:* 21
Brown, David, *7:* 47
Brown, Judith Gwyn, *1:* 45; *7:* 5; *8:* 167
Brown, Marcia, *7:* 30
Brown, Margery W., *5:* 32-33
Browne, Dik, *8:* 212
Browning, Coleen, *4:* 132
Brule, Al, *3:* 135
Bryson, Bernarda, *3:* 88, 146
Buck, Margaret Waring, *3:* 30
Buehr, Walter, *3:* 31
Bullen, Anne, *3:* 166, 167
Burchard, Peter, *3:* 197; *5:* 35; *6:* 158, 218
Burger, Carl, *3:* 33
Burn, Doris, *6:* 172
Burris, Burmah, *4:* 81
Burton, Virginia Lee, *2:* 43
Busoni, Rafaello, *1:* 186; *3:* 224; *6:* 126

Butterfield, Ned, *1:* 153
Byfield, Barbara Ninde, *8:* 18

Caddy, Alice, *6:* 41
Caraway, James, *3:* 200-201
Carle, Eric, *4:* 42
Carrick, Donald, *5:* 194
Carroll, Ruth, *7:* 41
Carty, Leo, *4:* 196; *7:* 163
Cary, *4:* 133
Cassel, Lili, *3:* 247
Cassels, Jean, *8:* 50
Castle, Jane, *4:* 80
Cather, Carolyn, *3:* 83
Cellini, Joseph, *2:* 73; *3:* 35
Chalmers, Mary, *3:* 145
Chambers, Mary, *4:* 188
Chapman, Frederick T., *6:* 27
Chappell, Warren, *3:* 172
Charlip, Remy, *4:* 48
Charlot, Jean, *1:* 137, 138; *8:* 23
Charmatz, Bill, *7:* 45
Chastain, Madye Lee, *4:* 50
Chen, Tony, *6:* 45
Chew, Ruth, *7:* 46
Cho, Shinta, *8:* 126
Chorao, Kay, *7:* 201; *8:* 25
Christensen, Gardell Dano, *1:* 57
Chute, Marchette, *1:* 59
Chwast, Jacqueline, *1:* 63; *2:* 275;
    6: 46
Chwast, Seymour, *3:* 128-129
Cirlin, Edgard, *2:* 168
Cleaver, Elizabeth, *8:* 204
Clevin, Jörgen, *7:* 50
CoConis, Ted, *4:* 41
Coerr, Eleanor, *1:* 64
Coggins, Jack, *2:* 69
Cohen, Alix, *7:* 53
Colby, C. B., *3:* 47
Cole, Olivia H. H., *1:* 134; *3:* 223
Connolly, Jerome P., *4:* 128
Cooke, Donald E., *2:* 77
Coombs, Patricia, *2:* 82; *3:* 52
Cooney, Barbara, *6:* 16, 50
Cooper, Marjorie, *7:* 112
Copelman, Evelyn, *8:* 61
Corcos, Lucille, *2:* 223
Corrigan, Barbara, *8:* 37
Cosgrove, Margaret, *3:* 100
Cox, Charles, *8:* 20
Crane, Alan H., *1:* 217
Credle, Ellis *1:* 69
Crowell, Pers, *3:* 125
Cruz, Ray, *6:* 55
Cuffari, Richard, *4:* 75; *5:* 98; *6:* 56;
    7: 13, 84, 153; *8:* 148, 155
Curry, John Steuart, *2:* 5

Darling, Lois, *3:* 59
Darling, Louis, *1:* 40-41; *2:* 63;
    3: 59
Dauber, Liz, *1:* 22; *3:* 266
Daugherty, James, *3:* 66; *8:* 178

d'Aulaire, Edgar, *5:* 51
d'Aulaire, Ingri, *5:* 51
de Angeli, Marguerite, *1:* 77
De Cuir, John F., *1:* 28-29
Delessert, Etienne, *7:* 140
Dennis, Wesley, *2:* 87; *3:* 111
de Paola, Tomie, *8:* 95
DeVille, Edward A., *4:* 235
Dewey, Ariane, *7:* 64
    See also Aruego, Ariane
Dick, John Henry, *8:* 181
Dillon, Corinne B., *1:* 139
Dillon, Diane, *4:* 104, 167; *6:* 23
Dillon, Leo, *4:* 104, 167; *6:* 23
Dines, Glen, *7:* 67
Dobrin, Arnold, *4:* 68
Dodd, Ed, *4:* 69
Dolson, Hildegarde, *5:* 57
Domanska, Janina, *6:* 67
Donahue, Vic, *2:* 93; *3:* 190
Donald, Elizabeth, *4:* 18
Doremus, Robert, *6:* 62
Dowd, Vic, *3:* 244
Dowden, Anne Ophelia, *7:* 70
Drummond, V. H., *6:* 70
du Bois, William Pene, *4:* 70
Duchesne, Janet, *6:* 162
Duke, Chris, *8:* 195
Dunnington, Tom, *3:* 36
Dutz, *6:* 59
Duvoisin, Roger, *2:* 95; *6:* 76;
    7: 197

Earle, Olive L., *7:* 75
Eaton, Tom, *4:* 62; *6:* 64
Edwards, Gunvor, *2:* 71
Eggenhofer, Nicholas, *2:* 81
Ehrlich, Bettina, *1:* 83
Eichenberg, Fritz, *1:* 79
Einzig, Susan, *3:* 77
Emberley, Ed, *8:* 53
Englebert, Victor, *8:* 54
Erhard, Walter, *1:* 152
Escourido, Joseph, *4:* 81
Estrada, Ric, *5:* 52, 146
Ets, Marie Hall, *2:* 102
Evans, Katherine, *5:* 64

Falls, C. B., *1:* 19
Faulkner, Jack, *6:* 169
Fava, Rita, *2:* 29
Fax, Elton C., *1:* 101; *4:* 2
Feelings, Tom, *5:* 22; *8:* 56
Feiffer, Jules, *3:* 91; *8:* 58
Fenton, Carroll Lane, *5:* 66
Fenton, Mildred Adams, *5:* 66
Fiorentino, Al, *3:* 240
Fisher, Leonard Everett, *3:* 6;
    4: 72, 86; *6:* 197
Fitschen, Marilyn, *2:* 20-21
Fitzhugh, Louise, *1:* 94
Flax, Zena, *2:* 245
Floethe, Richard, *3:* 131; *4:* 90

Floherty, John J., Jr., *5:* 68
Flora, James, *1:* 96
Floyd, Gareth, *1:* 74
Flynn, Barbara, *7:* 31
Foreman, Michael, *2:* 110-111
Fortnum, Peggy, *6:* 29
Foster, Genevieve, *2:* 112
Foster, Gerald, *7:* 78
Foster, Laura Louise, *6:* 79
Fox, Jim, *6:* 187
Frame, Paul, *2:* 45, 145
Frank, Lola Edick, *2:* 199
Frank, Mary, *4:* 54
Frasconi, Antonio, *6:* 80
Fraser, Betty, *2:* 212; *6:* 185; *8:* 103
Freeman, Don, *2:* 15
French, Fiona, *6:* 82
Fry, Guy, *2:* 224
Fry, Rosalie, *3:* 72
Fuchs, Erich, *6:* 84
Funk, Tom, *7:* 17, 7: 99

Galdone, Paul, *1:* 156, 181, 206;
    2: 40, 241; *3:* 42, 144; *4:* 141
Galster, Robert, *1:* 66
Gammell, Stephen, *7:* 48
Gannett, Ruth Chrisman, *3:* 74
Garnett, Eve, *3:* 75
Garraty, Gail, *4:* 142
Geary, Clifford N., *1:* 122
Geer, Charles, *1:* 91; *3:* 179; *4:* 201;
    6: 168; *7:* 96
Geisel, Theodor Seuss, *1:* 104-105,
    106
Genia, *4:* 84
George, Jean, *2:* 113
Gill, Margery, *4:* 57; *7:* 7
Giovanopoulos, Paul, *7:* 104
Githens, Elizabeth M., *5:* 47
Glanzman, Louis S., *2:* 177; *3:* 182
Glaser, Milton, *3:* 5; *5:* 156
Glattauer, Ned, *5:* 84
Gliewe, Unada, *3:* 78-79
Glovach, Linda, *7:* 105
Gobbato, Imero, *3:* 180-181; *6:* 213;
    7: 58
Goffstein, M. B., *8:* 71
Goldsborough, June, *5:* 154; *8:* 92
Goldstein, Leslie, *5:* 8; *6:* 60
Goldstein, Nathan, *1:* 175; *2:* 79
Goodall, John S., *4:* 92-93
Gordon, Margaret, *4:* 147; *5:* 48-49
Gorey, Edward, *1:* 60-61
Gorsline, Douglas, *1:* 98; *6:* 13
Gosner, Kenneth, *5:* 135
Gotlieb, Jules, *6:* 127
Gramatky, Hardie, *1:* 107
Gray, Reginald, *6:* 69
Green, Eileen, *6:* 97
Greenwald, Sheila, *1:* 34; *3:* 99;
    8: 72
Greiner, Robert, *6:* 86
Gretz, Susanna, *7:* 114
Gretzer, John, *1:* 54; *3:* 26; *4:* 162;
    7: 125

Grifalconi, Ann, *2:* 126; *3:* 248
Gringhuis, Dirk, *6:* 98
Gripe, Harald, *2:* 127
Grisha, *3:* 71
Groot, Lee de, *6:* 21
Guggenheim, Hans, *2:* 10; *3:* 37;
   8: 136

Hall, H. Tom, *1:* 227
Hamberger, John, *6:* 8; *8:* 32
Hamilton, Helen S., *2:* 238
Hammond, Elizabeth, *5:* 36, 203
Hampshire, Michael, *5:* 187; *7:* 110
Handville, Robert, *1:* 89
Hanley, Catherine, *8:* 161
Hanson, Joan, *8:* 76
Harlan, Jerry, *3:* 96
Harrington, Richard, *5:* 81
Harrison, Harry, *4:* 103
Hartshorn, Ruth, *5:* 115
Harvey, Gerry, *7:* 180
Hauman, Doris, *2:* 184
Hauman, George, *2:* 184
Hawkinson, John, *4:* 109; *7:* 83
Haydock, Robert, *4:* 95
Haywood, Carolyn, *1:* 112
Henneberger, Robert, *1:* 42; *2:* 237
Henry, Thomas, *5:* 102
Henstra, Friso, *8:* 80
Herrington, Roger, *3:* 161
Heyduck-Huth, Hilde, *8:* 82
Heyman, Ken, *8:* 33
Higginbottom, J. Winslow, *8:* 170
Hildebrandt, Greg, *8:* 191
Hildebrandt, Tim, *8:* 191
Himler, Ronald, *6:* 114; *7:* 162;
   8: 17, 84, 125
Hirsh, Marilyn, *7:* 126
Hoban, Lillian, *1:* 114
Hoberman, Norman, *5:* 82
Hodges, C. Walter, *2:* 139
Hofbauer, Imre, *2:* 162
Hogan, Inez, *2:* 141
Hogenbyl, Jan, *1:* 35
Hogner, Nils, *4:* 122
Hogrogian, Nonny, *3:* 221; *4:* 106-
   107; *5:* 166; *7:* 129
Holberg, Richard, *2:* 51
Holmes, Bea, *7:* 74
Holland, Marion, *6:* 116
Holmes, B., *3:* 82
Homar, Lorenzo, *6:* 2
Honigman, Marian, *3:* 2
Horder, Margaret, *2:* 108
Howe, Stephen, *1:* 232
Hughes, Shirley, *1:* 20, 21; *7:* 3
Hunt, James, *2:* 143
Hurd, Clement, *2:* 148, 149
Hustler, Tom, *6:* 105
Hutchinson, William M., *6:* 3, 138
Hyman, Trina Schart, *1:* 204;
   2: 194; *5:* 153; *6:* 106; *7:* 138,
   145; *8:* 22

Ilsley, Velma, *3:* 1; *7:* 55
Inga, *1:* 142
Ipcar, Dahlov, *1:* 124-125

Jacques, Robin, *1:* 70; *2:* 1; *8:* 46
James, Harold, *2:* 151; *3:* 62; *8:* 79
Janosch, *See* Eckert, Horst
Jansson, Tove, *3:* 90
Jaques, Faith, *7:* 11, 7: 132
Jauss, Anne Marie, *1:* 139; *3:* 34
Jefferson, Louise E., *4:* 160
Jeruchim, Simon, *6:* 173
John, Helen, *1:* 215
Johnson, Crockett, *See* Leisk,
   David
Johnson, Harper, *1:* 27; *2:* 33
Johnson, James Ralph, *1:* 23, 127
Johnson, Milton, *1:* 67; *2:* 71
Johnstone, Anne, *8:* 120
Johnstone, Janet Grahame, *8:* 120
Jones, Carol, *5:* 131
Jucker, Sita, *5:* 93
Jupo, Frank, *7:* 148

Kamen, Gloria, *1:* 41
Kaufmann, John, *1:* 174; *4:* 159;
   8: 43, 192
Kaye, Graham, *1:* 9
Keane, Bil, *4:* 135
Keats, Ezra Jack, *3:* 18, 105, 257
Keith, Eros, *4:* 98; *5:* 138
Kellogg, Steven, *8:* 96
Kennedy, Paul Edward, *6:* 190;
   8: 132
Kennedy, Richard, *3:* 93
Kent, Rockwell, *5:* 166; *6:* 129
Kessler, Leonard, *1:* 108; *7:* 139
Kettelkamp, Larry, *2:* 164
Key, Alexander, *8:* 99
Kiakshuk, *8:* 59
Kindred, Wendy, *7:* 151
Kirk, Ruth, *5:* 96
Knight, Hilary, *1:* 233; *3:* 21
Kocsis, J. C., *4:* 130
Koering, Ursula, *3:* 28; *4:* 14
Konigsburg, E. L., *4:* 138
Korach, Mimi, *1:* 128-129; *2:* 52;
   4: 39; *5:* 159
Koren, Edward, *5:* 100
Krahn, Fernando, *2:* 257
Kramer, Frank, *6:* 121
Kredel, Fritz, *6:* 35
Krush, Beth, *1:* 51, 85; *2:* 233;
   4: 115
Krush, Joe, *2:* 233; *4:* 115
Kubinyi, Laszlo, *4:* 116; *6:* 113
Kurelek, William, *8:* 107
Kuskin, Karla, *2:* 170

Laite, Gordon, *1:* 130-131; *8:* 209
Lambo, Don, *6:* 156
Lane, John R., *8:* 145

Langler, Nola, *8:* 110
Lantz, Paul, *1:* 82, 102
Larrea, Victoria de, *6:* 119, 204
Larsen, Suzanne, *1:* 13
Lasker, Joe, *7:* 187
Lattimore, Eleanor Frances, *7:* 156
Laune, Paul, *2:* 235
Lawson, Carol, *6:* 38
Lawson, Robert, *5:* 26; *6:* 94
Leacroft, Richard, *6:* 140; 7:
Lebenson, Richard, *6:* 209; *7:* 76
Le Cain, Errol, *6:* 141
Lee, Manning de V., *2:* 200
Lee, Robert J., *3:* 97
Lees, Harry, *6:* 112
Lehrman, Rosalie, *2:* 180
Leichman, Seymour, *5:* 107
Leisk, David, *1:* 140-141
Lenski, Lois, *1:* 144
Lent, Blair, *1:* 116-117; *2:* 174;
   3: 206-207; *7:* 168
Lewin, Ted, *4:* 77; *8:* 168
Liese, Charles, *4:* 222
Lilly, Charles, *8:* 73
Linell. *See* Smith, Linell
Lionni, Leo, *8:* 115
Lipinsky, Lino, *2:* 156
Lippman, Peter, *8:* 31
Lo, Koon-chiu, *7:* 134
Lobel, Anita, *6:* 87
Lobel, Arnold, *1:* 188-189; *5:* 12;
   6: 147; *7:* 167; *7:* 209
Loefgren, Ulf, *3:* 108
Lopshire, Robert, *6:* 149
Lorraine, Walter H., *3:* 110; *4:* 123
Lowrey, Jo, *8:* 133
Lubell, Winifred, *1:* 207; *3:* 15;
   6: 151
Luhrs, Henry, *7:* 123
Lupo, Dom, *4:* 204
Lyon, Elinor, *6:* 154
Lyons, Oren, *8:* 193

Maas, Dorothy, *6:* 175
Madden, Don, *3:* 112-113; *4:* 33,
   108, 155; *7:* 193
Maestro, Giulio, *8:* 124
Maitland, Antony, *1:* 100, 176;
   8: 41
Malvern, Corrine, *2:* 13
Manning, Samuel F., *5:* 75
Marino, Dorothy, *6:* 37
Mars, W. T., *1:* 161; *3:* 115; *4:* 208,
   225; *5:* 92, 105, 186; *8:* 214
Marsh, Christine, *3:* 164
Marshall, James, *6:* 160
Martin, Rene, *7:* 144
Martin, Stefan, *8:* 68
Martinez, John, *6:* 113
Matthews, F. Leslie, *4:* 216
Matulay, Laszlo, *5:* 18
Maxwell, John Alan, *1:* 148
Mayan, Earl, *7:* 193
Mayhew, Richard, *3:* 106

Mays, Victor, 5: 127; 8: 45, 153
McCann, Gerald, 3: 50; 4: 94; 7: 54
McClary, Nelson, 1: 111
McCloskey, Robert, 1: 184, 185;
    2: 186-187
McClung, Robert, 2: 189
McCrea, James, 3: 122
McCrea, Ruth, 3: 122
McCully, Emily, 2: 89; 4: 120-121,
    146, 197; 5: 2, 129; 7: 191
McDonald, Ralph J., 5: 123, 195
McGee, Barbara, 6: 165
McKay, Donald, 2: 118
McKie, Roy, 7: 44
McLachlan, Edward, 5: 89
Meyer, Renate, 6: 170
Micale, Albert, 2: 65
Middleton-Sandford, Betty, 2: 125
Miller, Marilyn, 1: 87
Miller, Shane, 5: 140
Mochi, Ugo, 8: 122
Mohr, Nicholasa, 8: 139
Montresor, Beni, 2: 91; 3: 138
Morrow, Gray, 2: 64; 5: 200
Morton, Marian, 3: 185
Murphy, Bill, 5: 138
Mutchler, Dwight, 1: 25

Navarra, Celeste Scala, 8: 142
Neebe, William, 7: 93
Negri, Rocco, 3: 213; 5: 67; 6: 91,
    108
Ness, Evaline, 1: 164-165; 2: 39;
    3: 8
Neville, Vera, 2: 182
Newberry, Clare Turlay, 1: 170
Niebrugge, Jane, 6: 118
Nielsen, Jon, 6: 100
Ninon, 1: 5
Noonan, Julia, 4: 163; 7: 207
Nordenskjold, Birgitta, 2: 208

Oakley, Graham, 8: 112
Obligado, Lilian, 2: 28, 66-67; 6: 30
Oechsli, Kelly, 5: 144-145; 7: 115;
    8: 83, 183
Ohlsson, Ib, 4: 152; 7: 57
Ohr, Judi, 7:
Olschewski, Alfred, 7: 172
Olsen, Ib Spang, 6: 178
Ono, Chiyo, 7: 97
Orbaan, Albert, 2: 31; 5: 65, 171
O'Sullivan, Tom, 3: 176; 4: 55
Oughton, Taylor, 5: 23
Owens, Carl, 2: 35
Oxenbury, Helen, 3: 150-151
Palazzo, Tony, 3: 152-153
Palladini, David, 4: 113
Palmer, Juliette, 6: 89
Panesis, Nicholas, 3: 127
Parker, Lewis, 2: 179
Parker, Robert, 4: 161; 5: 74
Parnall, Peter, 5: 137

Payne, Joan Balfour, 1: 118
Payson, Dale, 7: 34
Peet, Bill, 2: 203
Pendle, Alexy, 7: 159
Peppe, Rodney, 4: 164-165
Perl, Susan, 2: 98; 4: 231; 5: 44-45,
    118; 6: 199; 8: 137
Peterson, R. F., 7: 101
Peterson, Russell, 7: 130
Petie, Harris, 2: 3
Phillips, Douglas, 1: 19
Phillips, F. D., 6: 202
Pienkowski, Jan, 6: 183
Pincus, Harriet, 4: 186; 8: 179
Pinckney, Terry, 8: 218
Pinkwater, Manus, 8: 156
Pitz, Henry C., 4: 168
Politi, Leo, 1: 178; 4: 53
Polseno, Jo, 1: 53; 3: 117; 5: 114
Ponter, James, 5: 204
Poortvliet, Rien, 6: 212
Portal, Colette, 6: 186
Porter, George, 7: 181
Potter, Miriam Clark, 3: 162
Powers, Richard M., 1: 230; 3: 218;
    7: 194
Price, Christine, 2: 247; 3: 163, 253;
    8: 166
Price, Garrett, 1: 76; 2: 42
Prince, Leonora E., 7: 170
Pudlo, 8: 59
Purdy, Susan, 8: 162
Puskas, James, 5: 141
Pyk, Jan, 7: 26

Quackenbush, Robert, 4: 190;
    6: 166; 7: 175, 7: 178

Raible, Alton, 1: 202-203
Rand, Paul, 6: 188
Rappaport, Eva, 6: 190
Raskin, Ellen, 2: 208-209; 4: 142
Ravielli, Anthony, 1: 198; 3: 168
Ray, Deborah, 8: 164
Ray, Ralph, 2: 239; 5: 73
Relf, Douglas, 3: 63
Reschofsky, Jean, 7: 118
Rethi, Lili, 2: 153
Reusswig, William, 3: 267
Rey, H. A., 1: 182
Reynolds, Doris, 5: 71
Ribbons, Ian, 3: 10
Rice, Elizabeth, 2: 53, 214
Richardson, Ernest, 2: 144
Riger, Bob, 2: 166
Rios, Tere. See Versace, Marie
Ripper, Charles L., 3: 175
Roberts, Cliff, 4: 126
Roberts, Doreen, 4: 230
Robinson, Charles, 3: 53; 5: 14;
    6: 193; 7: 150; 7: 183; 8: 38
Robinson, Jerry, 3: 262
Robinson, Joan G., 7: 184
Rocker, Fermin, 7: 34

Rockwell, Anne, 5: 147
Rockwell, Gail, 7: 186
Rockwell, Norman, 7:
Roever, J. M., 4: 119
Rogers, Carol, 2: 262; 6: 164
Rojankovsky, Feodor, 6: 134, 136
Rose, Carl, 5: 62
Ross, Clare, 3: 123
Ross, John, 3: 123
Roth, Arnold, 4: 238
Rounds, Glen, 8: 173
Rud, Borghild, 6: 15
Ryden, Hope, 8: 176

Samson, Anne S., 2: 216
Sandin, Joan, 4: 36; 6: 194; 7: 177
Sapieha, Christine, 1: 180
Sargent, Robert, 2: 217
Saris, 1: 33
Savitt, Sam, 8: 66, 182
Scarry, Richard, 2: 220-221
Schindelman, Joseph, 1: 74; 4: 101
Schindler, Edith, 7: 22
Schlesinger, Bret, 7: 77
Schoenherr, John, 1: 146-147, 173;
    3: 39, 139
Schongut, Emanuel, 4: 102
Schramm, Ulrik, 2: 16
Schwartz, Charles, 8: 184
Schwartzberg, Joan, 3: 208
Schweitzer, Iris, 2: 137; 6: 207
Scott, Anita Walker, 7: 38
Sejima, Yoshimasa, 8: 187
Seltzer, Isadore, 6: 18
Sendak, Maurice, 1: 135, 190;
    3: 204; 7: 142
Seredy, Kate, 1: 192
Sergeant, John, 6: 74
Seuss, Dr. See Geisel, Theodor
Severin, John Powers, 7: 62
Sewell, Helen, 3: 186
Sharp, William, 6: 131
Shepard, Ernest H., 3: 193; 4: 74
Shepard, Mary, 4: 210
Sherwan, Earl, 3: 196
Shimin, Symeon, 1: 93; 2: 128-129;
    3: 202; 7: 85
Shortall, Leonard, 4: 144; 8: 196
Shulevitz, Uri, 3: 198-199
Sibley, Don, 1: 39
Siebel, Fritz, 3: 120
Sills, Joyce, 5: 199
Silverstein, Alvin, 8: 189
Silverstein, Virginia 8: 189
Simon, Eric M., 7: 82
Simon, Howard, 2: 175; 5: 132
Simont, Marc, 2: 119; 4: 213
Singer, Edith G., 2: 30
Slobodkin, Louis, 1: 200; 3: 232;
    5: 168
Slobodkina, Esphyr, 1: 201
Smalley, Janet, 1: 154
Smith, Alvin, 1: 31, 229
Smith, Edward J., 4: 224
Smith, Eunice Young, 5: 170

Smith, Linell Nash, *2:* 195
Smith, Ralph Crosby, *2:* 267
Smith, Robert D., *5:* 63
Smith, Virginia, *3:* 157
Smith, William A., *1:* 36
Sofia, *1:* 62; *5:* 90
Solbert, Ronni, *1:* 159; *2:* 232;
   5: 121; *6:* 34
Sorel, Edward, *4:* 61
Spanfeller, James, *1:* 72, 149; *2:* 183
Spier, Peter, *3:* 155; *4:* 200; *7:* 61
Spilka, Arnold, *5:* 120; *6:* 204;
   8: 131
Spivak, I. Howard, *8:* 10
Spring, Bob, *5:* 60
Spring, Ira, *5:* 60
Stahl, Ben, *5:* 181
Stanley, Diana, *3:* 45
Stein, Harve, *1:* 109
Steptoe, John, *8:* 197
Stewart, Charles, *2:* 205
Stobbs, William, *1:* 48-49; *3:* 68;
   6: 20
Stone, David K., *4:* 38; *6:* 124
Stone, Helen V., *6:* 209
Stubis, Talivaldis, *5:* 182, 183
Stuecklen, Karl W., *8:* 34, 65
Suba, Susanne, *4:* 202-203
Sugarman, Tracy, *3:* 76; *8:* 199
Summers, Leo, *1:* 177; *2:* 273
Sweet, Darryl, *1:* 163; *4:* 136
Szekeres, Cyndy, *2:* 218; *5:* 185;
   8: 85

Talarczyk, June, *4:* 173
Tallon, Robert, *2:* 228
Teason, James, *1:* 14
Tempest, Margaret, *3:* 237, 238
Thomson, Arline K., *3:* 264
Timmins, Harry, *2:* 171
Tolford, Joshua, *1:* 221
Tolkien, J. R. R., *2:* 243
Tomes, Jacqueline, *2:* 117
Tomes, Margot, *1:* 224; *2:* 120-121
Toothill, Harry, *6:* 54; *7:* 49
Toothill, Ilse, *6:* 54

Toschik, Larry, *6:* 102
Tripp, Wallace, *2:* 48; *7:* 28; *8:* 94
Troyer, Johannes, *3:* 16; *7:* 18
Tsinajinie, Andy, *2:* 62
Tudor, Bethany, *7:* 103
Tunis, Edwin, *1:* 218-219
Turkle, Brinton, *1:* 211, 213; *2:* 249;
   3: 226
Tusan, Stan, *6:* 58

Uchida, Yoshiko, *1:* 220
Unada. *See* Gliewe, Unada
Ungerer, Tomi, *5:* 188
Unwin, Nora S., *3:* 65, 234-235;
   4: 237
Utz, Lois, *5:* 190

Van Stockum, Hilda, *5:* 193
Vasiliu, Mircea, *2:* 255
Vavra, Robert, *8:* 206
Verrier, Suzanne, *5:* 20
Versace, Marie, *2:* 255
Viereck, Ellen, *3:* 242
Vilato, Gaspar E., *5:* 41
von Schmidt, Eric, *8:* 62
Vosburgh, Leonard, *1:* 161; *7:* 32

Wagner, John, *8:* 200
Wagner, Ken, *2:* 59
Walker, Charles, *1:* 46; *4:* 59; *5:* 177
Walker, Gil, *8:* 49
Walker, Mort, *8:* 213
Waltrip, Mildred, *3:* 209
Ward, Keith, *2:* 107
Ward, Lynd, *1:* 99, 132, 133, 150;
   2: 108, 158, 196, 259
Warren, Betsy, *2:* 101
Watkins-Pitchford, D. J.,
   6: 215, 217
Watson, Aldren, *2:* 267; *5:* 94
Watson, Wendy, *5:* 197
Watts, Bernadette, *4:* 227

Webber, Helen, *3:* 141
Weihs, Erika, *4:* 21
Weil, Lisl, *7:* 203
Weisgard, Leonard, *1:* 65; *2:* 191,
   197, 204, 264-265; *5:* 108
Weiss, Emil, *1:* 168; *7:* 60
Weiss, Harvey, *1:* 145, 223
Wells, Frances, *1:* 183
Wells, Rosemary, *6:* 49
Werth, Kurt, *7:* 122
Wetherbee, Margaret, *5:* 3
White, David Omar, *5:* 56
Whithorne, H. S., *7:* 49
Whitney, George Gillett, *3:* 24
Wiese, Kurt, *3:* 255; *4:* 206
Wiesner, William, *4:* 100; *5:* 200,
   201
Wiggins, George, *6:* 133
Wikland, Ilon, *5:* 113; *8:* 150
Wilde, George, *7:* 139
Wilkinson, Gerald, *3:* 40
Williams, Garth, *1:* 197; *2:* 49, 270;
   4: 205
Wilson, Edward A., *6:* 24
Wiseman, B., *4:* 233
Wishnefsky, Phillip, *3:* 14
Wiskur, Darrell, *5:* 72
Wondriska, William, *6:* 220
Wonsetler, John C., *5:* 168
Wood, Myron, *6:* 220
Wood, Ruth, *8:* 11
Worboys, Evelyn, *1:* 166-167
Worth, Wendy, *4:* 133

Yang, Jay, *1:* 8
Yap, Weda, *6:* 176
Young, Ed, *7:* 205
Young, Noela, *8:* 221

Zalben, Jane Breskin, *7:* 211
Zallinger, Jean, *4:* 192; *8:* 8, 129
Zallinger, Rudolph F., *3:* 245
Zemach, Margot, *3:* 270; *8:* 201

AUTHORS INDEX

(In the following index, the number of the volume in which an author's sketch appears is given *before* the colon, and the page on which it appears is given *after* the colon. For example, the sketch of Aardema, Verna, appears in Volume 4 on page 1).

Aardema, Verna, *4:* 1
Abbott, Alice. *See* Speicher, Helen Ross (Smith), *8:* 194
Abernethy, Robert G., *5:* 1
Abrahams, Robert David, *4:* 3
Adams, Adrienne, *8:* 1
Adams, Harriet S(tratemeyer), *1:* 1
Adams, Hazard, *6:* 1
Adams, Richard, *7:* 1
Adelberg, Doris, *See* Orgel, Doris, *7:* 173
Adkins, Jan, *8:* 2
Adler, Irving, *1:* 2
Adler, Ruth, *1:* 4
Adoff, Arnold, *5:* 1
Adshead, Gladys L., *3:* 1
Agle, Nan Hayden, *3:* 2
Aichinger, Helga, *4:* 4
Aiken, Conrad, *3:* 3
Aiken, Joan, *2:* 1
Ainsworth, Ruth, *7:* 1
Alderman, Clifford Lindsey, *3:* 6
Aldis, Dorothy (Keeley), *2:* 2
Aldon, Adair. *See* Meigs, Cornelia, *6:* 167
Alegria, Ricardo E., *6:* 1
Alexander, Anna Cooke, *1:* 4
Alexander, Frances, *4:* 6
Alexander, Linda, *2:* 3
Alexander, Lloyd, *3:* 7
Aliki. *See* Brandenberg, Aliki, *2:* 36
Allan, Mabel Esther, *5:* 2
Allen, Adam [Joint pseudonym]. *See* Epstein, Beryl and Samuel, *1:* 85
Allen, Allyn. *See* Eberle, Irmengarde, *2:* 97
Allen, Betsy. *See* Cavanna, Betty, *1:* 52

Almedingen, Martha Edith von. *See* Almedingen, E. M., *3:* 9
Almedingen, E. M., *3:* 9
Alsop, Mary O'Hara, *2:* 4
Ambrus, Victor G(tozo), *1:* 6
Amerman, Lockhart, *3:* 11
Ames, Lee J., *3:* 11
Amoss, Berthe, *5:* 4
Anckarsvard, Karin, *6:* 2
Anderson, Joy, *1:* 8
Anderson, (John) Lonzo, *2:* 6
Anderson, Mary, *7:* 4
Andrews, J(ames) S(ydney), *4:* 7
Andrews, Julie, *7:* 6
Anglund, Joan Walsh, *2:* 7
Angrist, Stanley W(olff), *4:* 9
Annixter, Jane. *See* Sturtzel, Jane Levington, *1:* 212
Annixter, Paul. *See* Sturtzel, Howard A., *1:* 210
Anno, Mitsumasa, *5:* 6
Anrooy, Frans van. *See* Van Anrooy, Francine, *2:* 252
Anthony, C. L. *See* Smith, Dodie, *4:* 194
Appleton, Victor [Collective pseudonym], *1:* 9
Appleton, Victor II [Collective pseudonym], *1:* 9
Arbuthnot, May Hill, *2:* 9
Archer, Jules, *4:* 9
Archibald, Joseph S. *3:* 12
Arden, Barbie. *See* Stoutenburg, Adrien, *3:* 217
Ardizzone, Edward, *1:* 10
Armstrong, William H., *4:* 11
Arnold, Elliott, *5:* 7
Arnold, Oren, *4:* 13
Arora, Shirley (Lease), *2:* 10
Arquette, Lois S(teinmetz), *1:* 13
Arthur, Ruth M., *7:* 6

Aruego, Ariane. *See* Dewey, Ariane, *7:* 63
Aruego, Jose, *6:* 3
Arundel, Honor, *4:* 15
Asch, Frank, *5:* 9
Ashabranner, Brent (Kenneth), *1:* 14
Asimov, Isaac, *1:* 15
Asinof, Eliot, *6:* 5
Atkinson, M. E. *See* Frankau, Mary Evelyn, *4:* 90
Atwood, Ann, *7:* 8
Austin, Elizabeth S., *5:* 10
Austin, Oliver L. Jr., *7:* 10
Averill, Esther, *1:* 16
Avery, Al. *See* Montgomery, Rutherford, *3:* 134
Avery, Gillian, *7:* 10
Avery, Kay, *5:* 11
Ayars, James S(terling), *4:* 17
Aylesworth, Thomas G(ibbons), *4:* 18

Baastad, Babbis Friis. *See* Friis-Baastad, Babbis, *7:* 95
Babbis, Eleanor. *See* Friis-Baastad, Babbis, *7:* 95
Babbitt, Natalie, *6:* 6
Bacon, Elizabeth, *3:* 14
Bacon, Margaret Hope, *6:* 7
Bacon, Peggy, *2:* 11
Bagnold, Enid, *1:* 17
Bailey, Matilda. *See* Radford, Ruby L., *6:* 186
Baity, Elizabeth Chesley, *1:* 18
Baker, Augusta, *3:* 16
Baker, Betty (Lou), *5:* 12

Baker, Charlotte, 2: 12
Baker, Elizabeth, 7: 12
Baker, Jeffrey J(ohn) W(heeler), 5: 13
Baker, Laura Nelson, 3: 17
Baker, Margaret, 4: 19
Baker, (Robert) Michael, 4: 20
Baker, Rachel, 2: 13
Balch, Glenn, 3: 18
Balducci, Carolyn Feleppa, 5: 13
Baldwin, Anne Norris, 5: 14
Ball, Zachary. See Masters, Kelly R., 3: 118
Ballard, (Charles) Martin, 1: 19
Balogh, Penelope, 1: 20
Bancroft, Griffing, 6: 8
Bannon, Laura, 6: 9
Barker, Albert W., 8: 3
Barker, Will, 8: 4
Barkley, James, 6: 12
Barnum, Richard [Collective pseudonym], 1: 20
Barr, George, 2: 14
Barry, Katharina (Watjen), 4: 22
Barry, Robert, 6: 12
Barth, Edna, 7: 13
Barthelme, Donald, 7: 14
Bartlett, Philip A. [Collective pseudonym], 1: 21
Barton, May Hollis [Collective pseudonym], 1: 21
Bartos-Hoeppner, Barbara, 5: 15
Bashevis, Isaac. See Singer, Isaac Bashevis, 3: 203
Bate, Norman, 5: 15
Batten, Mary, 5: 17
Battles, Edith, 7: 15
Baudouy, Michel-Aime, 7: 18
Bauer, Helen, 2: 14
Baum, Willi, 4: 23
Baumann, Hans, 2: 16
Bawden, Nina. See Kark, Nina Mary, 4: 132
BB. See Watkins-Pitchford, D. J., 6: 214
Beach, Charles Amory [Collective pseudonym], 1: 21
Bealer, Alex W(inkler III), 8: 6
Beatty, Hetty Burlingame, 5: 18
Beatty, Jerome, Jr., 5: 19
Beatty, John (Louis), 6: 13
Beatty, Patricia (Robbins), 1: 21
Bechtel, Louise Seaman, 4: 26
Beckman, Gunnel, 6: 14
Bedford, A. N. See Watson, Jane Werner, 3: 244
Bedford, Annie North. See Watson, Jane Werner, 3: 244
Beebe, B(urdetta) F(aye), 1: 23
Beech, Webb. See Butterworth, W. E., 5: 40
Behn, Harry, 2: 17
Behnke, Frances L., 8: 7
Bell, Corydon, 3: 19
Bell, Gina. See Iannone, Jeanne, 7: 139

Bell, Margaret E(lizabeth), 2: 19
Bell, Thelma Harrington, 3: 20
Bellairs, John, 2: 20
Bell-Zano, Gina, See Iannone, Jeanne, 7: 139
Belting, Natalie Maree, 6: 16
Belvedere, Lee. See Grayland, Valerie, 7: 111
Benary, Margot. See Benary-Isbert, Margot, 2: 21
Benary-Isbert, Margot, 2: 21
Benasutti, Marion, 6: 18
Benchley, Nathaniel, 3: 21
Benchley, Peter, 3: 22
Bendick, Jeanne, 2: 23
Benedict, Rex, 8: 8
Benet, Laura, 3: 23
Benson, Sally, 1: 24
Bentley, Phyllis Eleanor, 6: 19
Berelson, Howard, 5: 20
Berg, Jean Horton, 6: 21
Berger, Melvin H., 5: 21
Berger, Terry, 8: 10
Bernadette. See Watts, Bernadette, 4: 226
Bernard, Jacqueline (de Sieyes), 8: 11
Berrien, Edith Heal. See Heal, Edith, 7: 123
Berrington, John. See Brownjohn, Alan, 6: 38
Berry, B. J. See Berry, Barbara, J., 7: 19
Berry, Barbara J., 7: 19
Berry, Erick. See Best, Allena Champlin, 2: 25
Berson, Harold, 4: 27
Best, (Evangel) Allena Champlin, 2: 25
Best, (Oswald) Herbert, 2: 27
Bethell, Jean (Frankenberry), 8: 11
Bethers, Ray, 6: 22
Bettina. See Ehrlich, Bettina, 1: 82
Bialk, Elisa, 1: 25
Bierhorst, John, 6: 23
Biro, Val, 1: 26
Bishop, Curtis, 6: 24
Bisset, Donald, 7: 20
Bixby, William, 6: 24
Black, Irma S(imonton), 2: 28
Blaine, John. See Harkins, Philip, 6: 102
Blake, Walter E. See Butterworth, W. E., 5: 40
Blassingame, Wyatt (Rainey), 1: 27
Bleeker, Sonia, 2: 30
Blishen, Edward, 8: 12
Bliven, Bruce Jr., 2: 31
Bloch, Marie Halun, 6: 25
Blough, Glenn O(rlando), 1: 28
Blue, Rose, 5: 22
Blume, Judy (Sussman), 2: 31
Boardman, Fon Wyman, Jr., 6: 26
Bobbe, Dorothie, 1: 30
Bodecker, N. M., 8: 12
Boggs, Ralph Steele, 7: 21

Bolian, Polly, 4: 29
Bolliger, Max, 7: 22
Bolton, Carole, 6: 27
Bond, Michael, 6: 28
Bonham, Barbara, 7: 22
Bonham, Frank, 1: 30
Bontemps, Arna, 2: 32
Boone, Pat, 7: 23
Borland, Hal, 5: 22
Borland, Harold Glen, See Borland, Hal, 5: 22
Borten, Helen Jacobson, 5: 24
Borton, Elizabeth. See Trevino, Elizabeth B. de, 1: 216
Bothwell, Jean, 2: 34
Bova, Ben, 6: 29
Bowen, Catherine Drinker, 7: 24
Bradbury, Bianca, 3: 25
Brady, Irene, 4: 30
Bragdon, Elspeth, 6: 30
Brandenberg, Aliki Liacouras, 2: 36
Brandenberg, Franz, 8: 14
Brandon, Curt. See Bishop, Curtis, 6: 24
Branley, Franklyn M(ansfield), 4: 32
Bratton, Helen, 4: 34
Braymer, Marjorie, 6: 31
Brecht, Edith, 6: 32
Breck, Vivian, See Breckenfeld, Vivian Gurney, 1: 33
Breckenfeld, Vivian Gurney, 1: 33
Brennan, Joseph, 6: 33
Brenner, Barbara (Johnes), 4: 34
Brewster, Benjamin. See Folsom, Franklin Brewster, 5: 67
Brewton, John E(dmund), 5: 25
Bridges, William (Andrew) 5: 27
Bridwell, Norman, 4: 36
Brier, Howard M(axwell), 8: 15
Brindel, June Rachuy, 7: 25
Brink, Carol Ryrie 1: 34
Britt, Dell, 1: 35
Brock, Betty, 7: 27
Brock, Emma L(illian), 8: 15
Broderick, Dorothy M., 5: 28
Bronson, Lynn. See Lampman, Evelyn Sibley, 4: 140
Brooks, Anita, 5: 28
Brooks, Gwendolyn, 6: 33
Brooks, Lester, 7: 28
Broun, Emily. See Sterne, Emma Gelders, 6: 205
Brower, Millicent, 8: 16
Browin, Frances Williams, 5: 30
Brown, Bill. See Brown, William L., 5: 34
Brown, Dee (Alexander), 5: 30
Brown, Eleanor Frances, 3: 26
Brown, Irene Bennett, 3: 27
Brown, Ivor, 5: 31
Brown, Marcia, 7: 29
Brown, Margery, 5: 31
Brown, Marion Marsh, 6: 35
Brown, Myra Berry, 6: 36
Brown, Pamela, 5: 33

Brown, William L(ouis), 5: 34
Brownjohn, Alan, 6: 38
Bruce, Mary, 1: 36
Buchwald, Emilie, 7: 31
Buck, Margaret Waring, 3: 29
Buck, Pearl S(ydenstricker), 1: 36
Buckeridge, Anthony, 6: 38
Buckley, Helen E(lizabeth), 2: 38
Buckmaster, Henrietta, 6: 39
Budd, Lillian, 7: 33
Buehr, Walter, 3: 30
Bulla, Clyde Robert, 2: 39
Burch, Robert J(oseph), 1: 38
Burchard, Peter D(uncan), 5: 34
Burchardt, Nellie, 7: 33
Burford, Eleanor. See Hibbert,
　　Eleanor, 2: 134
Burgess, Robert F(orrest), 4: 38
Burgwyn, Mebane H., 7: 34
Burland, C. A. See Burland, Cottie
　　A., 5: 36
Burland, Cottie A., 5: 36
Burlingame, (William) Roger, 2: 40
Burman, Ben Lucien, 6: 40
Burn, Doris, 1: 39
Burnford, S. D. See Burnford,
　　Sheila, 3: 32
Burnford, Sheila, 3: 32
Burns, Paul C., 5: 37
Burns, William A., 5: 38
Burroughs, Polly, 2: 41
Burt, Olive Woolley, 4: 39
Burton, Hester, 7: 35
Burton, Virginia Lee, 2: 42
Butler, Beverly, 7: 37
Butters, Dorothy Gilman, 5: 39
Butterworth, Oliver, 1: 40
Butterworth, W(illiam) E(dmund
　　III), 5: 40
Byars, Betsy, 4: 40
Byfield, Barbara Ninde, 8: 19

Cadwallader, Sharon, 7: 38
Cain, Arthur H., 3: 33
Cain, Christopher. See Fleming,
　　Thomas J(ames), 8: 19
Caldwell, John Cope, 7: 38
Calhoun, Mary (Huiskamp), 2: 44
Call, Hughie Florence, 1: 41
Cameron, Edna M., 3: 34
Cameron, Eleanor (Butler), 1: 42
Cameron, Polly, 2: 45
Campbell, Bruce. See Epstein,
　　Samuel, 1: 87
Campbell, R. W. See Campbell,
　　Rosemae Wells, 1: 44
Campbell, Rosemae Wells, 1: 44
Carbonnier, Jeanne, 3: 34
Carey, Ernestine Gilbreth, 2: 45
Carle, Eric, 4: 41
Carlisle, Clark, Jr. See Holding,
　　James, 3: 85
Carlsen, Ruth C(hristoffer), 2: 47
Carlson, Bernice Wells, 8: 19

Carlson, Dale Bick, 1: 44
Carlson, Natalie Savage, 2: 48
Carol, Bill J. See Knott, William
　　Cecil, Jr., 3: 94
Carpelan, Bo (Gustaf Bertelsson),
　　8: 20
Carpenter, Allan, 3: 35
Carpenter, Frances, 3: 36
Carr, Harriett Helen, 3: 37
Carr, Mary Jane, 2: 50
Carrick, Carol, 7: 39
Carrick, Donald, 7: 40
Carroll, Curt, See Bishop, Curtis,
　　6: 24
Carroll, Latrobe, 7: 40
Carse, Robert, 5: 41
Carson, John F., 1: 46
Carter, Dorothy Sharp, 8: 21
Carter, (William) Hodding, 2: 51
Carter, Katharine J(ones), 2: 52
Carter, Phyllis Ann. See Eberle,
　　Irmengarde, 2: 97
Carter, William E., 1: 47
Case, Michael. See Howard,
　　Robert West, 5: 85
Casewit, Curtis, 4: 43
Cass, Joan E(velyn), 1: 47
Castillo, Edmund L., 1: 50
Catherall, Arthur, 3: 38
Catton, (Charles) Bruce, 2: 54
Caudill, Rebecca, 1: 50
Causley, Charles, 3: 39
Cavallo, Diane, 7: 43
Cavanah, Frances, 1: 52
Cavanna, Betty, 1: 54
Cerf, Bennett, 7: 43
Cerf, Christopher (Bennett), 2: 55
Cetin, Frank (Stanley), 2: 55
Chadwick, Lester [Collective
　　pseudonym], 1: 55
Chaffee, Allen, 3: 41
Chaffin, Lillie D(orton), 4: 44
Chalmers, Mary, 6: 41
Chambers, Aidan, 1: 55
Chambers, Margaret Ada
　　Eastwood, 2: 56
Chambers, Peggy. See Chambers,
　　Margaret, 2: 56
Chandler, Ruth Forbes, 2: 56
Channel, A. R. See Catherall,
　　Arthur, 3: 38
Chapman, Allen [Collective
　　pseudonym], 1: 55
Chappell, Warren, 6: 42
Charlip, Remy, 4: 46
Charlot, Jean, 8: 22
Charmatz, Bill, 7: 45
Charosh, Mannis, 5: 42
Chase, Alice. See McHargue,
　　Georgess, 4: 152
Chastain, Madye Lee, 4: 48
Chauncy, Nan, 6: 43
Chaundler, Christine, 1: 56
Chen, Tony, 6: 44
Chenault, Nell. See Smith, Linell
　　Nash, 2: 227

Cheney, Cora, 3: 41
Cherryholmes, Anne, See Price,
　　Olive, 8: 157
Chetin, Helen, 6: 46
Chew, Ruth, 7: 45
Chidsey, Donald Barr, 3: 42
Childress, Alice, 7: 46
Childs, (Halla) Fay (Cochrane),
　　1: 54
Chimaera, See Farjeon, Eleanor,
　　2: 103
Chipperfield, Joseph E(ugene),
　　2: 57
Chittum, Ida, 7: 47
Chorao, (Ann Mc)Kay (Sproat),
　　8: 24
Christensen, Gardell Dano, 1: 57
Christopher, Matt(hew F.), 2: 58
Chukovsky, Kornei (Ivanovich),
　　5: 43
Church, Richard, 3: 43
Chute, B(eatrice) J(oy), 2: 59
Chute, Marchette (Gaylord), 1: 58
Chwast, Jacqueline, 6: 46
Ciardi, John (Anthony), 1: 59
Clapp, Patricia, 4: 50
Clare, Helen, See Hunter Blair,
　　Pauline, 3: 87
Clark, Ann Nolan, 4: 51
Clark, Margaret Goff, 8: 26
Clark, Mavis Thorpe, 8: 27
Clark, Ronald William, 2: 60
Clark, Van D(eusen), 2: 61
Clark, Walter Van Tilburg, 8: 28
Clarke, Clorinda, 7: 48
Clarke, John. See Laklan, Carli,
　　5: 100
Clarke, Mary Stetson, 5: 46
Clarke, Michael. See Newlon,
　　Clark, 6: 174
Clarke, Pauline. See Hunter Blair,
　　Pauline, 3: 87
Clarke, Virginia. See Gray,
　　Patricia, 7: 110
Cleary, Beverly (Bunn), 2: 62
Cleaver, Carol, 6: 48
Cleland, Mabel. See Widdemer,
　　Mabel Cleland, 5: 200
Cleven, Cathrine. See Cleven,
　　Kathryn Seward, 2: 64
Cleven, Kathryn Seward, 2: 64
Clevin, Jöergen, 7: 49
Clewes, Dorothy (Mary), 1: 61
Clifford, Eth. See Rosenberg,
　　Ethel, 3: 176
Clifford, Margaret Cort, 1: 63
Clifford, Peggy. See Clifford,
　　Margaret Cort, 1: 63
Coates, Belle, 2: 64
Coatsworth, Elizabeth, 2: 65
Cobb, Vicki, 8: 31
Cober, Alan E., 7: 51
Cocagnac, Augustin, 7: 52
Cockett, Mary, 3: 45

Coe, Douglas [Joint pseudonym]. *See* Epstein, Beryl and Samuel, *1:* 87
Coerr, Eleanor, *1:* 64
Coffin, Geoffrey. *See* Mason, F. van Wyck, *3:* 117
Coffman, Ramon Peyton (Uncle Ray), *4:* 53
Coggins, Jack (Banham), *2:* 68
Cohen, Daniel, *8:* 31
Cohen, Joan Lebold, *4:* 53
Cohen, Peter Zachary, *4:* 54
Cohen, Robert Carl, *8:* 33
Coit, Margaret L(ouise), *2:* 70
Colby, C. B., *3.* 46
Cole, Davis, *See* Elting, Mary, *2:* 100
Collier, James Lincoln, *8:* 33
Collins, David, *7:* 52
Colman, Hila, *1:* 65
Colonius, Lillian, *3:* 48
Colt, Martin. *See* Epstein, Samuel, *1:* 87
Colver, Anne, *7:* 54
Colwell, Eileen (Hilda), *2:* 71
Comfort, Jane Levington. *See* Sturtzel, Jane Levington, *1:* 212
Comfort, Mildren Houghton, *3:* 48
Cone, Molly (Lamken), *1:* 66
Conford, Ellen, *6:* 48
Conklin, Gladys (Plemon), *2:* 73
Connolly, Jerome P(atrick), *8:* 34
Cook, Fred J(ames), *2:* 74
Cook, Joseph J(ay), *8:* 35
Cooke, David Coxe, *2:* 75
Cooke, Donald Ewin, *2:* 76
Coolidge, Olivia E(nsor), *1:* 67
Coombs, Charles, *3:* 49
Coombs, Chick. *See* Coombs, Charles, *3:* 49
Coombs, Patricia, *3:* 51
Cooney, Barbara, *6:* 49
Cooper, John R. [Collective pseudonym], *1:* 68
Cooper, Lee (Pelham), *5:* 47
Cooper, Susan, *4:* 57
Copeland, Helen, *4:* 57
Corbett, Scott, *2:* 78
Corbin, William. *See* McGraw, William Corbin, *3:* 124
Corby, Dan. *See* Catherall, Arthur, *3:* 38
Corcoran, Barbara, *3:* 53
Cordell, Alexander. *See* Graber, Alexander, *7:* 106
Corrigan, Barbara, *8:* 36
Cort, M. C. *See* Clifford, Margaret Cort, *1:* 63
Coskey, Evelyn, *7:* 55
Courlander, Harold, *6:* 51
Cousins, Margaret, *2:* 79
Cowie, Leonard W(allace), *4:* 60
Cowley, Joy, *4:* 60
Coy, Harold, *3:* 53

Craig, John Eland. *See* Chipperfield, Joseph, *2:* 57
Craig, Mary Francis, *6:* 52
Crane, William D(wight), *1:* 68
Crawford, Deborah, *6:* 53
Crawford, John E., *3:* 56
Crawford, Phyllis, *3:* 57
Crayder, Dorothy, *7:* 55
Crayder, Teresa. *See* Colman, Hila, *1:* 65
Crecy, Jeanne. *See* Williams, Jeanne, *5:* 202
Credle, Ellis, *1:* 68
Cresswell, Helen, *1:* 70
Cretan, Gladys (Yessayan), *2.* 82
Cromie, William J(oseph), *4:* 62
Crompton, Richmal. *See* Lamburn, Richmal Crompton, *5:* 101
Crone, Ruth, *4:* 63
Crosby, Alexander L., *2:* 83
Cross, Wilbur Lucius, III, *2:* 83
Crossley-Holland, Kevin, *5:* 48
Crouch, Marcus, *4:* 63
Crowe, Bettina Lum, *6:* 53
Crowell, Pers, *2:* 84
Cruz, Ray, *6:* 54
Cuffari, Richard, *6:* 55
Culp, Louanna McNary, *2:* 85
Cummings, Parke, *2:* 85
Cunningham, E. V. *See* Fast, Howard, *7:* 80
Cunningham, Julia W(oolfolk), *1:* 72
Curie, Eve, *1:* 73
Curry, Jane L(ouise), *1:* 73
Curry, Peggy Simson, *8:* 37
Curtis, Peter. *See* Lofts, Norah Robinson, *8:* 119
Cushman, Jerome, *2:* 86
Cutler, Samuel. *See* Folsom, Franklin, *5:* 67

Dahl, Borghild, *7:* 56
Dahl, Roald, *1:* 74
Dahlstedt, Marden, *8:* 38
Daly, Maureen, *2:* 87
Dangerfield, Balfour. *See* McCloskey, Robert, *2:* 185
Daniel, Hawthorne, *8:* 39
Daniels, Guy, *7:* 58
Darby, Ray K., *7:* 59
Daringer, Helen Fern, *1:* 75
Darling, Lois M., *3:* 57
Darling, Louis, Jr., *3:* 59
d'Aulaire, Edgar Parin, *5:* 49
d'Aulaire, Ingri (Maartenson Parin) *5:* 50
David, Jonathan. *See* Ames, Lee J., *3:* 11
Davidson, Jessica, *5:* 52
Davidson, Margaret, *5:* 53
Davis, Burke, *4:* 64
Davis, Christopher, *6:* 57
Davis, Julia, *6:* 58

Davis, Mary Octavia, *6:* 59
Davis, Russell G., *3:* 60
Davis, Verne T., *6:* 60
Dawson, Elmer A. [Collective pseudonym], *1:* 76
Dazey, Agnes J(ohnston), *2:* 88
Dazey, Frank M., *2:* 88
de Angeli, Marguerite, *1:* 76
Decker, Duane, *5:* 53
DeGering, Etta, *7:* 60
de Grummond, Lena Young, *6:* 61
de Jong, Dola, *7:* 61
De Jong, Meindert, *2:* 89
de Kay, Ormonde, Jr., *7:* 62
deKruif, Paul, (Henry) *5:* 54
Delaney, Harry, *3:* 61
Delaune, Lynne, *7:* 63
De Leeuw, Adele Louise, *1:* 77
Delving, Michael. *See* Williams, Jay, *3:* 256
Demarest, Doug. *See* Barker, Will, *8:* 4
deRegniers, Beatrice Schenk (Freedman), *2:* 90
Derleth, August (William) *5:* 54
Desmond, Alice Curtis, *8:* 40
Detine, Padre. *See* Olsen, Ib Spang, *6:* 177
Deutsch, Babette, *1:* 79
DeWaard, E. John, *7:* 63
Dewey, Ariane, *7:* 63
Dickens, Monica, *4:* 66
Dickinson, Peter, *5:* 55
Dickinson, Susan, *8:* 41
Dickson, Naida, *8:* 41
Dillon, Eilis, *2:* 92
Dines, Glenn, *7:* 65
DiValentin, Maria, *7:* 68
Dixon, Franklin W. [Collective pseudonym], *1:* 80 *Also see* Svenson, Andrew E., *2:* 238 Stratemeyer, Edward, *1:* 208
Dixon, Peter L., *6:* 62
Doane, Pelagie, *7:* 68
Dobler, Lavinia, *6:* 63
Dobrin, Arnold, *4:* 67
"Dr. A." *See* Silverstein, Alvin, *8:* 188
Dodd, Ed(ward) Benton, *4:* 68
Dodge, Bertha S(anford), *8:* 42
Doherty, C. H., *6:* 65
Dolson, Hildegarde, *5:* 56
Domanska, Janina, *6:* 65
Doob, Leonard W(illiam), *8:* 44
Dorian, Edith M(cEwen) *5:* 58
Dorian, Marguerite, *7:* 68
Dorman, Michael, *7:* 68
Doss, Margot Patterson, *6:* 68
Douglas, James McM. *See* Butterworth, W. E., *5:* 4
Douty, Esther M(orris), *8:* 44
Dowden, Anne Ophelia, *7:* 69
Downey, Fairfax, *3:* 61
Draco, F. *See* Davis, Julia, *6:* 68
Drewery, Mary, *6:* 69
Drummond, V(iolet) H., *6:* 71

du Bois, William Pene, *4:* 69
DuBose, LaRocque (Russ), *2:* 93
Ducornet, Erica, *7:* 72
du Jardin, Rosamond (Neal), *2:* 94
Duncan, Gregory. *See*
   McClintock, Marshall, *3:* 119
Duncan, Julia K. [Collective
   pseudonym], *1:* 81
Duncan, Lois. *See* Arquette, Lois
   S., *1:* 13
Dunlop, Agnes M. R., *3:* 62
Dunn, Judy. *See* Spangenberg,
   Judith Dunn, *5:* 175
Dunn, Mary Lois, *6:* 72
Dunnahoo, Terry, *7:* 73
Dupuy, Trevor N., *4:* 71
Durrell, Gerald (Malcolm), *8:* 46
Dutz. *See* Davis, Mary Octavia,
   6: 59
Duvoisin, Roger (Antoine), *2:* 95
Dwiggins, Don, *4:* 72

Earle, Olive L., *7:* 75
Eastwick, Ivy, *3:* 64
Eberle, Irmengarde, *2:* 97
Eckert, Horst, *8:* 47
Edmonds, I(vy) G(ordon), *8:* 48
Edmonds, Walter D(umaux), *1:* 81
Edmund, Sean. *See* Pringle,
   Laurence, *4:* 171
Edsall, Marian S(tickney), *8:* 50
Edwards, Dorothy, *4:* 73
Edwards, Harvey, *5:* 59
Edwards, Julie. *See* Andrews,
   Julie, *7:* 6
Edwards, Sally, *7:* 75
Eggenberger, David, *6:* 72
Ehrlich, Bettina (Bauer), *1:* 82
Eichner, James A., *4:* 73
Eifert, Virginia S(nider), *2:* 99
Elfman, Blossom, *8:* 51
Elkin, Benjamin, *3:* 65
Elkins, Dov Peretz, *5:* 61
Ellis, Ella Thorp, *7:* 76
Ellis, Mel, *7:* 77
Ellison, Virginia H(owell), *4:* 74
Ellsberg, Edward, *7:* 78
Elspeth. *See* Bragdon, Elspeth,
   6: 30
Elting, Mary, *2:* 100
Elwart, Joan Potter, *2:* 101
Emberley, Barbara A(nne), *8:* 51
Emberley, Ed(ward Randolph),
   8: 52
Embry, Margaret (Jacob), *5:* 61
Emerson, Alice B. [Collective
   pseudonym], *1:* 84
Emery, Anne (McGuigan), *1:* 84
Engdahl, Sylvia Louise, *4:* 75
Englebert, Victor, *8:* 54
Epstein, Beryl (Williams), *1:* 85
Epstein, Samuel, *1:* 87
Erdman, Loula Grace, *1:* 88

Ericson, Walter. *See* Fast,
   Howard, *7:* 80
Ervin, Janet Halliday, *4:* 77
Estep, Irene (Compton), *5:* 62
Estes, Eleanor, *7:* 79
Estoril, Jean. *See* Allan, Mabel
   Esther, *5:* 2
Ets, Marie Hall, *2:* 102
Eunson, Dale, *5:* 63
Evans, Katherine (Floyd), *5:* 64
Evarts, Hal, *6:* 72
Evernden, Margery, *5:* 65
Ewen, David, *4:* 78
Eyerly, Jeannette Hyde, *4:* 80

Faber, Doris, *3:* 67
Faber, Harold, *5:* 65
Fairfax-Lucy, Brian, *6:* 73
Faithfull, Gail, *8:* 55
Fanning, Leonard M(ulliken), *5:* 65
Farjeon, Eleanor, *2:* 103
Farley, Carol, *4:* 81
Farley, Walter, *2:* 106
Fast, Howard, *7:* 80
Fatio, Louise, *6:* 75
Faulhaber, Martha, *7:* 82
Fecher, Constance, *7:* 83
Feelings, Thomas, *8:* 55
Feelings, Tom. *See* Feelings,
   Thomas, *8:* 55
Feiffer, Jules, *8:* 57
Felsen, Henry Gregor, *1:* 89
Felton, Harold William, *1:* 90
Felton, Ronald Oliver, *3:* 67
Fenner, Carol, *7:* 84
Fenner, Phyllis R(eid), *1:* 91
Fenten, D. X., *4:* 82
Fenton, Carroll Lane, *5:* 66
Fenton, Edward, *7:* 86
Ferber, Edna, *7:* 87
Fergusson, Erna, *5:* 67
Fermi, Laura, *6:* 78
Ferris, James Cody [Collective
   pseudonym], *1:* 92
Fichter, George S., *7:* 92
Fidler, Kathleen, *3:* 68
Fiedler, Jean, *4:* 83
Field, Edward, *8:* 58
Finkel, George (Irvine), *8:* 59
Finlayson, Ann, *8:* 61
Fisher, Aileen (Lucia), *1:* 92
Fisher, Laura Harrison, *5:* 67
Fisher, Leonard Everett, *4:* 84
Fitzhardinge, Joan Margaret, *2:* 107
Fitzhugh, Louise, *1:* 94
Flash Flood. *See* Robinson, Jan
   M., *6:* 194
Fleischman, (Albert) Sid(ney),
   8: 61
Fleming, Thomas J(ames), *8:* 64
Fletcher, Charlie May, *3:* 70
Flitner, David P., *7:* 92
Floethe, Louise Lee, *4:* 87
Floethe, Richard, *4:* 89

Flora, James (Royer), *1:* 95
Folsom, Franklin (Brewster), *5:* 67
Forbes, Esther, *2:* 108
Forbes, Graham B. [Collective
   pseudonym], *1:* 97
Ford, Elbur. *See* Hibbert, Eleanor,
   2: 134
Ford, Marcia. *See* Radford, Ruby
   L., *6:* 186
Foreman, Michael, *2:* 110
Forman, Brenda, *4:* 90
Forman, James Douglas, *8:* 64
Forsee, (Frances) Aylesa, *1:* 97
Foster, Genevieve (Stump), *2:* 111
Foster, John T(homas), *8:* 65
Foster, Laura Louise, *6:* 78
Frankau, Mary Evelyn, *4:* 90
Franklin, Steve. *See* Stevens,
   Franklin, *6:* 206
Frasconi, Antonio, *6:* 79
Frazier, Neta Lohnes, *7:* 94
French, Dorothy Kayser, *5:* 69
French, Fiona, *6:* 81
French, Paul. *See* Asimov, Isaac,
   1: 15
Frick, C. H. *See* Irwin, Constance
   Frick, *6:* 119
Frick, Constance. *See* Irwin,
   Constance Frick, *6:* 119
Friedman, Estelle, *7:* 95
Friermood, Elisabeth Hamilton,
   5: 69
Friis, Babbis. *See* Friis-Baastad,
   Babbis, *7:* 95
Friis-Baastad, Babbis, *7:* 95
Friskey, Margaret Richards, *5:* 72
Fritz, Jean (Guttery), *1:* 98
Froman, Robert (Winslow), *8:* 67
Fry, Rosalie, *3:* 71
Fuchs, Erich, *6:* 84
Fujita, Tamao, *7:* 98
Fuller, Iola. *See* McCoy, Iola
   Fuller, *3:* 120
Funk, Thompson. *See* Funk, Tom,
   7: 98
Funk, Tom, *7:* 98

Gage, Wilson. *See* Steele, Mary
   Q., *3:* 211
Gallant, Roy A(rthur), *4:* 91
Galt, Thomas Franklin, Jr., *5:* 72
Galt, Tom. *See* Galt, Thomas
   Franklin, Jr., *5:* 72
Gannett, Ruth Stiles, *3:* 73
Gannon, Robert (Haines), *8:* 68
Gardner, Jeanne LeMonnier, *5:* 73
Garfield, James B., *6:* 85
Garfield, Leon, *1:* 99
Garnett, Eve C. R., *3:* 75
Garst, Doris Shannon, *1:* 100
Garst, Shannon. *See* Garst, Doris
   Shannon, *1:* 100
Garthwaite, Marion H., *7:* 100
Gates, Doris, *1:* 102

Gault, William Campbell, 8: 69
Geis, Darlene, 7: 101
Geisel, Theodor Seuss, 1: 104
Gelman, Steve, 3: 75
Gentleman, David, 7: 102
George, Jean Craighead, 2: 112
George, John L(othar), 2: 114
Georgiou, Constantine, 7: 102
Gibbs, Alonzo (Lawrence), 5: 74
Gibson, Josephine. See Joslin,
    Sesyle, 2: 158
Gidal, Sonia, 2: 115
Gidal, Tim N(ahum), 2: 116
Gilbert, Nan. See Gilbertson,
    Mildred, 2: 116
Gilbertson, Mildred Geiger, 2: 116
Gilbreth, Frank B., Jr., 2: 117
Gilfond, Henry, 2: 118
Gillett, Mary, 7: 103
Gilman, Dorothy. See Dorothy
    Gilman Butters, 5: 39
Ginsburg, Mirra, 6: 86
Giovanopoulos, Paul, 7: 104
Gipson, Frederick B., 2: 118
Gittings, Jo Manton, 3: 76
Gittings, Robert, 6: 88
Gliewe, Unada, 3: 77
Glovach, Linda, 7: 105
Glubok, Shirley, 6: 89
Godden, Rumer, 3: 79
Goffstein, M(arilyn) B(rooke), 8: 70
Goldfrank, Helen, 6: 89
Goldston, Robert Conroy, 6: 90
Goodall, John S(trickland), 4: 92
Gordon, Frederick [Collective
    pseudonym], 1: 106
Gordon, John, 6: 90
Gordon, Selma. See Lanes, Selma
    G., 3: 96
Gorham, Michael. See Folsom,
    Franklin, 5: 67
Gottlieb, Gerald, 7: 106
Goudge, Elizabeth, 2: 119
Goulart, Ron, 6: 92
Gould, Lilian, 6: 92
Graber, Alexander, 7: 106
Graff, Polly Anne. See Colver,
    Anne, 7: 54
Graham, Lorenz B(ell), 2: 122
Graham, Robin Lee, 7: 107
Gramatky, Hardie, 1: 107
Grange, Peter. See Nicole,
    Christopher, 5: 141
Grant, Bruce, 5: 75
Grant, Eva, 7: 108
Graves, Charles P(arlin), 4: 94
Gray, Elizabeth Janet, 6: 93
Gray, Genevieve S., 4: 95
Gray, Jenny. See Gray, Genevieve
    S., 4: 95
Gray, Nicholas Stuart, 4: 96
Gray, Patricia, 7: 110
Gray, Patsey. See Gray, Patricia,
    7: 110
Grayland, V. Merle. See Grayland,
    Valerie, 7: 111
Grayland, Valerie, 7: 111

Greaves, Margaret, 7: 113
Green, Adam. See Weisgard,
    Leonard, 2: 263
Green, D. See Casewit, Curtis,
    4: 43
Green, Morton, 8: 71
Green, Roger (Gilbert Lancelyn),
    2: 123
Green, Sheila Ellen, 8: 72
Greenberg, Harvey R., 5: 77
Greene, Bette, 8: 73
Greene, Carla, 1: 108
Greenleaf, Barbara Kaye, 6: 95
Greenwald, Sheila. See Green,
    Sheila Ellen, 8: 72
Grendon, Stephen. See Derleth,
    August (William), 5: 54
Gretz, Susanna, 7: 114
Grice, Frederick, 6: 96
Grifalconi, Ann, 2: 125
Griffith, Jeannette. See Eyerly,
    Jeanette, 4: 97
Griffiths, Helen, 5: 77
Gringhuis, Dirk. See Gringhuis,
    Richard H. 6: 97
Gringhuis, Richard H., 6: 97
Gripe, Maria (Kristina), 2: 126
Grohskopf, Bernice, 7: 114
Gruenberg, Sidonie M(atsner),
    2: 127
Gugliotta, Bobette, 7: 116
Guillaume, Jeanette G. (Flierl),
    8: 74
Guillot, Rene, 7: 117
Gunther, John, 2: 129
Gustafson, Sarah R. See Riedman,
    Sarah R., 1: 183

Habenstreit, Barbara, 5: 78
Hafner, Marylin, 7: 119
Haggerty, James J(oseph) 5: 78
Hagon, Priscilla. See Allan, Mabel
    Esther, 5: 2
Hahn, Emily, 3: 81
Hahn, Hannelore, 8: 74
Hale, Linda, 6: 99
Hall, Adele, 7: 120
Hall, Anna Gertrude, 8: 75
Hall, Elvajean, 6: 100
Hall, Lynn, 2: 130
Hall, Malcolm, 7: 121
Hall, Rosalys Haskell, 7: 121
Hallard, Peter. See Catherall,
    Arthur, 3: 38
Hallin, Emily Watson, 6: 101
Hamilton, Virginia, 4: 97
Hammer, Richard, 6: 102
Hamre, Leif, 5: 79
Hanson, Joan, 8: 75
Hardy, Alice Dale [Collective
    pseudonym], 1: 109
Harkins, Philip, 6: 102
Harnett, Cynthia (Mary), 5: 79
Harper, Wilhelmina, 4: 99

Harrington, Lyn, 5: 80
Harris, Christie, 6: 103
Harris, Colver. See Colver, Anne,
    7: 54
Harris, Janet, 4: 100
Harris, Leon A., 4: 101
Harris, Rosemary (Jeanne), 4: 101
Harrison, Harry, 4: 102
Haskell, Arnold, 6: 104
Haugaard, Erik Christian, 4: 104
Hautzig, Esther, 4: 105
Havighurst, Walter (Edwin), 1: 109
Haviland, Virginia, 6: 105
Hawes, Judy, 4: 107
Hawk, Virginia Driving. See
    Sneve, Virginia Driving Hawk,
    8: 193
Hawkins, Quail, 6: 107
Hawkinson, John, 4: 108
Hawley, Mable C. [Collective
    pseudonym], 1: 110
Haycraft, Howard, 6: 108
Haycraft, Molly Costain, 6: 110
Hayes, Will, 7: 122
Hayes, William D(imitt), 8: 76
Hays, Wilma Pitchford, 1: 110
Haywood, Carolyn, 1: 111
Headley, Elizabeth. See Betty
    Cavanna, 1: 54
Headstrom, Richard, 8: 77
Heady, Eleanor B(utler), 8: 78
Heal, Edith, 7: 123
Heaven, Constance. See Fecher,
    Constance, 7: 83
Heiderstadt, Dorothy, 6: 111
Helfman, Elizabeth S., 3: 83
Helfman, Harry, 3: 84
Hellman, Hal. See Hellman,
    Harold, 4: 109
Hellman, Harold, 4: 109
Helps, Racey, 2: 131
Henderley, Brooks [Collective
    pseudonym], 1: 113
Henderson, Zenna (Chlarson) 5: 81
Henry, Joanne Landers, 6: 112
Henstra, Friso, 8: 80
Herbert, Don, 2: 131
Herron, Edward A(lbert), 4: 110
Hess, Lilo, 4: 111
Heyduck-Huth, Hilde, 8: 81
Heyerdahl, Thor, 2: 132
Hibbert, Christopher, 4: 112
Hibbert, Eleanor Burford, 2: 134
Hicks, Eleanor B. See Coerr,
    Eleanor, 1: 64
Hieatt, Constance B(artlett), 4: 113
Higdon, Hal, 4: 115
Hightower, Florence, 4: 115
Hildick, E. W. See Hildick,
    Wallace, 2: 135
Hildick, (Edmund) Wallace, 2: 135
Hill, Grace Brooks [Collective
    pseudonym], 1: 113
Hill, Kathleen Louise, 4: 116
Hill, Kay. See Hill, Kathleen
    Louise, 4: 116

Hill, Monica. *See* Watson, Jane Werner, *3:* 244
Hill, Ruth A. *See* Viguers, Ruth Hill, *6:* 214
Hillerman, Tony, *6:* 113
Hillert, Margaret, *8:* 82
Hilton, Irene P., *7:* 124
Hilton, Ralph, *8:* 83
Hilton, Suzanne, *4:* 117
Himler, Ann, *8:* 84
Himler, Ronald, *6:* 114
Hirsch, S. Carl, *2:* 137
Hirsh, Marilyn, *7:* 126
Hiser, Iona Seibert, *4:* 118
Hoban, Russell C(onwell), *1:* 113
Hobart, Lois, *7:* 127
Hoberman, Mary Ann, *5:* 82
Hodges, C(yril) Walter, *2:* 138
Hodges, Elizabeth Jamison, *1:* 114
Hodges, Margaret Moore, *1:* 116
Hoexter, Corinne, *6:* 115
Hoffman, Phyllis M., *4:* 120
Hogan, Inez, *2:* 140
Hogarth, Jr. *See* Kent, Rockwell, *6:* 128
Hogg, Garry, *2:* 142
Hogner, Dorothy Childs, *4:* 121
Hogrogian, Nanny, *7:* 128
Hoke, John, *7:* 129
Holberg, Ruth Langland, *1:* 117
Holbrook, Stewart Hall, *2:* 143
Holding, James, *3:* 85
Holisher, Desider, *6:* 115
Holl, Adelaide (Hinkle), *8:* 84
Holland, Isabelle, *8:* 86
Holland, Marion, *6:* 116
Holm, (Else) Anne (Lise), *1:* 118
Holman, Felice, *7:* 131
Holt, Margaret, *4:* 122
Holt, Victoria. *See* Hibbert, Eleanor, *2:* 134
Holton, Leonard. *See* Wibberley, Leonard, *2:* 271
Honness, Elizabeth H., *2:* 145
Hood, Joseph F., *4:* 123
Hope, Laura Lee [Collective pseudonym], *1:* 119
Hopf, Alice L(ightner) *5:* 82
Hopkins, Lee Bennett, *3:* 85
Hopkins, Lyman. *See* Folsom, Franklin, *5:* 67
Horvath, Betty, *4:* 125
Hosford, Jessie, *5:* 83
Houghton, Eric, *7:* 132
Howard, Robert West, *5:* 85
Howarth, David, *6:* 117
Howell, Virginia Tier. *See* Ellison, Virginia Howell, *4:* 74
Howes, Barbara, *5:* 87
Hubbell, Patricia, *8:* 86
Hughes, Langston, *4:* 125
Hughes, Richard (Arthur Warren), *8:* 87
Hults, Dorothy Niebrugge, *6:* 117
Hume, Lotta Carswell, *7:* 133
Hunt, Irene, *2:* 146

Hunt, Mabel Leigh, *1:* 120
Hunter, Hilda, *7:* 135
Hunter, Mollie. *See* McIllwraith, Maureen, *2:* 193
Hunter Blair, Pauline, *3:* 87
Huntington, Harriet E(lizabeth), *1:* 121
Huntsberry, William E(mery), *5:* 87
Hurd, Clement, *2:* 147
Hurd, Edith Thacher, *2:* 150
Hutchins, Ross E(lliott), *4:* 127
Hutchmacher, J. Joseph, *5:* 88
Hyde, Margaret Oldroyd, *1:* 122
Hyde, Wayne F., *7:* 135
Hylander, Clarence J., *7:* 137
Hyman, Trina Schart, *7:* 137
Hymes, Lucia M., *7:* 139
Hyndman, Jane Andrews, *1:* 122

Iannone, Jeanne, *7:* 139
Ibbotson, M. C(hristine), *5:* 89
Ingraham, Leonard W(illiam), *4:* 129
Inyart, Gene, *6:* 119
Ionesco, Eugene, *7:* 140
Ipcar, Dahlov (Zorach), *1:* 125
Irving, Robert. *See* Adler, Irving, *1:* 2
Irwin, Constance, *6:* 119

Jackson, C. Paul, *6:* 120
Jackson, Caary. *See* Jackson, C. Paul, *6:* 120
Jackson, Jesse, *2:* 150
Jackson, O. B. *See* Jackson, C. Paul, *6:* 120
Jackson, Robert B(lake), *8:* 89
Jackson, Shirley, *2:* 152
Jacobs, Flora Gill, *5:* 90
Jacobs, Lou(is), Jr., *2:* 155
Jagendorf, Moritz (Adolf), *2:* 155
James, Dynely. *See* Mayne, William, *6:* 162
James, Josephine. *See* Sterne, Emma Gelders, *6:* 205
James, T. F. *See* Fleming, Thomas J(ames), *8:* 64
Jane, Mary Childs, *6:* 122
Janosch. *See* Eckert, Horst, *8:* 47
Jansson, Tove, *3:* 88
Jarman, Rosemary Hawley, *7:* 141
Jarrell, Randall, *7:* 141
Jeake, Samuel Jr. *See* Aiken, Conrad, *3:* 3
Jeffries, Roderic, *4:* 129
Jenkins, Marie M., *7:* 143
Jennings, S. M. *See* Meyer, Jerome Sydney, *3:* 129
Jennison, C. S. *See* Starbird, Kaye, *6:* 204
Jensen, Virginia Allen, *8:* 90
Jewett, Eleanore Myers, *5:* 90

Johns, Avery. *See* Cousins, Margaret, *2:* 79
Johnson, A. E. [Joint pseudonym] *See* Johnson, Annabell and Edgar, *2:* 156, 157
Johnson, Annabell Jones, *2:* 156
Johnson, Crockett. *See* Leisk, David Johnson, *1:* 141
Johnson, Dorothy M., *6:* 123
Johnson, Edgar Raymond, *2:* 157
Johnson, Elizabeth, *7:* 144
Johnson, Eric W(arner), *8:* 91
Johnson, Gaylord, *7:* 146
Johnson, James Ralph, *1:* 126
Johnson, Lois Smith, *6:* 123
Johnson, William Weber, *7:* 147
Johnston, Agnes Christine. *See* Dazey, Agnes J., *2:* 88
Johnston, Tony, *8:* 94
Jones, Adrienne, *7:* 147
Jones, Evan, *3:* 90
Jones, Mary Alice, *6:* 125
Jones, Weyman, *4:* 130
Jordan, June, *4:* 131
Jordan, Mildred, *5:* 91
Joslin, Sesyle, *2:* 158
Jucker, Sita, *5:* 92
Judd, Frances K. [Collective pseudonym], *1:* 127
Jumpp, Hugo. *See* MacPeek, Walter G., *4:* 148
Jupo, Frank J., *7:* 148
Juster, Norton, *3:* 91
Justus, May, *1:* 127

Kalnay, Francis, *7:* 149
Kark, Nina Mary, *4:* 132
Katz, Fred, *6:* 126
Kaufman, Mervyn D., *4:* 133
Kay, Helen. *See* Goldfrank, Helen Colodny, *6:* 89
Keane, Bil, *4:* 134
Keen, Martin L., *4:* 135
Keene, Carolyn. *See* Adams, Harriet S., *1:* 1
Keir, Christine. *See* Pullein-Thompson, Christine, *3:* 164
Keith, Carlton. *See* Robertson, Keith, *1:* 184
Keith, Harold (Verne), *2:* 159
Keller, Charles, *8:* 94
Keller, Gail Faithfull. *See* Faithfull, Gail, *8:* 55
Kellogg, Steven, *8:* 95
Kellow, Kathleen. *See* Hibbert, Eleanor, *2:* 134
Kelly, Ralph. *See* Geis, Darlene, *7:* 101
Kelly, Regina Z., *5:* 94
Kelsey, Alice Geer, *1:* 129
Kendall, Lace. *See* Stoutenburg, Adrien, *3:* 217
Kennell, Ruth E., *6:* 127
Kent, Margaret, *2:* 161

Kent, Rockwell, 6: 128
Kenworthy, Leonard S., 6: 131
Kenyon, Ley, 6: 131
Kerry, Lois. See Arquette, Lois S.,
    1: 13
Kettelkamp, Larry, 2: 163
Key, Alexander (Hill), 8: 98
Kiddell, John, 3: 93
Killilea, Marie (Lyons), 2: 165
Kilreon, Beth. See Walker, Barbara
    K., 4: 219
Kimbrough, Emily, 2: 166
Kindred, Wendy, 7: 15
King, Arthur. See Cain, Arthur H.,
    3: 33
King, Cynthia, 7: 152
King, Reefe. See Barker, Albert
    W., 8: 3
Kingman, (Mary) Lee, 1: 133
Kinney, C. Cle, 6: 132
Kirk, Ruth (Kratz), 5: 95
Kirtland, G. B. See Joslin, Sesyle,
    2: 158
Kleberger, Ilse, 5: 96
Klein, H. Arthur, 8: 99
Klein, Leonore, 6: 132
Klein, Mina C(ooper), 8: 100
Klein, Norma, 7: 152
Knott, Bill. See Knott, William
    Cecil, Jr., 3: 94
Knott, William Cecil, Jr., 3: 94
Knowles, John, 8: 101
Knudson, R. R. See Knudson,
    Rozanne, 7: 154
Knudson, Rozanne, 7: 154
Koch, Dorothy Clarke, 6: 133
Kohn, Bernice (Herstein), 4: 136
Komroff, Manuel, 2: 168
Konigsburg, E(laine) L(obl), 4: 137
Koning, Hans. See Koningsberger,
    Hans, 5: 97
Koningsberger, Hans, 5: 97
Koren, Edward, 5: 98
Kouts, Anne, 8: 103
Krasilovsky, Phyllis, 1: 134
Kraus, Robert, 4: 139
Krauss, Ruth, 1: 135
Krautter, Elisa. See Bialk, Elisa,
    1: 25
Kristof, Jane, 8: 104
Kroeber, Theodora (Kracaw),
    1: 136
Krumgold, Joseph, 1: 136
Krüss, James, 8: 104
Kurelek, William, 8: 106
Kuskin, Karla (Seidman), 2: 169
Kvale, Velma R(uth), 8: 108
Kyle, Elisabeth. See Dunlop,
    Agnes M. R., 3: 62

Lacy, Leslie A(lexander), 6: 135
Lader, Lawrence, 6: 135
Lady of Quality, A. See Bagnold,
    Enid, 1: 17

Laklan, Carli, 5: 100
Lamburn, Richmal Crompton,
    5: 101
Lampman, Evelyn Sibley, 4: 140
Land, Jane. See Speicher, Helen
    Ross (Smith), 8: 194
Land, Ross. See Speicher, Helen
    Ross (Smith), 8: 194
Landin, Les(lie), 2: 171
Lanes, Selma G., 3: 96
Lange, Suzanne, 5: 103
Langner, Nola, 8: 110
Langstaff, John, 6: 135
Langton, Jane, 3: 97
Larrick, Nancy, 4: 141
Latham, Frank B., 6: 137
Latham, Jean Lee, 2: 171
Latham, Mavis. See Clark, Mavis
    Thorpe, 8: 27
Latham, Philip. See Richardson,
    Robert S(hirley), 8: 164
Lattimore, Eleanor Francis, 7: 155
Lauber, Patricia (Grace), 1: 138
Laugesen, Mary E(akin), 5: 104
Laughlin, Florence, 3: 98
Laurence, Ester Hauser, 7: 156
Lavine, Sigmund A., 3: 100
Lawrence, Mildred, 3: 101
Laycock, George (Edwin) 5: 105
Leacroft, Helen, 6: 139
Leacroft, Richard, 6: 139
LeCain, Errol, 6: 141
Lee, Mary Price, 8: 111
Lee, Mildred, 6: 142
Lee, Tanith, 8: 112
Le Guin, Ursula K(roeber), 4: 142
Leichman, Seymour, 5: 106
Leighton, Margaret, 1: 140
Leisk, David Johnson, 1: 141
L'Engle, Madeleine, 1: 141
Lengyel, Emil, 3: 102
Lenski, Lois, 1: 142
Lent, Blair, 2: 172
Leong Gor Yun. See Ellison,
    Virginia Howell, 4: 74
LeSieg, Theo. See Geisel, Theodor
    Seuss, 1: 104
Leslie, Robert Franklin, 7: 158
Le Sueur, Meridel, 6: 143
Levitin, Sonia, 4: 144
Lewis, Claudia (Louise), 5: 107
Lewis, Francine. See Wells, Helen,
    2: 266
Lewis, Richard, 3: 104
Lewiton, Mina, 2: 174
Lexau, Joan M., 1: 144
Ley, Willy, 2: 175
Libby, Bill. See Libby, William M.,
    5: 109
Libby, William M., 5: 109
Liberty, Gene, 3: 106
Lifton, Betty Jean, 6: 143
Lighter, A. M. See Hopf, Alice L.
    5: 82
Lincoln, C(harles) Eric, 5: 111
Linde, Gunnel, 5: 112

Lindgren, Astrid, 2: 177
Lindop, Edmund, 5: 113
Lingard, Joan, 8: 113
Lionni, Leo, 8: 114
Lipsyte, Robert, 5: 114
Liss, Howard, 4: 145
List, Ilka Katherine, 6: 145
Liston, Robert A., 5: 114
Litchfield, Ada B(assett), 5: 115
Little, (Flora) Jean, 2: 178
Littledale, Freya (Lota), 2: 179
Lively, Penelope, 7: 159
Liversidge, (Henry) Douglas,
    8: 116
Livingston, Myra Cohn, 5: 116
Livingston, Richard R(oland),
    8: 118
Lobel, Anita, 6: 146
Lobel, Arnold, 6: 147
Lobsenz, Norman M., 6: 148
Lochlons, Colin. See Jackson, C.
    Paul, 6: 120
Locke, Clinton W. [Collective
    pseudonym], 1: 145
Loefgren, Ulf, 3: 106
Lofts, Norah (Robinson), 8: 119
Lomas, Steve. See Brennan,
    Joseph L., 6: 33
London, Jane. See Geis, Darlene,
    7: 101
Long, Helen Beecher [Collective
    pseudonym], 1: 146
Longman, Harold S., 5: 117
Loomis, Robert D., 5: 119
Lopshire, Robert, 6: 149
Lord, Beman, 5: 119
Lord, Nancy. See Titus, Eve,
    2: 240
Lord, Walter, 3: 109
Love, Katherine, 3: 190
Lovelace, Delos Wheeler, 7: 160
Lovelace, Maud Hart, 2: 181
Low, Elizabeth Hammond, 5: 120
Lowenstein, Dyno, 6: 150
Lowry, Peter, 7: 160
Lubell, Cecil, 6: 150
Lubell, Winifred, 6: 151
Luckhardt, Mildred Corell, 5: 122
Ludlum, Mabel Cleland. See
    Widemer, Mabel Cleland,
    5: 200
Lum, Peter. See Crowe, Bettina
    Lum, 6: 53
Lunn, Janet, 4: 146
Lutzker, Edythe, 5: 124
Luzzati, Emanuele, 7: 161
Lyle, Katie Letcher, 8: 121
Lynch, Lorenzo, 7: 161
Lynch, Patricia, 6: 153
Lyon, Elinor, 6: 154
Lyons, Dorothy, 3: 110

MacBeth, George, 4: 146
MacClintock, Dorcas, 8: 122

MacGregor-Hastie, Roy, *3:* 111
MacKellar, William, *4:* 148
MacMillan, Annabelle. *See* Quick,
    Annabelle, *2:* 207
MacPeek, Walter G., *4:* 148
Macrae, Hawk. *See* Barker, Albert
    W., *8:* 3
Macumber, Mari. *See* Sandoz,
    Mari, *5:* 159
Madden, Don, *3:* 112
Madison, Arnold, *6:* 155
Madison, Winifred, *5:* 125
Maestro, Giulio, *8:* 123
Mahony, Elizabeth Winthrop,
    8: 125
Maidoff, Ilka List. *See* List, Ilka
    Katherine, *6:* 145
Malcolmson, Anne. *See* Storch,
    Anne B. von, *1:* 221
Malcolmson, David, *6:* 157
Malo, John W., *4:* 149
Mangione, Jerre, *6:* 157
Mann, Peggy, *6:* 158
Manton, Jo. *See* Gittings, Jo
    Manton, *3:* 76
Manushkin, Fran, *7:* 161
Mapes, Mary A. *See* Ellison,
    Virginia Howell, *4:* 74
Margolis, Richard J(ules), *4:* 150
Markins, W. S. *See* Jenkins, Marie
    M., *7:* 143
Marlowe, Amy Bell [Collective
    pseudonym], *1:* 146
Marokvia, Mireille (Journet), *5:* 126
Mars, W. T. *See* Mars, Witold
    Tadeusz, Jr., *3:* 114
Mars, Witold Tadeusz, Jr., *3:* 114
Marshall, (Sarah) Catherine, *2:* 182
Marshall, Douglas. *See*
    McClintock, Marshall, *3:* 119
Marshall, James, *6:* 161
Martin, Eugene [Collective
    pseudonym], *1:* 146
Martin, Fredric. *See* Christopher,
    Matt, *2:* 58
Martin, Patricia Miles, *1:* 146
Martin, Peter. *See* Christine
    Chaundler, *1:* 56
Martini, Teri, *3:* 116
Mason, F. van Wyck, *3:* 117
Mason, Frank W. *See* Mason, F.
    van Wyck, *3:* 117
Mason, Miriam E(vangeline),
    2: 183
Mason, Tally. *See* Derleth, August
    (William), *5:* 54
Masters, Kelly R., *3:* 118
Masters, William. *See* Cousins,
    Margaret, *2:* 79
Mathis, Sharon Bell, *7:* 162
Matsui, Tadashi, *8:* 126
Matsuno, Masako, *6:* 161
Maxon, Anne. *See* Best, Allena
    Champlin, *2:* 25
Maxwell, Edith, *7:* 164
May, Charles Paul, *4:* 151

Mayne, William, *6:* 162
Mays, (Lewis) Victor, Jr., *5:* 126
McCaffrey, Anne, *8:* 127
McCain, Murray, *7:* 165
McCall, Edith S., *6:* 163
McCarthy, Agnes, *4:* 152
McClintock, Marshall, *3:* 119
McClintock, Mike. *See*
    McClintock, Marshall, *3:* 119
McCloskey, Robert, *2:* 185
McClung, Robert M., *2:* 188
McCoy, Iola Fuller, *3:* 120
McCoy, J(oseph) J(erome), *8:* 127
McCrea, James, *3:* 121
McCrea, Ruth, *3:* 121
McCullough, Frances Monson,
    8: 129
McCully, Emily Arnold, *5:* 128
McDole, Carol. *See* Farley, Carol,
    4: 81
McDonald, Gerald D., *3:* 123
McGee, Barbara, *6:* 165
McGiffin, (Lewis) Lee (Shaffer),
    1: 148
McGinley, Phyllis, *2:* 190
McGovern, Ann, *8:* 130
McGowen, Thomas E., *2:* 192
McGowen, Tom. *See* McGowen,
    Thomas, *2:* 192
McGrady, Mike, *6:* 166
McGraw, Eloise Jarvis, *1:* 149
McGraw, William Corbin, *3:* 124
McGregor, Craig, *8:* 131
McHargue, Georgess, *4:* 152
McIlwraith, Maureen, *2:* 193
McKown, Robin, *6:* 166
McMeekin, Clark. *See* McMeekin,
    Isable McLennan, *3:* 126
McMeekin, Isabel McLennan,
    3: 126
McNair, Kate, *3:* 127
McNeer, May, *1:* 150
McNeill, Janet, *1:* 151
Meade, Ellen (Roddick), *5:* 130
Meader, Stephen W(arren), *1:* 153
Meadowcroft, Enid LaMonte. *See*
    Wright, Enid Meadowcroft,
    3: 267
Means, Florence Crannel, *1:* 154
Medearis, Mary, *5:* 130
Mee, Charles L., Jr., *8:* 132
Meeks, Esther MacBain, *1:* 155
Mehdevi, Alexander, *7:* 166
Mehdevi, Anne (Marie) Sinclair,
    8: 132
Meigs, Cornelia (Lynde), *6:* 167
Meltzer, Milton, *1:* 156
Melzack, Ronald, *5:* 130
Memling, Carl, *6:* 169
Meredith, David William. *See*
    Miers, Earl Schenck, *1:* 160
Merriam, Eve, *3:* 128
Merrill, Jean (Fairbanks), *1:* 158
Meyer, Edith Patterson, *5:* 131
Meyer, Jerome Sydney, *3:* 129

Meyer, June. *See* Jordan, June,
    4: 141
Meyer, Renate, *6:* 170
Miers, Earl Schenck, *1:* 160
Miklowitz, Gloria D., *4:* 154
Miles, Betty, *8:* 132
Miles, Miska. *See* Martin, Patricia
    Miles, *1:* 146
Militant. *See* Sandburg, Carl
    (August), *8:* 177
Miller, Eddie. *See* Miller, Edward,
    8: 134
Miller, Edward, *8:* 134
Miller, Helen M(arkley), *5:* 133
Miller, John. *See* Samachson,
    Joseph, *3:* 182
Milne, Lorus J., *5:* 133
Milne, Margery, *5:* 134
Minier, Nelson. *See* Stoutenburg,
    Adrien, *3:* 217
Mintonye, Grace, *4:* 156
Mirsky, Jeannette, *8:* 135
Mirsky, Reba Paeff, *1:* 161
Moffett, Martha (Leatherwood),
    8: 136
Mohn, Viola Kohl, *8:* 138
Mohr, Nicholasa, *8:* 138
Molloy, Paul, *5:* 135
Montgomery, Elizabeth Rider,
    3: 132
Montgomery, Rutherford George,
    3: 134
Montresor, Beni, *3:* 136
Moody, Ralph Owen, *1:* 162
Moon, Sheila (Elizabeth), *5:* 136
More, Caroline. *See* Cone, Molly
    Lamken, *1:* 66
Morey, Walt, *3:* 139
Morgan, Lenore, *8:* 139
Morris, Robert A., *7:* 166
Morrison, Lillian, *3:* 140
Morrison, William. *See*
    Samachson, Joseph, *3:* 182
Morriss, James E(dward), *8:* 139
Morrow, Betty. *See* Bacon,
    Elizabeth, *3:* 14
Moscow, Alvin, *3:* 142
Mosel, Arlene, *7:* 167
Mowat, Farley, *3:* 142
Mulvihill, William Patrick, *8:* 140
Munzer, Martha E., *4:* 157
Murphy, Barbara Beasley, *5:* 137
Murphy, E(mett) Jefferson, *4:* 159
Murphy, Pat. *See* Murphy, E(mett)
    Jefferson, *4:* 159
Murray, Marian, *5:* 138
Murray, Michele, *7:* 170
Musgrave, Florence, *3:* 144
Mussey, Virginia T. H. *See*
    Ellison, Virginia Howell, *4:* 74

Nash, Linell. *See* Smith, Linell
    Nash, *2:* 227
Nash, (Frediric) Ogden, *2:* 194

Nast, Elsa Ruth. *See* Watson, Jane Werner, *3:* 244
Nathan, Robert, *6:* 171
Navarra, John Gabriel, *8:* 141
Nazaroff, Alexander I., *4:* 160
Neal, Harry Edward, *5:* 139
Needleman, Jacob, *6:* 172
Neimark, Anne E., *4:* 160
Nesbit, Troy. *See* Folsom, Franklin, *5:* 67
Nespojohn, Katherine V., *7:* 170
Ness, Evaline (Michelow), *1:* 165
Neufeld, John, *6:* 173
Neurath, Marie (Reidemeister), *1:* 166
Neville, Emily Cheney, *1:* 169
Neville, Mary. *See* Woodrich, Mary Neville, *2:* 274
Newberry, Clare Turlay, *1:* 170
Newlon, Clarke, *6:* 174
Newman, Robert (Howard), *4:* 161
Newton, Suzanne, *5:* 140
Nicole, Christopher Robin, *5:* 141
Nixon, Joan Lowery, *8:* 143
Noble, Iris, *5:* 142
Nodset, Joan M. *See* Lexau, Joan M., *1:* 144
Nolan, Jeannette Covert, *2:* 196
Noonan, Julia, *4:* 163
Nordstrom, Ursula, *3:* 144
North, Andrew. *See* Norton, Alice Mary, *1:* 173
North, Sterling, *1:* 171
Norton, Alice Mary, *1:* 173
Norton, Andre. *See* Norton, Alice Mary, *1:* 173
Nye, Robert, *6:* 174

Oakes, Vanya, *6:* 175
Oakley, Don(ald G.), *8:* 144
O'Connor, Patrick. *See* Wibberley, Leonard, *2:* 271
Oechsli, Kelly, *5:* 143
Ogburn, Charlton, Jr., *3:* 145
O'Hara, Mary. *See* Alsop, Mary O'Hara, *2:* 4
Ohlsson, Ib, *7:* 171
Olds, Elizabeth, *3:* 146
O'Leary, Brian, *6:* 176
Olschewski, Alfred, *7:* 172
Olsen, Ib Spang, *6:* 177
O'Neill, Mary L(e Duc), *2:* 197
Opie, Iona, *3:* 148
Opie, Peter, *3:* 149
Oppenheim, Joanne, *5:* 146
Orgel, Doris, *7:* 173
Osborne, Leone Neal, *2:* 198
Osmond, Edward, *7:* 174
Oxenbury, Helen, *3:* 151

Page, Eileen. *See* Heal, Edith, *7:* 123
Page, Eleanor. *See* Coerr, Eleanor, *1:* 64

Palazzo, Anthony D., *3:* 152
Palazzo, Tony, *3:* 152 *See* Palazzo, Anthony D., *3:* 152
Palder, Edward L., *5:* 146
Pape, D(onna) L(ugg), *2:* 198
Paradis, Adrian A(lexis), *1:* 175
Parker, Elinor, *3:* 155
Parks, Gordon (Alexander Buchanan), *8:* 145
Parlin, John. *See* Graves, Charles Parlin, *4:* 94
Parrish, Mary. *See* Cousins, Margaret, *2:* 79
Paton Walsh, Jill, *4:* 164
Pauli, Hertha, *3:* 155
Paulson, Jack. *See* Jackson, C. Paul, *6:* 120
Pearce, (Ann) Philippa, *1:* 176
Pease, Howard, *2:* 199
Peeples, Edwin A., *6:* 181
Peet, Bill. *See* Peet, William B., *2:* 201
Peet, William Bartlett, *2:* 201
Pender, Lydia, *3:* 157
Pendery, Rosemary, *7:* 174
Penn, Ruth Bonn. *See* Rosenberg, Ethel, *3:* 176
Pennage, E. M. *See* Finkel, George (Irvine), *8:* 59
Peppe, Rodney, *4:* 164
Percy, Charles Henry. *See* Smith, Dodie, *4:* 194
Perl, Lila, *6:* 182
Perlmutter, O(scar) William, *8:* 149
Perrine, Mary, *2:* 203
Peterson, Hans, *8:* 149
Peterson, Harold L(eslie), *8:* 151
Peterson, Helen Stone, *8:* 152
Petrovskaya, Kyra. *See* Wayne, Kyra Petrovskaya, *8:* 213
Petry, Ann (Lane), *5:* 148
Pevsner, Stella, *8:* 154
Pfeffer, Susan Beth, *4:* 166
Phelan, Mary Kay, *3:* 158
Phillips, Jack. *See* Sandburg, Carl (August), *8:* 177
Phillips, Louis, *8:* 155
Phipson, Joan. *See* Fitzhardinge, Joan M., *2:* 107
Phleger, Marjorie Temple, *1:* 176
Picard, Barbara Leonie, *2:* 205
Pienkowski, Jan, *6:* 182
Pierce, Ruth (Ireland), *5:* 148
Pilgrim, Anne. *See* Allan, Mabel Esther, *5:* 2
Pilkington, F(rancis) M(eredyth), *4:* 166
Pinkwater, Manus, *8:* 156
Piro, Richard, *7:* 176
Pitrone, Jean Maddern, *4:* 167
Pitz, Henry C., *4:* 167
Place, Marian T., *3:* 160
Plaidy, Jean. *See* Hibbert, Eleanor, *2:* 134
Plowman, Stephanie, *6:* 184
Plummer, Margaret, *2:* 206
Pohlmann, Lillian (Grenfell), *8:* 157

Polatnick, Florence T., *5:* 149
Polder, Markus. *See* Krüss, James, *8:* 104
Politi, Leo, *1:* 177
Polking, Kirk, *5:* 149
Polland, Madeleine A., *6:* 185
Pond, Alonzo W(illiam), *5:* 150
Poole, Gray Johnson, *1:* 179
Poole, Josephine, *5:* 152
Poole, Lynn, *1:* 179
Portal, Colette, *6:* 186
Posell, Elsa Z., *3:* 160
Potter, Miriam Clark, *3:* 161
Powers, Margaret. *See* Heal, Edith, *7:* 123
Price, Christine, *3:* 162
Price, Olive, *8:* 157
Prieto, Mariana B(eeching), *8:* 160
Pringle, Laurence, *4:* 171
Proctor, Everitt. *See* Montgomery, Rutherford, *3:* 134
Pryor, Helen Brenton, *4:* 172
Pugh, Ellen T., *7:* 176
Pullein-Thompson, Christine, *3:* 164
Pullein-Thompson, Diana, *3:* 165
Pullein-Thompson, Josephine, *3:* 166
Purdy, Susan Gold, *8:* 161
Purscell, Phyllis, *7:* 177

Quackenbush, Robert M., *7:* 177
Quammen, David, *7:* 179
Queen, Ellery, Jr. *See* Holding, James, *3:* 85
Quick, Annabelle, *2:* 207

Rabe, Berniece, *7:* 179
Radford, Ruby L(orraine), *6:* 186
Raebeck, Lois, *5:* 153
Ralston, Jan. *See* Dunlop, Agnes M. R., *3:* 62
Rand, Paul, *6:* 188
Randall, Florence Engel, *5:* 154
Randall, Janet *See* Young, Janet & Robert, *3:* 268-269
Randall, Ruth Painter, *3:* 167
Ranney, Agnes V., *6:* 189
Rappaport, Eva, *6:* 189
Raskin, Ellen, *2:* 209
Raucher, Herman, *8:* 162
Ravielli, Anthony, *3:* 169
Ray Deborah, *8:* 163
Ray, Irene. *See* Sutton, Margaret Beebe, *1:* 213
Ray, Mary (Eva Pedder), *2:* 210
Read, Elfreida, *2:* 211
Redding, Robert Hull, *2:* 212
Reed, Betty Jane, *4:* 172
Reed, Gwendolyn, *7:* 180
Reeder, Colonel Red. *See* Reeder, Russell P., Jr., *4:* 174
Reeder, Russell P., Jr., *4:* 174

Rees, Ennis, *3:* 169
Reeves, Ruth Ellen. *See* Ranney,
    Agnes V., *6:* 189
Reinfeld, Fred, *3:* 170
Renick, Marion (Lewis), *1:* 180
Renvoize, Jean, *5:* 157
Reuter, Carol (Joan), *2:* 213
Rey, H(ans) A(ugusto), *1:* 181
Rhys, Megan. *See* Williams,
    Jeanne, *5:* 202
Rice, Elizabeth, *2:* 213
Rich, Elaine Sommers, *6:* 190
Richard, Adrienne, *5:* 157
Richardson, Grace Lee. *See*
    Dickson, Naida, *8:* 41
Richardson, Robert S(hirley),
    8: 164
Richoux, Pat, *7:* 180
Richter, Conrad, *3:* 171
Richter, Hans Peter, *6:* 191
Ridge, Antonia, *7:* 181
Riedman, Sarah R(egal), *1:* 183
Rinkoff, Barbara Jean, *4:* 174
Rios, Tere. *See* Versace, Marie
    Teresa, *2:* 254
Ripley, Elizabeth Blake, *5:* 158
Ripper, Charles L., *3:* 174
Roberts, Terence. *See* Sanderson,
    Ivan T., *6:* 195
Robertson, Don, *8:* 165
Robertson, Keith, *1:* 184
Robinson, Adjai, *8:* 165
Robinson, Barbara (Webb), *8:* 166
Robinson, Charles, *6:* 192
Robinson, Jan M., *6:* 194
Robinson, Jean O., *7:* 182
Robinson, Joan (Mary) G(ale
    Thomas), *7:* 183
Robottom, John, *7:* 185
Rockwell, Thomas, *7:* 185
Rockwood, Roy [Collective
    pseudonym], *1:* 185
Rodgers, Mary, *8:* 167
Rodman, Maia. *See*
    Wojciechowska, Maia, *1:* 228
Rogers, (Thomas) Alan
    (Stinchcombe), *2:* 215
Rogers, Matilda, *5:* 158
Rolerson, Darrell A(llen), *8:* 168
Roll, Winifred, *6:* 194
Rollins, Charlemae Hill, *3:* 175
Rose, Anne, *8:* 168
Rosen, Sidney, *1:* 185
Rosen, Winifred, *8:* 169
Rosenbaum, Maurice, *6:* 195
Rosenberg, Ethel, *3:* 176
Rosenberg, Nancy Sherman, *4:* 177
Rosenberg, Sharon, *8:* 171
Rosenburg, John M., *6:* 195
Rothkopf, Carol Z., *4:* 177
Rothman, Joel, *7:* 186
Rounds, Glen (Harold), *8:* 171
Rowland, Florence Wightman,
    8: 173
Roy, Liam. *See* Scarry, Patricia,
    2: 218

Ruchlis, Hy, *3:* 177
Rudomin, Esther. *See* Hautzig,
    Esther, *4:* 105
Rushmore, Helen, *3:* 178
Rushmore, Robert William, *8:* 174
Ruskin, Ariane, *7:* 187
Russell, Helen Ross, *8:* 175
Russell, Patrick. *See* Sammis,
    John, *4:* 179
Russell, Solveig Paulson, *3:* 179
Ruthin, Margaret, *4:* 178
Rydell, Wendell. *See* Rydell,
    Wendy, *4:* 178
Rydell, Wendy, *4:* 178
Ryden, Hope, *8:* 176

Sachs, Marilyn, *3:* 180
Sage, Juniper. *See* Hurd, Edith,
    2: 150
St. Briavels, James. *See* Wood,
    James Playsted, *1:* 229
Samachson, Dorothy, *3:* 182
Samachson, Joseph, *3:* 182
Sammis, John, *4:* 179
Samson, Anne S(tringer), *2:* 216
Sandburg, Carl (August), *8:* 177
Sandburg, Charles A. *See*
    Sandburg, Carl (August),
    8: 177
Sandburg, Helga, *3:* 184
Sanderlin, George, *4:* 180
Sanderson, Ivan, *6:* 195
Sandoz, Mari (Susette), *5:* 159
Sanger, Marjory Bartlett, *8:* 181
Sargent, Robert, *2:* 216
Sattler, Helen Roney, *4:* 181
Savery, Constance (Winifred),
    1: 186
Savitt, Sam, *8:* 181
Savitz, Harriet May, *5:* 161
Sayers, Frances Clarke, *3:* 185
Scagnetti, Jack, *7:* 188
Scarf, Maggi. *See* Scarf, Maggie,
    5: 162
Scarf, Maggie, *5:* 162
Scarry, Patricia (Murphy), *2:* 218
Scarry, Patsy. *See* Scarry, Patricia,
    2: 218
Scarry, Richard (McClure), *2:* 218
Schaefer, Jack, *3:* 186
Schecter, Betty (Goodstein), *5:* 163
Scheer, Julian (Weisel), *8:* 183
Scheffer, Victor B., *6:* 197
Schiff, Ken, *7:* 189
Schlein, Miriam, *2:* 222
Schloat, G. Warren, Jr., *4:* 181
Schneider, Herman, *7:* 189
Schneider, Nina, *2:* 222
Scholastica, Sister Mary. *See*
    Jenkins, Marie M., *7:* 143
Scholefield, Edmund A. *See*
    Butterworth, W. E., *5:* 40
Schoor, Gene, *3:* 188
Schwartz, Alvin, *4:* 183

Schwartz, Charles W(alsh), *8:* 184
Schwartz, Elizabeth Reeder, *8:* 184
Sears, Stephen W., *4:* 184
Sechrist, Elizabeth Hough, *2:* 224
Sedges, John. *See* Buck, Pearl S.,
    1: 36
Seed, Jenny, *8:* 186
Segal, Lore, *4:* 186
Seidelman, James Edward, *6:* 197
Sejima, Yoshimasa, *8:* 186
Selden, George. *See* Thompson,
    George Selden, *4:* 204
Selsam, Millicent E(llis), *1:* 188
Sendak, Maurice (Bernard), *1:* 190
Seredy, Kate, *1:* 193
Serraillier, Ian (Lucien), *1:* 193
Seton, Anya, *3:* 188
Seuss, Dr. *See* Geisel, Theodor
    Seuss, *1:* 104
Severn, Bill. *See* Severn, William
    Irving, *1:* 195
Severn, William Irving, *1:* 195
Shapp, Martha, *3:* 189
Sharmat, Marjorie W(einman),
    4: 187
Sharp, Margery, *1:* 196
Shaw, Arnold, *4:* 189
Shaw, Ray, *7:* 190
Shay, Arthur, *4:* 189
Sheldon, Ann [Collective
    pseudonym], *1:* 198
Shelton, William Roy, *5:* 164
Shemin, Margaretha, *4:* 190
Shepard, Ernest Howard, *3:* 191
Shephard, Esther, *5:* 165
Shepherd, Elizabeth, *4:* 191
Sherburne, Zoa, *3:* 194
Sherman, Elizabeth. *See* Friskey,
    Margaret Richards, *5:* 72
Sherman, Nancy. *See* Rosenberg,
    Nancy Sherman. *4:* 177
Sherrod, Jane. *See* Singer, Jane
    Sherrod, *4:* 192
Sherry, (Dulcie) Sylvia, *8:* 187
Sherwan, Earl, *3:* 195
Shippen, Katherine B(inney), *1:* 198
Shotwell, Louisa R., *3:* 196
Shub, Elizabeth, *5:* 166
Shulevitz, Uri, *3:* 197
Shulman, Alix Kates, *7:* 191
Shura, Mary Francis. *See* Craig,
    Mary Francis, *6:* 52
Shuttlesworth, Dorothy, *3:* 200
Silver, Ruth. *See* Chew, Ruth,
    7: 45
Silverstein, Alvin, *8:* 188
Silverstein, Virginia B(arbara
    Opshelor), *8:* 190
Simon, Charlie May. *See* Fletcher,
    Charlie May, *3:* 70
Simon, Joe. *See* Simon, Joseph H.,
    7: 192
Simon, Joseph H., *7:* 192
Simon, Mina Lewiton. *See*
    Lewiton, Mina, *2:* 174
Simon, Norma, *3:* 201

Simon, Seymour, *4:* 191
Singer, Isaac. *See* Singer, Isaac
 Bashevis, *3:* 203
Singer, Isaac Bashevis, *3:* 203
Singer, Jane Sherrod, *4:* 192
Skinner, Cornelia Otis, *2:* 225
Skorpen, Liesel Moak, *3:* 206
Skurzynski, Gloria (Joan), *8:* 190
Sleator, William, *3:* 207
Sleigh, Barbara, *3:* 208
Slicer, Margaret O., *4:* 193
Slobodkin, Florence (Gersh),
 5: 167
Slobodkin, Louis, *1:* 199
Slobodkina, Esphyr, *1:* 201
Slote, Alfred, *8:* 192
Small, Ernest. *See* Lent, Blair,
 2: 172
Smaridge, Norah, *6:* 198
Smiley, Virginia Kester, *2:* 227
Smith, Betty, *6:* 199
Smith, Bradford, *5:* 168
Smith, Dodie, *4:* 194
Smith, Dorothy Stafford, *6:* 201
Smith, Eunice Young, *5:* 169
Smith, Frances C., *3:* 209
Smith, George Harmon, *5:* 71
Smith, Hugh L(etcher), *5:* 172
Smith, Jean. *See* Smith, Frances
 C., *3:* 209
Smith, Lafayette. *See* Higdon, Hal,
 4: 115
Smith, Linell Nash, *2:* 227
Smith, Norman F., *5:* 172
Smith, Ruth Leslie, *2:* 228
Smith, Sarah Stafford. *See* Smith,
 Dorothy Stafford, *6:* 201
Smith, William Jay, *2:* 229
Sneve, Virginia Driving Hawk,
 8: 193
Snyder, Anne, *4:* 195
Snyder, Zilpha Keatley, *1:* 202
Snyderman, Reuven K., *5:* 173
Sobol, Donald J., *1:* 203
Solbert, Romaine G., *2:* 232
Solbert, Ronni. *See* Solbert,
 Romaine G., *2:* 232
Sommer, Elyse, *7:* 192
Sommerfelt, Aimee, *5:* 173
Sonneborn, Ruth, *4:* 196
Sorensen, Virginia, *2:* 233
Sorrentino, Joseph N., *6:* 203
Soskin, V. H. *See* Ellison, Virginia
 Howell, *4:* 74
Soudley, Henry. *See* Wood, James
 Playsted, *1:* 229
Southall, Ivan, *3:* 210
Spangenberg, Judith Dunn, *5:* 175
Speare, Elizabeth George, *5:* 176
Speicher, Helen Ross (Smith),
 8: 194
Spencer, Cornelia. *See* Yaukey,
 Grace S. *5:* 203
Sperry, Armstrong W., *1:* 204
Sperry, Raymond, Jr.[Collective
 pseudonym], *1:* 205
Spiegelman, Judith M., *5:* 179

Spier, Peter (Edward), *4:* 198
Spilka, Arnold, *6:* 203
Stahl, Ben(jamin), *5:* 179
Stambler, Irwin, *5:* 181
Stankevich, Boris, *2:* 234
Stapp, Arthur D(onald), *4:* 201
Starbird, Kaye, *6:* 204
Stark, James. *See* Goldston,
 Robert, *6:* 90
Starkey, Marion L(ena), *8:* 194
Starret, William. *See* McClintock,
 Marshall, *3:* 119
Stearns, Monroe (Mather), *5:* 182
Steele, Mary Q., *3:* 211
Steele, William O(wen), *1:* 205
Stein, M(eyer) L(ewis), *6:* 205
Stein, Mini, *2:* 234
Steinberg, Fred J., *4:* 201
Stephens, Mary Jo, *8:* 196
Steptoe, John (Lewis), *8:* 198
Sterling, Dorothy, *1:* 206
Sterling, Philip, *8:* 198
Sterne, Emma Gelders, *6:* 205
Stevens, Franklin, *6:* 206
Stevens, Peter. *See* Geis, Darlene,
 7: 101
Stevenson, Augusta, *2:* 235
Stevenson, Janet, *8:* 199
Stewart, Elizabeth Laing, *6:* 206
Stewart, George Rippey, *3:* 213
Stewart, Robert Neil, *7:* 192
Stiles, Martha Bennett, *6:* 207
Stirling, Nora B., *3:* 214
Stoddard, Hope, *6:* 207
Stone, Alan [Collective
 pseudonym], *1:* 208. *See also*
 Svenson, Andrew E., *2:* 238
Stone, Eugenia, *7:* 193
Stone, Gene. *See* Stone, Eugenia,
 7: 193
Stone, Helen V., *6:* 208
Stone, Irving, *3:* 215
Stone, Raymond [Collective
 pseudonym], *1:* 208
Storch, Anne B. von. *See* von
 Storch, Anne B., *1:* 221
Stoutenburg, Adrien, *3:* 217
Stratemeyer, Edward L., *1:* 208
Strong, Charles. *See* Epstein,
 Samuel, *1:* 87
Stuart, (Hilton) Jesse, *2:* 236
Stubis, Talivaldis, *5:* 183
Sture-Vasa, Mary. *See* Alsop,
 Mary, *2:* 4
Sturtzel, Howard A(llison), *1:* 210
Sturtzel, Jane Levington, *1:* 212
Suba, Susanne, *4:* 202
Subond, Valerie. *See* Grayland,
 Valerie, *7:* 111
Suhl, Yuri, *8:* 200
Sullivan, George Edward, *4:* 202
Susac, Andrew, *5:* 184
Sutcliff, Rosemary, *6:* 209
Sutton, Margaret (Beebe), *1:* 213
Svenson, Andrew E., *2:* 238
Swarthout, Kathryn, *7:* 194

Swiger, Elinor Porter, *8:* 202
Syme, (Neville) Ronald, *2:* 239
Sypher, Lucy Johnston, *7:* 195
Szekeres, Cyndy, *5:* 184

Tannenbaum, Beulah, *3:* 219
Tashjian, Virginia A., *3:* 220
Tate, Ellalice. *See* Hibbert,
 Eleanor, *2:* 134
Tatham, Campbell. *See* Elting,
 Mary, *2:* 100
Taylor, Sydney (Brenner), *1:* 214
Taylor, Theodore, *5:* 185
Teale, Edwin Way, *7:* 196
Tennant, Kylie, *6:* 210
ter Haar, Jaap, *6:* 211
Terris, Susan, *3:* 221
Tharp, Louise Hall, *3:* 223
Thayer, Jane. *See* Woolley,
 Catherine, *3:* 265
Thomas, J. F. *See* Fleming,
 Thomas J(ames), *8:* 64
Thomas, John Gale. *See* Robinson,
 Joan G., *7:* 183
Thompson, Christine Pullein. *See*
 Pullein-Thompson, Christine,
 3: 164
Thompson, Diana Pullein. *See*
 Pullein-Thompson, Diana,
 3: 165
Thompson, George Selden, *4:* 204
Thompson, Josephine Pullein. *See*
 Pullein-Thompson, Josephine,
 3: 166
Thompson, Vivian L., *3:* 224
Thorndyke, Helen Louise
 [Collective pseudonym], *1:* 216
Thum, Marcella, *3:* 226
Titus, Eve, *2:* 240
Tobias, Tobi, *5:* 187
Todd, Anne Ophelia. *See* Dowden,
 Anne Ophelia, *7:* 69
Tolkien, J(ohn) R(onald) R(euel),
 2: 242
Tolles, Martha, *8:* 203
Tomfool. *See* Farjeon, Eleanor,
 2: 103
Tomlinson, Jill, *3:* 227
Tooze, Ruth, *4:* 205
Townsend, John Rowe, *4:* 206
Toye, William E(ldred), *8:* 203
Traherne, Michael. *See* Watkins-
 Pitchford, D. J., *6:* 214
Travers, P(amela) L(yndon), *4:* 208
Trease, (Robert) Geoffrey, *2:* 244
Treece, Henry, *2:* 246
Tregaskis, Richard, *3:* 228
Tresselt, Alvin, *7:* 197
Trevino, Elizabeth B(orton) de,
 1: 216
Tripp, Eleanor B., *4:* 210
Tripp, Paul, *8:* 204
Tucker, Caroline. *See* Nolan,
 Jeannette, *2:* 196

Tunis, Edwin (Burdett), *1:* 217
Turkle, Brinton, *2:* 248
Turlington, Bayly, *5:* 187
Turner, Josie. *See* Crawford,
    Phyllis, *3:* 57
Turngren, Ellen, *3:* 230
Tyler, Anne, *7:* 198

Ubell, Earl, *4:* 210
Uchida, Yoshiko, *1:* 219
Udry, Janice May, *4:* 212
Ullman, James Ramsey, *7:* 199
Unada. *See* Gliewe, Unada, *3:* 77
Uncle Gus. *See* Rey, H. A., *1:* 181
Uncle Ray. *See* Coffman, Ramon
    Peyton, *4:* 53
Ungerer, Jean Thomas, *5:* 187
Ungerer, Tomi. *See* Ungerer, Jean
    Thomas, *5:* 187
Unkelbach, Kurt, *4:* 213
Unnerstad, Edith, *3:* 230
Unsworth, Walt, *4:* 215
Untermeyer, Louis, *2:* 250
Unwin, Nora S., *3:* 233
Usher, Margo Scegge. *See*
    McHargue, Georgess, *4:* 152
Uttley, Alice Jane, *3:* 235
Uttley, Alison. *See* Uttley, Alice
    Jane, *3:* 235
Utz, Lois, *5:* 189

Valens, Evans G., Jr., *1:* 220
Van Anrooy, Francine, *2:* 252
Van Anrooy, Frans. *See* Van
    Anrooy, Francine, *2:* 252
Van der Veer, Judy, *4:* 216
Van Leeuwen, Jean, *6:* 212
Van Orden, M(erton) D(ick), *4:* 218
Van Riper, Guernsey, Jr., *3:* 239
Van Stockum, Hilda, *5:* 191
Van Wyck Mason. *See* Mason, F.
    van Wyck, *3:* 117
Van-Wyck Mason, F. *See* Mason,
    F. van Wyck, *3:* 117
Vasiliu, Mircea, *2:* 254
Vavra, Robert James, *8:* 206
Veglahn, Nancy (Crary), *5:* 194
Venable, Alan (Hudson), *8:* 206
Vernor, D. *See* Casewit, Curtis,
    4: 43
Versace, Marie Teresa Rios, *2:* 254
Vicker, Angus. *See* Felsen, Henry
    Gregor, *1:* 189
Victor, Edward, *3:* 240
Viereck, Phillip, *3:* 241
Viguers, Ruth Hill, *6:* 214
Vining, Elizabeth Gray. *See* Gray,
    Elizabeth Janet, *6:* 93
Viorst, Judith, *7:* 200
Voight, Virginia Frances, *8:* 208
von Almedingen, Martha Edith.
    See Almedingen, E. M., *3:* 9
von Storch, Anne B., *1:* 221

Wagner, Sharon B., *4:* 218
Wahl, Jan, *2:* 256
Walden, Amelia Elizabeth, *3:* 242
Walker, Barbara K., *4:* 219
Walker, David Harry, *8:* 210
Walker, (Addison) Mort, *8:* 211
Wallace, Barbara Brooks, *4:* 221
Wallace, John A., *3:* 243
Walsh, Jill Paton. *See* Paton
    Walsh, Gillian, *4:* 164
Walton, Richard J., *4:* 223
Warbler, J. M. *See* Cocagnac,
    A. M., *7:* 52
Ward, Lynd (Kendall), *2:* 257
Ward, Martha (Eads), *5:* 195
Ware, Leon (Vernon), *4:* 224
Warner, Frank A. [Collective
    pseudonym], *1:* 222
Warshofsky, Isaac. *See* Singer,
    Isaac Bashevis, *3:* 203
Waters, John F(rederick), *4:* 225
Watkins-Pitchford, D. J., *6:* 214
Watson, Clyde, *5:* 196
Watson, Jane Werner, *3:* 244
Watson, Sally, *3:* 245
Watson, Wendy (McLeod), *5:* 198
Watt, Thomas, *4:* 226
Watts, Bernadette, *4:* 226
Wayne, Kyra Petrovskaya, *8:* 213
Wayne, Richard. *See* Decker,
    Duane, *5:* 53
Weaver, Ward. *See* Mason, F. van
    Wyck, *3:* 117
Webb, Christopher. *See* Wibberley,
    Leonard, *2:* 271
Weber, Alfons, *8:* 215
Weber, Lenora Mattingly, *2:* 260
Webster, Frank V. [Collective
    pseudonym], *1:* 222
Weik, Mary Hays, *3:* 247
Weil, Lisl, *7:* 202
Weilerstein, Sadie Rose, *3:* 248
Weingarten, Violet, *3:* 250
Weingartner, Charles, *5:* 199
Weir, LaVada, *2:* 261
Weisgard, Leonard (Joseph), *2:* 263
Weiss, Harvey, *1:* 222
Weiss, Malcolm E., *3:* 251
Weiss, Miriam. *See* Schlein,
    Miriam, *2:* 222
Weiss, Renee Karol, *5:* 199
Welch, Ronald. *See* Felton, Ronald
    Oliver, *3:* 67
Wellman, Manly Wade, *6:* 217
Wellman, Paul I., *3:* 251
Wells, Helen, *2:* 266
Werner, Jane. *See* Watson, Jane
    Werner, *3:* 244
Werner, K. *See* Casewit, Curtis,
    4: 43
Wersba, Barbara, *1:* 224
West, Barbara. *See* Price, Olive,
    8: 157
West, Jerry. *See* Svenson, Andrew
    E., *2:* 238

West, Ward. *See* Borland, Hal,
    5: 22
Wheeler, Janet D. [Collective
    pseudonym], *1:* 225
White, Anne Terry, *2:* 267
White, Dale. *See* Place, Marian T.,
    3: 160
White, E(lwyn) B(rooks), *2:* 268
White, Ramy Allison [Collective
    pseudonym], *1:* 225
White, Robb, *1:* 225
Whitehead, Don(ald) F., *4:* 227
Whitinger, R. D. *See* Place,
    Marian T., *3:* 160
Whitney, Phyllis A(yame), *1:* 226
Wibberley, Leonard, *2:* 271
Widdemer, Mabel Cleland, *5:* 200
Wier, Ester, *3:* 252
Wiese, Kurt, *3:* 254
Wiesner, William, *5:* 200
Wilkinson, Burke, *4:* 229
Willey, Robert. *See* Ley, Willy,
    2: 175
Williams, Beryl. *See* Epstein,
    Beryl, *1:* 85
Williams, Charles. *See* Collier,
    James Lincoln, *8:* 33
Williams, Clyde C., *8:* 216
Williams, Frances B. *See* Browin,
    Frances Williams, *5:* 30
Williams, J. R. *See* Williams,
    Jeanne, *5:* 202
Williams, Jay, *3:* 256
Williams, Jeanne, *5:* 202
Williams, Patrick J. *See*
    Butterworth, W. E., *5:* 40
Williams, Slim. *See* Williams,
    Clyde C., *8:* 216
Williams, Ursula Moray, *3:* 257
Williamson, Joanne Small, *3:* 259
Wilson, Beth P(ierre), *8:* 218
Wilson, Carter, *6:* 218
Wilson, Hazel, *3:* 260
Winders, Gertrude Hecker, *3:* 261
Winthrop, Elizabeth. *See* Mahony,
    Elizabeth Winthrop, *8:* 125
Wise, William, *4:* 230
Wise, Winifred E., *2:* 273
Wiseman, B(ernard), *4:* 232
Wizard, Mr. *See* Herbert, Don,
    2: 131
Wohlrabe, Raymond A., *4:* 234
Wojciechowska, Maia, *1:* 228
Wolfe, Burton H., *5:* 202
Wolfe, Louis, *8:* 219
Wolkstein, Diane, *7:* 204
Wondriska, William A., *6:* 219
Wood, James Playsted, *1:* 229
Wood, Nancy, *6:* 220
Woodrich, Mary Neville, *2:* 274
Woods, Margaret, *2:* 275
Woody, Regina Jones, *3:* 263
Woolley, Catherine, *3:* 265
Woolsey, Jannette, *3:* 266
Worth, Valerie, *8:* 220
Wright, Enid Meadowcroft, *3:* 267

Wright, R(obert) H., *6: 220*
Wrightson, Patricia, *8; 220*
Wyndham, Lee. *See* Hyndman,
    Jane Andrews, *1: 122*

Yamaguchi, Marianne, *7: 205*
Yates, Elizabeth, *4: 235*
Yaukey, Grace S(ydenstricker),
    5: 203
Yep, Laurence M., *7: 206*

Yolen, Jane H., *4: 237*
York, Andrew. *See* Nicole,
    Christopher Robin, *5: 141*
York, Carol Beach, *6: 221*
Young, Bob. *See* Young, Robert
    W., *3: 269*
Young, Clarence [Collective
    pseudonym], *1: 231*
Young, Edward. *See* Reinfeld,
    Fred, *3: 170*
Young, Jan. *See* Young, Janet
    Randall, *3: 268*
Young, Janet Randall, *3: 268*

Young, Margaret B(uckner), *2: 275*
Young, Miriam, *7: 208*
Young, Robert W., *3: 269*
Young, Scott A(lexander), *5: 204*

Zalben, Jane Breskin, *7: 211*
Zemach, Harve, *3: 270*
Zim, Herbert S(pencer), *1: 231*
Ziner, (Florence) Feenie, *5: 204*
Zolotow, Charlotte S., *1: 233*